Conrad's Narrative Method

Conrad's Narrative Method

*

JAKOB LOTHE

CLARENDON PRESS · OXFORD
1989

Oxford University Press, Walton Street, Oxford OX2 6DP
Oxford New York Toronto
Delhi Bombay Calcutta Madras Karachi
Petaling Jaya Singapore Hong Kong Tokyo
Nairobi Dar es Salaam Cape Town
Melbourne Auckland
and associated companies in
Berlin Ibadan

Oxford is a trade mark of Oxford University Press

Published in the United States
by Oxford University Press, New York

© Jakob Lothe 1989

British Library Cataloguing in Publication Data
Lothe, Jakob
Conrad's narrative method.
1. Fiction in English. Conrad, Joseph,
1857–1924. Critical studies
I. Title
823'.912
ISBN 0-19-812961-0

Library of Congress Cataloging in Publication Data
Lothe, Jakob.
Conrad's narrative method.
Includes index.
1. Conrad, Joseph, 1857–1924—Technique.
2. Narration (Rhetoric) I. Title.
PR6005.04Z7664 1989 823'.912 88-29144
ISBN 0-19-812961-0

Typeset by Colset Private Limited,
Printed in Great Britain
by Biddles Ltd.
Guildford & King's Lynn

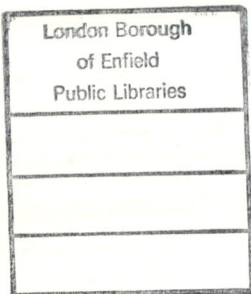

To the memory of
Georg Roppen

Acknowledgements

THIS study of Conrad's narrative method is based in large part on work done at the University of Sussex in 1980–1 and at Oxford in 1981–3. My most important academic contact both at Sussex and when I worked in Oxford was Cedric Watts of the University of Sussex, to whose encouragement and constructive criticisms I remain greatly indebted. When I returned to Norway I was fortunate, though I lived in Oslo, to make contact with Jeremy Hawthorn of the University of Trondheim; and his genuine interest in my work and numerous comments on it have also been invaluable. Although my obligations to Watts and Hawthorn are quite different in type, I feel them to be about equal in scope.

Additionally, the remarks made on the study by Ian Watt, Zdzisław Najder, and John Batchelor have been particularly helpful. Hans van Marle and Bjørn Tysdahl have read an earlier version of the manuscript and made a number of detailed and useful suggestions. I am also most grateful to David Leon Higdon, who not only responded encouragingly to an early outline of the project, but whose wise advice also led to the contact with Cedric Watts. To my wife, Elin Toft, I owe a debt of gratitude too extensive to be easily specified.

My studies in Britain were made possible by a three-year grant from the Norwegian Research Council for Science and the Humanities. I would like to express my gratitude to the Council for its support of my work, which included a generous grant to cover some of the costs of publication. As much of the research has been carried out in various university libraries, I am grateful to the staffs and facilities of Sussex University Library, the Bodleian Library at Oxford, the British Library, the Henry Green Library at Stanford, and Oslo University Library.

Earlier versions of Chapters 3, 4, and 6 have appeared in *L'Epoque Conradienne* (1981), 33–48; *The Conradian*, 8 (1983), 22–9; and *Conradiana*, 16 (1984), 215–24. A section of Chapter 12 has appeared in Jeremy Hawthorn (ed.), *Narrative: From Malory to Motion Pictures* (London: Edward Arnold, 1985), 124–7. I thank the editors and publishers of these for permission to reprint.

This book was completed in 1987.

J.L.

Contents

Textual Notes and Abbreviations

REFERENCES to Conrad's works are to Dent's Collected Edition (London, 1946–55). The pagination of this edition is often identical to that of the World's Classics Conrad (Oxford University Press).

In any quotation, a row of three unspaced dots (...) indicates an elision that I have made, whereas a row of three spaced dots (. . .) indicates an ellipsis present in the material being quoted. First letters are capitalized in 'Part First', 'Part Second', etc., which refer to Conrad's divisions of *Nostromo* and *Under Western Eyes*, and in 'Part I' and 'Part II', which refer to the bipartite division of *Chance*. If not capitalized, 'part' or 'section' refers to a textual division introduced by me.

The following abbreviations are used:

CMP   Jacques Berthoud, *Joseph Conrad: The Major Phase* (Cambridge: CUP, 1978).

CN   Albert J. Guerard, *Conrad the Novelist* (Cambridge, Mass.: Harvard University Press, 1958).

CNC   Ian Watt, *Conrad in the Nineteenth Century* (London: Chatto & Windus, 1980).

CWD   H. M. Daleski, *Joseph Conrad: The Way of Dispossession* (London: Faber and Faber, 1977).

ND   Gérard Genette, *Narrative Discourse*, trans. Jane E. Lewin (Oxford: Blackwell, 1980).

OED   *Oxford English Dictionary*.

xi

1
Introduction

I

This book will investigate the narrative method observable in the fiction of Joseph Conrad. Its primary focus is on this method's devices, functions, variations, and thematic effects or implications. 'Narrative method' is here seen as an integral aspect of textual structure, but the study is not narrowly or exclusively 'structuralist' as it is concerned with the complicated, and partly reciprocal, relationship in Conrad's fiction between narrative method and the complex thematics shaped through this diverse method. The study analyses a dozen Conrad texts of varying lengths. It attempts to identify and evaluate the narrative techniques of these texts, and on this basis suggests narrative and thematic generalizations about them.

Most Conrad criticism to date appears to have proceeded from the critical assumption (it is seldom thematized as a theoretical problem) that literary content precedes form,[1] that the writer of fiction starts from certain ideas and concerns to which he or she then attempts to give as convincing and effective a form as possible. Jacques Berthoud, for instance, reasserting the literary relevance of the philosophical distinction between causes and reasons, emphasizes Conrad's reasons for applying a particular narrative method, and regards him as a reflective modernist writer largely in control of

---

[1] 'Form' and 'content' are here used as imprecise, explanatory terms in order to place the study within a broader critical context. Although, as will become apparent in the textual analyses, the theoretical validity of the form/content distinction is questionable with reference to Conrad, it still retains some usefulness for practical criticism of his fiction. If we provisionally define 'form' as the manner in which a fictional text is structured and dramatized, then it can be seen as an inclusive concept subsuming various others that are more closely related to narrative method. Examples of such terms are 'sjužet' (Russian formalists), 'composition' (Uspensky), 'récit' (Barthes, Genette), 'discourse' (Chatman), and 'plot' (Peter Brooks). Full reference to the theorists using these concepts is given below.

his own medium.[2] This book certainly does not dispute the modernity or the remarkable fictional self-consciousness of Conrad. But rather than probing into Conrad's reasons (as variously manifested in his non-fictional writings such as letters and prefaces) for adopting, implementing, and modifying a certain technique, it ventures to analyse the narrative method of the fictional texts themselves. Rather than proceeding from ideas about fictional content to considerations of the form this content assumes, my book focuses instead on Conrad's narrative method as a most significant constituent aspect of his fiction. It also includes comments on the intriguing interplay of form and content in Conrad, or more specifically of narrative method and the thematics this method helps to shape.

Very broadly, then, this book evinces—in contrast to most earlier Conrad criticism—a shift of emphasis from content to form. As a corollary to this changed critical emphasis it follows that the larger part of the study is concerned with analysis of narrative method. Yet this distribution of criticism does not imply that the concluding, more thematic generalizations about the texts are considered as unimportant. On the contrary, it is a main critical premiss here that previous discussions of Conrad's fictional ideas and concerns have tended to be too general and abstract. Such discussions, it seems to me, are often based on insufficient consideration of textual examples of the narrative method from which much of the texts' reverberating suggestiveness derives.

The form/content dichotomy is here seen as a most complicated relationship which can be observed, though not easily delineated and systematized, in Conrad's fictional texts. When the relationship is productive and successful, as in 'Heart of Darkness', it becomes particularly difficult to discriminate between constituent aspects of form and content. Although this difficulty is partly due to the narrative economy of this particular novella, it is also, as we shall see in

---

[2] According to the philosophical distinction between causes and reasons, it is a logical error to treat reasons in terms of causes. If we ask, for instance, with Berthoud, why Conrad wrote *Lord Jim*, the answer may be subsumed under 'cause' or 'reason' depending on the assumptions we make. 'In the former case we will reply: "Because of the biographical, psychological and social conditions that determined his actions", and we will undertake a programme of research into his life and times. In the latter case we will answer: "Because he saw, felt, understood, imagined something which he wished to explore and communicate", and we will address ourselves to the work in order to discover what it is.' See Jacques Berthoud, *Joseph Conrad: The Major Phase* (Cambridge: C U.P, 1978), 3. Abbreviated as *C M P* hereafter.

Chapter 2, closely related to sophisticated modulations of the narrative method employed. In other tales by Conrad the relationship is more strained—as in *Chance*, where the narrative function of Marlow invites adverse commentary (cf. Chapter 2), or in *Victory*, where the thematic purpose of the heavy allegorizing seems unclear.

As these introductory observations have, I hope, indicated, the central thesis of this study can be set out as a twofold argument. First, it argues that the narrative method of Conrad's fiction is an important field of study in itself. This author's fiction is, as Edward W. Said comments, 'great for its presentation, not only for what it was representing'.[3] Applying to Conrad potentially helpful critical concepts and notions introduced by recent narrative theory, I shall attempt to investigate the 'presentation' of his fiction in some detail.

Secondly, thematic generalizations about Conrad's fiction might become more nuanced and convincing if based on analyses of the narrative method which serves to constitute it. Once this is said, an interpretative problem is actualized, for there is a sense in which a sustained critical emphasis on Conrad's narrative method also *complicates* thematic generalizations about his fiction. A further implication of this second argument is that the critical usefulness of the following interpretations of Conradian narrative is not necessarily wholly dependent on the validity of the generalizations for which they serve as basis here. There is a strong general need for analyses of Conrad's narrative method. Such analyses or interpretations are relevant to several of the questions Conrad's fiction raises, and not just the more strictly technical ones.

As I hope this outline of the book's critical focus has made clear, it introduces a set of critical concepts and applies them to the analyses of Conrad's narrative method. In order to highlight the importance and potential usefulness of such concepts I have chosen to present the most basic of them in the Introduction. It might be mentioned here that although this book is primarily intended as a contribution to Conrad studies, this does not preclude the possibility that it may—in more indirect and perhaps paradoxical ways—throw some light on more general problems of narrative as well. There seems to be too wide a gap between the recent advances made in narrative theory and the application of this theory to studies of individual

---

[3] Edward W. Said, 'Conrad: The Presentation of Narrative', ch. 4 of his *The World, the Text, and the Critic* (London: Faber and Faber, 1984), 90, cf. 101.

authors. This study attempts to bridge part of that gap as far as Conrad studies are concerned. This is another reason for my focusing on narrative concepts: the following analyses demonstrate the necessity of interrelating the critical concepts and the texts to which they are applied.

Before introducing these basic narrative terms two additional aspects of the book's main critical focus need briefly to be commented on: the selection of fictional texts (from the total Conrad canon) subjected to textual analysis, and the historical dimension of the kind of narrative analysis and interpretation presented here. As the study aims at some more general conclusions not only about each of the dozen texts that are analysed but also about Conrad's narrative method as such, it is imperative that the discussions and evaluations should be based on a reasonably wide range of works, and that the choice of texts should not be allowed to become unrepresentative. At the same time there is broad critical consensus that Conrad's fiction is of a distinctly uneven quality, and this must be taken into account when deciding which texts to subject to closer analysis. One of the first to comment on the relative inferiority of Conrad's late work was Virginia Woolf,[4] but although I share her preference for the earlier fiction, it is essential that a study of narrative method analyse works written at different stages of the author's writing career. A related problem is that caused by my interest in the various devices and variations of Conrad's narrative method: clearly, some Conrad texts are more interesting in this respect than others. Broadly, the textual selection is made on the grounds of literary quality and narrative variety, but it does not follow that I am uncritical of all aspects of narrative in the texts analysed. Neither do the texts exhibit the same degree of narrative sophistication and complexity—the narrative method of 'Typhoon', for example, is very simple compared to that of *Lord Jim* or *Nostromo*.

A final criterion of selection is that of varying textual length. On the basis of this criterion Conrad's fiction can be divided into short stories, novellas, and novels. Although Conrad's best narratives often tend towards textual expansion, some of his shorter texts are

---

[4] Unsigned review, *The Times Literary Supplement* (1 July 1920); included in Norman Sherry (ed.), *Conrad: The Critical Heritage* (London: Routledge & Kegan Paul, 1973), 332–5.

also remarkably rich and suggestive. Still, we shall see that essential aspects of Conrad's narrative method require a certain textual length in order to allow for the productive narrative variation of which his fiction is capable.

The relation of a systematic investigation of Conrad's narrative method to literary characteristics connected with, though not necessarily directly conditioned by, historical developments is very complicated, and cannot be other than summarily considered here. But for this very reason two interconnected points need to be emphasized. First, and quite obviously, a study of narrative method requires rather detailed close readings which complicate, though they may invite, consideration of interpretative problems that are historical, sociological, and cultural rather than structural and textual. However, the borderlines between different forms of criticism are blurred, and more so in current post-structuralist criticism than previously. This book's textual emphasis certainly does not imply a deprecatory view of the important question of the historical and socio-cultural dimensions of Conrad's fiction.

Secondly, because of its focus on narrative method this study of Conrad can also be seen as a serious, though somewhat curtailed and indirect, attempt to contribute to our understanding of a major writer's fictional achievement at a crucially transitional point in the history of the English novel, and, more widely, in early modernism. As David Lodge and others have noted, 'Modernist fiction is pioneered in England by James and Conrad.'[5] If we go on to ask how this fiction, which reached its fullest development in the work of Joyce and Woolf, was 'pioneered', then we have to consider, as indeed Lodge does, questions of structure and narrative method. There is a sense, then, in which the opposition between 'structure' and 'method' on the one hand and 'history' on the other is factitious, possibly even theoretically untenable. As Tzvetan Todorov argues, 'it is only on the level of structures that we can describe literary development; not only

[5] David Lodge, *The Modes of Modern Writing: Metaphor, Metonymy, and the Typology of Modern Literature* (London: Edward Arnold, 1977), 45. See also Lodge, *Working with Structuralism: Essays and Reviews on Nineteenth- and Twentieth-Century Literature* (London: Routledge & Kegan Paul, 1981) and *Language of Fiction: Essays in Criticism and Verbal Analysis of the English Novel*, 2nd edn., (London: Routledge & Kegan Paul, 1984).

does the knowledge of structures not impede that of variability, but indeed it is the sole means we possess of approaching the latter'.[6]

II

One difficulty in the presentation of critical concepts is to avoid simplifying their attendant theoretical problems which, if properly considered, would demand their own full-length study. This is perhaps one reason why Conrad critics, with a certain heuristic justification, have tended to refrain from applying recent narrative research to Conrad's fiction. It seems to me, however, that although in one sense insurmountable, this difficulty is outweighed by the possibilities which such research suggests for increased insight into the complexity of Conrad's narrative method. Further difficulties are those of simplification and arbitrary selection of complicated, and quite often conflicting, narrative theories. But again, these are general problems whose danger can be exaggerated: critical terms can retain much of their usefulness in spite of being adopted from different theories of narrative. The primary theoretical basis for this study is provided by Gérard Genette's excellent *Narrative Discourse*.[7] Though it obviously has to be much shorter and more selective than his, the following presentation draws on Genette. Following Shlomith Rimmon-Kenan's *Narrative Fiction*, it is organized around the *differentia specifica* of Conrad's fiction;[8] and my focus on Conrad makes it necessary to introduce supplementary concepts Genette does not employ.

[6] Tzvetan Todorov, *Introduction to Poetics*, trans. Richard Howard (Brighton: Harvester, 1981), 61. An important collection of Todorov's essays is *The Poetics of Prose*, trans. Howard (Oxford: Blackwell, 1977), which includes discussions of such issues as narrative grammar, character, and narrative transformations. Todorov is also the editor of *French Literary Theory Today: A Reader*, trans. R. Carter (Cambridge: CUP, 1982).

[7] Gérard Genette, *Narrative Discourse*, trans. Jane E. Lewin (Oxford: Blackwell, 1980), abbreviated as *ND* hereafter; orig. publ. as 'Discours du récit', *Figures III* (Paris: Seuil, 1972). His more recent *Nouveau discours du récit* (Paris: Seuil, 1983) is a sensible commentary on *Narrative Discourse* (and the reactions it provoked) rather than a new study of narrative theory.

[8] Shlomith Rimmon-Kenan, *Narrative Fiction: Contemporary Poetics* (London: Methuen, 1983), 5. This is an accessible and informative introduction to the wide-ranging field of contemporary narrative theory. See also her article, 'A Comprehensive Theory of Narrative: Genette's *Figures III* and the Structuralist Study of Fiction', *Poetics and Theory of Literature*, 1 (1976), 33–62.

Author—Conrad. The critical status and position of the author, though once unproblematic, have recently been subjected to negative comment by theorists with leanings towards critical schools as different as Marxism and deconstruction. Michel Foucault, for instance, who himself resisted being placed within a given school or trend, problematizes the word 'author' to the extent of asking, in the conclusion of his influential essay 'What is an Author?': 'What difference does it make who is speaking?'[9] In Conrad it makes a significant difference; and this can be said without exaggerating the importance of Conrad's roots and literary intentions. To employ a suggestive term introduced by Albert J. Guerard, we can identify an insistent and forceful 'Conradian voice' in Conrad's fiction.[10] It is this 'voice' (which is different from the more technical definition of voice given below) that lends such pervasive thematic urgency to Conrad's best fiction. As Zdzislaw Najder's authoritative biography of Conrad demonstrates,[11] it would have been unthinkable without Conrad's particular roots, interests, and preoccupations; and it proceeds from, and is founded upon, the author's keen historical experience and existential awareness. Relating Guerard's notion to the critical concerns of this book, we could say that Conrad's narrative method is one of the most essential constituent aspects of the 'Conradian voice' observable in the fiction he wrote.[12]

[9] Michel Foucault, 'What Is an Author?', in Josué Harari (ed.), *Textual Strategies: Perspectives in Post-Structuralist Criticism* (London: Methuen, 1980), 160. See also Roland Barthes, 'The Death of the Author', in *The Rustle of Language* (Oxford: Blackwell, 1986), 49–55; cf. n. 31 below.

[10] Albert J. Guerard, 'The Conradian Voice', in Norman Sherry (ed.), *Joseph Conrad: A Commemoration* (London: Macmillan, 1976), 1–16, esp. 4–7.

[11] Zdzislaw Najder, *Joseph Conrad: A Chronicle* (Cambridge: CUP, 1983). Reliable and meticulously researched, this biography supports a main notion in Norman Sherry's *Conrad's Eastern World* and *Conrad's Western World* (Cambridge: CUP, 1966 and 1971), that Conrad often used aspects of his own wide and varied experience as the basis or raw material for his fiction. Yet Najder adds a pertinent warning: 'the finished product should not be treated in the same way as raw material' (493).

[12] It must be noted that such an understanding of Conrad's 'voice' relates it, albeit indirectly, to the difficult issues of 'intention' and 'artistic control' of 'literary meaning'. Although I do not address the issue of Conrad's intentions directly, it is probably true to say that in my critical practice I tend to assume artistic control and that, given my sustained emphasis on narrative method, it would indeed have been virtually impossible not to have done so. However, although some form of authorial intention is necessarily manifested in the literary text, the intrinsic narrative and thematic variation in Conrad's fiction which this study demonstrates would seem to indicate that it is doubtful whether one can talk about Conrad's intentions as 'limited' or 'original' in relation to his intentions as observable in the fictional texts. If the concept

Text—narrative. The concept of text has also become more problematic in contemporary criticism, and especially in decontructionist
post-structuralism. The status of the primary text now appears
reduced; Geoffrey Hartman, for instance, has suggested that it may
be more valuable to read Derrida *on* Balzac than to read Balzac.[13]
Although I accept George Steiner's comment that this is irrefutable
as a claim, I share his doubts about a too-blurred distinction between
commentary/interpretation on the one hand and the primary text
towards which the interpretative effort is directed on the other.[14] My
book aims to improve the reader's understanding of Conrad's fiction
by analysing his narrative method; it hopes to encourage reappraisal
of the primary text, not to suppress it or supersede it.

Though obviously more specific than text, 'narrative' as used here

---

of intention is to be applied to Conrad, it must be remembered that for him it is very
much a process, as his intentions often became more complex and nuanced in the
process of writing. Understood in this way the concept of intention becomes more
closely related both to narrative method and to 'thematics' (a term to be introduced
below). This understanding of intention is partly compatible with that of Jan
Mukařovský: see 'Intentionality and Unintentionality in Art', ch. 8 in his *Structure,
Sign, and Function*, trans. and ed. John Burbank and Peter Steiner (New Haven: Yale
University Press, 1978), 89–128. For a different view on intention and an extended
theoretical discussion of the issue, see P. D. Juhl, *Interpretation: An Essay in the
Philosophy of Literary Criticism* (Princeton, New Jersey: Princeton University Press,
1980). More recently, Juhl has interestingly argued that even in the interpretative
practice of a deconstructionist critic such as Paul de Man certain ties remain between
the meaning of a literary work and the author's intention with the same work. See his
'Playing with Texts: Can Deconstruction Account for Critical Practice?', in Jeremy
Hawthorn (ed.), *Criticism and Critical Theory* (London: Edward Arnold, 1984),
59–71. For a lucid discussion of literary meaning see Stein Haugom Olsen, 'The
"Meaning" of a Literary Work', in his *The End of Literary Theory* (Cambridge: CUP,
1987), 53–72.

[13] This example was used by George Steiner in a lecture on the theory of reading.
Cf. Hartman, *Saving the Text: Literature/Derrida/Philosophy* (Baltimore: Johns
Hopkins University Press, 1981) and id. (ed.), *Deconstruction and Criticism*
(London: Routledge & Kegan Paul, 1979). It might be noted here that although, as
these comments make clear, I am sceptical about certain notions associated with
deconstruction, it does not follow that all post-structuralist theory is uninteresting in
relation to Conrad's narrative method. Thus the broadly structuralist basis of this
study is supplemented by aspects of post-structuralist theory. This applies in particular to the work of Edward Said and Hillis Miller, both of whom have contributed
significantly to Conrad studies as well as to critical post-structuralism.

[14] For an elaboration of George Steiner's views on literary language and criticism
see e.g. his *Language and Silence: Essays 1958–1966* (London: Faber and Faber,
1967).

is also an inclusive concept, probably best described as one which both designates and incorporates the various constituent aspects of Conrad's complex narrative method. Building on Seymour Chatman,[15] we could say that while style deals with the form of the surface of narratives (verbal nuance, for instance), narrative form indicates the larger and more abstract devices that not only structure the fictional text, but are also more clearly related to its thematics. However, borderlines are blurred here—I am certainly not suggesting that stylistic variations cannot be thematically significant. One complicating factor about Conrad is the extent to which the complexity of his narrative method varies. A critical consequence of this variation is that the chapter on such a technically complex novel as *Lord Jim* has to concentrate on the most noticeable narrative variations, whereas the chapter on a much simpler text such as 'Typhoon' can be more responsive to the interplay of narrative and style.

Story and plot. The distinction between story and plot corresponds to that urged by the Russian formalists between *fabula* and *sjužet*. While *fabula* (or story) indicates the chronological order of the text's events, *sjužet* designates these events as they are actually presented and dramatized as plot. The difference between story and plot can reveal much about the narrative method of a Conrad text. Yet the extrapolation of the story is, as we shall see, an artificial and reductive manoeuvre which easily results in overt simplifications. One interesting aspect of Conrad's fiction is that the varying differences between story and plot often have important thematic implications. When, for example, the difference is a small one in the short story 'The Secret Sharer', this is partly because of the importance attached to the narrative principle of suspense in this text (see Chapter 4).

Because of the common association of plot (more, it must be added at once, among literary theorists than among Conradians) with traditional thematic criticism, the concept has been discredited for quite a long while. Very interestingly, however, it is reintroduced in Peter Brooks's recent *Reading for the Plot*. His general definition of plot as 'the dynamic shaping force of the narrative

---

[15] Seymour Chatman, *Story and Discourse: Narrative Structure in Fiction and Film* (Ithaca and London: Cornell University Press, 1978), 15–42. A useful study of Conrad's style is Werner Senn, *Conrad's Narrative Voice: Stylistic Aspects of his Fiction* (Berne: Francke Verlag, 1980).

discourse'[16] approximates to that adopted in this study of Conrad. Brooks's description is influenced by Paul Ricoeur's emphasis on 'the plot's connecting function between an event or events and the story. A story is *made out of* events to the extent that plot *makes* events *into* a story. The plot, therefore, places us at the crossing point of temporality and narrativity.'[17] Brooks is right to stress the usefulness of Ricoeur's notion of the shaping function of plot. This function can be related not only to my concern with the variations and extensions of narrative in Conrad, but also to Cedric Watts's productive distinction between overt and covert plots in Conrad's fiction.[18] As used in this study, then, narrative and plot are virtually synonyms, but the former term is slightly more technical, while the latter has a clearer bias towards action and characterization.

Narrator. The critical focus on the status and function of the narrator is one of the major gains of structuralist literary theory. As an integral part of the fictional creation, the narrator (or the combination of narrators) is the author's primary means of presenting and developing his text, which is constituted through the various activities and functions the narrator is made to perform. Although it is now a commonplace in narrative theory that author and narrator must not be confused, some Conrad critics continue to do so. One reason for the confusion may be that several of Conrad's narrators function as characters as well. In 'Heart of Darkness', for instance, it is difficult to discriminate between Marlow's roles as narrator and character. A related reason for this problem is that Conrad often endows his narrators with an ability or tendency to generalize; and

---

[16] Peter Brooks, *Reading for the Plot: Design and Intention in Narrative* (Oxford: Clarendon Press, 1984), 13. Brooks's study is an important addition to the work of American theorists of narrative such as Chatman, Booth, and Scholes. See Wayne C. Booth, *The Rhetoric of Fiction* (Chicago: University of Chicago Press, 1961), 2nd edn. 1983 with a new Afterword and a supplementary bibliography; Robert Scholes and Robert Kellogg, *The Nature of Narrative* (Oxford: OUP, 1966); R. Scholes, *Structuralism in Literature: An Introduction* (New Haven: Yale University Press, 1974); and id., *Semiotics and Interpretation* (New Haven: Yale University Press, 1982). One of the best introductions to Russian formalism is still Victor Erlich, *Russian Formalism: History—Doctrine* (The Hague: Mouton, 1955).

[17] Paul Ricoeur, 'Narrative Time', in W. J. T. Mitchell (ed.), *On Narrative* (Chicago: University of Chicago Press, 1981), 167. See also Ricoeur, 'Structure and Hermeneutics', in Don Ihde (ed.), *The Conflict of Interpretations: Essays in Hermeneutics* (Evanston: Northwestern University Press, 1974), 27–61. Cf. ch. 10 n. 22.

[18] Cedric Watts, *The Deceptive Text: An Introduction to Covert Plots* (Brighton: Harvester, 1984).

such generalizations may appear to approach the author's own views. In actual fact, however, this is not necessarily the case— compare the discussion in Chapter 12 about the personal narrator's generalizations in *Under Western Eyes*.

Authorial and personal narrators. Throughout this study a distinction between authorial and personal narrators is upheld. The basic formal criterion I use is the grammatical one of pronominal reference: third-person personal pronouns signify an authorial narrator, first-person pronouns a personal narrator. Although the distinction is not unproblematic (this applies in particular to the association of authorial narrator with the third-person personal pronoun), I hope to be able to show that there is much to be gained by applying it to narrative analysis. Moreover, there is, as both Todorov and Franz K. Stanzel observe, a crucial point involved here concerning the ontological status of the narrator.[19] As summarized by Stanzel:

The contrast between an embodied narrator and a narrator without such bodily determination, that is to say, between a first-person narrator and an authorial third-person narrator, accounts for the most important difference in the motivation of the narrator to narrate. For an embodied narrator, this motivation is existential; it is directly connected with his practical experiences, with the joys and sorrows he has experienced, with his moods and needs... For the third-person narrator, on the other hand, there is no existential compulsion to narrate.[20]

Conrad's fiction, which exhibits a large variety of authorial and personal narrators, generally serves to confirm the validity of this critical distinction. We shall see that Conrad's fictional works are most interesting in terms of the relationships between authorial and personal narrative. The narrative and thematic effects that ensue from the sophisticated manner in which these relationships are combined are not only wide-ranging, but frequently surprising and paradoxical as well.

Frequency and repetition. Narrative frequency (concerning the relations between the narrative and the story) has been relatively little studied by theorists of narrative or by Conrad critics. Still, as

---

[19] See Todorov, *Introduction to Poetics*, 39, and n. 20.
[20] Franz K. Stanzel, *A Theory of Narrative* (Cambridge: CUP, 1986), 93, cf. 98. This is a revised, English version (trans. Charlotte Goedsche) of his *Theorie des Erzählens* (Göttingen: Vandenhoeck & Ruprecht, 1979).

Genette points out, this is a main feature of narrative temporality, known in linguistics as *aspect* and repeatedly observable in Conrad's fiction. The fact that three of the four types of frequency Genette lists are relevant to Conrad's fiction exemplifies alone some of its narrative variation. Very briefly, these types are:

1. Narrating once what happened once (singulative narrative, cf. the 'Typhoon' chapter below);
2. narrating *n* times what happened once (repeating narrative, cf. the chapters on *Lord Jim*, *Nostromo*, and *Under Western Eyes*);
3. narrating once what happened *n* times (iterative narrative, which Genette considers typical of Proust, but which can also be seen as a possible implication of the narrative of *Nostromo*).[21]

The relation between narrative frequency and repetition is in one sense obvious, and yet most complicated. Used as a critical concept, repetition is one of the best examples of a term which has both a narrative and a thematic dimension; and the borderline between the two dimensions is often unclear. This applies to both ways in which 'repetition' is used here. First, it refers in a fairly straightforward manner to the repetition of, for instance, a narrative device, either in the same text or from one text to another. Secondly, in the interpretations of four Conrad novels, it designates a distinction between two more thematic, complex forms of repetition. This distinction, which builds on J. Hillis Miller's *Fiction and Repetition*,[22] is explained when it is introduced and applied to the discussion of *Lord Jim* below (see Chapter 9).

Distance. Considered as a whole the fiction of Conrad strongly supports the view of distance as one of the most basic characteristics of narrative fiction. As used in this book, distance is a modal category that denotes, essentially, the relation between the narrator and the characters and events he describes. Additionally, distance may also refer to the relationship between the narrator and the author, or more precisely between the understanding, views, and sensations of the narrator and the thematics the author presents through his narrator(s). This aspect of distance will become clearer

---

[21] Cf. *ND* 113–17.
[22] J. Hillis Miller, 'Two Forms of Repetition', ch. 1 of his *Fiction and Repetition: Seven English Novels* (Oxford: Blackwell, 1982), 1–21. Cf. ch. 9 n. 57.

in the discussions of such novels as *Lord Jim* and *Under Western Eyes*. Distance may be spatial or temporal; and it can also indicate a difference between narrator and character in matters of information, insight, and attitude. Conrad's fiction exhibits intricate modulations of distance—from the detached, ironic stance of the authorial narrators of *The Secret Agent* and *Nostromo* to the lyric interludes to be identified and discussed in the chapters on *The Nigger of the 'Narcissus'* and *The Shadow-Line*, where attitudinal distance may sometimes decrease. Different sorts of distance can also vary very considerably within a single text, as in *Lord Jim*. Like repetition, distance too is a critical term that has not only a narrative, but also a thematic dimension. One of my main critical notions is that there is a close relationship between Conrad's narrative method and his general need for distance from his fictional material.

Perspective and voice. This mode of regulating narrative information arises from the choice of 'point of view'. Genette is clearly right to observe that earlier theory of narrative has suffered from a confusion of what he calls mood and voice, a confusion (or failure to discriminate) between these two questions:

1. Who is the character whose point of view orients the narrative perspective? or *who sees?*; and
2. who is the narrator? or *who speaks?*[23]

Genette finds that narrative theorists as influential as Stanzel and Wayne C. Booth fail to discriminate between these questions. With regard to Conrad, the basic variants of perspective are:

1. Non-focalized narrative, where the omniscient narrator is outside the story; and
2. internal perspective, with the focal character in the story.

Lord Jim, for instance, has multiple internal perspectives, but in the early part of the novel there is, additionally, non-focalized narrative. Broadly, this latter variant is used synonymously with authorial narrative; and the two most important examples of this form that I analyse are *Nostromo* and *The Secret Agent*. If perspective refers to the instance that 'sees', voice indicates for Genette the narrating instance, the speaker of the fictional text. This narrating instance is considered to have produced the narrative discourse, but

[23] *ND* 186, cf. 187–9.

it does not necessarily remain constant and invariable in the course of a single narrative work. Genette refers to *Lord Jim* as a novel with 'complex situations'; and in this text there is indeed, as we shall see in Chapter 9, a sophisticated interplay of different narrative voices.

Narratee and reader. If we, following Rimmon-Kenan, describe the narratee as 'the agent which is at the very least implicitly addressed by the narrator',[24] then we can immediately specify the function this agent has in Conrad by saying that he or she is frequently explicitly addressed—particularly by the personal narrators Conrad employs. Although the varied function of Conrad's narratees cannot be considered in as much detail as that of his narrators, it is not wholly ignored. Surely Gerald Prince's characterization of the narratee's function also applies to Conrad's narratees: '[the narratee] constitutes a relay between narrator and reader; he helps specify the context of the narration, he serves to characterize the narrator, he puts certain themes in relief'.[25] However, one interesting characteristic of Conrad's narrative method is that although quite often addressed, the Conradian narratee tends to preserve a meditative silence—pondering, as it were, both the implications and the validity of the narrator's utterances and reflections.

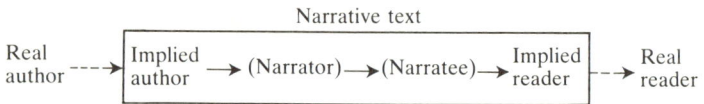

Narrative text

Real author ---→ Implied author → (Narrator) → (Narratee) → Implied reader --→ Real reader

Suggesting a semiotic model of narrative communication related not only to Booth but also to Roman Jakobson,[26] Chatman presents the accompanying diagram.[27] Accepting Rimmon–Kenan's argumentation, I too regard two of the participants enumerated in this diagram, the implied author and the implied reader, as redundant in the model of narrative communication serving as a theoretical basis

24 Rimmon-Kenan, *Narrative Fiction*, 89.

25 Quoted in Todorov, *Introduction to Poetics*, 40. See also Gerald Prince, *Narratology: The Form and Functioning of Narrative* (Berlin: Mouton Publishers, 1982) and 'Narrative Analysis and Narratology', *New Literary History*, 13 (1982), 179–88.

26 Cf. Booth, *The Rhetoric of Fiction, passim*, and Jakobson, 'Closing Statement: Linguistics and Poetics', in T. A. Sebeok (ed.), *Style in Language* (Cambridge, Mass.: MIT Press, 1960), 350–77.   27 Chatman, *Story and Discourse*, 151.

for the following analyses.[28] Only four of Chatman's six participants are thus relevant to my conception of narration in Conrad: the real author (Conrad), the narrator(s), the narratee(s), and the reader. As far as the role of the reader of Conrad is concerned, this is also a complex question which cannot be other than superficially discussed here.[29] But it is necessary to comment briefly on one aspect which is related to the question of fictional coherence and fragmentation in Conrad—a question repeatedly addressed in the textual interpretations. The reader of Conrad assimilates the text, more or less consciously, to various models that are needed to make it intelligible. Arguably, this assimilation process is exceptionally important in the reading of Conrad because of the inherent difficulty of many of his fictional texts. Jonathan Culler calls the process 'naturalization',[30] a term which can be connected with Roland Barthes's description of codes: 'The code is a perspective of quotations, a mirage of structures... so many fragments of something that has always been *already* read, seen, done, experienced; the code is the wake of

---

[28] It does not follow that the concepts of implied author and implied reader are unimportant or unnecessary. But as Rimmon-Kenan convincingly argues, 'If the implied author is only a construct, if its defining property (as opposed to the narrator) is that it has "no voice, no direct means of communicating" [Chatman, *Story and Discourse*, 148], then it seems a contradiction in terms to cast it in the role of the addresser in a communication situation... the notion of the implied author... is best considered as a set of implicit norms rather than as a speaker or a voice (i.e. a subject).' *Narrative Fiction*, 88. In this study such 'implicit norms' are seen as more problematic and conflicting than in Booth and Stanzel; and they are related to, and abstracted from, the various constituent aspects of Conrad's narrative method. Defining narrative fiction as 'the narration of a succession of fictional events', Rimmon-Kenan rightly stresses both the communication process implicit in a narrative and its verbal nature. See *Narrative Fiction*, 2. It follows that it represents, as Boris Tomashevsky pointed out as early as 1925, a *succession* of events, so that 'narrative' as used in this study usually consists of more than one event. See Tomashevsky, 'Thematics', in Lee T. Lemon and Marion J.Reis (eds.), *Russian Formalist Criticism: Four Essays* (Lincoln, Nebr.: University of Nebraska Press, 1965), 61–95, esp. 66–71. Cf. Ian MacKenzie, 'Narratology and Thematics', *Modern Fiction Studies*, 33 (1987), 535–44.

[29] Three important studies of the reading of fiction are Wolfgang Iser, *The Act of Reading: A Theory of Aesthetic Response* (Baltimore: Johns Hopkins University Press, 1978); Umberto Eco, *The Role of the Reader: Explorations in the Semiotics of Texts* (London: Hutchinson, 1981); and J. Hillis Miller, *The Ethics of Reading* (New York: Columbia University Press, 1987).

[30] Jonathan Culler, *Structuralist Poetics: Structuralism, Linguistics and the Study of Literature* (London: Routledge & Kegan Paul, 1975), 138. See also Culler, *The Pursuit of Signs: Semiotics, Literature, Deconstruction* (London: Routledge & Kegan Paul, 1981).

that *already*.[31] One indication of the complexity, sophistication, and modernity of Conrad's fiction is the extent to which his narratives frustrate or counteract the reader's codes, so that we—in order to obtain a fuller understanding of the text—have to reread it, and in that second reading process modify or change our initial assumptions.

Thematics. One of the main conclusions in this study of Conrad's narrative method is that its intrinsic variation and complexity are correlated with a wide range of thematic and ideological elements. It is essentially this characteristic that makes the concept of thematics preferable to 'theme' or 'norm': thematics is a more open, inclusive term which can incorporate, though it does not necessarily unify, the various aspects of content and literary meaning present in Conrad's fiction.[32] Understood in this way, Conrad's thematics is closely related not only to the complexity of his fictional ideas, but more specifically to two other facets of his work, the philosophical and the ideological. My reasons for avoiding the term 'philosophy' are intimated below; they are also implicit in my concern with Conrad's fictional texts only. As far as the ideological facet is concerned, it consists, according to Boris Uspensky, of 'a general system of viewing the world conceptually';[33] and the text's characters and events are then evaluated in accordance with this system.

A major implication for Uspensky is that the ideology of the narrator-focalizer is normally taken as authoritative. In Conrad's fiction, however, this is not necessarily the case, as the interpretation of *Under Western Eyes* demonstrates. My understanding of Conrad's most complex fiction would rather suggest an ideological affinity with M. M. Bakhtin's 'polyphonic' reading of Dostoevsky,[34] whom

---

[31] Roland Barthes, *S/Z*, trans. Richard Miller (New York: Hill and Wang, 1974), 20; orig. publ. 1970 (Paris: Seuil). Though of varying relevance, the work of Barthes is exceptionally suggestive, both generally and with regard to Conrad. Cf. n. 9 above, ch. 4 n. 18, ch. 10 n. 27, and ch. 11 n. 18.

[32] Such an understanding of thematics deviates markedly from a basic, if sometimes implicit, critical assumption of New Criticism, that discordant opposites be reconciled to form an artistically 'unified' literary work. Cf. David Robey, 'Anglo-American New Criticism', in Ann Jefferson and D. Robey (eds.), *Modern Literary Theory: A Comparative Introduction*, 2nd edn. (London: Batsford Academic, 1986), 73–91; and Frank Lentricchia, *After the New Criticism* (London: Athlone Press, 1980). Cf. n. 28 above and ch. 9 n. 57.

[33] Boris Uspensky, *A Poetics of Composition: The Structure of the Artistic Text and Typology of a Compositional Form*, trans. Valentina Zavarin (Berkeley: University of California Press, 1973), 8.

[34] See M. M. Bakhtin, *Problems of Dostoevsky's Poetics* (Ann Arbor, Mich.: Ardis, 1973), orig. publ. in Russian 1929; cf. Michael Holquist (ed.), *The Dialogic Imagination: Four Essays by M. M. Bakhtin* (Austin: University of Texas Press, 1981).

Conrad resented, but whose *Crime and Punishment* in particular is interestingly related to *Under Western Eyes*. According to Bakhtin a single text can accommodate different ideological positions which are not necessarily, or at least not unproblematically, subsumed under a single or predominant one; such an understanding of ideology could be fruitfully applied to all the four novels analysed here. It must be emphasized, however, that although the following analyses of Conrad's narrative method both complicate and extend the thematics of the fiction constituted by this method, my critical concern with narrative necessarily precludes a correspondingly sustained consideration of thematic issues.

III

These issues have already been explored by many Conrad critics. What seems reasonable to attempt here with regard to Conradian thematics, then, is first to suggest possible thematic effects and implications of Conrad's narrative method, and then to relate, or invite the reader to relate, such suggestions to main points in earlier Conrad criticism. As it is essential to put my study into the context of this criticism, I have attempted to acknowledge my debt to earlier relevant contributions in the notes.[35] Here I shall merely draw attention to a lasting paradox in Conrad studies: that many of the most suggestive insights into Conrad's narrative method are to be found in studies which must be described as predominantly thematic, such as those by Albert Guerard, H. M. Daleski, Jacques Berthoud, and Ian Watt.[36] The most impressive section in Guerard's *Conrad the Novelist*, for instance, is a series of paradoxes that Guerard abstracts from Conrad's works, and that establish some of the most original thematic tensions in his fiction. One of the paradoxes is this: 'A

---

[35] A useful (selective and evaluative) bibliography of Conrad studies is Ferdinand Schunck, *Joseph Conrad* (Darmstadt: Wissenschaftliche Buchgesellschaft, 1979). There are additional bibliographies in *Conradiana*, published by Texas Tech University Press (Lubbock), and in the MLA International Bibliographies. The editor of *The Conradian* (Journal of the Joseph Conrad Society [UK]) regularly presents critical surveys of supplementary periodical literature on Conrad.

[36] Albert J. Guerard, *Conrad the Novelist* (Cambridge, Mass.: Harvard University Press, 1958), abbreviated as C N hereafter; H. M. Daleski, *Joseph Conrad: The Way of Dispossession* (London: Faber and Faber, 1977), abbreviated as C W D hereafter; Ian Watt, *Conrad in the Nineteenth Century* (London: Chatto & Windus, 1980), abbreviated as C N C hereafter.

declared fear of the corrosive and faith-destroying intellect—
doubled by a profound and ironic skepticism'.[37] On the whole, there
are a number of important links between the sort of thematic tensions Guerard and other critics identify and discuss in Conrad and
the observations to be made here on narrative variations and effects.

As an example of a study that has proved usefully provocative in
specifying and implementing my own approach, I shall briefly discuss
Torsten Pettersson's *Consciousness and Time*,[38] which investigates
philosophical and aesthetic questions dramatized in Conrad's work.
An important similarity between Pettersson's study and mine is that
both attempt to investigate the interplay between Conrad's thematics
(the term I prefer to Pettersson's 'philosophy') and narrative method.
One of my main arguments, however, is that this interplay or interrelationship is not only more complicated, but also more reciprocal
than Pettersson seems to think. He is certainly right to stress that
Conrad was an exceptionally reflective writer; and many of the
observations he makes on the relationship of Conrad's epistemological convictions to his narrative experimentation are both
illuminating and convincing. Still, if it were clear that Conrad
consciously and consistently attempted to express his philosophy
through his fiction, it would also seem evident that we have to
discriminate between varying degrees of success in these attempts.
Furthermore, the fictional works themselves—as constituents of
meaning through a remarkable variety of narrative devices and
techniques—engender a thematics which is far more complex than
any thematic extrapolation from Conrad's non-fictional writings
would suggest. In consistence with this view the following interpretations, focused on the diverse functions of Conrad's narrative
method, are less concerned with the relation of this method to
Conrad's philosophy than to the complex thematics they themselves
serve to present, shape, intensify, and extend. I am sceptical, therefore, about Pettersson's curiously direct and unmodified application
of Conrad's philosophy, established on the basis of his *non-fictional*
writings, to the following discussion of the *fictional* works. He gives
an account of this philosophy which is persuasive enough in itself,
but less so when used as an explanantion of the strategies and

---

[37] CN 57.
[38] Torsten Pettersson, *Consciousness and Time: A Study in the Philosophy and Narrative Technique of Joseph Conrad* (Åbo: Åbo Akademi, 1982).

achievements of the fictional texts. Now Pettersson is certainly not the first to employ this form of critical procedure; similar criticisms could be made of studies by such influential critics as Berthoud and Said.[39] However, the theoretical problems associated with the procedure become particularly conspicuous in Pettersson's case because of the direct combination of philosophy and narrative technique.

The main critical aim of this book, then, is to describe and evaluate Conrad's narrative method as presented by, and observable in, his fictional work. I propose to do so by subjecting to narrative analysis a dozen of Conrad's most interesting fictional texts. To say that these works are 'interesting' is to suggest that, in addition to including most of the characteristics of Conrad's fiction, they illustrate not only the range of his narrative method, but also varying degrees of narrative success and thematic suggestiveness. Conrad's narrative strategies are not only more or less sophisticated and nuanced, but also variously productive thematically. Narrative method is here understood as an inclusive and, unavoidably, a rather imprecise concept. It serves as a collective term under which the various constitutive aspects of Conrad's narrative method are subsumed and interrelated. There is a relation, however, between the relative imprecision of the initial thesis of this study and what might be termed its critical flexibility, which allows not only for an investigation of the range of Conrad's narrative method, but also for an exploration of the relationship between narrative method and Conradian thematics.

It would seem consistent with my main critical concerns as outlined above that considerable emphasis should be placed on the commentary on the individual texts. I shall start by comparing, in summary and rather curtailed fashion, two Conrad texts which not only illustrate several of the main characteristics of his narrative method, but also reveal different degrees of narrative success in relation to the thematics explored. In the ten following chapters, which present more detailed analyses of three short stories, three novellas, and four novels, the critical commentary on the works in question proceeds progressively—identifying and discussing the narrative devices, functions, variations, and effects as they are introduced, modified, and extended. The critical flexibility attempted in

---

[39] Cf. n. 2 above and Edward Said, *Joseph Conrad and the Fiction of Autobiography* (Cambridge, Mass.: Harvard University Press, 1966).

these chapters is confirmed and supplemented by a certain 'openness' of approach which implies that I allow the textual characteristics of the fictional text under consideration to influence the choice and application of narrative terminology. This is a main reason why the critical concepts are taken from several studies of narrative: as the narrative terms and notions of different theorists may indicate and clarify various aspects of Conrad's narrative, so the intrinsic variation and complexity of his narrative actualize a variety of narrative problems more extensive than those treated by any single theorist. Although, as already indicated, this kind of conceptual eclecticism is not unproblematic, the critical challenges of Conrad's complex and diverse narrative method seem to go quite far towards justifying it.

If the borderlines between textual commentary and interpretation are blurred in this study, this is not only another indication of methodological flexibility, but also, at a different level, of the inter-relationship of narrative and thematics in Conrad's fiction. The functions and effects of Conrad's narrative method cannot, in a majority of cases, be persuasively investigated unless the devices and variations are put into relation not only to each other, but also to the narrative and thematic effects of the text as a whole. This variant of my critical approach is most noticeable at the end of the various chapters, where I attempt some concluding generalizations about the narrative method of the text in question.

2

'Heart of Darkness' Contrasted with *Chance*: Narrative Success and Narrative Failure

In order to see more clearly some of the most characteristic strengths and weaknesses of Conrad's narrative method it may be useful to contrast 'Heart of Darkness', one of his most successful narratives, with *Chance*, a relative failure. In contrasting these two texts, a novella from 1899 and a novel (Conrad's first popular success) from 1913,[1] more critical attention has to be given to 'Heart of Darkness' than to *Chance* because of the greater complexity of the former work.[2] To compare these two narratives is to provide this study with a concrete starting-point that may prove a helpful supplement to the more theoretical Introduction above; furthermore, we thus enlarge the study's textual points of reference. Very briefly, and in no way attempting a full analysis of the two texts, I shall identify some essential aspects of the narrative method of each of them—discussing how productive the various narrative devices and functions are in relation to the thematics developed. Particular attention will be paid to the introduction and function of Marlow as a narrator.

---

[1] 'Heart of Darkness' was serialized in *Blackwood's Magazine* in 1899 and published in *Youth: A Narrative and Two Other Stories* in 1902; *Chance* was serialized in *New York Herald* in 1912 and published in book form in 1913.

[2] The two best and most exhaustive discussions of 'Heart of Darkness' are those in Cedric Watts, *Conrad's 'Heart of Darkness': A Critical and Contextual Discussion* (Milan: Mursia, 1977), and CNC 126–253. There are helpful chapters on the novella in CWD 51–76; CMP 41–63; C. B. Cox, *Joseph Conrad: The Modern Imagination* (London: Dent, 1974), 45–59; Jeremy Hawthorn, *Joseph Conrad: Language and Fictional Self-Consciousness* (London: Edward Arnold, 1979), 7–36; and Suresh Raval, *The Art of Failure: Conrad's Fiction* (Boston: Allen & Unwin, 1986), 19–44. See also the selection of criticism in C. B. Cox (ed.), *Conrad: 'Heart of Darkness', 'Nostromo' and 'Under Western Eyes'. A Casebook* (London: Macmillan, 1981). An example of a thematically oriented essay which includes perceptive observations on Marlow's narrative function and attitudinal position is Hunt Hawkins, 'Conrad's Critique of Imperialism in *Heart of Darkness*', *PMLA* 94 (1979), 286–99.

I

'Heart of Darkness' has the additional advantage of having been considered by two of the narrative theorists whose work has influenced my approach to Conrad: Tzvetan Todorov and Peter Brooks.[3] For Todorov, 'Heart of Darkness' superficially resembles an adventure story, but then takes the form of a process of gradually deepening insight (both for Marlow, the novella's narrator-character, and the reader), which, however, ends in nothingness or disillusionment. The process culminates after Marlow's meeting with Kurtz, the other main character, whose experience, actions, and attitudes paradoxically embody this emptiness: 'Kurtz est bien le centre du récit, et sa connaissance, la force motrice de l' intrigue... Kurtz est le cœur des ténèbres mais ce cœur est vide'.[4]

If we regard Todorov's last point as a possible formulation of an essential aspect of the thematics of 'Heart of Darkness', it becomes apparent at once that the credibility of this thematics is dependent on the success or persuasiveness of the narrative method employed in the novella. If the thematic centre of the text is an instance of vacuity or emptiness, then the narrative process towards this emptiness—with its implications of a profound disillusionment—is inevitably accentuated. It takes a persuasive narrative method indeed to ensure the reader's assent to, and acceptance of, such an uncompromisingly pessimistic view of one of the two main characters in the novella. For although Kurtz is portrayed as exceptionally ruthless, a strong and distressing implication of 'Heart of Darkness' is that there is, at a deep level, a certain attitudinal affinity not only between Kurtz and Marlow, but also between Kurtz and the reader.

In addition to the frame narrator, the most essential elements of the narrative method of 'Heart of Darkness' are constituted by Marlow's functions as narrator and character. Like *Lord Jim*, to whose narrative method that of 'Heart of Darkness' is most clearly related, the novella is a framed text, which Brooks illustrates as in the accompanying diagram.[5] The diagram is useful as a simplified

---

[3] See Tzvetan Todorov, 'Connaissance du vide: *Coeur des ténèbres*', *Les Genres du discours* (Paris: Seuil, 1978), 161–73; and Peter Brooks, 'An Unreadable Report: Conrad's *Heart of Darkness*', ch. 9 of his *Reading for the Plot*, 238–63.

[4] 'Kurtz is certainly the centre of the narrative, and his knowledge, the driving force of the plot... Kurtz is the heart of darkness but this heart is empty.' My trans. from Todorov, *Les Genres du discours*, 167, 169.

[5] Brooks, *Reading for the Plot*, 351.

illustration of the basic narrative structure of the novella—a framed tale presented as a set of nested boxes. Yet, as Brooks himself notes, it is a false diagram in that 'the inner frame of Kurtz's narrative has no such shapely coherence [as that of the classic framed tale], and—perhaps as consequence—neither Marlow's narrative nor the first narrator's appears to "close" in satisfactory fashion'.[6]

First Narrator [Marlow [Kurtz [ ] K's death] end M's narrative] First Narrator / final paragraph

As I agree only partly with this comment, my dissent may provide the starting-point for a somewhat closer consideration of the narrative method at the beginning and end of 'Heart of Darkness'. My critical response is provoked by Brooks's apparent equation of the degree of fictional closure in Marlow's narrative and in that of the personal frame narrator who functions both as narratee (he is one of the group of sailors addressed by Marlow aboard the *Nellie*) and as the narrator who relays Marlow's tale to the reader, For if there is, as I would suggest, an essential difference of understanding and insight between Marlow and the personal narrator, then this difference would seem to include a dissimilar attitude to the problems of coherence and closure, and by implication also to the related complex issues of origin, beginning, and repetition in fiction. It is certainly important to observe, as Brooks does,[7] that the ending of the novella is 'open' in a way which relates it to the reflective and problematic attitude to language characteristic of modernist writing. However, if we link Brooks's suggestive notion specifically both to Marlow and the personal narrator, then we can see more clearly how different they really are. Broadly, the personal narrator's opening remarks indicate a more unproblematic, simplifying attitude to the text's main thematic concerns than that of Marlow, whose story he transmits. This is another way of suggesting that the exceptional thematic complexity of 'Heart of Darkness' is in part dependent on the varying degrees of insight shown by the novella's narrators. To make this point is to reaffirm the necessity of discussing Conrad's

[6] Ibid.
[7] Ibid. 251–3.

narrative method by relating it to the different functions the narrators perform. A main characteristic of this method is suggested by the way in which the narrators can not only supplement but also contradict one another, so that the combined effect becomes more paradoxical, ironic, and complex.

There is a general danger attached to the narrative technique of interposing a 'simpler' narrator between the reader and the text's major (and more authoritative) one: the views of the frame narrator may reduce or distort the complexity of the narrative he presents. Variants of this problem are, as we shall see, observable in texts as dissimilar as 'The Tale' and *Under Western Eyes*. In the case of 'Heart of Darkness', however, the danger is controlled by the structural function of the personal narrator: he provides a contrast with the subsequent narrative which paradoxically enhances the complexity of the novella as a whole.

The potential advantages of the personal frame narrator's presence at the beginning and ending of 'Heart of Darkness' are fully exploited. As Cedric Watts notes, 'the bizarre events recounted gain vividness through the apparently respectable and sociable normality of the contrasting outer narrative'.[8] Furthermore, there is an important 'tentacular effect' at work here: 'the initial impression of contrast is disturbed by the implication that there may be some complicity between the apparently respectable "outer" group and the brutalities of the "inner" narrative'.[9] Although the most important connection between the outer group and the inner narrative is, as already indicated, Marlow, it is also in part established through the mediating function of the frame narrator.

The complexity of the novella necessitates delimitation of this short discussion, which is introductory and does not constitute a narrative analysis in the same way as the subsequent chapters do. I choose, therefore, to comment in some detail on one particular aspect of the frame narrator's function that has hitherto been insufficiently considered. This will enable us to specify the references to Watts's study, thus offering additional critical support for the emphasis he places on the productive sophistication of the novella's narrative method. Briefly, the narrative variation to be considered is this: although the personal narrator at first appears to be strikingly

---

[8] Watts, *Conrad's 'Heart of Darkness'*, 26.
[9] Ibid.

simple compared to Marlow, this simplicity (both in attitude and insight) is more noticeable at the very beginning of his narrative than it is later on. This change increases the narrative and thematic significance of the function the frame narrator performs.

Read in the light of our knowledge of the action of the novella as a whole, the personal narrator's opening description of the setting of his narration is very evocative and yet highly selective:

The sea-reach of the Thames stretched before us like the beginning of an interminable waterway... The air was dark above Gravesend, and farther back still seemed condensed into a mournful gloom, brooding motionless over the biggest, and the greatest, town on earth. (45)

What greatness had not floated on the ebb of that river into the mystery of an unknown earth! . . . The dreams of men, the seed of commonwealths, the germs of empires.

The sun set; the dusk fell on the stream, and lights began to appear along the shore. The Chapman lighthouse, a three-legged thing erect on a mud-flat, shone strongly. Lights of ships moved in the fairway—a great stir of lights going up and going down. And farther west on the upper reaches the place of the monstrous town was still marked ominously on the sky, a brooding gloom in sunshine, a lurid glare under the stars.

'And this also,' said Marlow suddenly, 'has been one of the dark places of the earth.' (47–8)

This narrative variation is one of the most effective in all of Conrad's writings. Marlow's quiet remark not only exposes the relative naïvety and limited insight of the frame narrator, but also prefigures the complex, sombre implications of the story he is about to tell. Rather overtly, Marlow's comment anticipates his following reflection on the arrival of the Romans in Britain 'nineteen hundred years ago— the other day . . .' (49). More importantly, his introductory comment functions as a complex prolepsis of 'darkness', the central metaphor in the text.[10] 'But darkness was here yesterday,'(49) Marlow says at the beginning of his tale. When the reader has reached the end of it, he or she is likely to conclude that darkness is here today as well—it has merely assumed a different, less overt form.

[10] 'Prolepsis' and 'analepsis' are for Genette variants of 'anachrony', which in *Narrative Discourse* indicates the different types of discordance between the two orderings of story and plot. They are subsumed under the broad concept of 'order', the term Genette uses to describe the temporal duality which German theorists of narrative commonly refer to as the opposition between *Erzählzeit* (time of narration)

It must be noted, however, that the relative simplicity of the frame narrator's introductory description does not preclude the presence of proleptic elements here too. The name of the town Gravesend suggests seriousness and death: and the air above it is 'dark... condensed into a mournful gloom'. Although London is seen as 'the greatest town on earth', the adjective 'monstrous' is applied to it in the second passage quoted. Even at this early stage, then, the narrative of the personal frame narrator oscillates between a somewhat naïve nationalism and a more complex and disillusioned view which can be related to the insights provoked by Marlow's story. Interestingly, the narrator himself seems unconscious of both these positions.

The indirect characterization of the frame narrator is extended as he goes on to introduce Marlow:

> The yarns of seamen have a direct simplicity, the whole meaning of which lies within the shell of a cracked nut. But Marlow was not typical (if his propensity to spin yarns be excepted), and to him the meaning of an episode was not inside like a kernel but outside, enveloping the tale which brought it out only as a glow brings out a haze, in the likeness of one of these misty halos that sometimes are made visible by the spectral illumination of moonshine. (48)

There are two interrelated ways in which the personal narrator seems to reveal more understanding and insight here than in the former quotation. First, his introduction to Marlow goes quite far to affirm the difference between them that we have already noted, and recognition of limited knowledge surely implies some wisdom. Secondly, and more interestingly, the passage tells us something important not only about the narrative and thematic characteristics of the tale we are about to hear, but also about the narrator's surprising understanding of Marlow's presentation of it. This relative insight increases his

---

and *erzählte Zeit* (narrated time). A prolepsis is 'any narrative manœuvre that consists of narrating or evoking in advance an event that will take place later', see N D 40, cf. 67–79. Conrad's fiction contains numerous examples of prolepsis, which are often thematically productive. They are variously observable in the text; frequently they can be seen and appreciated only on a second reading. More frequent than prolepsis, analepsis designates 'any evocation after the fact of an event that took place earlier than the point in the story where we are at any given moment', see N D 40, cf. 48–67. Analepses can be internal or external. If external the entire extent of the analepsis remains external to the extent of the first narrative, while the extent of an internal analepsis is internal to the extent of the first narrative. In Conrad the internal analepses are the more important. They are mostly 'homodiegetic' in that they deal with the same line of action as the first narrative. See N D 49–51.

reliability, which is essential in order to preserve the narrative and thematic effects of Marlow's narrative. The kind of inconsistency and unreliability associated with the language teacher as narrator in *Under Western Eyes* (cf. Chapter 12) would seriously have impaired the impact of 'Heart of Darkness'.

Hillis Miller's notion of the narration of the novella as a 'process of unveiling' is relevant here.[11] Although this process includes both paradoxical and ironic elements (the combined effects of which support the kind of thematic conclusion reached by Todorov), its structure as a relay of narrators or witnesses establishes the characteristic tentacular effect which again enhances the moral complexity of the tale and the reader's involvement in it. For Miller, the personal narrator's distinction between the yarns of seamen and those of Marlow 'is made in terms of two figures, two versions of the relation of inside to outside, outside to inside. The hermeneutics of parable is presented here parabolically, according to a deep and unavoidable necessity'.[12] As Miller sees 'Heart of Darkness' as a 'parabolic text',[13] the passage is to him essentially a constituent of the novella's 'preordained correspondence to... the meaning',[14] however partial and obscure this meaning may be.

For Marlow, as the personal narrator suggests in this passage, the meaning conditions and envelops the story rather than the other way round. However, even though these words by the narrator suggestively characterize the novella and support Miller's generic classification of it as parabolic, it must be emphasized that this understanding of enveloping meaning is a textual characteristic presented by a fictional character, and not a critical point which interferes with the capacity of narrative method to generate a thematics which, in an

[11]   J. Hillis Miller, '*Heart of Darkness* Revisited', in Ross C. Murfin (ed.), *Conrad Revisited: Essays for the Eighties* (Alabama: University of Alabama Press, 1985), 43.

[12]   Ibid. 33. For Miller, 'The distinctive feature of a parable, whether sacred or secular, is the use of a realistic story, a story in one way or another based firmly on what Marx calls man's "real conditions of life, and his relations with his kind," to express another reality or truth not otherwise expressible' (31). See Karl Marx, 'Manifesto of the Communist Party', in *The Marx–Engels Reader*, 2nd edn., ed. Robert C. Tucker (New York: Norton, 1978), 476. Miller then goes on to relate his understanding of parable to that of apocalypse: 'My contention is that *Heart of Darkness* fits, in its own way, the definitions of both parable and apocalypse, and that much illumination is shed on it by interpreting it in the light of these generic classifications' (33).

[13]   Ibid. 31 and *passim*.

[14]   Ibid. 34–5.

obvious and yet complicated way, is related to the problem of meaning. What this semantically dense passage essentially does, in addition to its strong suggestion of the personal narrator's improved understanding, is to specify two characteristic qualities of Marlow's ensuing narrative. These qualities are, as Ian Watt observes, suggested metaphorically; and they can be described, to adopt his concepts, as 'symbolist and impressionist'.[15]

The personal narrator's reflections, then, not only function as nuanced introduction to Marlow's narrative, but also as qualification of the position he has formerly assumed. Watt regards the reflections as 'Conrad's'.[16] It would be more accurate to say that what is remarkable about the passage is the surprising insight the personal narrator reveals into the preconditions and characteristics of his own narrative. From this observation we could go on to suggest that in 'Heart of Darkness' the views of the frame narrator are interestingly influenced by the process of learning which the novella dramatizes. The passage considered here is better attuned to the main tenor of Marlow's narrative than the personal narrator's opening, more simplifying views. This is another way of saying that one constituent element of the success of 'Heart of Darkness' resides in its narrative flexibility, and in the way this flexibility is correlated with the thematic development of the tale.

In the early part of 'Heart of Darkness', then, there is a characteristic duality in the personal narrator's attitude and insight. A similar doubleness seems at first to be observable in the paragraph with which the novella ends:

Marlow ceased, and sat apart, indistinct and silent, in the pose of a meditating Buddha. Nobody moved for a time. 'We have lost the first of the ebb,' said the Director, suddenly. I raised my head. The offing was barred by a black bank of clouds, and the tranquil waterway leading to the uttermost ends of the earth flowed sombre under an overcast sky—seemed to lead into the heart of an immense darkness. (162)

In one sense, these concluding words of the personal narrator's appear to trivialize the climactic ending of Marlow's preceding description of his meeting with Kurtz's fiancée, caught 'in the triumphant darkness from which I could not have defended her—from which I could not even defend myself' (159). And yet Marlow's story

---

[15] CNC 169.
[16] Ibid.

has evidently left a deep impression on the personal narrator. He appears wiser here than at the very beginning of his tale; and the change becomes particularly noticeable in the words and imagery he attaches to the Thames and the sea.

Clearly, some of the personal narrator's functions are best understood in relation to Marlow, whose story he transmits. A key characteristic of this relation is his response, as frame narrator, to Marlow's act of narration. This response is notably different from that of the other listeners aboard the *Nellie*; and, as Dorice W. Elliott puts it, it 'indicates the powerful effect of [Marlow's] voice on his consciousness'.[17] If the frame narrator's strong response to Marlow's narrative is connected with his variable, and increasing, insight, then this particular form of narrative variation becomes more immediately understandable. There is also, in this exceptionally dense fictional text, an interesting relation between the frame narrator's response and the tentacular effect Cedric Watts has described. To judge from his opening remarks, the narrator's capacity for the kind of response we are considering here seems only remotely possible. However, as his response is a consequence of his learning process, the reader of the novella is manipulated into a kind of response which resembles, or is at least influenced by, that of the frame narrator. This kind of response (concerning both the frame narrator and the reader) may incorporate glimpses of insight and a serious attention that are all too easily suppressed by more systematic, critical discourse. Although (and also because it is) inconsistent and partial, the frame narrator's response seems exceptionally honest.

While the frame narrator commands, then, more respect than at first seems warranted, his individualization is limited by his primary role as reliable transmitter of Marlow's narrative. Broadly, the narrative and thematic function of Marlow in 'Heart of Darkness' is most complex, and can be only summarily considered here.[18] I shall, however, comment briefly on the two main characteristics of his narrative that Ian Watt identifies and discusses: narrative impressionism and symbolism.

As Watt notes, 'Marlow's emphasis on the difficulty of understanding and communicating his own individual experience aligns

---

[17] Dorice W. Elliott, 'Hearing the Darkness: The Narrative Chain in Conrad's *Heart of Darkness*', *English Literature in Transition 1880–1920*, 28 (1985), 166.

[18] See in particular Cedric Watts's two chs. on 'Marlow's Narrative', *Conrad's 'Heart of Darkness'*, 48–127.

Heart of Darkness with the subjective relativism of the impressionist attitude.'[19] A chief characteristic of Marlow's narrative is the way in which it repeatedly puts the reader into direct, sensory contact with the dramatic events as they unfold through the act of narration. As formulated by Watt, this means that 'the physical impression must precede the understanding of cause. Literary impressionism implies a field of vision which is not merely limited to the individual observer, but is also controlled by whatever conditions—internal and external—prevail at the moment of observation.'[20]

Relating Watt's important point to this study, I would suggest that one reason for the narrative success of the 'subjective moral impressionism'[21] of 'Heart of Darkness' is to be sought in the productive correlation of Marlow's personal narration, which takes the form of an ordering and existentially motivated re-experience, and that of the frame narrator, which proceeds from an unexpected involvement and a surprising understanding. Paradoxically, the frame narrator's involvement increases as a result of the impressionist narrative he himself transmits. Watt has coined the term 'delayed decoding' to describe one constituent aspect of Conrad's impressionist narrative. As he puts it, through the narrative device of delayed decoding the author attempts 'to present a sense impression and to withhold naming it or explaining its meaning until later... This takes us directly into the observer's consciousness at the very moment of the perception, before it has been translated into its cause'.[22] Conrad had used this device prior to 'Heart of Darkness', but one of its notable textual manifestations here is Marlow's confusion when his boat is attacked just below Kurtz's station. Only later does he discover the cause of the various odd changes he observes: 'We cleared the snag clumsily. Arrows, by Jove! We were being shot at!' (110).

A minor dissent from Watt is provoked by his tendency, as he continues his excellent discussion of literary impressionism in 'Heart of Darkness', to connect only one of the two constituent aspects of

---

[19] CNC 179.

[20] Ibid. 178.

[21] Ibid. 174.

[22] Ibid. 175. Cf. Cedric Watts, 'Conrad and Delayed Decoding', *The Deceptive Text*, 43–46. For Genette, the term which approximates to delayed decoding is 'completing analepsis', which 'comprises the retrospective sections that fill in, after the event, an earlier gap in the narrative'. See *ND* 51.

delayed decoding to the text's aspects of meaning. While this connection is valid as far as it goes, it would seem that meaning need not necessarily be wholly excluded from the actual impression either. The concept of delayed decoding, as Watt uses it, is probably most productive as narrative description of relatively simple and easily identifiable instances of temporarily inexplicable impressions and occurrences. A larger problem such as Marlow's impression of Kurtz is not decoded, but it does not follow from this form of obscurity that Marlow's encounter with the other protagonist of the novella may not contain some meaning.

The symbolism developed through Marlow's narrative can be briefly considered in relation to the central metaphor of darkness and the 'yarns of seamen' passage quoted above. Although the earliest sense of 'symbol' was 'a creed of confession or faith' (*OED*), in modernist literature it is distinguished, some would say negatively, by a pervasive ambiguity of meaning. Thus the symbolism of 'Heart of Darkness' is definitely not of a fixed and conventional kind; it is rather constituted by the novella's combined devices of imagery, metaphor, paradox, and irony—all of which are intimately related to the relay of narrators through whom the story is presented to the reader.[23]

One important qualification follows from this observation. A variant on the thematics of the novella, the symbolism lags behind the narrative development of Marlow's story in the sense that its characteristics and implications cannot be properly appreciated until the text has been reread. An example is Marlow's opening sentence: ' "And this also," said Marlow suddenly, "has been one of the dark places of the earth" ' (48). Its full meaning cannot possibly be grasped on a first reading, but as we reread the text the adjective 'dark' almost unavoidably makes us think not only of the darkness surrounding Kurtz, but also of the dusk (fading into darkness) of the sitting-room where Marlow meets (and perhaps falls in love with) Kurtz's fiancée, and of the frame narrator's last, suggestive reference to 'an immense darkness' (162).

As the ambiguity of the darkness metaphor adumbrates the range of the symbolism of the novella, it should be pointed out how closely the constituent elements of the metaphor are connected with the

---

[23] See ch. 6 n. 4 for explanatory comments on the concepts of 'metaphor' and 'symbol'.

progression of Marlow's narrative, and particularly the section which describes the 'empty' centre occupied by Kurtz. As Brooks has pointed out, Kurtz's story has a curiously non-narrated form, 'And since [it] in its telling becomes bound up with Marlow's, it never is clearly demarcated from its frames'.[24] While explication of a metaphor (or symbol) will all too often reduce its thematic suggestiveness, the way in which the darkness metaphor is intertwined with the story's narrative method promotes instead a generalization of it which extends, rather than delimits, these implications.

If we now return to the 'yarns of seamen' passage, we are in a better position to evaluate the frame narrator's characterization of Marlow's narrative and notion of meaning. Read in the light of the whole text, the frame narrator's description seems remarkably accurate. Marlow's tale has indeed revealed itself to be, in Watt's phrase, 'typically "centrifugal": the relation of the spheres is reversed; now the narrative vehicle is the smaller inside sphere; and its function is merely to make the reader go outside it in search of a circumambient universe of meanings which are not normally visible, but which the story, the glow, dimly illuminates'.[25] As Miller's discussion of the passage demonstrates, its thematic implications—and, as a corollary, the interpretative possibilities which it actualizes and encourages—are almost infinite. These possibilities cannot be explored here, but it is essential to specify and extend one point made above: rereading the passage, it strikes one as a succinct description not only of Marlow's narrative but also of the thematics which is developed, modified, and generalized through the progressive act of narration. For instance, the vacuity associated with Kurtz as thematic centre bears a significant relation to the absence of a determinable 'kernel'. Furthermore, the generalizing movements of the text—generalizations of the kind that promote ambiguity and repetition but complicate conclusion—point to a version of 'outside' meaning which is partial and unstable, but not wholly obliterated and not without some moral purpose. If this openness or avoidance of narrative and thematic closure furthers a shift of emphasis from the narrative itself to the act of narration, it also complicates this narration by implying the possibility of a potentially never-ending pattern which conforms to what can be called a second form of repetition.[26]

---

[24] Brooks, *Reading for the Plot*, 257.

[25] *CNC* 180.

[26] The distinction between two forms of repetition is introduced and explained in ch. 9 (on *Lord Jim*); see ch. 9 n. 57.

Marlow may be telling his tale again, perhaps with a somewhat changed emphasis. And, at the different levels of reading, response, and interpretation, the reader will formulate his or her version of this searching exploration of human exploitation, power, loneliness, and dispossession. These versions will not only change from reader to reader, but will also depend on how many times the text has been read.

Several critics have drawn attention to the human qualities of Marlow; and it is certainly true that there is a close functional link between his capacities as narrator and his honest, courageous, and sceptical attitude as character. In a curious way the reader of 'Heart of Darkness' not only comes to sympathize with Marlow, but is also—even as the novella is reread—manipulated into a kind of response which incorporates, or seems to us to incorporate, some of his suffering. We respond, for instance, to the problem of distance Marlow is confronted with as he embarks on his narrative venture. On the one hand, the need to clarify distance might be seen as one motivating factor for his narrative, and this in spite of the inadequacies of language which his narration reveals.[27] On the other hand, Marlow's narration inevitably reduces distance by reintroducing him to the irresistible force of the recurrent experience. Again, the novella goes far to dramatize the tension of this conflict, which is generalized rather than resolved by the act of narration Marlow performs.

I have said that the thematics of 'Heart of Darkness' is obscure; this form of obscurity can be related to Frank Kermode's understanding of secrecy in narrative:

It is... a paradox applying to all narrative that although its function is mnemonic it always recalls different things. The mode of recall will depend in some measure on the fashion of a period—what it seems natural or reasonable to expect a text to say. This is another way of affirming that all narratives possess 'hermeneutic potential,' which is another way of saying that they must be obscure... the narrative inhabits its proper dark, in which the interpreter traces its lineaments as best he can.[28]

[27] Cf. Henry Staten, 'Conrad's Mortal Word', *Critical Inquiry*, 12 (1986), 720–40. This essay is in part a response to Garrett Stewart's article, 'Lying as Dying in *Heart of Darkness*', *P M L A* 95 (1980), 319–31.

[28] Frank Kermode, *The Genesis of Secrecy: On the Interpretation of Narrative* (Cambridge, Mass.: Harvard University Press, 1979), 45. See also Kermode's *The Sense of an Ending: Studies in the Theory of Fiction* (Oxford: OUP, 1966). His *Essays on Fiction: 1971–82* (London: Routledge & Kegan Paul, 1983) includes discussions of *The Secret Agent* and *Under Western Eyes*.

As Allon White writes, commenting perceptively on this passage, one must beware of misreading Kermode as suggesting that obscurity and hermeneutic potential be equated. Still, White is right to note that 'if ever a narrative inhabited "its proper dark" as the metaphor of its own textual obscurity, it is Conrad's tale of the Congo'.[29] This is not to suggest that the novella does not incorporate a strong critique of European imperialism in Africa, but it also transcends such a critique in that it dramatizes a series of more or less covert or obscure connections between imperialism as one particular form of human activity and characteristics of the human psyche which may lead human beings of Kurtz's calibre ('All Europe contributed to the making of Kurtz' (117)) to engage in this kind of activity. Thus 'Heart of Darkness' is not essentially, and definitely not only, a story about imperialism, but rather a fictional statement on the human condition and the human psyche provoked by a specific form of exposure to imperialism (and its consequences). However, what needs to be stressed is that the novella offers abundant intrinsic justification, both at the narrative and thematic levels, of its own fictional obscurity. At the level of interpretation too, the text does a lot to guide the reader towards accepting its inherent obscurity: as we as readers attempt to follow Marlow's story we discover that much of his narration takes the form of an interpretative re-experience; and we are impressed by his ardent, sustained attempt to reveal, in White's phrase, 'the nature of enigmatic concealment' surrounding his journey.[30]

II

As we now, in order to establish the basis required for a comparison, move on to a short discussion of the narrative method of *Chance*, it must be remembered that the critical aim of this chapter is primarily introductory: it presents a short, evaluative comparison essentially designed to serve as a transition from the theoretical Introduction to the analyses in the following chapters. The brevity of this chapter unavoidably entails simplifications, and the textual commentary (which I see as a prerequisite for generalizations about Conrad's

---

[29] Allon White, 'Conrad and the Rhetoric of Enigma', ch. 5 of his *The Uses of Obscurity: The Fiction of Early Modernism* (London: Routledge & Kegan Paul, 1981), 126.

[30] Ibid. 127.

narrative method) is necessarily less systematic and exhaustive here than elsewhere. Another interpretative problem actualized by the structure of this chapter must also be made explicit: while I hope that this form of evaluative comparison can be clarifying and critically useful, it may imply too appreciative a view of 'Heart of Darkness' and too depreciatory a view of *Chance*. Still, the critical concept of 'narrative success' is clearly relative, and compared with the narrative method of 'Heart of Darkness' that of *Chance* seems distinctly inferior.[31]

In his 'Author's Note' to the novel (written several years after its publication), Conrad emphasizes that 'In doing this book my intention was to interest people in my vision of things which is indissolubly allied to the style in which it is expressed' (p. x). This remark tells us something about the weight Conrad attached to the narrative method of *Chance*; paradoxically, however, his 'intention' seems better realized in 'Heart of Darkness' than in the later novel. Implicit in Conrad's assertion, then, is the problem of *Chance* which Graham Hough has diagnosed thus: 'The complexities of the narrative method are... layers of protecting covering to an essentially simple heroic vision.'[32] In *Chance* there is, to extend Hough's point, a problematic relation between the intricate narrative method and the thematics it develops.[33] Both readers and critics have complained of this over-

---

[31] It should be noted that the form of fictional obscurity represented by 'Heart of Darkness' has also provoked rather adverse critical commentary. F. R. Leavis may have phrased this criticism most succinctly when he says, in reference to another passage from the novella, that Conrad 'is intent on making a virtue out of not knowing what he means'. See Leavis, *The Great Tradition: George Eliot, Henry James, Joseph Conrad* (Harmondsworth: Penguin, 1962), 199. This book (orig. publ. 1948; the section on Conrad first appeared in *Scrutiny* in 1941) is probably the most influential critical assessment of Conrad's fiction prior to Guerard's *Conrad the Novelist*. However, while some of Leavis's comments on Conrad are very perceptive, this one on 'Heart of Darkness' reveals at least two failures of perception: not only failing to draw the crucially important distinction between Conrad and Marlow, it also reveals a failure to recognize the intrinsic complexity of the thematics the novella explores.

[32] Graham Hough, *Image and Experience: Studies in a Literary Revolution* (London: Duckworth, 1960), 220.

[33] One of the first to criticize *Chance* for its artificial construction was Henry James, in a long article on 'The Younger Novelists' which appeared in the *Times Literary Supplement*, 19 Mar. and 2 Apr. 1914. As Najder puts it, 'According to James, the method of indirect narration in *Chance* is almost an aim in itself, and a driving force of presented events.' See Najder, *Chronicle*, 391. Najder also notes that Conrad 'was conscious that the novel comprised elements of two different books, written at different times' (385); and he finds that '*Chance* was the first of Conrad's books not to have a clearly defined thematic center' (386).

sophistication: the narrative technique of the novel seems designed to engender a much more complex thematics than that actually associated with its simple 'heroic vision', which is notably less interesting and thought-provoking than Marlow's presentation of his experiences and reflections in 'Heart of Darkness'.

In a manner which bears some structural resemblance to 'Heart of Darkness', the narration of *Chance* is transmitted by means of three frames. The story is told by young Powell, a member of the 'sea' group of characters which is contrasted with the 'land' people, to Marlow, who at first seems to resemble the Marlow of 'Heart of Darkness' since he, too, occupies a central position both as narrator and character. Marlow, in his turn, tells the story of *Chance* to an anonymous personal narrator who organizes it into the narrative we read. As in 'Heart of Darkness', then, we have here a narration presented through a chain of personal narrators. In *Chance* too, Marlow is the most important of these narrators, but in the later novel both his narrative and human characteristics are strikingly different from those we have identified and discussed in the section on 'Heart of Darkness'. This change indicates a central problem which must be considered in some detail, but first it might be useful to give a broad outline of the action of *Chance*.

As the narrative of the novel slowly unfolds it presents two related issues: a love motif involving Roderick Anthony and Flora de Barral, and a power motif presented through the typically, though greatly simplified, Conradian bipartite division of land and sea. This land/sea dichotomy is correlated with the attempt to establish an opposition of materialism and idealism: the sea people are described as courageous and loyal, whereas the land group is characterized by a damaging tendency to obstruct both love and friendship.[34] Convinced that she is unlovable, Flora marries Anthony partly in order to help herself and her father, de Barral, when he is released after seven years imprisonment. Flora's misguided belief that she cannot be loved has been forced on her by her governess, one of the novel's most successful characters, who, as John Batchelor puts it in his persuasive discussion of *Chance*, 'has cherished her envious hatred of Flora'.[35] The latter then turns to Mrs Fyne, Anthony's sister, for

[34] Cf. Stephen K. Land, *Conrad and the Paradox of Plot* (London: Macmillan, 1984), 177–91; and John Batchelor, *The Edwardian Novelists* (London: Duckworth, 1983), 81–5.
[35] Batchelor, *Edwardian Novelists*, 82.

help, but this lady, a feminist, proves equally obstructive. Anthony, on his part, is also guilty of compromise. He is, as Marlow says, 'a simple soul' (340), whose independence is greatly reduced by the influence exerted upon him by his father, the poet Carleon Anthony. The characterization of Anthony is weak. He remains too much of a type—barely individualized, passive, and hard to visualize. As, late in the novel, he and Flora set to sea in the *Ferndale* we expect the simplified land/sea division to be diversified, but much of the negative influence of the land group remains.

As the constellation of characters in *Chance* is exceptionally symmetrical, Stephen Land has suggested that they can be grouped in pairs beside the central pair of hero and heroine.[36] Whereas the governess, for instance, exerts her influence upon Flora as heroine, Mrs Fyne influences Anthony as hero. Generally, such a symmetrical structure of characters is not necessarily a narrative weakness. In this particular case, however, it suggests some of the damagingly static (because gradually less interesting) relations of the various characters. Actually, Land's grouping leaves out only Marlow, 'who, as the principal sub-narrator, is neutral with respect to the conflict in which hero and heroine are engaged'.[37] Although the adjective 'neutral' provides an inaccurate description of Marlow's attitude to the characters of his story (compare his sweeping generalizations and pervasive cynicism), Land is right to imply that his detached 'neutrality' epitomizes a central problem in the narrative method of the novel. For the Marlow of *Chance* is not personally and existentially involved in his narrative in the way Marlow is in 'Heart of Darkness' (or *Lord Jim*); and this lack of serious involvement makes the narrative of *Chance* at once less intense and less persuasive.

Marlow is described by the personal narrator in Chapter 1 of Part I in *Chance*:

But Marlow was not put off. He was patient and reflective. He had been at sea many years, and I verily believe he liked sea-life because upon the whole it is favourable to reflection. I am speaking of the now nearly vanished sea-life under sail. To those who may be surprised at the statement I will point out that this life secured for the mind of him who embraced it the inestimable advantages of solitude and silence. Marlow had the habit of pursuing general ideas in a peculiar manner, between jest and earnest. (23)

36 Land, *Paradox of Plot*, 187.
37 Ibid.

As Marlow's narrative progresses, the personal narrator's (or the frame narrator's) introductory characterization is shown to be valid enough. The last sentence in particular brings out some of Marlow's tendency to use his story as a basis for generalized statements. Most of them do not possess the searching, even haunting, quality of the generalizations in 'Heart of Darkness'; and neither is the relation between narrative and thematic generalization as close and convincing as in the novella. A recurrent narrative pattern in *Chance* is that Marlow first relates a dramatic (or melodramatic) occurrence, then attempts to explain this occurrence (or a character's reaction to it) psychologically, and then finally generalizes on the basis of the occurrence and his own explanation. The pattern seems increasingly mechanical: as we read on, several of the generalizations become repetitious and self-assertive. This applies, for instance, to his denunciations of women, about which many critics have complained.[38]

The Marlow of *Chance* is, in fact, so different from the Marlow of 'Heart of Darkness' that the identical name is misleading. The essential differences between the two 'versions' of this transtextual character have been summarized by Bernard Meyer: 'The early Marlow is a thoughtful, troubled man endowed with a remarkable capacity for sympathy and understanding... [the Marlow of *Chance* is] transformed into a stuffy, cantankerous, and opinionated man, given to sweeping generalizations and particularly to intemperate misogyny'.[39] Curiously, there is a passage in the text where the frame narrator—whose position is, generally, more stable and less intriguing than that of his counterpart in 'Heart of Darkness'—describes Marlow in a manner which resembles the judgement of Meyer and other critics: 'I had seldom seen Marlow so vehement, so pessimistic, so earnestly cynical before' (212). Here the frame narrator seems to feel the need for a certain distance from Marlow, for whom he normally has great respect, and whom he even characterizes, with no apparent irony though with the obvious intention of flattery, as 'the expert in the psychological wilderness' (311).

---

[38] See, for instance, Helen Funk Rieselbach, *Conrad's Rebels: The Psychology of Revolution in the Novels from Nostromo to Victory* (Ann Arbor, Michigan: UMI Research Press, 1985), 91–4.

[39] Bernard Meyer, *Joseph Conrad: A Psychoanalytic Biography* (Princeton: Princeton University Press, 1967), 235. Cf. Thomas Moser, *Joseph Conrad: Achievement and Decline* (Cambridge, Mass.: Harvard University Press, 1957), 165.

On the whole, the problem of distance is much less productive in *Chance* than in 'Heart of Darkness'. For the Marlow of 'Heart of Darkness', the act of narration is motivated by his strong need for an ordering, linguistically structured distance from his trying Congo experience; and yet, paradoxically and effectively, the force of this experience is actualized through his narration. In *Chance*, by contrast, Marlow's detached, distanced attitude is of an altogether different and less problematic kind. Similarly, his irony and scepticism are also different from those suggested by the narrative of 'Heart of Darkness'. In this novella, irony is observable not only on all the narrative levels but even, due to the tentacular effect we have noted, on the level of reading. In *Chance*, the function of irony is more limited and predictable; it serves essentially to characterize Marlow's non-committal distance from his narrative. Broadly, then, the initial impression of similarity with 'Heart of Darkness' gives way to a lasting sense of profound dissimilarity between the two works. Generalizing from the very different thematic impact of the two texts, we must conclude that the narrative method of *Chance* is distinctly inferior to that of the earlier novella. Neither is the method of *Chance* comparable qualitatively to that of *Lord Jim*—where the narrative function of Marlow is crucial, though more unevenly successful than in 'Heart of Darkness'—but it exhibits an interesting affinity with that of 'Youth', an important short story Conrad completed in 1898.

Although this study is systematic (in the sense of considering the narrative method of a dozen Conrad texts of varying lengths) rather than developmental (in the sense of discussing Conrad's works in chronological order), it should be pointed out that the fiction Conrad wrote from 1896 to 1900 is particularly interesting with regard to narrative method. In the works from this period—*The Nigger of the 'Narcissus'*, *Tales of Unrest*, 'Youth', 'Heart of Darkness', and *Lord Jim*—we can see Conrad experimenting with various devices and techniques, attempting not only to find a method that would prove generative thematically, but also groping for one that would enable him to handle the fundamental problem of distance from his fictional material. When I say that the narrative of *Chance* interestingly resembles that of 'Youth', this observation can be specified by suggesting that the narrative function of Marlow, who is first introduced in 'Youth', is rather simple in both these texts in comparison with his diverse functions in 'Heart of Darkness' and

Lord Jim. Once this affinity is indicated, however, the point must be qualified by noting that Marlow's narrative function in 'Youth' is more successful than in *Chance* not only because it is more immediately understandable, but also because it establishes a vantage-point or basis of narrative method from which Conrad could go on to employ Marlow as narrator-character in two of his major works.

The introduction of Marlow, then, marks a turning-point in Conrad's narrative method; and it is a shift that is not merely technical, but intimately related to Conrad's uncertainty and experimentation as a writer of fiction. Although I make little use of biographical material, it is helpful here to quote Najder's persuasive explanation of Marlow's importance for Conrad's writing:

> Marlow, a model English gentleman, ex-officer of the merchant marine, was the embodiment of all that Conrad would wish to be if he were to become completely anglicized. And since that was not the case, and since he did not quite share his hero's point of view, there was no need to identify himself with Marlow, either emotionally or intellectually. Thanks to Marlow's duality, Conrad could feel solidarity with, and a sense of belonging to, England by proxy, at the same time maintaining a distance such as one has toward a creation of one's imagination. Thus, Conrad, although he did not permanently resolve his search for a consistent consciousness of self-identity, found an integrating point of view that enabled him, at last, to break out of the worst crisis of his writing career.[40]

Two implications of this view of Marlow must be briefly commented on. First, it suggests an important, though indirect and problematic, relationship between the modulations of distance to be identified and discussed in the following interpretations of Conrad's fiction and his *need for distance* in order to write at all. And, as a corollary, the author's need for distance from his fiction (and also, in a complex way, from his audience) would seem to lend support to the distinction drawn here not only between Conrad and Marlow, but also between Conrad and his narrators in general.

As Cedric Watts observes, the Marlow of 'Heart of Darkness' clearly has 'biographical continuity' with the Marlow of 'Youth';[41] the biography of Captain Charles Marlow is indeed the most important example of fictional transtextuality in the Conrad

---

40 Najder, *Chronicle*, 231.
41 Watts, *Conrad's 'Heart of Darkness'*, 32.

canon.[42] However, one characteristic of Marlow as a narrative device is the extent to which complexity as character and productive sophistication as narrator are correlated: in essentials (as presented through the narrative) the Marlow of 'Heart of Darkness' and of *Lord Jim* is strikingly different from his counterparts in 'Youth' and *Chance*. There seems to be a connection here between Marlow's narrative and thematic complexity and his personal, existential involvement in his narrative. As the Marlow of 'Youth' is, as Watts puts it, 'reminiscing with mainly patronising nostalgic relish about his romantic earlier self',[43] so Marlow's narration in *Chance* is, as I have suggested, similarly patronising and non-committal, although (partly due to the larger scope of *Chance*) less nostalgic and not so much focused on his own past experience as in 'Youth'.[44]

There is a form of obscurity about *Chance* which is very different from that dramatized in 'Heart of Darkness'. In other works— *Nostromo* may be the best example—Conrad can frustrate the reader's initial responses and expectations and then, at a later stage of the narrative or even on a second reading, make him or her appreciate the thematic effect of, for instance, delayed decoding or distorted chronology. Reading *Chance*, however, our search for textual explanation of the various narrative deviations and digressions is but very partially rewarded. The intrinsic motivation for the novel's narrative method (including its excessive length) is obscure, but obscure in a relatively superficial sense. There is not the kind of searching, thematically motivated and serious obscurity (existential,

---

[42] Cf. Watts, 'Transtextual Narratives', ch. 9 of *The Deceptive Text*, 138. By a 'transtextual narrative' Watts means 'one which exists in, across and between two or more texts. It is covert in proportion to the reader's unawareness of the relevant material' (133). He points out that 'Since it is a matter of a coherent narrative (generally given coherence by continuity of characterization), transtextuality is much more specific... than "intertextuality" ' (194). Julia Kristeva has defined 'intertextuality' (an imprecise term with varying usage) as the vast sum of linguistic and cultural knowledge that makes it possible for texts to have meaning: 'tout texte se construit comme mosaïque de citations'. See Kristeva, *Semeiotikè* (Paris: Seuil, 1969), 146.

[43] Watts, *Conrad's 'Heart of Darkness'*, 32.

[44] Although this study works from published versions of Conrad's fictional texts, it might be noted that the revisions of 'Youth' not only support my view of this narrative as a relatively simple record of Marlow's past experience, but also demonstrate to what extent Conrad—particularly at this crucial stage of his writing career— was experimenting with different narrative techniques even within a single text. See Ernest W. Sullivan, 'The Genesis and Evolution of Joseph Conrad's "Youth": A Revised and Copy-edited Typescript Page', *The Review of English Studies*, 36 (1985), 522.

epistemological, linguistic, and interpretative) so strikingly present in 'Heart of Darkness'.

Some tentative conclusions can be attempted on the basis of this summary comparison. First, the variant of personal narrative which the device of Marlow represents has a more effective and persuasive function if it is not just centred on his earlier life experience in a wide sense (as in *Chance*), but on a specific experience which has strongly and seriously engaged him (and, in the case of 'Heart of Darkness', even threatened him).

Secondly, with regard to the narrative and thematic effects obtained, it seems decisive that this experience has not just been a trying and serious one for Marlow, but also one that has somehow shaped his attitude to it and his way of narrating it. This point is related to the general problem of intrinsic, thematic justification of narrative method in Conrad. It is another way of saying that in 'Heart of Darkness' Marlow's narrative, which is sophisticated and yet relatively simple and chronological, increases its persuasiveness in proportion to the gradual development of the story it dramatizes. Narrative method and thematic concern are nicely correlated. In *Chance*, the relation between narrative method and thematics is more problematic. The three narrative frames seem an over-sophisticated device in relation to the simplicity of the 'heroic vision' associated with Anthony.

Thirdly, the issues of narrative length and economy are actualized here. In 'Heart of Darkness', the narrative texture is exceptionally condensed and economical. Some would regard the narrative and thematic density of the novella as excessive; it is a demanding text which insists on attentive rereading. This is not a question of length only: *Nostromo*, Conrad's longest novel, is also one of his most economical. But in order to avoid the damaging effects of mechanical repetition and too detailed description, the novelist must achieve a convincing balance between length and thematic potential. Very evident in 'Heart of Darkness', such a balance is less apparent in *Chance*.

Fourthly, the narrative function of the frame narrator is much more productive in 'Heart of Darkness' than in *Chance*. Although he does not reach Marlow's level of insight, the frame narrator of 'Heart of Darkness' undergoes a process of learning which—and this is important in our critical context—is furthered by the problems and characteristics of the narrative he loyally transmits. In *Chance* too, the frame narrator is influenced by Marlow's narration, but while his attitude may be as consistent as that of his counterpart in 'Heart of Darkness', it seems less appealing and persuasive.

Fifthly, in both these Conrad texts there is a close relation between the degree of success in the narrative method employed and the thematic suggestiveness of the work as a whole. In 'Heart of Darkness' there is an exceptionally productive correlation between the searching narrative method and the sombre thematics which gradually evolves as the story progresses. The characteristically tentacular effect of the novella's narrative serves to provoke and seriously engage the reader; gradually we come to realize that we are more strongly implicated in its thematics than we would like to be. Though largely unsolved, the questions posed by 'Heart of Darkness' are generalized in a manner which increases their relevance. A problem with the narrative method of *Chance* is that the explanations and generalizations offered by Marlow seem all too simple, but although it becomes very clear that his views have to be distinguished from Conrad's, it remains unclear whether the text suggests the possibility of an alternative, authorial position against which Marlow's generalizations could be measured and qualified.

The list might be extended; the use of irony, for instance, is much more suggestive in 'Heart of Darkness' than in *Chance*, where Marlow's irony is an integral part of his detached cynicism. Concluding, then, it would seem that although no narrative method is perfect, that of 'Heart of Darkness' succeeds better than that of *Chance*. The combination of lucidity and profundity of 'Heart of Darkness', combined with its compressed narrative structure, recessive adroitness, and remarkable thematic range, impress and engage us as readers and manipulate us into a thought-provoking form of narrative participation. There is a dynamic and suggestive quality about the narrative of 'Heart of Darkness' that is highly rewarding.

With regard to the difficult question of narrative success, the Conrad texts to be analysed in the following ten chapters would seem to occupy intermediate positions between 'Heart of Darkness' and *Chance*. If the interpretations give a general impression of being perhaps too sympathetic to the narrative method analysed (particularly in relation to the rather adverse commentary on *Chance* above), it must be remembered that one criterion underlying the textual selection is—in addition to narrative variety—that of literary quality. As the brief discussion of *Chance* indicates, this quality is variable in Conrad, and it is doubtful whether all his works (including, for instance, *The Arrow of Gold*) deserve serious critical consideration. This is not to suggest that all his successful narratives are analysed here—*Victory* (1914), for example, is an important Conrad novel, and so is the first one he published, *Almayer's Folly* (1895). But the selection of Conrad's fictional works considered in this study is representative and varied enough to justify the generalizations about his narrative method which are attempted in the concluding chapter.

3

'An Outpost of Progress': Distanced Authorial Narrative as Textual Concentration

One of the most striking characteristics of Conrad's narrative method is its tendency towards textual expansion. Works begun as short stories (*Lord Jim* and *Nostromo* are two obvious examples) in the course of Conrad's painful writing process inevitably became much longer than originally planned. Like William Faulkner, that major modernist writer so strongly influenced by him, Conrad often started from a relatively isolated memory, an impression, an image—and it was difficult, if not impossible, for him to foresee the eventual result of dramatization of the initial idea. This is not to suggest that there are not, in Conrad as in Faulkner, important differences between the narrative method of shorter and longer texts. Furthermore, Conradian narratives of approximately the same length can display remarkable variation in narrative economy. In Conrad's fiction textual length is not only a strictly formal question, but an aspect of narrative method that is related to the author's subject matter—to his thematic concerns and the narrative presentation of these concerns.[1]

Perhaps the best illustration of Conrad's narrative as textual concentration is provided by 'An Outpost of Progress' (part of *Tales of Unrest*, 1898), at 31 pages one of Conrad's shortest stories and yet a pregnant and in some ways a surprisingly complex one. Its brevity enables us to consider its narrative development in some detail. I shall focus on two of the text's narrative characteristics: the function of the authorial narrator and of irony. By way of

---

[1] With this most would agree, but some critics take surprising views on the question of textual length in Conrad. Lawrence Graver, for instance, talks about the 'excessive length' of the most economical, in one sense even (as I shall suggest in ch. 4) too economical 'The Secret Sharer'. See Graver, *Conrad's Short Fiction* (Berkeley: University of California Press, 1969), 158. In a different critical context, Edward Said sees a connection between 'economy' as fictional representation of Conrad's 'deeply felt experience' and his use of the short-story genre. See Said, *Conrad and the Fiction of Autobiography*, 3, 45.

concluding this chapter some of the observations made on the short story are related to 'Heart of Darkness', and to the comments on this novella made above.

In order to establish a point of departure, and of reference, it might be useful to summarize the main action of 'An Outpost of Progress':

Two Europeans, Kayerts and Carlier, are left in charge of a run-down trading station in the Congo by the Managing Director of a large trading company. The only other inhabitants are a Negro clerk, Makola, his family, and ten Negro workers. As chief and assistant, Kayerts and Carlier run the station in a haphazard way, trading for food and ivory with the local natives. Then, through the machinations of Makola, ten Negro workers are sold to some itinerant slave-dealers for ivory. At first appalled, Kayerts and Carlier gradually ease their consciences by blaming Makola and by telling themselves that they must make the best of the situation. As the natives fear that more of them may be taken to the slave-dealers, they stay away, so that trade at the post dries up completely, and the white men's supply of food consequently fails. Their relationship is strained; then, in a quarrel that starts from a petty beginning, one of the men is accidentally shot by the other. The following morning the Managing Director, who has been delayed two months beyond his promised return, arrives at the station—to find that Kayerts has hanged himself from the cross on the grave of the previous chief.[2]

This summary indicates to some extent the story's effective combination of two concerns: description of the unbearably static and meaningless life experienced by Kayerts and Carlier at the trading station; and the dramatically depicted degeneration of the situation, ending in the two deaths, a killing and a suicide. Conrad had good reason to be dissatisfied with the superimposed bipartite division of the story.[3] Not only is the reader's first impression strongly dependent on the pointed ending; rereading 'An Outpost of Progress' we find that much in its main textual body is oriented towards the ending and takes on additional meaning if read in the light of it.

[2] This summary largely follows, but condenses, that given by J. Hilson and D. Timms in their fine essay, 'Conrad's "An Outpost of Progress" or, The Evil Spirit of Civilization', in Claude Thomas (ed.), *Studies in Joseph Conrad* (Montpellier: Université Paul-Valéry, 1975), 115.

[3] See Frederick R. Karl and Laurence Davies (eds.), *The Collected Letters of Joseph Conrad*, I (Cambridge: CUP, 1983), 330.

Considering the short story as a relatively coherent text,[4] I prefer to suggest a tripartite structure based on, and underlining, the continual regressive development of Kayerts and Carlier. The story's first part would be from the opening to the moment when the two white men notice the strangers in the trading station: 'They both, for the first time, became aware that they lived in conditions where the unusual may be dangerous, and that there was no power on earth outside of themselves to stand between them and the unusual' (98). Indicating the frailty of their new life and anticipating the later unintentional killing, this authorial comment is exceptional for 'An Outpost of Progress' in granting the two main characters at least *some* insight. The concession becomes all the more noticeable because it is stated just before that 'being constantly together, they did not notice the change that took place *gradually* in their appearance, and also in their dispositions' (96, my emphasis).

The second part of the story would be from this point in the narrative to the sudden revelation experienced by Kayerts just before the quarrel over the sugar:

Carlier was smiling with marked insolence. And suddenly it seemed to Kayerts that he had never seen that man before. Who was he? He knew nothing about him. What was he capable of? There was a surprising flash of violent emotion within him, as if in the presence of something undreamt-of, dangerous, and final. (110)

Confirming the earlier anticipation of danger and violence, this flash of limited insight on Kayerts's part serves as a forewarning of his killing of Carlier—an absurd act of despair and confusion, void of rational motivation. The story's third and final part, then, would be from the above quotation to the end.

It is telling that even this outline of the structural development of 'An Outpost of Progress' includes a comment on its authorial narrator. The function of this narrative device in the story is crucial, and closely linked to the text's concentration. Discussing the device, I shall pay particular attention to the authorial narrator's distance from the characters, his omniscience, and his generalizations. All

---

[4] In a 1906 number of *The Grand Magazine*, which in that year ran a series called 'My best story and why I think so', Conrad writes that he 'aimed at a scrupulous unity of tone' with 'An Outpost of Progress'. See R. W. Hobson, 'A Textual History of Conrad's "An Outpost of Progress" ', *Conradiana*, 11 (1979), 148.

these characteristics are observable in the first part of the story, and reaffirmed and extended later.[5]

In several of Conrad's major works there are notable modulations of narrative distance, but not in 'An Outpost of Progress': here, on the other hand, there is a wide, and largely constant, gap between the authorial narrator and the characters of the short story. The thematic effect is partly comparable to *Nostromo* (where the narrative method considered as a whole is much more complicated): the characters appear small and vulnerable, with severely restricted control over their own lives. As an impersonal, unindividualized entity the story's authorial narrator is entirely separated from the lives of the characters he describes; and though he may share some of their sensations, this is at a very general level, and linked to his generalizations. The combination of narrative distance and objective information is indicated at the very beginning of the story: 'There were two white men in charge of the trading station. Kayerts, the chief, was short and fat; Carlier, the assistant, was tall' (86). It is as though the device of the authorial narrator, who seems so removed both temporally and spatially from the main characters, enables Conrad to employ relatively strict relevance criteria for the information provided: it is carefully selected on the grounds of effective combination of information value and dramatic and evocative potency.

Throughout the short story the authorial narrator's distance is integrated with his omniscience. The narrator is not only removed from the characters in time and space; he is also capable of entering their minds and explaining what they themselves do not comprehend. In the first paragraph we are told that 'Makola, taciturn and impenetrable, despised the two white men. He had charge of a small clay storehouse with a dried-grass roof, and pretended to keep a correct account...' (86). In a strikingly economical manner, Conrad here uses the authorial narrator to bring out the fact that Makola, who appears impenetrable and certainly *is* to Kayerts and Carlier, actually despises his superiors. But beyond this discrepancy, which is established on the basis of contrast between personal ignorance and authorial omniscience, there are reverberant implications—and

---

[5] The story's commentators have tended to pass lightly over the device of the authorial narrator. See, for instance, CN 64–5; CNC 75; Graver, *Conrad's Short Fiction*, 10–14; and A. T. Tolley, 'Conrad's "Favourite" Story', *Studies in Short Fiction*, 3 (1966), 314–20.

more on a second reading than on a first. There is the suggestion of opposition between the black and white; there is also the possible implication that Makola may in fact be more in control of the situation than his two white chiefs (and also the more intelligent and cunning of the two parties); and already at this stage there is implicit ironic play on 'progress', the key-word in the story's title.

Both narrative distance and omniscience are linked to the authorial narrator's tendency to generalize. As the combination of distance and omniscience enables the narrator to obtain an overview not possessed by any of the characters, one aspect of his generalizations is a widening of perspective beyond the limited setting of the African outpost. This tendency, however, has a second characteristic, which is both more complicated and more intriguing than the first. It is indirectly suggested by Guerard's comment that the 'omniscient author pauses to deliver brief intelligent essays'.[6] Guerard seems to be thinking of what is here subsumed under the narrator's generalizations; and while the word 'essay' suggests too strong a separation from the surrounding narrative, it is certainly justifiable to note the reflective element in the generalizations.

Some major characteristics of the narrator's tendency to generalize are already brought out in the first part. In order to indicate the outward, generalizing movement of the relevant section it is necessary to quote at some length:

They were two perfectly insignificant and incapable individuals, whose existence is only rendered possible through the high organization of civilized crowds. Few men realize that their life, the very essence of their character, their capabilities and their audacities, are only the expression of their belief in the safety of their surroundings. The courage, the composure, the confidence; the emotions and principles; every great and every insignificant thought belongs not to the individual but to the crowd: to the crowd that believes blindly in the irresistible force of its institutions and of its morals, in the power of its police and of its opinion. But the contact with pure unmitigated savagery, with primitive nature and primitive man, brings sudden and profound trouble into the heart. (89)

Beginning with an informative statement on Kayerts and Carlier, the paragraph blends into philosophical reflection on, and evaluation of, the conditions of human existence. Although we cannot

6 CN 65.

consider all the thematic implications of this passage, it should be noted that it is not Conrad but his authorial narrator who, in his eagerness to generalize, becomes categorical and inclined towards overstatement and simplification here. If we were to suggest a norm or a set of values adhered to by Conrad in 'An Outpost of Progress', then the above passage would certainly have to be taken into account, but it would also have to be related to the surrounding context, and still the conclusions reached would have to be rather tentative. The categorical and somewhat condescending attitude in the passage is partly counteracted by the sheer extent of the generalization: ultimately, it is related to both the narrator and the reader.

The narrative characteristics of the first part of 'An Outpost of Progress' also apply to the text as a whole. Having established the central position of the authorial narrator in part one, Conrad confirms it in the two following parts; and there is little of the intricate narrative variation that helps promote the textual expansion of such a work as *Lord Jim*. Narrative distance remains very substantial. Authorial omniscience is retained, but with two noteworthy modulations. The first is one that the short story's commentators have partly overlooked, partly regarded as essentially stylistic. However, its thematic functions and effects justify its status as a narrative variation as well. I am thinking of the 'narrated monologue' which is used to portray Kayerts's bewildered state of mind after the killing of Carlier in part three. Significantly, but also problematically, the linguistic features of narrated monologue indicate a combination of direct and indirect discourse: the reporting verb of indirect discourse is omitted and so is the conjunction 'that', but the third-person reference is retained.[7] Compare this example

---

[7] 'Narrated monologue' is defined by Dorrit Cohn as 'the technique for rendering a character's thought in his own idiom while maintaining the third-person reference and the basic tense of narration'. See her *Transparent Minds: Narrative Modes for Presenting Consciousness in Fiction* (Princeton: Princeton University Press, 1978), 100. Cohn specifies this definition by noting that 'in its meaning and function, as in its grammar, the narrated monologue holds a mid-position between quoted monologue and psycho-narration, rendering the content of a figural mind more obliquely than the former, more directly than the latter' (105). While 'psycho-narration' or referential narrative statement identifies both the subject matter and the activity it denotes, in 'quoted monologue' a character's successive encounters and experiences are accompanied by direct citations of his of her thoughts. Broadly, Cohn's understanding of narrated monologue corresponds to Roy Pascal's term 'free indirect speech', which he investigates in *The Dual Voice: Free Indirect Speech and its Functioning in the Nineteenth-Century European Novel* (Manchester: Manchester

from the relevant section on Kayerts: 'He knew! He was at peace; he was familiar with the highest wisdom!' (115). Here the narrated monologue enhances· the text's complexity or polyvocality by bringing into play the attitudes of both Kayerts and the authorial narrator simultaneously. The narrated monologues of this short story function as a productive variant on its pervasive authorial narrative.

Secondly, the way in which the authorial narrator employs his all-embracing knowledge to comment authoritatively on minor characters, too, contributes to the narrative economy of the story. Following an account of how Kayerts and Carlier anxiously await the delayed return of the steamer, Conrad abruptly makes his narrator give the reader the relevant information: 'But one of the Company's steamers had been wrecked, and the Director was busy with the other, relieving very distant and important stations on the main river' (109). Then, characteristically, there is an immediate switch from this outer state of affairs into the mind of the Managing Director: 'He thought that the useless station, and the useless men, could wait.' Both these pieces of information, outer and inner, are (for all their simplicity and abruptness) relevant as well as plausible— wholly in keeping with the textual concentration of the short story, and consistent with the earlier description of the director as 'a man ruthless and efficient' (87).

The most important generalization in part two is this:

The wicked people were gone, but fear remained. Fear always remains. A man may destroy everything within himself, love and hate and belief, and

---

University Press, 1977). An alternative understanding of narrated monologue is developed by Ann Banfield in her closely-argued *Unspeakable Sentences: Narration and Representation in the Language of Fiction* (London: Routledge & Kegan Paul, 1982). Building on Brian McHale's article, 'Free Indirect Discourse: A Survey of Recent Accounts', *Poetics and Theory of Literature*, 3 (1978), 249–87, Rimmon-Kenan lists seven types of speech presentation, ranging from 'Diegetic summary' to 'Free direct discourse... the typical form of first-person interior monologue'. See Rimmon-Kenan, *Narrative Fiction*, 109–10. It should be pointed out that although this progressive scale ranges from relatively diegetic to more mimetic narrative, the crucial distinction in narrative fiction is not between diegesis and mimesis (or telling and showing), but, as Genette persuasively argues, between different degrees and kinds of telling. See *ND* 163–4. Both in Genette, Rimmon-Kenan, and this study, the 'diegetic level' refers to the story of the fictional text, and an 'extradiegetic' narrator is thus ' "above" or superior to the story he narrates'. See Rimmon-Kenan, *Narrative Fiction*, 94, 91.

even doubt; but as long as he clings to life he cannot destroy fear: the fear, subtle, indestructible, and terrible, that pervades his being; that tinges his thoughts; that lurks in his heart; that watches on his lips the struggle of his last breath. (107)

It is interesting that, in spite of the narrator's distance from Kayerts and Carlier, there is, at this deep and general level, the suggestion of fear as a basic and unifying aspect of human experience. Clearly, fear is here related to the increasing loneliness and despair of the two main characters. But in the passage following the quotation it is also connected with old Gobila; and there is even the implication that the narrator makes this generalization not only on the basis of his knowledge of Kayerts and Carlier, but on the basis of his own life experience as well. It might be suggested that at this point, that is, in this generalization, the narrator's attitudinal distance from the characters is somewhat reduced; and the suggestion is supported by the absence of irony in the passage.

While the first two parts treat Kayerts and Carlier as a pair, the emphasis in part three is on Kayerts—first as killer and then as victim of a situation found unbearable. That Kayerts is the killer and Carlier the one killed is of minor importance—it might have been the other way round. The stress is put on the violent act as the absurd outcome of a desperate situation, and on Kayerts's reactions to what he has done. Here too there is a marked attitudinal distance between authorial narrator and character, as in this passage: 'He argued with himself about all things under heaven with that kind of wrong-headed lucidity which may be observed in some lunatics' (114–5).

The narrator's omniscience is still very noticeable, but with one important qualification: we are not given any direct explanation of Kayerts's suicide. If this seems to run counter to the point made above on the authorial narrator's omniscience, it must be remembered that there is no one-to-one correlation between narrative omniscience and explanation. The relevant information which the reader of the story receives often establishes an alliance between him or her and the narrator, above the characters. But for all its directness the short story leaves important questions unanswered; and Kayerts's reasons for suicide are left for the reader to ponder, on the basis of the information given about outer circumstances and inner states of mind, and also on the basis of the narrator's generalizations. In a way it is surprising that the narrator's categorical and self-assured statements should promote uncertainty and encourage reflection, but combined with the story's action they may do so. The questions are basic ones in Conrad's fiction, such as motivation for human action, human egotism, loneliness and fear, violence, the idea of equality versus that of superiority and inferiority, the question of what is civilized and what is primitive, and the question of progress. Given more extended treatment in Conrad's longer narratives, all these central questions are not only touched on, but to some extent developed, in 'An Outpost of Progress'. This is a remarkable achievement for so short a story.

That the final generalization is given within parentheses does not reduce its significance: 'The Managing Director of the Great Civilizing Company (since we know that civilization follows trade) landed first, and incontinently lost sight of the steamer.' (116) The generalization is ironic because if 'An Outpost of Progress' has demonstrated anything at all it is that civilization does *not* follow trade: though not entirely resulting from it, the deterioration and downfall of Kayerts and Carlier are strongly connected with their trade duties and the setting in which they are placed by trade. There is, then, an implied contrast between the narrator's scepticism about 'civilizing' ventures of the kind dramatized in the short story and the adduction of the 'civilizing' argument in support of imperialism. This is one of the story's main ironies; and the discrepancy between authorial and personal attitude is here dramatized as that between the scepticism of the authorial narrator and the attitude of those equating civilization with trade.

If the above example illustrates how a generalization can incorporate irony, there are also instances where it is brought out through the narrator's omniscience. In these cases the irony is not only dependent on a discrepancy in attitude to a given problem, but also on varying degrees of knowledge and insight on the part of the characters. Thus some of the irony becomes more apparent when the story is reread, for instance that arising from the description of Kayerts's reaction to the director's appointment of him as the chief of the trading post:

Kayerts was moved almost to tears by his director's kindness. He would, he said, by doing his best, try to justify the flattering confidence, &c., &c. Kayerts had been in the Administration of the Telegraphs, and knew how to express himself correctly. (88)

The amount of irony concentrated in these few sentences is another indication of narrative economy, First, very little in this new situation is dependent on manner of expression; secondly, the director is not at all kind, but a brutal and ruthless man; thirdly, Kayerts is in fact a lazy and ineffective chief; and finally, there is a nice irony in the mention of his previous occupation: as a means of communication, 'Telegraphs' are a striking contrast to the isolation of Kayerts's outpost, whose real administrator is Makola.

Another example to similar effect occurs towards the end of part one: 'For days the two pioneers of trade and progress would look on their empty courtyard in the vibrating brilliance of vertical sunshine' (93). The authorial irony here arises from a difference between what Kayerts and Carlier regard themselves as and what they actually are, in the judgement of the authorial narrator (and with the implication that his judgement be accepted). Beyond this obvious irony there is, however, the play on 'progress', with the suggestion of an ironic contrast between the common meaning of the word in such a context ('advance to better and better conditions, continuous improvement': OED) and the action referred to as 'progress' in 'An Outpost of Progress'. This aspect of irony forms part of the scepticism inherent in some of the narrator's generalizations, a scepticism that, it seems reasonable to suggest, contributes decisively to the thematics of the work.

The irony in 'An Outpost of Progress' is varied: indeed the introductory characterization of the story as 'surprisingly complex' is essentially an implicit reference to the range of irony in it. Part of this range may be indicated by suggesting that irony here operates at different levels. Clearly, discrepancies between authorial and personal attitude account for many of the story's ironies. However, the diversity of the authorial narrative commentary—from simplifying, sweeping comments to shrewd philosophical reflections—implies that aspects of this commentary are not exempt from irony either. For there is a considerable distance between some of the narrator's overt simplifications and a generalization such as that on fear, where the momentary absence of irony seems to reduce the authorial narrator's distance both from the characters and from Conrad. If not implying self-irony, the story's irony does include self-criticism, merged with scepticism and resignation. The range of irony in 'An Outpost of Progress', then, anticipates the narrative and thematic suggestiveness of the sophisticated irony in two of Conrad's most complex works, *Nostromo* and *The Secret Agent*.[8]

Norman Sherry concludes his brief but illuminating chapter on this short story by noting that it 'would appear to be based much more upon Conrad's reading and much less upon his direct experience than *Heart of Darkness*, but it treats themes that were to be dealt with more fully and skilfully in the later novel'.[9] This discussion of Conrad's fiction in 'An Outpost of Progress' as narrative concentration would suggest only a partial agreement with Sherry's conclusion. Literary influences may be more apparent in 'An Outpost of Progress' than in 'Heart of Darkness';[10] and the thematic issues briefly considered above are certainly more exhaustively explored in the later novella. The question of skill, however, is more complicated, involving the evaluating comparison not only of thematic concerns in two works but also of their dissimilar narrative methods. Although the oblique narrative technique of 'Heart of Darkness' could be regarded as more skilful in that its searching complexity proves strikingly congenial to the thematics of the novella, we have seen that the authorial narrative strategy of 'An Outpost of Progress' is impressively effective as well, within the obvious limitations of this much shorter story. The very substantial difference in length and narrative method between the two texts is a warning against too directly evaluative a comparison of them.

'Heart of Darkness' explores in greater depth the problem of hunman action and its motivations, and dramatizes the problem through Marlow's relation to Kurtz on the one hand and the frame narrator on the other. In 'An Outpost of Progress' the distance between the authorial narrator and the characters, as well as the narrator's omniscience and generalizations, are all linked to the use of irony, but a narrative characteristic of this story is the fluctuation between irony and merely detached, informative commentary. A distinctive feature of the story is the sharp focus on one particular situation, closely related to rendering of monotony, futility, and absurdity; a central paradox in it is the interpretation of categorical assertions and an accumulative suggestiveness—of questions Conrad was to explore further in 'Heart of Darkness'. Turning from this major work and back to 'An Outpost of Progress', we find so

---

[8] For discussion (including theoretical notes on irony) see chs. 10–11 below.

[9] Sherry, *Conrad's Western World*, 133.

[10] Graver detects the influence of Flaubert and Kipling, and mentions in particular Flaubert's *Bouvard et Pécuchet*. See *Conrad's Short Fiction*, 11.

much suggested and anticipated in the short story that we must agree with the author's assessment of it: 'in its essentials'—as textual concentration—'An Outpost of Progress' appears 'true enough'.[11]

Although it may be tempting to read Conrad himself into the utterances and reflections of the authorial narrator in 'An Outpost of Progress', this discussion has indicated that Conrad's position and attitude are not easily pinpointed, but must be sought in the textual structure, with its different narrative devices. We then find that the author's position is by no means unambiguous. It is a paradoxical position: incorporating some very firm standpoints and criticisms (as of white trading companies' exploitation of Africa), the authorial narrator's attitude to the two main characters of the story is more ambiguous than it at first seems. There are suggestions of Kayerts and Carlier as both mediocre and representative specimens—as exceptional and remote, but also as surprisingly, even uncomfortably, close to the reader. Indicative of narrative complexity, such conflicting suggestions promote tension and a sense of unease—a disturbing combination of scepticism and ambiguity which is enhanced through the diverse use of irony. The irony of 'An Outpost of Progress' is not only sophisticated but also remarkably wide-ranging; and in this capacity it modifies the authority of the authorial narrator while at the same time increasing the story's overall complexity and suggestiveness.

[11] 'Author's Note' to *Tales of Unrest*, p. vii.

4

'The Secret Sharer':
Economical Personal Narrative

The thematic tendency of Conrad criticism is evident in several of the most influential essays on 'The Secret Sharer' (part of *'Twixt Land and Sea*, 1912).[1] It is already observable in two of the first interpretations of this relatively long short story, those by R. W. Stallman in 1949 and Douglas Hewitt in 1952;[2] and since then numerous critics have linked their predominantly thematic analyses to a discussion of the strange relationship between the story's captain-narrator and Leggatt, the ship's intruder and the captain's 'secret sharer'. Such discussions frequently employ terms such as 'parable', 'archetype', 'symbol/symbolic', and 'psychological'. Stallman finds 'The Secret Sharer' 'charged with symbolic purpose';[3] Guerard considers it as the 'most frankly psychological of Conrad's shorter works';[4] and Porter Williams sees the story of Cain in Genesis as 'a precise symbol of Leggatt's predicament'.[5] Granted that such concepts may helpfully be applied to discussions of the work, and not only to thematic ones, their usefulness for a better understanding of 'The Secret Sharer' is not given a priori; and there are instances where uncritical use of such abstract terms hinders, rather than promotes, the reader's ability to grasp the complex meanings of Conrad's tale. An example of such an essay is Louis H. Leiter's 'Echo Structures'[6]—a confusing article which, however, contains one interesting implication. 'The fundamental thematic

---

[1] A selection of these essays is included in Bruce Harkness (ed.), *Conrad's Secret Sharer and the Critics* (Belmont, Calif.: Wadsworth, 1962).

[2] R. W. Stallman, 'Conrad and "The Secret Sharer" ', *Accent*, 9 (1949), 131–43; rpt. in Stallman (ed.), *The Art of Joseph Conrad: A Critical Symposium* (Athens, Ohio: Ohio University Press, 1982), orig. publ. 1960, 275–88. Douglas Hewitt, *Conrad: A Reassessment* (London: Bowes & Bowes, 1952), 70–9.

[3] Stallman (ed.), *The Art of Joseph Conrad*, 277.

[4] *CN* 21.

[5] Porter Williams, Jr, 'The Brand of Cain in "The Secret Sharer" ', *Modern Fiction Studies*, 10 (1964), 27.

[6] Louis H. Leiter, 'Echo Structures: Conrad's "The Secret Sharer" ', *Twentieth-Century Literature*, 5 (1960), 159–75; rpt. in Harkness (ed.), *Conrad's Secret Sharer*, 133–50.

tensions in "The Secret Sharer", he writes, 'are embodied in and conveyed by these overlapping archetypal patterns.'[7] If we disregard the problematic word 'archetypal' (and thus in one sense invalidate Leiter's point), what he seems to be considering here is the importance of overlapping patterns—or structures established through narrative method—in the generation and development of the 'thematic tensions' of the story. The implication, then, is that in 'The Secret Sharer' structure and narrative method perform a crucial thematic function. Tension, suspense, paradox, and ambiguity are indeed the key characteristics of 'The Secret Sharer' and, as Cedric Watts has shown in his perceptive analysis of the story, 'tension is generated by the interplay of such effects with the diachronic narrative thrust'.[8] By 'such effects' Watts means 'mirror-effects' which become 'recessive spiral-effects', but, as his essay demonstrates, these effects are both varied and complementary. They are also, *qua* effects, the result of some narrative technique or method, even though, in such a tightly-structured text as 'The Secret Sharer', narrative motivation and narrative effect may appear inseparable and the distinction thus perhaps too theoretical.

The purpose of this chapter is to identify the main narrative characteristics and peculiarities of 'The Secret Sharer', to attempt to discern essential thematic functions of these characteristics, and to indicate how the ambiguous thematics of the short story is shaped through its interplay of narrative devices, functions, and effects. The text invites a consecutive commentary as—in the words of Guerard, whose brief comments on the story's narrative method are very much to the point—it 'carries us consecutively from the beginning of the experience to its end'.[9] In Guerard's view 'The Secret Sharer' is Conrad's 'most successful experiment by far with the method of nonretrospective first-person narration. The nominal narrative past is, actually, a harrowing present which the reader too must explore and survive.'[10] The story's personal narration is,

[7] Ibid. 150.

[8] Cedric Watts, 'The Mirror-Tale: An Ethico-Structural Analysis of Conrad's "The Secret Sharer"', *Critical Quarterly*, 19 (1977), 26. Cf. the perceptive comments on this short story in Karl Miller, *Doubles: Studies in Literary History* (Oxford: OUP, 1987), 255–7; and in Jeremy Hawthorn, *Multiple Personality and the Disintegration of Literary Character: From Oliver Goldsmith to Sylvia Plath* (London: Edward Arnold, 1983), 84–90.

[9] CN 27.

[10] Ibid.

indeed, all-pervasive, but Guerard's term 'nonretrospective' is misleading since the whole story is related with the advantage of hindsight and also contains three incorporated, ordered, and qualified analepses: two are constituted by Leggatt's accounts of the killing aboard the *Sephora* and his escape (101–3 and 107–9); the third (short) one is introduced by the narrator's 'And I told him a little about myself' (110). However, in spite of this hindsight, possible conclusions and gained insights are largely suppressed—they are known by the narrator but told only selectively and not until arrived at in due course via the chronological narrative movement of the story. Thus narrative simplicity here promotes suspense since answers to the reader's questions are deferred and partly withheld.

As one of Conrad's densest stories, 'The Secret Sharer' illustrates well his ability to use not only authorial (as in 'An Outpost of Progress') but also personal narrative to achieve thematic pregnancy through textual concentration. The story is divided into two chapters of similar length. Chapter 1 can be further divided into four sections; the first consists of three paragraphs conveying the introductory thoughts and reflections of the narrator before he joins his officers at supper. He joins them as the ship's captain, and his status as responsible commander is reflected in the narrative ('alone with my ship' (92)). Yet there is a paradoxical complication. Pinpointing his status as captain, the narrative also epitomizes his professional deviation: there is a discrepancy between the expected (a captain) and the actual (this captain) which provides a partial explanation of the captain-narrator's unstable state of mind and goes some way to motivate the development of the peculiar relationship between him and Leggatt. This convenient term, 'captain-narrator', is somewhat problematic since the functions and characteristics of the story's 'I' as narrator and character are not wholly compatible. Because of my critical focus on narrative method, and because most critics of 'The Secret Sharer' have dealt with the captain as a character, I shall refer to him as 'narrator' hereafter (but inevitably several of the comments on the narrator also apply to the narrator as character): the story's predominant 'I', then, is the omnipresent, but not omniscient, personal narrator—in its diverse functions the major technical device selected and developed by Conrad in this short story.

There is a finely-struck balance in this text between the exclusion of overt prolepses (an exclusion related to the importance of suspense) and the implied or covert prolepses detectable in the narrator's opening reflections. The beginning takes the reader directly into the situation of the narrating 'I'. Three comments must be made on the narrative at this initial stage. First, there is the emphasis on departure: 'we had just left on the first preparatory stage of our homeward journey' (91). Although departure as described here does not in itself suggest personal change and the possibility of (outer and inner) conflict, it not only functions well as background for the narrator's meditative thoughts, but also sparks off his learning or initiation process. Departure and travel may intensify human awareness and alert us to details otherwise missed. On his departure from the river Meinam the narrator's thoughts are intensified by visual impressions: 'the grove surrounding the great Paknam pagoda, was the only thing on which the eye could rest from the vain task of exploring the monotonous sweep of the horizon' (91–2). Visual impression constitutes the narrator's primary source of information; it is what he relies on and what he feels he *has to* rely on. There is a close link between the emphasis on seeing at the beginning of the story and the third narrative characteristic of its opening: the narrator's loneliness, which is engendered partly by the (principally psychological) sense of estrangement aboard a new ship, partly by his (more existential) sense of 'the solemnity of perfect solitude' (92).

While the narrator's reflections in section one are continued and further developed in section three, the second gives his account of himself in the company of his officers. This interposed statement serves to break up the relatively monotonous, continuous narrative movement of sections one and three; it also enhances the narrator's reliability as it dramatizes the sense of novelty and solitude already indicated. The motif of loneliness is diversified through a twofold modification: the narrator is not only 'a stranger to the ship', but 'if all the truth must be told, I was somewhat of a stranger to myself' (93). His inexperience and uncertainty are related to his obsessive concern with what sort of impression he is making on the crew as master new to the ship. There are suggestions of a suspense-provoking tension between his actual situation and 'that ideal conception of one's own personality every man sets up for himself secretly' (94). It is thematically enriching that suspense is here established both at the psychological level (the narrator's thoughts and doubts) and at the level of outer narrative action. The *Sephora* is an enigmatic ship first seen by the lonely captain, although, significantly, the second mate is better informed. This uneven distribution of relevant, potentially even vital, information among the ship's officers enhances the curious precariousness or vulnerability of the narrator's controlling position as commander.

Section three of Chapter 1 is framed by the narrator's 'my strangeness, which had made me sleepless' (95) and his first words to Leggatt: ' "What's the matter?" I asked in my ordinary tone' (98). The section is essentially characterized by an elaboration of the relationship between the narrator and the crew. His self-conscious reflections concerning the possible effects of his decisions become even more apparent: he is worried that 'my action might have made me appear eccentric' (97). There is repetition of, and renewed stress on, the narrator's (more subjective) loneliness and (more objective) isolation: 'My strangeness, which had made me sleepless, had prompted that unconventional arrangement, as if I had expected in those solitary hours of the night to get on terms with the ship of which I knew nothing, manned by men of whom I knew very little more' (95). It is noteworthy, however, that the narrator's feelings are not wholly despondent; they may also contain joy and excitement. In a manner reminiscent of passages in *The Nigger of the 'Narcissus'*, a contrast is suggested between land and sea: 'And suddenly I rejoiced in the great security of the sea as compared with the unrest of the land' (96). This is not just a respite from the narrator's anguish, but a sensation which forms an integral part of his personality and which is related to his reflections at the very end of the story. The emphasis on the visual is retained right up to the discovery of Leggatt. Significantly, this discovery is made by the lonely narrator (not by the crew, which would of course have made the subsequent action impossible); and the loneliness of both men serves as a basis for their immediate, 'mysterious communication' (99).

In the fourth and last, and by far the longest, section of Chapter 1 (98–115), the peculiar alliance between the narrator and Leggatt is firmly established. The narrative method in the opening of section four is characterized by abruptness. The two characters appear yoked together, by coincidence certainly, but in the dynamics of the story also by need, since the narrator's initiation process is dependent on the problems and challenges presented by Leggatt's arrival and presence.

The relationship of the story's two main characters has been subjected to many critical considerations, several of which focus on the
status and characteristics of Leggatt in relation to those of the
narrator. In his illuminating thematic interpretation of the story,
Daleski notes that critics tend to take widely divergent views of
Leggatt,[11] and he adds useful comments on the ethical issue dramatized through this character's attitude and earlier homicidal action.
We must agree with Daleski that there *is* a moral problem in the
attitude of Leggatt, and implicitly in that of the narrator as well.
One of the clearest indications of the problem comes early in the
fourth section of Chapter 1, when Leggatt confesses, 'I've killed a
man,' and the narrator offers the confident explanation, 'Fit of
temper' (101). The suggestion of a bluff arrogance on the narrator's
part here is disturbing, particularly as this does not seem to be in
accordance with the usual 'fineness of Conrad's moral discrimina-
tion'.[12] On the level of narrative, a partial explanation might be that
the narrator's striking impression of similarity or even identity
between himself and Leggatt blurs the moral issue.

Leggatt's account of the earlier events and the confrontation which
led to the killing aboard the *Sephora* is rendered as an incorporated
analepsis, divided into two by the movement from the deck of the ship
to Leggatt's hiding-place, the narrator's L-shaped cabin. The narrative form of the analepsis confirms the main narrative method of 'The
Secret Sharer': lucid and chronological, it seems to have been carefully
edited on the principle of relevance for narrative economy and suspense. This reaffirmation of narrative strategy is not surprising—it
appears consistent that the resemblance between the story's two main
characters should be extended to include a similarity in narrative procedure. A noteworthy distinction between the two constituent parts
of the analepsis is that while the first is told by Leggatt in an introductory, background-providing manner ('and he told me the story
roughly in brusque, disconnected sentences' (102)), the final part is
his response to the narrator's more direct inquiry.

Leggatt's last analepsis not only continues in sequence the story of
his escape, but also contains some further explanations. It is followed by a short analeptic account on the part of the narrator, but it
is striking how, in a most economical manner, this complementary

[11] *CWD* 172–3.
[12] Ibid. 173.

information (from the narrator to Leggatt) is linked to the alliance established between the two characters: 'For the rest, I was almost as much of a stranger on board as himself, I said. And at the moment I felt it most acutely' (110). The remainder of section four is gradually focused on the present situation, whose danger and challenge are most directly presented by the arrival of the investigating captain of the *Sephora*.

Chapter 2 can be subdivided into three sections. The first is constituted by the dialogue or confrontation between the narrator and the visiting captain (116–22). The dialogue further strengthens the bond between the narrator and Leggatt:

> I had become so connected in thoughts and impressions with the secret sharer of my cabin that I felt as if I, personally, were being given to understand that I, too, was not the sort that would have done for the chief mate of a ship like the *Sephora*. I had no doubt of it in my mind. (119)

This is a remarkable statement. Not just reaffirming the narrator's strong sense of alliance with and intuitive understanding of Leggatt, it invites the reader to infer that if the narrator were chief mate of the *Sephora* he might have committed a comparable criminal act. If this implication seems forced, a possible riposte could be that it is not as imaginative as the narrator's own thoughts. The pressing question is how the mere arrival of another person can spark off such an insistent impression of shared personal characteristics, and even of identical life experience. I shall return to this question when discussing the relationship between narrative method and thematics in the conclusion of this chapter.

An interesting aspect of narrative method in this section is the relatively explicit reference to temporal distance—the difference in time between the experience and the narrative act. The *Sephora* captain 'gave his name (it was something like Archbold—but at this distance of years I hardly am sure)' (116). Four pages later there is another passage which indicates temporal distance, although a less substantial one: 'But, strangely enough—(I thought of it only afterwards)—I believe that... ' (120). Given this temporal distance the reader more readily accepts and understands some of the text's main narrative characteristics: the exceptional concentration on relevant material, the well-ordered story, the stress on suspense, and the great significance attached to Leggatt (at the time of the experience the function of Leggatt as catalyst of the narrator's much-needed initiation and test could not possibly be seen).

The second section of Chapter 2 consists of the dialogue between the narrator and Leggatt after the *Sephora* captain has left. The emphasis of the dialogue is increasingly on the 'nerve-trying situation' (123) in which the two seem trapped, but the section also includes a brief elaboration of the analepses in part one. Then the last section opens thus:

This is not the place to enlarge upon the sensations of a man who feels for the first time a ship move under his feet to his own independent word. In my case they were not unalloyed. I was not wholly alone with my command; for there was that stranger in my cabin. (125)

Again, we note the terseness of the personal narrator's narrative— the focus of his story on the characteristics and consequences of the relationship between himself and Leggatt. The gradual complication of the situation with Leggatt in hiding serves to motivate the Koh-ring venture and leads to a shift in suspense, away from the question : will Leggatt be discovered? to: will the Koh-ring plan succeed? This modulation of suspense becomes a means of promoting the concluding movement of the story. It is in one sense a circular movement (ending with the departure of the intruder), but it is also one in the course of which the narrator undergoes a profound and lasting change.

The ending of 'The Secret Sharer' places a renewed emphasis on the importance of the visual. Sight, and the ability to manoeuvre, are required if the Koh-ring plan is to succeed. Had the white hat not been spotted on the black water, catastrophe would inevitably have occurred: '—behold—[the hat] was saving the ship, by serving me for a mark to help out the ignorance of my strangeness. Ha!' (142). This exclamation is indicative of the firmness and self-possession the narrator has gained by helping Leggatt, and through their peculiarly intimate partnership. The question of his loneliness has not been solved, and problems are still to confront him, but his ability to handle them (and, in a wider sense, to live by performing responsible work) has greatly improved.

A major feature of Conrad's narrative method in 'The Secret Sharer' is the combination of the suspense principle and various forms of likeness, complement, and contrast. Throughout the story, strict criteria of relevance (the focus on the narrator/Leggatt relationship and the importance of the suspense of the story) are applied. This consistent limitation to relevant material helps first to generate, then to sustain, an exceptionally economical fictional text. A related reason for the story's narrative economy is the temporal distance between the narrated events and the act of narration. If the distance in time makes the narrator understand more fully how important this particular experience was for him, it also enables him to concentrate on the most essential constituent aspects of the experience. In the narrative tension and progression of 'The Secret Sharer', the narrator and Leggatt both operate at the diegetic level of action. However, their equal statuses—with the combined emphasis on contrast, complement, and similarity—do not preclude a far-reaching psychological likeness. Neither does this affinity exclude the possibility of a supernatural coloration of the *doppelgänger* motif in the story. This motif is made very explicit indeed; the originality of 'The Secret Sharer' resides rather in the combination of likeness with contrast and complement. Furthermore, it is suggested by the way in which various characteristics of the relationship are controlled by the emphasis on suspense, by the advantages and consequences of temporal distance, and by the guiding principles of narrative economy and tight structuring.

If we try to summarize 'The Secret Sharer' we realize that its simplicity is deceptive: such a summary is certain to over-simplify the thematics of the story, two key elements of which are the problems of human identity and loneliness. If a main narrative characteristic of 'The Secret Sharer' is the interplay of structural similarities and differences on the one hand and principles of suspense, narrative economy, and distance on the other, a major thematic characteristic of the story is that the combination of technical virtuosity and psychological emphasis tends to blur, rather than resolve, the most pressing moral questions which it dramatizes. A qualification must follow immediately. Although 'moral questions' are central to the thematics of Conrad's fiction, and although such questions could also be seen as one constituent aspect of his narrative method, they are rarely, if ever, unambiguously 'resolved' but are, at best, rephrased or transformed into strongly qualified moral recommendations. What might be suggested with regard to this short story, then, is that it evinces a problematic relationship between the seriousness of the moral problems it seems to address and the relative superficiality noticeable in the narrator's attitude to, and presentation of, these problems.

As this concluding point would appear to need some development,

I shall substantiate it by considering more closely two of the short story's narrative elements: structural similarities and differences on the one hand, and the narrative principle of suspense on the other. As far as the first element is concerned, a helpful basis for discussion is provided by the 'structural table' Cedric Watts presents in his essay on 'The Secret Sharer', which he regards as 'a Janiform work'.[13] The suggestiveness of this description becomes clear when we consider his structural table for the short story,[14] and then relate it to the above observations.

Now this table certainly cannot be regarded as an exhaustive illustration of the remarkably mirror-like or reciprocal relationship between the captain-narrator and Leggatt. I concede partial agreement with Watts's scepticism about certain consequences of structuralist criticism as practised in the 1960s and 1970s: 'Structuralism often tends to halt the kinesis of a narrative by freezing diachronic tensions into a synchronic pattern.'[15] My emphasis on narrative modulations and interest in thematic effects can be seen as a corollary to scepticism of this kind: both these constituent elements of narrative are significantly related to its 'diachronic tensions'. Yet some narratives invite the kind of structuralist schematization illustrated here. This is another way of saying that in certain texts—and 'The Secret Sharer' is a case in point in the Conrad canon—structural similarities and contrasts become so striking as to threaten the reader's (or critic's) appreciation of other, perhaps equally important, narrative and thematic elements. Not only does 'The Secret Sharer' contain 'some interesting symmetrical contrasts';[16] these contrasts are combined with the text's suspense principle in such an effective manner that the moral or ethical issues which the short story presents are considerably, and even problematically, blurred. This is not to say that the story should necessarily resolve, or suggest unambiguous answers to, the moral problems it presents (compare Leggatt's killing a man and the captain's risking a shipwreck)—complex ethical issues defy easy answers, and indeed such answers are rarely given in

---

[13] 'As Janus is the two-headed god, so a Janiform work is a two-faced work: morally it seems to be centrally or importantly paradoxical or self-contradictory. Not merely ambiguous or complex, but paradoxical or self-contradictory... Conrad called himself "homo duplex"; and "The Secret Sharer" is a fine example of a Janiform tale.' Watts, 'The Mirror-Tale', 26.

[14] Ibid. 29.

[15] Ibid. 31.

[16] Ibid. 29.

JANUS		
face 2 mirroring	face 1 mirrored	Mirror-relationship:
Leggatt	Hero	
young (in his twenties);	young (in his twenties);	Likeness
same build as hero;	same build as Leggatt;	Likeness
ex-*Conway* boy;	ex-*Conway* boy;	Likeness
'a stranger on board'—	'the only stranger on board'—	Likeness
alienated from crew—	alienated from crew—	Likeness
distrusted by them.	distrusted by them.	Likeness
'A headless corpse!'	'my head over the rail'.	Complement
Kills one man	To save life of one man	Contrast
to avert shipwreck.	risks a shipwreck;	Contrast
	the man is Leggatt.	Recession/spiral
Élitist ethic	Fraternal ethic	Complement
subordinates seaman's	subordinates seaman's	Likeness
and landsman's.	and landsman's;	Likeness
	endorses élitist ethic.	Recession/spiral
The ship is imperilled;	The ship is imperilled;	Likeness
the captain is fearful;	the captain is bold;	Contrast
the first mate is bold.	the first mate is fearful	Contrast

Conrad's fiction. But there is a certain negligence noticeable in the way the problems are dramatized in 'The Secret Sharer'.

Compared to the serious exploration of similar questions in, say, *Lord Jim*, this may seem a surprising observation. Still, it seems sensible to consider the relative thematic superficiality of 'The

Secret Sharer' as a consequence of the combination of narrative strategies identified and discussed above. Yet this explanation also needs to be qualified: quite obviously the possibility of thematic diversity and complexity is delimited by the text's narrative economy and suspense. Still, in relation to its modest length the thematics of 'The Secret Sharer'—and especially the questions and unresolved problems implied in this thematics—are surely quite complex. Moreover, the effect of thematic superficiality would probably have been reduced were not the suspense principle such an important element in the narrative method of this short story. According to Watts, who has suggested that the suspense principle be seen as the basis of all narratives, it operates as follows:

> From the information presented in the initial stages of the narrative we elicit a salient problem; and in the act of formulating the problem we are simultaneously (virtually as a matter of logical entailment) formulating our prediction of the solution which the narrative will eventually supply.[17]

I have rephrased two aspects of the 'salient problem' of this text as two questions: will Leggatt be discovered? and: will the Koh-ring plan succeed? Both of these questions are unambiguously answered by the text. However, my discussion has suggested that the central problem of the short story is its insistence on the mirror-relationship between the narrator and Leggatt, and that the complications and issues that follow from this insistence remain largely unresolved.

Although Watts does not himself refer to Barthes's discussion of suspense in the classic essay 'An Introduction to the Structural Analysis of Narrative', his conception of suspense as a basic element of narrative becomes even more thought-provoking if related to Barthes's perceptive comment on it:

> Suspense is evidently but a privileged, or, if one prefers, an exasperating form of distortion: on the one hand, by keeping a sequence open... it secures the contact with the reader, thus managing an obviously communicative function; on the other hand, it holds over him the threat of an uncompleted sequence, of an open paradigm... that is to say, a logical disorder.[18]

17 Watts, *The Deceptive Text*, 184.

18 Roland Barthes, 'An Introduction to the Structural Analysis of Narrative', *New Literary History*, 6 (Winter 1975), 267. The essay first appeared as 'Introduction à l'analyse structurale des récits', in the issue of *Communications*, 8 (1966) entitled *L'analyse structurale du récit* (Paris: Seuil, 1981), 7–33. A. J. Greimas, Claude

For Barthes, the 'distortion' is the logical, generalized distortion which constitutes the language of narrative. As a variant on distortion, suspense problematizes language. Keeping a sequence open, the suspense principle may also imply the possibility or 'threat' of an uncompleted one; 'we elicit a salient problem' in the narrative, but both the problem and its possible solution have to be adjusted (modified or extended) as the reading process evolves.

In 'The Secret Sharer' the structural and thematic affinity between the narrator and Leggatt, combined with the story's shortness, entails an increasing emphasis on the aspect of suspense connected with the 'overt' closure of the tale—Leggatt's escape. Extending Barthes's point, we could say that the narrative device of suspense both simplifies and problematizes fictional language here: if the sequence associated with Leggatt's escape seems simplified, that revolving round the moral and ethical problems we have noted remains more problematically open than in a longer text such as *Lord Jim*. It must be added, though, that 'The Secret Sharer' is not only a much shorter narrative; it is also one which is consistently centred on the narrator's test-like experience with Leggatt as a crucial constituent aspect of his learning—and not only as narrator but also as main character. If the personal narrative of 'The Secret Sharer' somewhat ambiguously and perhaps unsatisfactorily suggests rather then convincingly explores its own thematic implications, it evokes successfully the visual impressions, doubts, loneliness, and learning of the narrator.

There are two complicating implications of learning or initiation as presented in 'The Secret Sharer'. First, although the short story definitely dramatizes an important learning process on the part of the narrator, problems arise if we inquire into the terms and possible result of this learning; and these problems are closely related to the thematic or moral ambiguity of the text. This point may be substantiated by comparing the learning process of the narrator in 'The Secret Sharer' with that of the personal narrator in *The*

Bremond, and Todorov are further contributors to the 1966 issue of *Communications*, which marks a turning-point not only in the development of French structuralism, but also in the study of narrative generally. Two of the best books on Barthes are Annette Lavers, *Roland Barthes: Structuralism and After* (London: Methuen, 1982) and Jonathan Culler, *Barthes* (Glasgow: Fontana Paperbacks, 1983).

Shadow-Line, the novella to be discussed in Chapter 7. Both narrators occupy central positions in their respective texts; both are lonely, and confront, though in dissimilar ways, the danger of dispossession; and both are engaged in dramatic actions which serve to influence and shape their learning. Contrary to his counterpart in 'The Secret Sharer', however, the narrator of *The Shadow-Line* is, for all his loneliness, part of a social context with a set of norms attached to it. He is able to follow the wise advice of a more experienced character such as Giles; and his learning process is, in a much less problematic way than that of the narrator in 'The Secret Sharer', correlated with a movement towards a form of self-possession which incorporates professional competence and responsibility.

The second implication to be noted extends the first: as the narrator of 'The Secret Sharer' is removed from the social context (compare his suspicions of the crew and his élitist ethic), his egocentricity as narrator makes him less appealing as a character. As Michael P. Jones observes, the narrator is gradually 'driven further into himself, into his imagination, wondering "how far I should turn out faithful to that ideal conception of one's own personality every man sets up for himself secretly" ' (94).[19]

This observation provides a helpful specification of the narrator's loneliness. However, a major critical difference between the interpretation presented here and Jones's reading of the story is that for him the fictional reality of Leggatt is questionable: Jones sees Leggatt as the likely product of the narrator's imagination. While it is certainly true that Leggatt is sometimes described as curiously unreal (compare the narrator's 'Can it be... that he is not visible to other eyes than mine?' (130)), I am more inclined to relate this doubt of the narrator's to his fundamental insecurity and problems of epistemological orientation than to consider it as an indication of Leggatt's non-existence as character. As Jones emphasizes 'the captain's unreliability as narrator',[20] the possibility of extending this 'unreliability' to include the narrator's doubts about Leggatt's existence would seem to make Jones's reading less persuasive.

Although the narrator's vivid imagination and extreme egocentricity make him less than reliable, his unreliability is delimited

[19] Michael P. Jones, *Conrad's Heroism: A Paradise Lost* (Ann Arbor, Michigan: UMI Research Press, 1985), 105.
[20] Ibid. 109.

by the absence from the text of firmer indications of authorial authority. Furthermore, if the narrator and Leggatt did not function at the same textual level, the effects of narrative suspense as discussed above would be severely reduced, as would indeed the fictional reality of the text's insistence on various forms of likeness, contrast, paradox, tension, and ambiguity. This is not to deny that Leggatt, as Jones suggests, has a metaphorical function in addition to that as character: given the personal colouring and imaginative quality of the narrator's discourse, the role of Leggatt as metaphor (also of the narrator's unconscious and semi-conscious ideals) is quite evident.

This discussion of 'The Secret Sharer' would, broadly speaking, seem to bring us close to agreement with Jones's view of the narrator's initiation 'into an ideal'[21] rather than, as in the case of the narrator in *The Shadow-Line*, into society. Dissenting from Jones, however, I shall conclude by suggesting that the story's ambiguous thematics is paradoxically enriched by the way in which its narrative method problematizes this idealism. It does so partly by refraining from specifying the idealism (not relating it to the demands of society), partly by questioning (however indirectly, and under the guise of heroism) its ethical implications, and partly by revealing how dependent the narrator's idealism is on his loneliness and social isolation. Up to a point, then, the narrative method of 'The Secret Sharer' is comparable to those of 'The Tale' and *Under Western Eyes* (cf. Chapters 5 and 12): in these personal narratives the absence of a stable, correcting position of authorial authority presents difficult problems of interpretation. It must be added, however, that although such authorial instability and distance complicate both the reading and interpretative process, this is not necessarily a narrative weakness but may instead enrich and extend an otherwise fairly simple thematics. Still, the possibility of authorial distance from the personal narrator of 'The Secret Sharer' does not suffice to remove the relative thematic superficiality and problematic moral ambiguity from this text. Essentially, this short story is characterized by its insistence on narrative suspense and by its equally insistent focus on the interplay of similarity and contrast between the two main characters.

[21] Ibid.

5

'The Tale':
Epistemological Uncertainty Dramatized through Three Concentric Tales

While both 'An Outpost of Progress' and 'The Secret Sharer' definitely rank among the masterpieces of Conrad's short fiction, the status of 'The Tale' is more uncertain. Still, this is clearly one of the two most interesting stories in *Tales of Hearsay*, Conrad's last collection of short stories, which appeared posthumously in 1925. The narrative method of 'The Tale' is exceptionally sophisticated for late Conrad, contrasting with that of 'Prince Roman', the other outstanding short story in *Tales of Hearsay*, which is distinguished by an effective simplicity of narrative. This simplicity becomes understandable if we consider how closely the story of Prince Roman, the only Pole in Conrad's fiction, resembles the passage in *A Personal Record* which recounts how Conrad as a child met, and was deeply impressed by, Prince Roman Sanguszko, who participated in the 1830 insurrection, and on whose dramatic life the short story is based. If the combination of personal recollection and Polish setting and main character is connected with the story's narrative simplicity, then one explanation of this simplicity might be to regard it as a manifestation of Conrad's lasting need for distance from his fictional material. The problem of distance in Conrad is complicated and paradoxical; and it is by no means solved by his inclusion of certain autobiographical elements in his fiction.[1] In the case of 'Prince Roman', it would seem that simplicity serves as a means of preserving distance: the proximity of setting, history, and protagonist to the story's author limits the extent to which its thematic issues can be explored.

If we begin by identifying some of the narrative elements that make 'The Tale' a more elaborately-structured text than 'Prince Roman', it may be helpful to present the *fabula* of the short story:

---

[1] Cf. Najder, *Chronicle*, 127, 358–9.

The commanding officer is in charge of a British warship searching for neutral ships suspected of refuelling enemy submarines. An empty barrel is seen floating on the water, indicating that a submarine may have refuelled in the vicinity. As fog comes down, the commander edges his ship into a nearby cove. When the fog partially lifts, a neutral ship is discovered in the entrance to the cove; the commander boards the ship to interview its captain, can unearth no evidence that it has actually assisted a submarine, but suspects that the captain (a Northman) and his log-book are lying. The commander accordingly orders the neutral ship to leave the cove, giving the Northman directions that will run him on to a ledge of rocks. Later the commander learns that the ship, contrary to what he had assumed, had taken his false directions and sunk without survivors.

Given the inevitable shortcomings of such summaries of action, this one of 'The Tale' provides the basis for two initial points, both of which are connected with my opening remarks about 'Prince Roman'. First, although summaries of both these texts drastically simplify matters, there is a marked difference in the degrees of simplification. While it is possible to summarize the action of 'Prince Roman' without seriously distorting it, the above summary of 'The Tale' is more like a summary of what the commander tells his mistress. It is a summary, in other words, of the tale within 'The Tale', and definitely not of the complete fictional text with its authorial frame.

The second observation to be made here extends the first: even though this summary simplifies the text almost to the extent of indicating a different one, still we cannot say, as William W. Bonney does in a stimulating discussion of this short story, that its title is 'misleading'.[2] Conrad is of course perfectly justified in using the commander's tale as the short story's title; moreover, it economically enhances the commander's centrality, as the other tales of the text are inseparable from the one he relates. For Bonney, 'there exist four concentric tales' in 'The Tale',

each of which involves its own narrative perspective, auditor, sphere of experience, and rhetorical logic. The nonhuman narrative voice of the story presents the entire aesthetic fabrication to the reader; the commanding officer presents his confessional tale to his mistress; the Northman recounts his misadventures to the commanding officer; and, while listening to the

[2] William W. Bonney, *Thorns & Arabesques: Contexts for Conrad's Fiction* (Baltimore: Johns Hopkins University Press, 1980), 208.

Northman, the commanding officer listens simultaneously to a 'grave murmur in the depth of his very own self, telling another tale' (73).[3]

Referring to an important essay Edward Said wrote on Conrad's 'Presentation of Narrative' in 1974, Bonney regards 'The Tale' as 'an excellent example of how in Conrad's work the "inner continuity of each tale... derives from the utterance's sense of its own differences [from] conflicting or complementary utterances",[4] how Conrad insistently substitutes an intermediate discourse for the referent'.[5] There is much to be said for such a view of the story, but Bonney's application of Said is distorted by his tendency, further on in the discussion, to substitute semantic categories such as 'meaning' and 'logical coherence' for Said's 'continuity'—a more inclusive concept which incorporates both semantic, thematic, and formal elements. Furthermore, Bonney's equation of four tales in the text seems to me to imply a failure to take its surface narrative seriously, for there is an essential distinction to be drawn between the commander's suspicion (which for Bonney constitutes the fourth tale) and the three tales that are manifestly part of the narrative structure. Bonney is, however, quite right to note that the tales are concentric: as readers we have little difficulty in identifying three tales—or narratives—that are interrelated and embedded in one another: the all-encompassing authorial narrative, the commander's story to his mistress, and the Northman's story which the commander does not believe. The commander's personal narrative, which constitutes the first and second tales, is framed by the authorial one. There are also occasional authorial comments inserted into the personal narrative.

According to its narrative structure, then, 'The Tale' can be divided into three. The first part is the authorial introduction to the narrative situation and setting. The transition from this authorial opening to the commander's tale is gradual: authorially-presented dialogue blends into a dramatized, personal story with the commander as both narrator and protagonist. The second part is by far the longest of the three. It starts with the words 'As you will. In that world, then, there was once upon a time a Commanding Officer

[3] Ibid.

[4] Edward W. Said, 'Conrad: The Presentation of Narrative', *Novel*, 7 (1974), 122. This essay is an earlier version of that referred to in ch. 1 n. 3.

[5] Bonney, *Thorns & Arabesques*, 208.

and a Northman' (61). The third and final part, according to this suggestion of a tripartite narrative structure, would start at the break introduced by 'The narrator bent forward towards the couch, where no movement betrayed the presence of a living person' (80).

The most interesting problem of narrative method in 'The Tale' is probably that of attitudinal (and partly also temporal) narrative distance; and I shall lay emphasis upon the variations and functions of this aspect. One striking functional feature of distance in this short story is the extent to which it is both a constituent element of narrative method and, at the thematic level, a pressing moral problem for the commander-narrator. Since this problem is closely related to his narrative and thematic functions, it is not very noticeable in the first, authorial part. As the authorial narrator introduces us to a male speaker and female listener or narratee, hints are given of a love affair that appears also to have involved some estrangement and resignation. While the latent tension and instability of the relationship adumbrate central thematic issues of the tale the speaker is about to tell (and also of 'The Tale' as a whole), the second paragraph is also both proleptic and stylistically representative of the opening of the story:

It was a long room. The irresistible tide of the night ran into the most distant part of it, where the whispering of a man's voice, passionately interrupted and passionately renewed, seemed to plead against the answering murmurs of infinite sadness. (59)

One may be struck, or even irritated, by the ornate style of this paragraph, and indeed of the authorial opening as a whole. The authorial discourse is not only characterized by rhythmical patterns which include repetition and alliteration ('passionately interrupted and passionately renewed'). It includes disturbing elements of cliché too, as when, in the following paragraph, the commander is described as 'masculine and mysterious in his immobility'.

However, the paragraph also incorporates the first mention of the verb 'seem', which, recurring throughout the text, increasingly epitomizes the narrator's epistemological uncertainty. As the title of this chapter indicates, the particular form of uncertainty which 'The Tale' evinces is here seen as an essential aspect of its narrative method as well as of its thematics, which will be specified below. One interesting implication of this first use of 'seem' is that the authorial narrator employs the word in a sense not altogether different from the commander's later application of it. Thus the text offers an early suggestion of affinity between the authorial and the personal narrator, which goes some way towards reducing the attitudinal distance between them. This affinity suggests that the text's basic problems of epistemological orientation and moral dilemma are not limited to the particular story of the commander which 'The Tale' dramatizes. Thus the opening authorial narrative not only introduces the subsequent personal one, but also extends its thematic implications.

In the dialogue of the authorial narrative, the narratee's reference to the commander's 'professional—tales' (60) prefigures the challenge of the 'supreme test' (80) in which the following story culminates. 'The Tale' leaves the reader in little doubt as to whether the central dilemma of this test is a real one; it is indeed one of the pivots on which the dramatic tension and suspense of the story depend. As a consequence of this recognition of the commander's dilemma I shall avoid such a word as 'murder' when describing his action towards the crew of the neutral ship.[6] The text's wartime setting is an additional reason why our moral judgement of the commander must be qualified, especially as the moral complications of wartime actions are referred to by the narrator himself. They are also confirmed by his narratee, about whom some selective information is given at the end of the first part. As the commander has only five days' leave, so she has also 'taken a five days' leave from—from my duties' (61). Providing the impression of a certain disillusionment, this remark by the narratee strengthens the attitudinal affinity between her and the commander. The 'leave from... my duties' probably refers to her marital duties and is suggestive in a double sense: not just indicating, and probably exaggerating, the similarity between the commander's wartime situation and her present one, it cautiously questions the validity of the former's distinction between the moral criteria of war and those of peacetime. Although this modification does not take the form of an authorial criticism or assessment of the characters' lives and their present affair, it serves as an integral part of the text's narrative method in that it extends the thematic linkage between the commander's tale and the frame narrative.

---

[6] Cf. ibid. 209.

As part two of 'The Tale' begins, the commander's consciously distancing efforts become more noticeable:

'As you will. In that world, then, there was once upon a time a Commanding Officer and a Northman. Put in the capitals, please, because they had no other names. It was a world of seas and continents and islands—'
'Like the earth,' she murmured, bitterly. (61)

The first observation to make here is that as the commander starts narrating his tale, he employs the third person singular in referring to himself.[7] The text's failure, or refusal, to state explicitly how conscious this choice of pronominal reference is provides an interesting example of narrative specification through ellipsis. This form of specification is paradoxical and indirect: rather than explicating a given narrative element of the text (or, alternatively, adding another to those already introduced) it confirms and extends the interpretative observation above on the short story's characteristic tension and epistemological uncertainty.

Once this point is made, however, it immediately needs to be qualified by referring to the problem of reading as evidenced by this particular kind of narrative structure. As indicated in the Introduction, one of the critical premisses of my approach to Conrad's narrative method is that it cannot be properly appreciated unless the interpretations are based on careful rereading of the texts under consideration. This critical premiss, which is also an interpretative and hermeneutic one,[8] is a precondition for the kind of point I have just made. The need for qualification is accentuated in the two following paragraphs of the text, where the changing pronominal references to the commander seem to imply, even on a first reading, that the narrating 'I' and the 'he' whose story is to be related are in fact identical.

During the first six pages of part two (62–8), the commander outlines the ship's movements up to the confrontation with the neutral vessel. As his function as narrator gradually becomes more evident in this section, the presence of the authorial narrator is correspondingly reduced; and the narratee's interruptions increasingly take the form of brief, encouraging comments serving to

---

[7] We might also note the commander's use of the conventional fairy-tale opening 'once upon a time' and his claim that the actors of his story had no proper names. Both are distancing devices which supplement his use of the third person singular.
[8] Cf. ch. 1 nn. 12, 29.

remind the reader of the story's frame narrative. However, these comments have an additional function too, which is related to that of the relatively rare authorial intrusions in the section. Though brief, the narratee's remarks—which either are or pretend to be appreciative of the commander's actions and reflections—can be read as textual instalments which question the validity of the distinction the personal narrator is trying to establish between the commander of his tale and the commander of 'The Tale', in other words between two versions or manifestations of self. This notion would appear to be supported by the restriction of authorial knowledge in a comment accompanying the narratee's intrusions: ' "No. We won't," she said, in a neutral tone which concealed perfectly her relief—or her disappointment' (62).[9]

Throughout the short story, both the necessity of seeing and the attempts to see are stressed, but so are the various complications involved. 'The Tale' provides an illustration of the double meaning of 'seeing' in Conrad's fiction—that he, in Hillis Miller's phrase, 'means to make the reader see not only the vivid facts of the story he tells but the evasive truth behind them, of which they are the obscure revelation'.[10] And Miller goes on to make this interesting point: 'All Conrad's work turns on this double paradox, first the paradox of the two senses of seeing, seeing as physical version and seeing as seeing through, as penetrating to or unveiling the hidden invisible truth, and second the paradox of seeing the darkness in terms of the light.' As the commander's (and, to some extent, the crew's) seeing 'as physical vision' is repeatedly referred to, his frustration arising from the impossibility of 'seeing through' gradually increases. One illustrative, though relatively simple, textual manifestation of the problem is the officers' failure to determine the significance of the barrel which is discovered floating on the water. Furthermore, the text suggests a connection between the commander's inability to see and his growing suspicions. If 'seeing through' is related to knowledge and certainty, suspicions are related

[9] The authorial narrator's use of the adjective 'neutral' is interesting: not only implying a certain attitudinal affinity between her and the Northman, it also suggests that the commander's generally suspicious attitude is a problem in their relationship as well. These suggestions constitute a thematic link between the commander's story and the frame narrative.

[10] J. Hillis Miller, 'Heart of Darkness Revisited', in Murfin (ed.), Conrad Revisited, 37.

to frustration and uncertainty, both accentuated by the narrator's responsibility as commander and by the wartime setting. Miller's second paradox is also relevant, particularly if considered in the light of the whole text. Although no complete 'light' is offered by 'The Tale', there is a partial clarification of the problem at the end as the commander learns about the wreckage of the neutral ship. This information, which could be regarded as a glimpse of 'light', paradoxically increases the narrator's self-criticism and tormenting doubt, thus making at least one aspect of his 'darkness' more obvious.

As the commander's story approaches the culminating, dramatic account of the challenge presented by the neutral ship, part of the distancing, more critical function of the earlier authorial commentary is taken over by the commander's remarks *as narrator*. There is surely a very considerable temporal and spatial distance between the setting of the frame narrative and that of the commander's tale; this distance is indicated quite explicitly in the authorial opening of the story. The temporal distance is probably the more important, making the narrator conscious of his attitudinal distance from his own actions at the time of the confrontation. However, as the 'supreme test' approaches, the personal commentary modulates between factual information about the commander's tale and more reflective, even critical, comments *on* the tale—and on its thematic implications. As the narrative function of these reflections is similar to that of the authorial generalizations at the beginning of the short story, a balance is established between the reduction of authorial commentary and the increase of personal reflection. This functional correlation strengthens the resemblance between the text's authorial and personal narrators. For instance, the main tenor of the personal narrator's generalization, ' "Curiosity is the great motive power of hatred and love" ' (71), is similar to the authorial narrator's 'As usual, it was the woman who had the courage' (59). Such simplifying generalizations have their own distancing effect. Additionally, attitudinal distance between the narrator's narration and the experience he is recounting is also established by means of a form of irony that is not exclusively authorial, but also includes elements of distancing self-irony. Consider the commander's rendering, as narrator, of his own reaction to the boarding officer's report: 'The commanding officer, after communing with his suspicions for a time, called his second aside' (71).

Boarding the neutral ship the commander is met by its master, 'a robust Northman' (72), who recapitulates the explanation already given to the boarding officer:

'The commanding officer listened to the tale. It struck him as more plausible than simple truth is in the habit of being. But that, perhaps, was prejudice. All the time the Northman was speaking the commanding officer had been aware of an inward voice, a grave murmur in the depth of his very own self, telling another tale, as if on purpose to keep alive in him his indignation and his anger with that baseness of greed or of mere outlook which lies often at the root of simple ideas.' (73)

In the analysis presented here, this explanatory story constitutes, as already indicated, the text's third concentric tale, distinct from that related by the commander and yet embedded in it. Although not given in full, this story qualifies as a narrative in its own right: it describes, and explains in order to justify, the neutral ship's movements and activities, stating its professional purpose, cargo, and destination. In contrast, the commander's 'inward voice... telling another tale' has few of the characteristics of a narrative proper: indeed his inability to construct an alternative narrative further reduces the factual basis that might exist for his suspicions of the neutral ship. Hence the 'tale' of his 'inward voice' can best be understood as a manifestation of his generally suspicious outlook on life, an outlook engendered at least in part by the trying wartime situation and his pressing epistemological uncertainty.

The speculative quality of the commander's suspicions is strengthened by the quoted monologues inserted into the two officers' jerky conversation. Although the quoted monologues may appear rather contrived here too, it must be granted that as textual manifestations of the commander's suspicions they greatly reduce the possibility of a real dialogue between him and the Northman. For the commander, their confrontation serves as catalyst of a much larger problem—that of existential orientation in a world of confusing visual impressions, unreliable appearances, and partial knowledge. The meeting does, however, entail a dramatic actualization of this general problem since it forces the commander to make a definite choice with regard to the neutral ship. Although this choice is made more difficult by the scarcity of relevant knowledge, the need for a firm decision is also paradoxically enhanced by the commander's uncertainty. The combination of wartime setting and all-pervasive tension puts a strong pressure on the protagonist to act in accordance with his supposed role as commander of a warship. Rather than reducing his suspicions, this pressure serves as an additional catalyst for them, and they take on a more definite form: 'The certitude was strong within him. "But I am going to clear all you fellows off this coast at once. And I will begin with you. You must leave in half an hour." ' (79)

The commander's 'certitude' can be considered as a metaphor which, ironically as well as paradoxically, pinpoints his epistemological uncertainty at the culminating point of an exceptionally trying experience. The metaphor signifies a strange stabilization of his suspicions which allows him to make the decision he thinks is required of him in the given context. But although the certitude which the commander now claims to possess implies a very substantial simplification of the problems of knowledge and certainty as experienced and presented earlier in the short story, this simplification ironically highlights these central issues rather than excluding them as irrelevant or unimportant. Indeed, at this stage of the narrative the problems are restated and further developed.

A narrative variation which contributes to this thematic development is narrated monologue, which functions as a supplement to the text's instances of quoted monologue. Now the border-line between referential narrative statement and narrated monologue may sometimes be blurred, especially if, as in this particular text, character and narrator are identical in a narrative which is concerned with both maintaining and questioning attitudinal distance, and in which the personal narrator even pretends to present an authorial narrative through his refusal to identify himself with the commander. Still, sentences such as the following qualify as narrated monologue: ' "At least, it seemed elaborated. Nothing could be trusted" ' (76), and ' "Was this significant, or of no meaning whatever?" ' (77). Tellingly, both these narrated monologues emphasize the problem of appearance versus knowledge. Unable to remove his suspicion, the commander searches for elements of verification of it in the Northman's talk and gestural behaviour. The narrated monologues convey the commander's dubious reflections during the Northman's concluding explanation.

Because of its characteristically intermediate position between referential narrative statement and quoted monologue, narrated monologue brings out, in more condensed form, not only the commander's suspicions but also his more self-critical doubts concerning the factual basis for, and justification of, these suspicions. Moreover, narrated monologue functions here as a link between the commander's actions and thoughts at the time of the ordeal of the confrontation and the narrator's situation and reflections in the setting of the frame narrative. Increasing the relevance of the commander's tale as presented by the narrator, the narrated monologues thus confirm the point I have made about the necessity of recognizing the seriousness of the commander's dilemma. If the quoted monologues are indicative of the narrator's attempt to increase the attitudinal distance between the action-provoking thoughts of the commander and his own reflections, the narrated monologues serve to reduce that distance because they are expressed in the narrator's own style and idiom. Thus the narrated monologues at the end of the second part could be seen as anticipating the breakdown of the narrator's distancing efforts in the third.

This concluding part of 'The Tale' is very short (less than a page long), and is introduced by an intrusive authorial comment: 'The narrator bent forward towards the couch, where no movement betrayed the presence of a living person' (80). Reminding the reader of the text's frame narrative and confirming the commander's dual function as both personal narrator and protagonist, this authorial intrusion contributes to the concluding, structurally circular, movement of part three, where the narrative situation is dissolved upon the completion of the commander's story. Provoked by his suspicion or 'certitude' into giving the wrong course to the neutral ship, the commander finds that his doubts remain:

He abandoned all pretence.
    'Yes, I gave that course to him. It seemed to me a supreme test. I believe—no, I don't believe. I don't know. At the time I was certain. They all went down; and I don't know whether I have done stern retribution—or murder; whether I have added to the corpses that litter the bed of the unreadable sea the bodies of men completely innocent or basely guilty. I don't know. I shall never know.' (80)

Three critical observations must be made on this central passage in the concluding part of 'The Tale'. First, the authorial statement that the personal narrator abandons 'all pretence' confirms and emphasizes the consistently distancing effort of the commander's narrative right up to this point. The authorial narrator's use of 'pretence' refers implicitly both to the personal narrator's refusal or inability to identify himself with the protagonist and to the more critical quality of some of his observations and reflections (especially towards the end of part two and through the narrative modulations of narrated monologue).

Secondly, the personal narrator's abandonment of his self-imposed, distancing posture results not in just one single reference to 'I' (which here alone would have been sufficient to indicate a significant narrative variation), but in as many as ten instances of 'I' in one and the same paragraph. If all these first person references increase the artificiality of the narrative stance the narrator has formerly assumed, they also remind the reader of his need for distance in order to tell the tale at all. His sudden identification with the commander suggests not just resignation, but also a certain courage which to some extent increases our respect for him.

Thirdly, the elimination of the distinction which the text, through the personal narrator, has established between its protagonist and narrator emphasizes, rather than reduces, the problems of appearance versus reality, limited knowledge, and trying uncertainty. Characterizing the confrontation with the neutral ship as a 'supreme test', the narrator himself not only stresses its significance but also implies, in the reflections that follow, that the essence of this test revolved around the problems of action and decision on the one hand and suspicion, doubt, and uncertainty on the other.

The narrator's only (and last) remark after the passage discussed here is a repetition of its concluding sentence, ' " shall never know" ' (81). This last reference to his continuing, frustrating speculations and doubts not only occurs at the very end of the frame narrative: there is the suggestion that these thoughts will accompany the narrator all his life and greatly complicate his relationships with others, including the narratee. The return to the frame narrative in part three both specifies and extends the main thematic elements identified in my discussion of the text's two preceding parts. If the commander's tale culminates, as I have indicated, with his account of the confrontation with the neutral ship, the narrative and thematic climax of 'The Tale' is the first-person passage of part three where the identities of commander and narrator coalesce.

In contrast to *The Nigger of the 'Narcissus'* (cf. Chapter 6), the shift to, or rather relapse into, first-person references is immediately justifiable here, not just thematically but also in relation to the narrative structure of the text as a whole. As the narrator abandons his 'pretence', his personal narrative is diversified; this diversification is correlated with the change of pronominal reference. Paradoxically, the abrupt introduction of 'I' references, which in this study are generally seen as indications of personal narrative, reduces the commander's status and function as personal narrator. The whole of part three can be regarded as an authorial narrative in which the personal narrator is, to a greater extent than in parts one and two, portrayed as a character. This narrative modulation leads to an additional paradox, for the narrator's role as commander is played down here at the end.

If the conflict or dilemma of 'he' (the commander) is between limited knowledge, uncertainty, and suspicion on the one hand and the pressure to make potentially deadly decisions on the other, the problem or tragedy of 'I' (the narrator and earlier commander) is that his doubts concerning the factual foundation and justification of his decision remain, and will remain indefinitely. Although the 'supreme test' occurred at one particular point in time, the questions it posed for the commander are general and existential, or more precisely epistemological. Conrad was no professional philosopher, but this does not preclude the possibility of some interesting affinities between the narrative and thematic structure of his fiction and central issues posed in the history of epistemology. What is important is that such affinities be qualified, particularly by referring to the differences in genre. Even more strikingly than in 'The Secret Sharer', the thematics of 'The Tale' remains problematically open— it indicates the existence of doubts and questions rather than dramatizing and exploring them in the manner of *Lord Jim* or *Nostromo*. As in epistemology, one of the main questions asked by 'The Tale' is the very general one of whether knowledge can be related to some class of truth, or indeed whether knowledge is possible at all.[11] As epistemology is related to a general scepticism as regards knowledge, so the thematic tenor of the commander's uncertainty and suspicion in 'The Tale' is related to the pervasive scepticism of Conrad's fiction.

However, to connect the main character's uncertainty and suspi-

---

[11] See Paul Edwards (ed.), *The Encyclopedia of Philosophy*, III (London: Collier-Macmillan, 1967), 9.

cion with epistemological problems only would be to over-simplify. The thematics of the short story is more complex than such a relation would indicate; it includes a moral aspect which the narrative both plays down and affirms. It could be suggested, therefore, that a major characteristic of the commander is his tendency to delimit the problem of the 'supreme test' by re-defining it in epistemological terms. This applies in particular to the confrontation itself; at the time of his narration of it, a distancing process has taken place which has made the commander (as narrator) more aware of the dubious morality implicit in the decision he makes concerning the neutral ship. His phrase 'It seemed to me a supreme test' could be seen as pointing indirectly (though as directly as the narrator is able) to the serious moral flaw in a decision which, since the Northman would probably not have followed the Commander's directions if he were guilty, in one sense seems designed to kill the innocent and let the guilty go.

Even though such an interpretation of the 'supreme test' may appear to run counter to some of the main points already made in this chapter, it is also in part anticipated by them. The phrase 'supreme test' takes on a distinctly ironic colouring if read in the light of the above specification of the moral flaw associated with this test, but it does not follow that the commander's uncertainty and suspicion cast doubt on the reliability of his narrative. If, as already noted, the commander's problems are not recognized as real in the textual structure of the story, both its narrative suspense and main thematic thrust would be undermined. Moreover, it would seem that if we were intended fundamentally to distrust or reject the commander's narrative, the text would have had to suggest an alternative authorial evaluation different from that actually contained in it. However, the possibility of such an alternative authorial position is reduced by the elements of melodrama in the frame narrative. As we can read both self-criticism and self-irony into the narrator's last words, I would suggest that his growing awareness of the moral complications of his decision increases rather than reduces his narrative reliability.

The authorial narrator's final reference to the narratee complicates rather than clarifies the problems of interpretation which this text presents: 'She knew his passion for truth, his horror of deceit, his humanity' (81). If isolated from its context and related specifically to the moral flaw of the commander's decision, the word 'humanity' in this authorial remark might be seen as containing both authorial and dramatic irony. But such a reading is not supported by the text itself, and its validity is further reduced by the disturbing elements of melodrama at the end. Rather than speculating about possible loss of narrative control on Conrad's part here, I shall conclude by regarding 'The Tale' as an interesting late example in the Conrad canon of a modernist text offering conflicting interpretative possibilities. 'The Tale' is a short story where the narrative generates a thematics which remains tantalizingly unresolved.

6

The Nigger of the 'Narcissus': Problematic but Effective Combination of Authorial and Personal Narrative

Critics of Conrad's narrative in *The Nigger of the 'Narcissus'* (1897) have tended to be either appreciative or sceptical of the narrative method of the novella.[1] Placing itself in the first group, this chapter will argue that one important reason for Conrad's fictional achievement with *The Nigger of the 'Narcissus'* is suggested by a more considerable narrative variation, especially of perspective and distance, than most of the text's commentators have noted. I shall present a systematization of the novella's narrative variations, but it must be based on a commentary on the narrative method of relevant textual passages. My concluding comments focus on the importance of the novella for the development of Conrad's narrative method.

The introduction of Mr Baker in the first paragraph of *The Nigger of the 'Narcissus'* introduces an authorial narrative which, as John Lester has pointed out,[2] predominates in the account of the

---

[1] According to this broad and inevitably approximate distinction, the group of appreciative or sympathetic commentators would include such as Guerard, Berthoud, Watt, and Michael. See *NC* 100–25; *CMP* 23–40; *CNC* 68–125; and Marion C. Michael, 'James Wait as Pivot: Narrative Structure in *The Nigger of the "Narcissus"* ', in W. T. Zyla and W. M. Aycock (eds.), *Joseph Conrad: Theory and World Fiction* (Lubbock: Texas Tech Press, 1974), 89–102. Among those more sceptical about the narrative technique of the novella are Young, Mudrick, and Foulke. See Vernon Young, 'Trial by Water: Joseph Conrad's *The Nigger of the "Narcissus"* ', *Accent*, 12 (1952), 67–81; Marvin Mudrick, 'The Artist's Conscience and *The Nigger of the "Narcissus"* ', *Nineteenth-Century Fiction*, 11 (1957), 288–97; and Robert Foulke, 'Postures of Belief in *The Nigger of the "Narcissus"* ', *Modern Fiction Studies*, 17 (1971), 249–63, included in Robert Kimbrough (ed.), *The Nigger of the 'Narcissus'* (New York: Norton, 1979), 308–21. Kimbrough's edn. features several of the most influential essays on the novella. Intermediate positions between these two groups of critics are occupied by William Bonney, *Thorns & Arabesques*, 162–74, and Jeremy Hawthorn, 'The Incoherences of *The Nigger of the "Narcissus"* ', *The Conradian*, 11 (1986), 98–115.

[2] John Lester, 'Conrad's Narrators in *The Nigger of the "Narcissus"* ', *Conradiana*, 12 (1980), 166. See also David Manicom, 'True Lies/False Truths: Narrative Perspective and the Control of Ambiguity in *The Nigger of the "Narcissus"* ', *Conradiana*, 18 (1986), 105–18, which includes some helpful criticisms of an earlier version of this chapter.

beginning of the voyage. Already in Chapter 1 there are, however, more narrative variations than Lester notes. The hint of a personal narrator in the parenthetical comment, '(as we had calculated from his papers)' (7), is relatively insignificant; more important is the description of Old Singleton engaged in the reading of Bulwer Lytton. As the authorial account blends into appreciative character- ization, we get the first indication of a narrator who not only tells a story but also reflects on it, compares, and generalizes. To the narrator, Singleton 'resembled a learned and savage patriarch' (6). Then widening the perspective, he asks: 'What meaning their rough, inexperienced souls can find in the elegant verbiage of his pages? What excitement?—what forgetfulness?—what appeasement? Mystery!' Certainly the narrator of these reflective questions does not, as Lester has it, strike one as 'omniscient',[3] and yet the fact that he ponders the appeal of Lytton's 'Pelham' reveals interest and knowledge exceeding that of a common crewman. The exclamation 'Mystery!' qualifies the narrator's knowledge further, but it also suggests a capacity for excited wonder and reveals an appealing combination of incomprehension and respect.

The focal point of the narrative is still Singleton in the important paragraph towards the end of the first chapter. Here Singleton is portrayed as the representative of a disappearing generation of seamen whose ethic and 'fate' are endorsed by the authorial narra- tor. The narrator seems now more self-assured, firmer in his opinions, but also more resigned: 'The sea and the earth are unfaithful to their children: a truth, a faith, a generation of men goes—and is forgotten, and it does not matter!' (25). The elevated tone makes this exclamation almost hymnic. The narrator, though technically authorial, expresses his personal views, but these views need to be qualified if critically compared with the surrounding narrative context. The artistic quality of the passage then appears weakened: in Conrad elevation of tone does not necessarily improve artistic quality: there are certain similarities between this quotation and rather journalistic passages in *The Mirror of the Sea*.

The two sections with relatively overt authorial commentary at the beginning and end of Chapter 1 constitute an essential narrative and thematic supplement to the more straightforward account of

---

[3] Lester, 'Conrad's Narrators', 166.

the *Narcissus* and her crew. They also function as a structural frame
round the climax of the first chapter, the introduction of James
Wait. In the fictional universe of the novella, this introduction is
factual, but the facts rapidly merge with the curiously menacing
influence Wait exerts on the crew from the very outset. Rereading
The Nigger of the 'Narcissus' it is difficult not to read proleptic
elements into the introduction of Wait; and this variant of prolepsis
seems here to be at work at two interrelated levels. First, there is the
prefiguration of the dominant thematic position of the 'nigger' in
the story—both in the importance attached to his appearance and
initial influence and, more explicitly, in the mention of the cook's
later remark about him: 'The poor fellow had scared me. I thought I
had seen the devil' (19). Secondly, since the stress on the crew's
reaction to Wait prepares us for the introduction of the personal
crewman-narrator in the following chapter, the impression of a
conspicuous combination of authorial and personal narrative is
somewhat reduced.

The narrative variations at the beginning of Chapter 2 include
authorial passages that rank among the most suggestive and visually
striking in the early Conrad. In its opening description there are
three different, and yet closely related, focuses. First, there is the
Narcissus herself. Then there is nature, and especially the sea—with
the implied suggestion of harmony and peace at sea, and the ship as
integral part of nature, separated from and contrasted with life
ashore. Thirdly, there is the crew, and Captain Allistoun as 'the
ruler of that minute world' (31). The first paragraph in particular
demonstrates how these three focuses are fused through technical
devices more commonly associated with poetry than narrative
fiction:

Next morning, at daylight, the *Narcissus* went to sea.
   A slight haze blurred the horizon. Outside the harbour the measureless
expanse of smooth water lay sparkling like a floor of jewels, and as empty
as the sky... The loose upper canvas blew out in the breeze with soft round
contours, resembling small white clouds snared in the maze of ropes. Then
the sheets were hauled home, the yards hoisted, and the ship became a high
and lonely pyramid, gliding, all shining and white, through the sunlit mist.
(27)

The suggestive simile of the water 'sparkling like a floor of jewels, and as empty as the sky' is followed by a powerful identification metaphor: 'the ship became a high and lonely pyramid'.[4] The human attributes suggested by 'lonely' are developed in a further comparison with another living creature: 'She resembled an enormous and aquatic black beetle, surprised by the light, overwhelmed by the sunshine'. The different modes of perception discussed by Robert Foulke are fused early in Chapter 2.[5] Direct, visual observation blends into reflection, while the third mode—the clusters of metaphors that to Foulke suggest a mythical voyage—becomes a constituent of both. The narrative variations here, and indeed throughout the novella, are variations of narrative perspective and distance more than of voice. In contrast to such a novel as *Lord Jim*, where, as we shall see in Chapter 9, there are several distinct and supplementary narrative voices, the whole of *The Nigger of the 'Narcissus'* is told by an unnamed narrator. As explained in the Introduction, however, narrative perspective concerns not the speaker but the one who sees. It indicates the vantage points of the narrative vision; and here *The Nigger of the 'Narcissus'* exhibits considerable variation.

In this novella perspective operates in close contact with narrative distance. As used here, 'distance' indicates not only the problematic relationship in this text between the unnamed narrator and the characters, but also the (partly indeterminable) relationship between Conrad as author and the text's combination of authorial and personal narrative—a combination which includes what Ian Watt calls 'Conrad's intrusive authorial commentary',[6] and which also incorporates char-

---

[4] My use of the term 'simile' here is synonymous with 'image': both concepts indicate a comparison introduced by 'like' or 'as though'. In the 'identification metaphor', however, Conrad's use of the verb 'become' to interlink its constitutive elements strengthens the sense of identification and intensified, lyric description. For a learned and illuminating discussion of the concepts of metaphor and symbol, see Umberto Eco, *Semiotics and the Philosophy of Language* (London: Macmillan, 1984), 87–163. It must be added that not all metaphors are identification metaphors; like most critics I also use the term to indicate a significant image, such as 'darkness' in 'Heart of Darkness'. Metaphor and symbol are two of the most complex concepts commonly used not only in literary criticism, but in linguistics and philosophy of language as well. As Eco says, 'To speak of metaphor, therefore, means to speak of rhetorical activity in all its complexity' (87). And as far as the concept of the symbol is concerned, Eco even refuses to consider it as a particular sort of sign, or as a modality of sign production: 'It is a *textual modality*, a way of producing and of interpreting the aspects of a text.' (162) Cf. the application of Eco's theories to the discussion of metaphors and symbols in *Nostromo*, ch. 10 below.

[5] Foulke, 'Postures of Belief', 309–10.

[6] *CNC* 99.

acteristics of 'The Conradian Voice' as Albert Guerard understands it.[7] Although some of the authorial narrator's generalizations may seem to approach Conrad's own views, this is not necessarily the case. However, the decreasing attitudinal distance in the opening of Chapter 2 is of a different kind: the imaginative intensity resulting from the combination of the different descriptive focuses and the application of the poetic devices we have noted promotes the impression of an incorporated prose poem with lyric elements.[8] If excerpts of the beginning of Chapter 2 (particularly in the second, third, and fifth paragraphs) are read as lyric interludes, then it might be suggested that—for a limited stretch of the narrative—the attitudinal distance between Conrad and his authorial narrator is reduced, thus establishing a sense of the narrator as lyric voice transmitting a particular visual sensation as intensified memory:[9]

The passage had begun, and the ship, a fragment detached from the earth, went on lonely and swift like a small planet. Round her the abysses of sky and sea met in an unattainable frontier. A great circular solitude moved with her, ever changing and ever the same, always monotonous and always imposing... She had her own future; she was alive with the lives of those beings who trod her decks; like that earth which had given her up to the sea, she had an intolerable load of regrets and hopes. On her lived timid truth and audacious lies; and, like the earth, she was unconscious, fair to see—and condemned by men to an ignoble fate. The august loneliness of her path lent dignity to the sordid inspiration of her pilgrimage. (29–30)

Part of the lyric effect here (and it must be stressed that such an effect will in part depend on the reader's response) is associated with the combination of visual intensification and the metaphor 'a fragment detached from the earth', suggesting both the vulnerability of the *Narcissus* and the sense of isolation of her crew. Although it would be an over-simplification to cite an excerpt such as this one (from the fifth paragraph of Chapter 2) as a narrative instance of intensified memory only, the term 'lyric interlude' seems apt if

---

[7] Cf. ch. 1 n. 10.

[8] The poetic qualities of *The Nigger of the 'Narcissus'* were noted early. In a review in *Academy* (1 January 1898), I. Zangwill comments thus on the descriptive authorial paragraphs of the novella: 'In vision this is poetry.' See Sherry (ed.), *Conrad: The Critical Heritage*, 94.

[9] Such a reading could receive critical support from Emil Staiger's definition of the lyric as intensified memory. See Staiger, 'Lyrischer Stil: Erinnerung', ch. 2 of his *Grundbegriffe der Poetik* (Zürich: Atlantis Verlag, 1946), 13–88, esp. 55–69.

combined with the observation that it is merged with authorial reflection. Interestingly, although the lyric sensation of intensified, visual memory is in a sense simple, the incorporated reflections (such as that indicated by 'circular solitude') point to thematic concerns that are among the most central in Conrad. More specifically, we shall see in Chapter 8 that there are some noteworthy affinities between this kind of authorial description and personal descriptions in another novella Conrad wrote some twenty years later, *The Shadow-Line*. Finally, in addition to their importance as descriptive passages in their own right, the lyric interludes also establish a contrast with the later storm and the problems aboard the *Narcissus*; on a second reading, a phrase such as 'On her lived timid truth and audacious lies' takes on a proleptic quality which we cannot appreciate if unaware of the approaching conflict.

The character who initiates the conflict is James Wait, but in spite of the crew's intuitive perception of Wait as a potential adversary, the latter part of Chapter 2 also includes the suggestion of a special alliance between him and the crew: 'He seemed to hasten the retreat of departing light by his very presence; the setting sun dipped sharply, as though fleeing before our nigger' (34). With the introduction of this 'our' the authorial narrative situation in the novella breaks down; and an influx of *we*, *us*, and *our* follows. Although the significance of this change is not to be minimized, it does not necessarily imply the introduction of a second narrator. Another possible explanation is that the authorial narrator identifies himself as one of the crew and thus technically becomes personal, so that while the narrative voice remains constant a change of perspective takes place. Once this suggestion is made, however, I should add that the identity of the narrative voice in *The Nigger of the 'Narcissus'* is often obscure. There are numerous occasions later in the text when the first-person pronouns temporarily disappear and the narrative again seems authorial.

The use of a personal narrator enables Conrad to dramatize parts of the story more convincingly and to establish its thematic focus more firmly. The frantic effort to save Wait at the very culmination of the gale, for instance, could not have been presented so directly and forcefully had not the personal narrator himself been an active participant in the rescue. The identification of the personal narrator with the crew and its tasks helps to dramatize the novella's concern with human solidarity, the united group, and the work ethic, both when at sea generally and in times of crisis. Two indications of this narrative function are the oppositions that are established, first between Donkin and *we* (38), and then between *we* and Singleton (41). These contrasts show the crew's wavering and precarious position: distanced from and critical of Donkin, it can still be manipulated into feeling comtempt for Singleton.

Chapter 3, which includes the colourful description of the gale and the dramatic account of the rescue of Wait, productively combines authorial and personal narrative. The immediate effect of the suffusion of first-person pronouns in the appraisal of the *Narcissus* is to reaffirm the alliance between the crew and the ship that the authorial narrator has been stressing earlier. But the chapter also contains generalizing, associative descriptions reminiscent of the early authorial narrative. If these two formal variations supplement each other in a thematically unifying manner here, they also increase the authorial narrator's reliability by confirming his previous observations on the relationship between crew and ship. The main effect of the introduction of 'they' (57–8), a further narrative elaboration, is that while the personal narrative situation is retained, a new modulation of distance is introduced between the crewman-narrator and the other members of the crew. There are even variations within this particular form of modulation: *They* may signal the crewman's personal recollections of the actions of others as he saw them aboard the *Narcissus*, but *they* may also indicate that the narrator is seeking some detachment in his ruminative descriptions. The thematic importance of this distinction is comparatively slight. It might be seen as an indication of hampered solidarity due to the influence of Wait, but overall, this narrative variation seems one of the least rewarding in the novella.

With regard to narrative method, the latter part of Chapter 3 is less interesting than the first. The textual length of the crew's reaction to the rescue of Wait is probably excessive, and the narrative suffers from a sense of anticlimax following this culminating action. Then, in the much-discussed first paragraph of Chapter 4, there are significant similarities with the opening of Chapter 2. The paragraph begins thus:

On men reprieved by its disdainful mercy, the immortal sea confers in its justice the full privilege of desired unrest. Through the perfect wisdom of its grace they are not permitted to meditate at ease upon the complicated and acrid savour of existence. (90)

Here, as early in Chapter 2, the narrative perspective is authorial; the whole paragraph is reflective, thought-provoking, and generalized. More isolated from the surrounding narrative context than the opening of Chapter 2, the statement is less lyric and more intellectual. It is perhaps because of its reflective or philosophical character that this paragraph has been seen as embodying central thematic concerns of *The Nigger of the 'Narcissus'*. It certainly points to some of them,[10] but its explicit and rather isolated position in the text somewhat reduces its thematic relevance and effectiveness. It is perhaps, at this stage of the narrative, too overtly authorial.

The structure of this chapter of the novella is tripartite. Carrying on from Chapter 3, the first part is a subdued and prolonged statement on the ship and the sailors in the aftermath of the gale. Then comes the strange encounter of Donkin and Wait, where a curious combination of alliance and opposition is established between two very different characters. An interesting variation of perspective occurs in this scene: the crew considers Wait selfish and so does the narrator as a member of it, but at the same time the detached, authorial narrator is so knowledgeable here that he can even reveal Wait's thoughts: 'He thought:—That lunatic Belfast will bring me some water if I ask. Fool. I am very thirsty...' (113) Those sceptical about the novella's narrative method have found this omniscience disturbing, and in one sense it certainly is, particularly because Wait's thoughts are related to the attitude of the crew here, which the reader by now naturally associates with the personal crewman-narrator. Objections of this kind must, however, be measured against possible gains resulting from this sudden revelation of Wait's scheme. One striking consequence is that the mystery surrounding Wait is dispelled, his ordinariness is revealed, and the crew realize that his influence on them has been more subtle and indirect than formerly assumed—that he is a symbol, in Ian Watt's phrase, 'not of death but of the fear of death'.[11]

In the third part of the chapter, dealing with the unrest of the crew and the impending danger of mutiny, the narrator's attitude and degree of involvement are unclear. The use of *they* suggests some removal and detachment on his part; and there is a shift to the consequences of Wait's (and Donkin's) presence and influence. At

[10] Cf. *CNC* 98–9.
[11] Ibid. 106.

the same time, the narrator must to some extent be involved in, or at least confused by, the row, since only Singleton's practical wisdom and Captain Allistoun's professional authority remain supremely undisturbed by it. A narrative problem here is that in some sections the perspective appears to be that of an officer rather than a crewman. Thus one could speculate that the personal narrator is the ship's third mate, who, contrary to Mr Baker and Mr Creighton (the first and second mates) is nowhere named and described, and who as the lowest-ranking officer would be relatively close to the crewmen. However, such a suggestion would seem contradicted not only by the numerous instances where the personal narrator appears to be a crewman, but also by the reference to 'his two big officers' (125), which implies that Captain Allistoun has only two mates under his command.

Order aboard the *Narcissus* is not restored until well into the final fifth chapter, whose first paragraph again fluctuates between authorial and personal narrative. The opening, starting from the activities of the crew, unexpectedly includes a reflection reminiscent of earlier authorial passages: 'The problem of life seemed too volu-minous for the narrow limits of human speech' (138). Thoughts on the sea accompany the reflection; then there are rather categorical authorial notes on the effects of Wait's influence; and then the introduction of *we* follows. This kind of juxtaposition of personal and more authorial narrative is problematic: the transitions are abrupt and the attendant technical problems made conspicuous. In a passage such as this one, the reversion to authorial omniscience (from a personal narrator's limited knowledge) may make the reader ask what kind of authority the narrator in *The Nigger of the 'Narcissus'* actually has, and what the relationship is between personal and authorial authority. There is a linkage between uncer-tainty in the answers to such questions and ambiguity in the thematics of the novella.

In the scene describing Wait's death (structurally comparable to the Donkin/Wait scene in Chapter 4), the authorial omniscience of the narrative is emphasized once again. In the final pages of the novella, however, there are great variations of both authorial and personal narrative. Authorial elements are noticeable in the account of the ship's rapid return to England after the burial of Wait. They also emerge in the description of England as 'A great ship!' (163)—a problematically ambiguous metaphor since the suggestion of affinity between the country and the ship seems to contradict the earlier emphasis on the *Narcissus* as a small, cut-off world. Then at the very end the collective *we* is abandoned, and for the first time the crewman-narrator refers to himself by the use of 'I': 'As I came up I saw a red-faced, blowsy woman' (170). Underlining the disruption and dispersal of the crew once ashore, and suggesting that the virtues of solidarity, unifying work, and stoic simplicity are both rarer and harder to come by if separated from the *Narcissus*, this concluding narrative variation is of substantial thematic importance.

On the basis of the above observations we can now attempt a systematization of the narrative variations in *The Nigger of the 'Narcissus'*. In one sense the novella resists such a critical ordering, and an excessively technical consideration of it probably reduces its thematic impact. At the same time *The Nigger of the 'Narcissus'* does, as we have seen, invite considerations of form and method; more than most of Conrad's fictional texts, this particular one provokes both appreciative and adverse commentary on its narrative strategies. The basis for the following systematization is the broad distinction drawn between authorial and personal narrative in *The Nigger of the 'Narcissus'*, and the observation that the novella has more significant variations of perspective than of voice. We have noted only one narrative voice, that of the crewman-narrator who eventually emerges as the narrating 'I' of the story. When Ian Watt says that the whole text is told by 'an unnamed and uncharacterised narrator',[12] he is giving a broad description of the novella's combination of authorial and personal narrative. However, it would seem that, though unnamed, the personal narrator is not wholly uncharacterized: at several stages of the narrative he clearly functions and speaks as a crewman.

If we say that there are two narrative voices in *The Nigger of the 'Narcissus'*, one unnamed and one identified, then we make a distinction which approximately corresponds to that between authorial and personal narrative. But then we would also have to say that it is often unclear which voice is speaking. Generally Conrad succeeds, partly because of his powerful narrative rhetoric, in diverting the reader's attention from this difficult point. Instead our interest is focused on the novella's variations of mood, constituted by an elaborate interplay of changes in perspective and

12 *CNC* 99.

distance. As the productive interrelationship of these two devices makes it difficult to employ them as a basis for narrative systematization, it may be more helpful to use the variation of personal pronouns as indication of the text's overall narrative variation. The two extreme positions in *The Nigger of the 'Narcissus'* would then be 'narrator as character' (*I* as personal pronoun) and 'detached and reflective authorial narrator' (*they* as personal pronoun). In the narrative, however, these two positions are repeatedly modified and blended: building on the above observations we can list six narrative variations which supplement and enrich one another:

1. *I*: personal recollection of a crewman who was there, involved in the action aboard the *Narcissus*, but who is now left alone after the completion of the voyage.

2. *we*: personal recollection by a crewman who was there, involved in the action during the voyage.

3. *they*: (*a*) personal recollection by a crewman who was there, involved in the action, but who is now recalling the actions of others as he saw them;
   (*b*) personal recollection by a crewman seeking a detached perspective;
   (*c*) detachment of a reflective, authorial narrator;
   (*d*) reduced attitudinal distance with narrator as lyric voice.

Technically, 1 and 2 constitute the personal narrative and 3 the authorial, but as we have seen, there are affinities between the personal *we* and the authorial *they*(*a*). The transition from 3(*a*) to (*b*) may also be blurred, and is partly dependent on the reader's alertness. There does, however, seem to be a significant difference between the narrator's attitude to *they* in parts of Chapter 3 (especially on page 58) and parts of Chapter 4 (especially on page 134). This difference illustrates the distinction between 3(*a*) and (*b*): in the first case, the factual recollection is that of an observer; in the second case, it seems that the narrator is seeking a more detached perspective because of disagreement with the crew's grumbling and possibly in order to understand the reason for their unrest.

In 3(*c*) the narrative perspective is more characteristically authorial. Although this narrative variant is most apparent in the early chapters of the novella, it is reintroduced later; and then the fluctuations of voice may be disturbing. This particular narrative problem is much more noticeable in *The Nigger of the 'Narcissus'* then in a later work such as *The Shadow-Line*, where we have a competent captain as personal narrator. For this reason the lyric elements I shall identify in the discussion of *The Shadow-Line* (cf. Chapter 8) may be easier to respond to, but then it must be added that this late novella has fewer narrative variations and tends more unambiguously towards fictional memory than does *The Nigger of the 'Narcissus'*. The narrative variation of 3(*d*) is primarily one of narrative distance—a temporary reduction of the attitudinal distance between Conrad and his authorial narrator, whose narrative function may thus also become a lyric one. This lyric variation is different from an authorial description such as that in the first paragraph of Chapter 4, where the function of the authorial narrator approximates 'Conrad's tendency to editorialise'.[13] It might be added that the response to the lyric quality will depend, for instance, on how much irony the reader finds in the general narrative movement of the text. One reason why I emphasize the lyric element is that the variant of Conradian irony found in *The Nigger of the 'Narcissus'* seems relatively simple, and is modified by an undertone of nostalgia and collective loss.

The irony of the novella is most obviously associated with the characterization of Donkin, whom the narrator strongly resents, and whose views and attitudes represent a threat to the community of the *Narcissus* which supplements that of Wait. Although this narrative variation is not included in the above systematization into six narrative situations (which are so close that they may appear inseparable in the reading process), the listed variations clearly indicate some of the complexity of Conrad's narrative method in *The Nigger of the 'Narcissus'*. I would suggest, then, that the powerful narrative rhetoric of the novella is closely related to a method which, through a successful combination of memory and imagination, enables Conrad to dramatize some of his deepest concerns with human solidarity, work in the well-defined setting of a ship, human loneliness, vulnerability, and fear. The combination of authorial and personal perspective is used to emphasize the thematic significance of the crew; its collective consciousness and

[13] *CNC* 97.

characteristics are central to the thematics of *The Nigger of the 'Narcissus'*. It is important for Conrad to convey a whole view of the ship, and the narrative devices and functions we have noted contribute to this end in a rhetorically effective (if not technically consistent) manner. The use of Marlow as a narrator would, for instance, have been incompatible with the need for a method capable of characterizing all the crew. The narrative potential of Marlow resides essentially in his ability to explore and present the problems and experiences of a particular individual. In 'Heart of Darkness' this individual is, as we have seen in Chapter 2, Marlow himself: he is telling the story of his Congo experience from the vantage point of a later, safer existence in 'civilized' London, but the dramatic intensity of the experience is accentuated rather than reduced. In *Lord Jim* Marlow is admittedly not telling us about himself, but still there is, as remains to the demonstrated in Chapter 9 below, an important sense in which Marlow's strange interest in Jim (it surprises even himself) is explicable only as a strong, existential need to investigate aspects of his own personality hitherto unknown.

In contrast to 'Heart of Darkness' and *Lord Jim*, the focus of *The Nigger of the 'Narcissus'* is not just on one character (or more precisely on two: the protagonist and the narrator-interpreter); it is rather, as we have seen, on the crew of the *Narcissus*. The description of the crew (and some of its venerable members such as Singleton) serves to constitute a thematics that is less complex than in the two other works, but is still an essential part of the thematics observable in Conrad's fiction as a whole. *The Nigger of the 'Narcissus'* dramatizes some of its more 'positive' aspects: the value of solidarity, the relatively unproblematic (but not therefore valueless) meaning to be found in the prosecution of hard, manual work, the peculiar intensity of life experienced at sea. In order to establish, dramatize, and develop these constituent aspects of Conradian thematics (and there are more than those mentioned here) the combination of authorial and personal narrative achieves much. The outside authorial perspective is an efficient means of describing the ship and the crew at sea—with the problems, challenges, and assets of this particular form of human existence. The fact that the kind of life led aboard the *Narcissus* is, as the ending of the novella suggests, temporally limited not only augments its value but also enhances, in Jacques Berthoud's apposite phrase, 'the nostalgic

seductiveness of an achievement seen in retrospect'.[14] The linkage
between different narrative devices and variations of distance helps
to make parts of the authorial narrative remarkably suggestive, and
sometimes generates a lyric intensity not often found in narrative
fiction. The work is not flawless, but its achievements are exceptional despite its flaws and narrative inconsistencies. The abandonment of the narrator's collective *we* at the end, for instance, is technically conspicuous; yet it forms the narrative basis for the narrator's
somewhat sentimental, elegiac appraisal of his fellow sailors with
which the novella ends. In *The Nigger of the 'Narcissus'* we can see
Conrad 'in process of learning'.[15] Combined with the authorial
narrative, the personal narrative perspective—diversified through
the varying use of personal pronouns—contributes to the dramatic
effectiveness of the narration, and also proves a productive method
of constituting, developing, and confirming the book's thematic
concerns.

Given the critical emphasis of this study on narrative method,
these concerns cannot be explored here. Interestingly, however,
two recent considerations of *The Nigger of the 'Narcissus'* specify
the thematics of the novella in a manner which presupposes greater
awareness of its narrative devices and variations than has been
customary. One of these critical contributions is Berthoud's excellent introduction to his edition of *The Nigger of the 'Narcissus'* in
the World's Classics edition of Conrad; the other is Michael P.
Jones's chapter on the novella in his study *Conrad's Heroism.* As
Berthoud shows that greater attention to the 'historical context'[16] of
The Nigger of the 'Narcissus' prompts an increased awareness of its
thematic complexity, one implication of his argument is that this
complexity is to a considerable extent dependent on the text's
variations of narrative perspective, which make the authorial position more nuanced. Jones concludes his stimulating interpretation
by regarding the novella as 'Conrad's farewell to the past and the
only time among his greatest works that he deals extensively with an
heroic community in its resistance to history and society and the

[14] Jacques Berthoud, 'Conrad and the Sea', intro. to the World's Classics edn. of
The Nigger of the 'Narcissus' (Oxford: O U P, 1984), p. vii.

[15] The phrase is coined by J. Warren Beach, one of of the first critics to make this
observation, in *The Twentieth-Century Novel: Studies in Technique* (New York:
Appleton–Century–Crofts, 1960; orig. publ. 1932), 352.

[16] Berthoud, 'Conrad and the Sea', p. xiv.

modern world,' and adds—in consort with the general tenor of his argument—that 'In finally evaluating this tale, we would probably agree that it is not a story that leaves us thinking about its failures.'[17] It certainly does not; and the main reasons for this are the exceptional narrative intensity, the ethical persuasiveness, and the collective focus of this classic of the sea.

[17] Michael P. Jones, *Conrad's Heroism: A Paradise Lost* (Ann Arbor, Michigan: UMI Research Press, 1985), 63.

7
'Typhoon':
Thematically Productive Narrative
Simplicity

Critical evaluations of 'Typhoon' (part of *Typhoon and Other Stories*, 1903) can be grouped in two broad categories. First, there are the critics who underestimate the work—either implicitly by limiting their critical attention to other Conrad texts,[1] or through their explicit commentary on this particular narrative. In her early study of Conrad, M. C. Bradbrook considers 'Typhoon' a mere 'yarn'.[2] Douglas Hewitt finds that in this novella 'Nothing happens which... seems "to throw a kind of light" on moral or spiritual issues'.[3] Guerard admires the text for its characterization and evocative prose, but claims that its 'preoccupations are nearly all on the surface... Thus *Typhoon* requires no elaborate interpreting'.[4] F. R. Leavis too regards 'Typhoon' as a minor work, yet interestingly goes on to single it out as a text in which Conrad's 'strength may be found in its purest form'.[5]

This appreciation, one of the first influential ones of the novella, establishes a point of transition to the more favourably-disposed view characteristic of the second group of critics. John H. Wills emphasizes what he calls the 'organic nature' of 'Typhoon', and gives an unconvincing formulation of the story's thematic concern: 'the ironic victory of modern society over a world it cannot understand'.[6] It must be added, however, that Wills also observes that

[1] Berthoud, for instance, does not discuss 'Typhoon', and neither does C. B. Cox; see his *Joseph Conrad: The Modern Imagination* (London: Dent, 1974). A recent exception to the general tendency to dismiss the novella is Francis A. Hubbard, *Theories of Action in Conrad* (Ann Arbor, Michigan: UMI Research Press, 1984). Hubbard provides an extended discussion of 'Typhoon' in his first chapter, 1–22, before proceeding to 'Heart of Darkness' and *The Secret Agent*.

[2] M. C. Bradbrook, *Joseph Conrad: Poland's English Genius* (New York: Russell & Russell, 1966), orig. publ. 1941, 32.

[3] Hewitt, *Conrad: A Reassessment*, 113.

[4] CN 294.

[5] Leavis, *The Great Tradition*, 203.

[6] John H. Wills, 'Conrad's *Typhoon*: A Triumph of Organic Art', *The North Dakota Quarterly*, 30 (1962), 62.

'Typhoon' 'is a complex of centrifugal, as well as centripetal forces' and that 'Theme is dissolved also in the structural and stylistic elements of the novel.'[7] Combined with the useful analysis of Jukes's function and personal growth, such observations firmly place Wills in the second group, to which critics such as Paul S. Bruss and H. M. Daleski also belong.[8] Following Wills, they are both eager to revaluate the thematic importance of Jukes in the story. Of the two essays Daleski's is clearly the more perceptive. Arguing that 'Typhoon' brings to an end the phase in which Conrad was 'primarily concerned with the question of physical self-possession',[9] he makes the important, if rather obvious, point that 'the crew of the *Nan-Shan*, like that of the *Patna*, are subjected to a sudden and unexpected test',[10] and that this particular test (the typhoon) not only reveals what is hidden in a character, 'but also exposes hitherto unrealized dimensions of the universe in which he lives'.[11]

If I can agree with Daleski this far, the way in which he goes on to compare 'Typhoon' with *Lord Jim* gives reason for dissent. Although he qualifies the comparison by noting some of the ways in which MacWhirr is differentiated from Jim, he pushes the analogy of the two characters (who are really very different) too far. And although the comparison he draws between Jim and Jukes is potentially interesting, it is not sufficiently developed to become persuasive. Seeing Jukes as a 'potential Jim, a man who would indubitably have gone the way of Jim were it not for the grace of his captain',[12] Daleski makes a point which is too speculative to be critically cogent.

Such a provisional grouping into two main critical attitudes to 'Typhoon' makes it easier to delineate the critical focus of this chapter. My critical concern remains narrative method, which in this particular case essentially means investigation of the diversified functions of the text's authorial narrative. Even if it is true that 'Typhoon' is a relatively straightforward Conrad text, still its omniscient authorial narrator performs functions more varied and

[7] Ibid. 69.
[8] Paul S. Bruss, '*Typhoon*: The Initiation of Jukes', *Conradiana*, 5 (1973), 46–55; *C WD* 104–12.
[9] *C WD* 104.
[10] Ibid. 105.
[11] Ibid.
[12] Ibid. 107.

sophisticated than critics have generally noted. Once the particular form of narrative sophistication which 'Typhoon' evinces is appreciated, then the thematic generalizations briefly summarized above are revealed as simplifying or even misleading. The main critical focus is on Jukes and MacWhirr. As much of the novella's central action revolves around these two characters, and as they receive about the same amount of authorial commentary, they gradually emerge as the two main characters of the text. There is a particular thematics attached to each of them; a larger and more ambiguous thematics arises from the striking contrast between these two personalities, and from their divergent relations to the crew and to the typhoon with which the ship is confronted.

I

At 100 pages, 'Typhoon' consists of six chapters of approximately equal length. Several critics have noted that Chapters 1 and 6 frame the novella's central action, which is basically constituted by the ordeal of the typhoon which Captain MacWhirr decides to meet head-on. Wills finds that the first and last chapters are 'primarily comprised of observations by others upon the character and actions of MacWhirr'.[13] In actual fact, however, these two chapters are really quite different. It is thematically significant that the novella ends with Jukes's letter, with no authorial comment appended to it. In the first chapter, in contrast, authorial prominence is striking and must be considered in some detail, but first the narrative pattern of the beginning of the text must be discussed.

The first paragraph immediately establishes an authorial narrative situation where attention is focused on MacWhirr in order to give an introductory characterization of him. The authorial omniscience becomes apparent at once: MacWhirr's 'physiognomy... was the exact counterpart of his mind: it presented no marked characteristics of firmness or stupidity; it had no pronounced characteristics whatever; it was simply ordinary, irresponsive, and unruffled' (3). This early example of authorial omniscience prefigures what is gradually established as one of the chief narrative characteristics of the novella. Its effects are, as we shall see, varied.

13 Wills, 'Conrad's *Typhoon*', 69.

A general point to be made already, however, is that in this text there is a crucial linkage between authorial omniscience and narrative authority: there is no narrative instance or device in the text which gives the reader reason to doubt the veracity of the authorial narrator's pronouncements. To emphasize the narrator's authority—which is strengthened, but not directly verified, by his omniscience—is not to suggest that all his statements and views should be accepted uncritically. Still, most of the narrative and thematic effects of 'Typhoon' are intimately related to the authority of the authorial narrative.[14]

In this connection I shall draw attention to a sentence in the third paragraph whose significance critics appear to have overlooked. Having given a preliminary characterization of MacWhirr as non-imaginative, reliable and factual, the narrator adds: 'Yet the uninteresting lives of men so entirely given to the actuality of the bare existence have their mysterious side' (4). If narrative authority is taken, as it must be, to include the view of MacWhirr and his likes voiced here, then the sentence not only gives a partial explanation of the authorial narrator's sincere interest in the type of character and work ethic MacWhirr represents, but also advises the reader not to take too dismissive a view of MacWhirr (and certainly not, as both Wills and Bruss tend to do, to ridicule him by way of contrasting him with Jukes). At this early stage of the narrative these implications may seem strained, but we shall see that they are borne out by its development, and also that the generalization is effectively related to the novella's curiously modified use of irony.

More immediately, however, it introduces an analeptic narrative movement outlining MacWhirr's background. The function of this analepsis is essentially twofold. First, it incorporates the first of the several letters which throughout the novella serve as an important, though somewhat mechanical, variant on the authorial narrative. The length and thematic significance of the letters, which in a relatively unsophisticated manner provide personal perspectives on the events related by the authorial narrator, vary greatly. The first one belongs, with the next two following sult, among the shortest: 'We had very fine weather on our passage out' (5). In addition to the narrative variation it provides, the letter represents, with the following

---

[14] Thus it is debatable if Bruss is justified in talking, for example, about MacWhirr's 'verbal absurdity'—a phrase the authorial narrator would never have employed. See Bruss, 'Typhoon', 46.

description of the parents' reaction to it, an early example of humour in 'Typhoon'. Secondly, the analepsis establishes a contrast which is to be substantiated later on in the narrative, that between life ashore and aboard the *Nan-Shan*. This contrast serves as a structural basis for two of the novella's thematic concerns, the problems of human communication and loneliness.

The analepsis is followed by a strikingly economical 'reach':[15] 'All these events had taken place many years before the morning when, in the chart-room of the steamer *Nan-Shan*, he stood confronted by the fall of a barometer he had no reason to distrust' (6). This transition to the novella's main narrative focus introduces a distinct element of suspense, which is simply but effectively generated by the warning the fall of the barometer gives. Generally, the narrative function of suspense is less intricate here than in 'The Secret Sharer' (cf. Chapter 4). One reason for this relative simplicity is suggested by the early authorial characterization of MacWhirr and made almost excessively explicit in the authorial commentary following the quotation; already at this early stage of the narrative it seems doubtful whether even a violent storm can bring about any pro-found change in the main character. Suspense thus becomes exter-nalized; it is focused principally on what will happen to the ship, only secondarily on the possibility of some profound alteration in the character of MacWhirr. However, with the introduction of Jukes, the contrastive character to MacWhirr, the function of suspense is nuanced and extended.

In the remaining part of Chapter 1 information is provided on the *Nan-Shan*, her chief engineer Solomon Rout, and her first mate Jukes. The quarrel over the change of flag (from British to Siamese) is exceptionally well rendered. Even if MacWhirr's inability to understand Jukes's consternation seems to reveal an almost incred-ible naïvety, the captain's attitude is still quite consistent with the initial authorial characterization of him. Furthermore, the scene gives Conrad the opportunity to exploit the humorous aspects of the tale. The comedy of the failure of the ship's two senior officers to understand each other also accentuates the problem of communi-cation. Thus suspense is increased: we wonder whether the two men

---

[15] 'Reach' corresponds to Genette's term 'portée', which indicates the temporal distance or extension of the anachronic variation in a narrative, whether into the past or into the future. The concept is thus closely related to both analepsis and prolepsis. See *ND* 48, and cf. ch. 2 n. 10.

can work together if the ship is exposed to danger, as the falling barometer indicates she will be. As the narrative progresses the challenge of the typhoon leads to a diversification of the problem of communication.

Of the two letters which bring Chapter 1 to its conclusion, Jukes's is by far the more interesting, particularly if related to the authorial commentary that accompanies it. Sharing with a friend his impression of MacWhirr, Jukes considers his captain 'jolly innocent' (18) and elaborates upon his dullness and queerness. His description substantiates rather than contradicts the earlier authorial characterizations. The phrase ' "He doesn't do anything actually foolish" ' (17), for instance, is consonant with the authorial 'his mind... presented no marked characteristics of firmness or stupidity' (3). Once Jukes's letter is given (in full, presumably), the authorial narrator proceeds to comment to it:

Thus wrote Mr. Jukes to his chum in the Western ocean trade, out of the fullness of his heart and the liveliness of his fancy.

He had expressed his honest opinion. It was not worth while trying to impress a man of that sort... He was not alone in his opinion. (18)

This is somewhat clumsy and qualitatively uneven writing for the mature Conrad, but it tells much about the way in which the authorial commentary functions in this text. Although Jukes may appear closer to the authorial narrator than the other characters are, yet the narrator takes care to distance himself from him. Then the awkwardly explicit 'He had expressed his honest opinion' is followed by a passage of narrated monologue, which again serves as starting-point for authorial reflections. What is interesting about the narrated monologue applied to Jukes here ('It was not worth while trying to impress a man of that sort') is that it seems to indicate authorial distance from Jukes, and to subject his views to irony by imitating them. Authorial attitude to Jukes is curiously suspended at this stage of the narrative; and the narrator's evaluation of MacWhirr is similarly indeterminate.

Starting from Jukes's 'opinion', the authorial reflections of the final paragraph of Chapter 1 explicity confirm that in spite of his wide and varied experience MacWhirr has never been put to the test. The authorial narrator does not himself use the word 'test', but the implication of the pointedly direct commentary is clear enough:

Captain MacWhirr had sailed over the surface of the oceans as some men go skimming over the years of existence to sink gently into a placid grave, ignorant of life to the last, without ever having been made to see all it may contain of perfidy, of violence, and of terror. There are on sea and land such men thus fortunate—or thus disdained by destiny or by the sea. (19)

The reader's sense of suspense is obviously reinforced here, and extended from a mere outward indication (falling barometer) of a major challenge approaching the story's main character. Equally if not more intriguing is the suspense related to the tension which is established between the authorial narrator's description of MacWhirr's ignorance of life and his inarticulateness. Building on the first chapter alone we cannot, for instance, know whether MacWhirr will experience the challenge *as* a test; and although this may be a minor difficulty, it is clearly one which is related to Conrad's use of authorial narrative.

The most notable achievement of Chapter 2 is to establish a gradually strengthened impression of looming threat, the ominously approaching typhoon. The manner in which this effect is obtained is similar to that already observed in Chapter 1. There is, however, one important addition to the text's narrative method, constituted by two atmospheric authorial descriptions of the *Nan-Shan* as she draws nearer and nearer to the storm. The narrative technique of these descriptions must be considered in some detail.

(*a*) At its setting the sun had a diminished diameter and an expiring brown, rayless glow, as if millions of centuries elapsing since the morning had brought it near its end. A dense bank of cloud became visible to the northward; it had a sinister dark olive tint, and lay low and motionless upon the sea, resembling a solid obstacle in the path of the ship. She went floundering towards it like an exhausted creature driven to its death. The coppery twilight retired slowly, and the darkness brought out overhead a swarm of unsteady, big stars, that, as if blown upon, flickered exceedingly and seemed to hang very near the earth. At eight o'clock Jukes went into the chart-room to write up the ship's log. (26)

(*b*) The far-off blackness ahead of the ship was like another night seen through the starry night of the earth—the starless night of the immensities beyond the created universe, revealed in its appalling stillness through a low fissure in the glittering sphere of which the earth is the kernel. (29)

Passage (*a*) is striking for its efflorescence of similes. The sun looks smaller and has 'an expiring... glow', 'as if millions of centuries elapsing since the morning had brought it near its end'; there is a bank of cloud 'resembling a solid obstacle in the path of the ship', which she approaches 'like an exhausted creature driven to its death', while the stars 'as if blown upon, flickered exceedingly and seemed to hang very near the earth'. The most obvious function of the imagery employed here is to intensify the reader's sense of imminent drama and danger. In this capacity it functions effectively as an integral part of the novella's narrative method, whose sophistication is thus enhanced. To start with the simplest simile, the strictly factual second one prefigures the dispute MacWhirr and Jukes later have as to whether the ship should turn eastward or continue north towards the 'solid obstacle'. The way in which this matter-of-fact simile is interposed between the others increases the proximity of all of them to the story of the *Nan-Shan*. Suggesting a return to this story, the second simile delimits the implications of the first, which would otherwise have seemed more contrived. As they now stand, modified not only by the second simile but also by the narrative preceding and following them, the first and third similes significantly widen the thematic scope of the novella by giving it a more universal or cosmic dimension of ominous finality. In a sense it is surprising that such a range of problems can be suggested in what is for Conrad a rather simple narrative, but at the same time it is precisely the simplicity of the setting which assures that this can be done without too great a loss of credibility.

The third simile is also remarkable. As the final 'its death' echoes and extends 'its end' of the first, the cosmic or universal dimension of the ship's confrontation with the typhoon is brought closer to the narrative itself. Furthermore, the sense of seriousness and danger is intensified both through the suggested link between the first and third similes and through the content of the third one. Then the final simile of passage (*a*) suggests increased authorial affinity with Jukes's frame of mind. It becomes noticeable in the verb *seem* and in the description of the 'big stars', which are also watched by Jukes (page 27). Although this authorial slanting into Jukes's perspective illustrates a problematic element in the novella's narrative method, it serves here as a transition from the descriptive interlude back to the narrative proper.

The imagery of passage (*b*) extends the thematic implications of the first. Its apocalyptic aspects are related to an existential anguish provoked by the threat of the typhoon. When a Conrad character is put to the test, the problematic and enigmatic nature of his or her life experience tends to be accentuated. In spite of the authorial basis for the description, there is here, too, an authorial slanting into Jukes's thought. We have just been told that 'Jukes reflected rapidly...'; and although these reflections concern the second mate and not the image itself, his following comment is—for all its casualness—clearly related to the content of the imagery. It would seem, then, that the imagery identified and briefly discussed here not only intensifies and extends the thematic range of 'Typhoon', but also modulates the authorial narrative by suggesting a strangely intimate relationship with Jukes.

This authorial alliance with the first mate increases his narrative and thematic importance. MacWhirr's position is correspondingly weakened; there is a shift of emphasis and Jukes appears to emerge as the central character of the novella. This change seems confirmed by the curious theory MacWhirr advances about facing the storm: 'A gale is a gale, Mr. Jukes... and a full-powered steam-ship has got to face it' (34). This 'gale philosophy', to which the captain returns in Chapter 5 (89), is consistent with the earlier authorial descriptions of MacWhirr, but becomes more problematic now, since the narrator has meanwhile established greater intimacy with Jukes, who is a more reflective and well contrasted character.

In the next chapter, however, the authorial descriptions are better balanced in that while attitudinal distance between the narrator and Jukes increases somewhat, that between the narrator and MacWhirr appears to decrease. The way in which this decrease is achieved is quite sophisticated, and has at least two constitutive aspects. First, the characterization of MacWhirr changes. If, as Daleski finds, his 'decision to meet the typhoon head-on must be adjudged rash to the point of irresponsibility',[16] his actions and perseverance during the ordeal are portrayed as consistent with the decision, for which he is ready to take full responsibility. This responsibility, which includes both the ship and her crew, is coupled with the 'deep concern' (53) he has for the Chinamen when informed by the boatswain that they have started fighting amongst themselves. The concern indicated here, which is verified by Jukes's realization that he will have to obey orders and attempt to solve the problem presented by the Chinamen, is an important addition to the previous authorial characterization of MacWhirr. It is surprising when compared with his earlier outburst: 'The Chinamen!... Never heard a lot of coolies spoken of as passengers before. Passengers, indeed!' (31); and it goes quite far to present MacWhirr as a

---

[16] CWD 107.

character whose qualities should be appreciated on the basis of his actions and attitudes rather than his words. As the narrator says, 'To be silent was natural to him, dark or shine' (40).

Secondly, a certain rehabilitation of MacWhirr's textual position is also suggested indirectly through an increased attitudinal distance between the authorial narrator and Jukes. This distance, which is related to a difference in age and experience, is particularly noticeable at the beginning of Chapter 4:

Jukes, however, had no wide experience of men or storms. He conceived himself to be calm—inexorably calm; but as a matter of fact he was daunted; not abjectly, but only so far as a decent man may, without becoming loathsome to himself... Jukes was benumbed much more than he supposed. (51–2)

A related constituent aspect of this increased distance is that if Jukes has previously appeared to be more concerned about the Chinamen than his captain, the tables are now turned: 'Jukes remained indifferent, as if rendered irresponsible by the force of the hurricane, which made the very thought of action utterly vain' (51). At this stage, MacWhirr seems to be passing the test better than Jukes.

In Chapter 3, then, the descriptions and generalizations are more independently authorial than previously. Authorial slanting into Jukes's perspective is less apparent; and this has the effect of qualifying the earlier impression of Jukes's privileged proximity to the narrator. The sixth paragraph of Chapter 3, for instance, is obviously connected with Jukes in the sense that he is mentioned both before and after it, but it is authorially authoritative in a manner more reminiscent of Chapter 1 than Chapter 2; and this tendency is further strengthened in the succeeding paragraph:

It was something formidable and swift, like the sudden smashing of a vial of wrath. It seemed to explode all round the ship with an overpowering concussion and a rush of great waters, as if an immense dam had been blown up to windward. In an instant the men lost touch of each other. This is the disintegrating power of a great wind: it isolates one from one's kind. (40)

As one of the most poignant generalizations in 'Typhoon', the final sentence of this quotation pinpoints both the narrative and the thematic significance of the authorial narrator's commentary. Not just descriptive but also interpretative, the generalization emphasizes the utmost seriousness of the human drama enforced on the crew by the typhoon. Furthermore, it forms the constitutive basis for a central paradox which is established and affirmed through the new sense of companionship and mutual respect MacWhirr and Jukes come to experience. If the wind creates barriers among the men that appear insurmountable, leaving each isolated with his fear, it also unites them as they realize that it is only through common effort they can possibly survive. As MacWhirr is inevitably the pivot of this effort, his position at the centre of the narrative is strengthened.

If part of the funtion of the authorial narrative here is to suggest a more balanced attitude to, and evaluation of, the two main characters, it also provides a convincing description of the violent storm. The most important additional narrative variant is the use of personification:

1. 'The *Nan-Shan* was being looted by the storm with a senseless, destructive fury...' (44)
2. 'They held hard. An outburst of unchained fury, a vicious rush of the wind absolutely steadied the ship...' (46)
3. 'There was hate in the way she was handled, and a ferocity in the blows that fell. She was like a living creature thrown to the rage of a mob: hustled terribly, struck at, borne up, flung down, leaped upon.' (47)
4. '[MacWhirr] had to fight the gale for admittance...' (63)

When we consider these descriptive, authorial passages we must conclude that the personifications help to intensify the typhoon as human challenge and drama. It is one of the potential effects or implications of personification as a rhetorical device that authorial description becomes invested with an unidentified personal element, which is here related to the crew and to the personified *Nan-Shan*. In this case the effect is distinctly less lyric than in the example from *The Nigger of the 'Narcissus'* considered above. It serves essentially to strengthen the sense of alliance between crew and ship. Both are engaged in a desperate attempt to survive the fight against what the personifications—through a blend of authorial and unidentified personal perspective—portray as a mighty adversary endowed with human feelings of fury and hatred.

The culmination of the storm comes at the beginning of Chapter 5:

Nobody—not even Captain MacWhirr, who alone on deck had caught sight of a white line of foam coming on at such a height that he couldn't believe his eyes—nobody was to know the steepness of that sea and the awful depth of the hollow the hurricane had scooped out behind the running wall of water... She dipped into the hollow straight down, as if going over the edge of the world. (74)

Part of the climactic effect of this passage obviously depends on the intensification of earlier descriptions, but it is also generated through the authorial insistence on a more exhaustive knowledge of the storm's dimensions than that possessed by any character, including MacWhirr. The imagery in the following paragraph confirms this stress on authorial knowledge. The information provided about the characters is marked by pointed authorial distance, even from Jukes, whose face is 'like the face of a blind man' (74).

The middle section of Chapter 5 is taken up with Jukes's attempt to settle the fight (which has aspects of the absurd, the grotesque, and the comic) which the Chinamen have started over some 'scattered dollars' (78). It could be argued that these passages, where the authorial narrative is related first to the perspective of the boatswain and then to that of Jukes, are shallow and monotonous compared to the intensity of the storm description. The section does, however, widen the thematic scope of the novella. The fact that the human drama enacted below the deck of the *Nan-Shan* is only superficially described seems at first to increase the affinity of the perspective of the authorial narrative and that of the crew. When the row has been settled the sailors are relieved: 'There is something horribly repugnant in the idea of being drowned under a deck' (80). Yet in this narrative statement the distance between the authorial narrator and the crew again seems to increase. Far from suggesting a derogatory view of the Chinamen, the authorial implication is that their suffering during the ordeal of the typhoon must have been even greater than that of that crew. An implied sympathy on the part of the authorial narrator with the crew does not necessarily mean that he vouches for all the views they pronounce. Moreover, an interesting shift of perspective is observable in the middle of the account of the Chinamen's struggle: 'The coming of the white devils was a terror. Had they come to kill?' (78). This narrated monologue provides an illuminating narrative variation: although the perspective does not remain with the Chinamen for long, the shift is clearly sufficient to indicate that the authorial narrator's knowledge and sympathy exceed that of the crew.

The last part of the chapter returns to MacWhirr in order to modify and extend authorial characterization of him. This applies in particular to the passage which starts with the 'incredibly low' (84) reading of the barometer and then proceeds to give the most extended characterization of MacWhirr in the whole novella. Three aspects of the narrative method of this passage may be noted. First, omniscient authorial observation of MacWhirr's reading of the barometer is accompanied by effectively interposed narrated monologue: 'Perhaps something had gone wrong with the thing!' (84). Combined with the authorial observations, the instances of narrated (and quoted) monologue are then employed as a basis for explanatory reflection: 'These instantaneous thoughts were yet in their essence heavy and slow, partaking of the nature of the man' (85). The persuasiveness of this comment is enhanced by its textual position: it summarizes a quality of MacWhirr's character that the action has already dramatized.

More importantly, the passage makes the reader more aware of MacWhirr's loneliness and sense of responsibility. This is achieved through a narrative combination of the authorial reflections with the third constitutive aspect of the passage, the sparing but effective use of quoted monologue. If we introduce a potentially useful distinction here between quoted thought and quoted monologue,[17] then we can immediately note two instances of the former, ' "It'll be terrific," he pronounced, mentally' and ' "I wouldn't have believed it," he thought' (84). But then these two examples of quoted thought are followed by two of quoted monologue that are not only distinctly less cumbersome, but also indicative of a substantial maturing of MacWhirr's character: ' "I shouldn't like to lose her," he said half aloud' and 'Then a murmur arose. "She may come out of it yet" ' (86). The banality of the first remark is striking; yet paradoxically so is its narrative effect because of MacWhirr's deeply ingrained taciturnity and because the remark comes just after an authorial statement on MacWhirr: 'By this awful pause the storm penetrated the defences of the man and unsealed his lips. He spoke out in the solitude and the pitch darkness of the cabin, as if addressing another being awakened within his breast' (86). Combined with this powerful authorial statement, the remark not only improves the reader's understanding of MacWhirr's sense of responsibility and sincere concern for his ship, but also suggests increased self-knowledge on his part.

In addition to these modulations of quoted thought and monologue, the most noteworthy aspect of narrative method here is the omission of a second gale description. Conrad seems to have

[17] Cf. ch. 3 n. 7.

concluded, and no doubt rightly, that it would not have added substantially to the very effective first one but would instead, unavoidably, have seemed anticlimactic. As the second half of the ship's struggle with the typhoon is passed over in silence, the reader is left to infer—on the basis of the description of the first part of the ordeal—what it must have been like. Temporally, the ellipsis must be located in the reach between the fifth and the last chapter, which takes the form of an epilogue to the story proper.

In this final chapter, the description of Mrs MacWhirr and her daughter ironically reaffirms and strengthens the contrast between two extremely different ways of life that has already been indicated earlier in the novella. Irony mingles with humour and resignation; the two parties are in every sense—not just geographically—miles apart. Underneath the humorous presentation of the failure to communicate, however, a more serious implication can be detected in this particular approach to what is a major problem in Conrad: his fiction contains few examples of genuine and mutually rewarding human communication. Considering these relatively rare instances, it does not take long to notice that they are often related to a sense of communication through shared work—not least in the well-defined and limited setting of a ship. It is important, therefore, that MacWhirr and Jukes, who embody very different personal charac-teristics, are helped, if not forced, to co-operate and communicate during such a major crisis as that of the typhoon.

Once the crisis is over, however, former positions are all too easily resumed—as Jukes's seems to be in the letter of his which effectively concludes the narrative of 'Typhoon'. The use of letters—both MacWhirr's and Jukes's—is an important variation in a narrative that at times appears somewhat monotonously authorial. Providing both information and personal views, Jukes's concluding letter reduces authorial focus on MacWhirr, but not without stress-ing his crucial role and impressive professional skills. The very last sentence again contains an example of curiously modified irony. There is an obvious authorial distance from Jukes here, for MacWhirr's performance during the storm clearly does not corres-pond with Jukes's adjective 'stupid' (102); and yet there is some truth in the characterization, as the simplicity of MacWhirr's 'face it' philosophy may appear to verge on stupidity. It seems just right that Jukes's letter concludes the novella; Conrad wisely refrained from adding an authorial comment to it.

Francis Hubbard argues that MacWhirr is fundamentally changed by his experience of the typhoon.[18] If my interpretation of the novella suggests agreement with Hubbard's thesis, it has also—through the critical focus on the modulations of the text's authorial narrative, and the thematic effects of these modulations—shown in greater detail than Hubbard does how MacWhirr's change is indicated and dramatized. Although the narrative method of 'Typhoon' is distinctly less sophisticated than that of, say, 'Heart of Darkness', the various constituent aspects of this method—the authorial omniscience, the shifts of perspective, the use of letters, imagery, and personification—present several thematic concerns that are both persuasive and suggestive. In the narrative discourse of 'Typhoon', thematic simplicity promotes thematic suggestiveness: as the elemental drama of the *Nan-Shan* struggling with the typhoon accentuates human qualities such as courage, perseverance, and the ability to face up to loneliness, so it is precisely this lone, test-like fight on the part of MacWhirr that constitutes the basis for his change and makes him emerge as a wiser and more imaginative human being at the end of the novella.

[18] Hubbard, *Theories of Action*, 11–12.

8
The Shadow-Line:
Ultimate, Intense Personal Narrative

F. R. Leavis, with characteristic critical assurance, finds *The Shadow-Line* (1917) 'central to [Conrad's] genius'.[1] This assessment would seem a valid one, yet its validity is not altogether easy to demonstrate. Leavis's own, modestly psychoanalysing explanation is only partially convincing: the novella is, he says, 'clearly something Conrad *had* to write. It comes out of experience that was intimately and urgently personal; when we read it we can't doubt that.'[2] We certainly cannot, and yet *The Shadow-Line* is obviously—as a novella, a work of prose fiction—an elaborately-structured text involving various forms of distance and mediation.

This chapter argues that one of the chief narrative characteristics of *The Shadow-Line*, and hence a constituent element of Conrad's fictional achievement in this tale, is to be sought in the reciprocal relationship between narrative distance and a striking immediacy sometimes approaching the lyric (cf. Leavis's 'intimately and urgently personal [experience]'). This relationship, which gradually takes the form of a tension experienced by the narrator and transmitted from him to the reader (as the reader is invited to share the protagonist's experience) is correlated with the narrator's gradual learning process in the course of the narrative—a process that is here, as Jeremy Hawthorn shows in his introduction to the World's Classics edition of the novella, centred on a test enabling 'the protagonist to find the self which, at the start of the tale, he has so conspicuously lost'.[3]

In his 'Author's Note' to *The Shadow-Line*, Conrad expresses his view of the novella as 'in its brevity a fairly complex piece of work', and goes on to outline his thematic purpose with it: 'Primarily the aim of this piece of writing was the presentation of certain facts

---

[1] Leavis, 'Joseph Conrad', *The Sewanee Review*, 66 (1958), 188.
[2] Ibid.
[3] Jeremy Hawthorn, intro. to the World's Classics edn. of *The Shadow-Line* (Oxford: OUP, 1985), p. xii. See also Jacques Berthoud's intro. to the Penguin edn. of this novella (Harmondsworth: Penguin, 1986), 7–24.

which certainly were associated with the change from youth... to the more self-conscious and more poignant period of maturer life'.[4] Like all assertions in Conrad's 'Author's Notes', and like all his notoriously unreliable and inaccurate extratextual comments on his own fiction for that matter, this description cannot be accepted uncritically, but must be compared with the thematic implications of the narrative as it is actually presented and developed. If we proceed to do so, however, then it would appear that the above characterization is one of the most persuasive, and least reductive, ever given by Conrad on a piece of fiction of his. Part of the reason for the commentary's aptness may be suggested by the relative proximity in time (approximately two years) between the publication of the novella and the writing of the 'Author's Note'. A partial explanation may also be implicit in the text's sub-title, 'A Confession', which indicates an exceptionally close relationship between author and narrator-protagonist.

I

The prominence of the narrator is central to Conrad's narrative method in *The Shadow-Line*. The narration is consistently personal throughout: the protagonist relates a particular succession of experiences—revolving round a sea voyage during which he exercises his first command—that constitutes his crucial transition from youth to adulthood. The tale is the story of its narrator, at a particularly challenging and difficult point in life. And yet there are, as Ian Watt touches on when reflecting on the change of title from 'First Command' to 'Shadow-Line',[5] far-reaching thematic implications attached to the subjective, introverted personal account. The most important implications obviously result from a complex combination of the various constituent elements of the narrative, and thus cannot be fully appreciated until the text is finished, or preferably reread. Even so, there are characteristics of the narrator's discourse that are more immediately observable. The most noticeable instance of these 'visible' narrative characteristics is probably the narrator's striking generalizations, one of which opens the story:

---

[4] 'Author's Note' to *The Shadow-Line*, pp. v, vi.

[5] Ian Watt, 'Story and Idea in Conrad's *The Shadow-Line*', *Critical Quarterly*, 2 (1960), 144. This remains one of the best essays on the novella.

Only the young have such moments. I don't mean the very young. No. The very young have, properly speaking, no moments. It is the privilege of early youth to live in advance of its days in all the beautiful continuity of hope which knows no pauses and no introspection.

One closes behind one the little gate of mere boyishness—and enters an enchanted garden... One knows well enough that all mankind has streamed that way. It is the charm of universal experience from which one expects an uncommon or personal sensation—a bit of one's own. (3)

This beginning not only contains searching generalizations; it also tells us something important about their form and content. There are three points to be made here. First, the opening or prologue, constituted by the first four paragraphs, adumbrates a central thematic concern of the tale as a whole: a troubled experience of existence in time, and of life as a process not only towards adulthood but also towards death—a painfully self-conscious awareness of the ageing process. There is a logical progression in the reflective generalizations. Early youth is idealized for its lack of temporal consciousness. Then follows one of the text's most striking metaphors: the transition from boyishness to youth is to enter 'an enchanted garden'. Simplifying somewhat, we could say that what the metaphor primarily signifies is the coming, the unstoppable approach, of temporal and existential consciousness. As the warning of its ending is 'a shadow-line', the novella's title, like the story background which follows, is eloquently incorporated into its thoughtful prologue.

Secondly, an interesting narrative characteristic is observable in the way these introductory reflections are presented. For they presuppose experience and hindsight; they presuppose, in fact, successful handling of the challenge facing the narrator in the main action of *The Shadow-Line*. One aspect of the generalizations here at the beginning of the story is that they are based, in a fairly straightforward manner, on the narrator's own experiences. This is, indeed, the main reason why they are so convincing—they are to a large extent verified by the incidents (and the narrator's response to them) later dramatized. This point bears some relation to a key one in this chapter: it is the distance—not only in time, but also in knowledge—which enables the narrator to focus his story on its essential aspects and to intensify the central experience.

Thirdly, the use of 'one' in the prologue should be noted. It certainly does not signal a change of narrative voice—throughout

The Shadow-Line there is just one, that of the personal narrator. Neither does the change from 'I' to 'one' suggest a radically new perspective. Rather, it could be described as a subtle modulation of a stable narrative situation: a formalized (textually visible) invitation to the narratee to relate the insight suggested by the generalizations to those procured in his or her own life. The thematic significance of such an objectification can of course be exaggerated, but it should not be overlooked. A side-effect of this particular form of narrative modulation is that the liberal use of 'one' here at the beginning invites the reader to participate in the rather different, albeit related, generalizations later on in the narrative.

The introductory narrative reflections function well as background to the narrator's abrupt and unmotivated act of throwing up his berth. The lack of external motive is total: there was nothing particularly wrong with the ship and there is no appointment awaiting him ashore. The resultant mode is one of hesitant disengagement: 'I had never in my life felt more detached from all earthly goings on' (19). It is in the dialogue with Captain Giles, and through the young narrator's relationship to this old, sagacious sailor, that his tense state of mind is most persuasively conveyed. One reason for the narrator's mistrust of Giles is of course his irritatingly direct question, 'Why did you throw up your berth?' (14). But the essential critical point to make here is that the question, and the ensuing dialogue, enable Conrad to objectify through conversation the indirect characterization of the narrator which has earlier filtered through his own reflections and generalizations, and this even before the novella's action has got under way.

Part of the first chapter's statement on the narrator's inertia is presented implicitly through the reputation of Giles ('For Captain Giles had prestige' (14)) and the narrator's first impression of him, 'I thought he was the most dull, unimaginative man I had ever met,' (15) which is one of the narrator's typical exaggerations at this initial stage of his learning process. Interspersed with such rash judgements there are, however, certain narrative elements that reveal traces of the analeptic hindsight briefly indicated above. Two examples will illustrate this point. On page 18, the reaction provoked by Giles is described by the narrator himself as 'childish irritation'. Clearly, this must be a self-description at the time of writing, from the vantage point of a shadow-line already crossed. The second example combines the temporal modulation noticeable in the first with a subtle prolepsis: 'It never occurred to me then that I didn't know in what soundness of mind exactly consisted and what a delicate and, upon the whole, unimportant matter it was' (21). Indicating the addition of a later reflection, the 'then' of this passage epitomizes the narrator's relative ignorance when at the Sailors' Home. The reflections here contain analeptic elements related to the test which the protagonist is about to undergo, but this subtle narrative modulation cannot possibly be appreciated on a first reading.

It is on page 25 of the first chapter that its turn or climax is reached. The narrator follows Giles's advice after all: spontaneously acting on 'an impulse of some sort', he initiates that series of events which rapidly leads not only to his first command, but also to the trying voyage during which he has to exercise it. If this seems a rather self-evident observation, it is necessary as a basis for the following one: the suggested affinity between this impulse, which results in the narrator's command, and the earlier one to depart from his ship is not only striking for the reader, but presented as uncomfortably strong for the narrator as well. It is a strength of the personal narrative here, and one which increases the novella's over-all narrative economy, that while the first impulse fits in well with the characteristic deliberateness of the first chapter, the second initiates command, work, responsibility, and dynastic duty. Through effective combination of factual account and reflection coloured by later insight, the passage demonstrates how similar, if not identical, impulses may entail very different consequences.

It is essentially due to the proleptic elements in the narrator's reflections that one implication of the established contrast between Giles's advice and the narrator's response is a decrease of this distance at the time of writing. A related implication is that the self-criticism scattered through the narrator's discourse increases the reader's belief in his honesty and reliability, both of which prove important for the thematic effect of his tale. It is consistent with the text's immediacy and autobiographical colouring that the use of irony is restricted, and its narrative and thematic importance rela-tively limited. Irony is not, however, entirely absent from the first chapter, and its primary function is to contribute to the narrative formation of the contrast and implications outlined above. An illustrative example occurs on page 20: 'I began to pity him pro-foundly. And in a tone which I tried to make as little sarcastic as possible I said that I was glad he had found something to occupy his morning hours.' There is a twofold irony at work here. First, irony is observable in the actual words spoken by the narrator; and it is no doubt perceived by Giles as well. An interesting thing about this narrative variant is the speaker's explicit mention of the term 'sarcastic', which reveals how conscious he is of the effect of the remark on his listener—and not only of the words themselves but also of their 'tone'. A profounder irony, however, arises from the fact that the outcome of Giles's meditations shows the narrator's intended irony to be entirely pointless. Instead it is turned back on the narrator himself—who stands corrected, and humbler and wiser, at the end of the novella.

II

Several of the main narrative characteristics of *The Shadow-Line*, then, are indicated at an early stage: the predominance of the narrator as protagonist, not only relating the story of a turning-point of his life but also adding to the facts the reflections and insights provoked by them; the narrator's unqualified frankness coupled with utter reliability, addressing no identified narratee; and finally the tension generated not only by the temporal gap between the time of the actual experience and the time of writing, but also by the learning process the narrator goes through.

There is a paragraph towards the end of Chapter 1 which plays a key role not only by serving as transition to the following chapter, but also by suggesting a possible remedy to the narrator's early inertia:

But it was not hesitation on my part. I had been, if I may express myself so, put out of gear mentally. But as soon as I had convinced myself that this stale, unprofitable world of my discontent contained such a thing as a command to be seized, I recovered my powers of locomotion. (28)

It is one of the interpretative principles of this study that generalizations about the thematics of Conrad's fiction should not only be more closely related to his narrative method than has been customary, but should also preferably be based on a wide range of textual references. Generalizations based on a single reference must therefore be cautious. Still, this passage does seem to suggest that the prospect of work is a positive challenge—a challenge in the nature of an opportunity. That the command is accompanied by enormous problems does not in the least blur the distinction between the narrator's experience of his situation before and after it has been seized. Conrad critics have made too little of the text's invitation to understand the call to command as a call to human activity—and of the fact that a strong sense of meaning or purpose may arise through the conscientious and competent exercise of such an activity.

The narrator's attainment of a command is accompanied by a new, or at least renewed, sense of identity. 'I, the Captain' (33) experiences a 'feeling of wonder—as if I had been specially destined for that ship I did not know...' (36). Almost ecstatically exclaiming, 'A ship! My ship!' (40), he is struck by 'such a sense of the intensity of existence as I have never felt before or since' (40). The contrast with the bored detachment of Chapter 1 is striking; yet it is noteworthy how this contrast lends psychological verisimilitude to the narrator's later, temporarily ecstatic, mood.

The transition from the static situation of Chapter 1 to the challenges implicit in the command and the following voyage is closely correlated with the narrator's mental growth. The change is dramatized in the dialogue between the narrator and Giles in the middle of Chapter 2. It seems logical enough that the narrator should, now that Giles has secured the command for him, pay greater respect to the venerable sage. But he is still easily provoked into disagreeing with Giles and particularly—which creates a nice self-irony—when Giles makes a statement which the subsequent narrative reveals to be especially profound. The best illustration of this is probably Giles's comment on the more or less obscure intentions of the steward: 'As to that, I believe everybody in the world is a little mad' (42). Apart from the interesting echo of *Hamlet* here,[6] and apart from the more general truth of the reflection if related to Conrad's non-fictional ideas, the statement is important within the context of the novella itself—if, that is to say, the text is reread. Although heightened by irony, the effect is not wholly dependent on this device only; the irony aimed at the narrator is modified by his self-criticism at the time of narration, and also

---

[6] Echoes of *Hamlet* (cf. III. i and V. ii) reverberate throughout *The Shadow-Line*, cf., for instance, the quotation above from p. 28 of the novella. There are also echoes of Coleridge's 'Rime of the Ancient Mariner'.

by the seriousness of his later ordeal. What should be stressed, rather, is that the full significance of Giles's utterance cannot be appreciated unless the reader is in a position to relate it to the occurrences that succeed it.

Some pages further on, the narrator makes a statement whose critical interest is increased if it is related to my notion that *The Shadow-Line* evinces a reciprocal relationship between lyric immediacy and epic distance: 'My education was far from being finished, though I didn't know it. No! I didn't know it' (47). Paradoxically, it is the temporal gap between narration and the narrated (and the incidents whch have taken place in between) that enables the narrator to make such an exclamation. The way in which the statement is emphasized (the repeated negation, the use of an exclamation mark after 'No') tells us something about the importance the narrator attaches to the experience. Furthermore, it gives a partial psychological explanation of the striking immediacy of the story he recounts: there is a relation between the individual's need for human communion on the one hand and the narrator's youthful, restless mood followed by the loneliness and responsibility of his first command on the other. Even though such a relation offers no verifiable explanation of the narrative immediacy and directness of *The Shadow-Line*, it serves to make these constituent aspects of the text's narrative method more plausible and hence more effective.

In Chapter 3 the narrator reports Burns's story of the ship's late captain, with whom Burns is evidently obsessed. The account is incorporated into the personal narrative as an edited analepsis which partly adds to the characterization of Burns, and partly ironically modifies the narrator's strong impression of tradition and dynastic continuity. The inserted account, which is supposedly the narrator's shortened version of what Burns has already told him, clearly has a thematic function beyond that of providing a welcome comic interlude. Stressing the need for a distinction between tradition as such and some of its less venerable human representatives, the incorporated story of the narrator's predecessor ominously anticipates the approaching external threat to his own sanity: 'It appeared that even at sea a man could become the victim of evil spirits. I felt on my face the breath of unknown powers that shape our destinies' (62).

As Chapter 3 primarily serves as a transition from the narrator's inactive state ashore to the beginning of the actual voyage, the emphasis which the narrator places on the word 'delay' is pertinent indeed. The delay he experiences at the opening of this chapter is correlated with the deliberateness or stasis of Chapter 1; and it also provides the necessary background for the narrator's impatience and accompanying reflections. Some of these reflections reveal an insight which once again reminds the reader of the temporal distance between narration and narrated: 'People have a great opinion of the advantages of experience. But in that connection experience means always something disagreeable as opposed to the charm and innocence of illusions' (65). This reflection is exceptionally interesting for two reasons. First, 'experience' and 'illusions' are two of the most noteworthy constituent elements of Conradian thematics. The emphasis given to them here—and the fact that this generalization is also, as is almost invariably the case in this work, plausible if related to the surrounding narrative context—indicates the proximity of the novella to the basic thematic concerns of Conrad's fiction. Secondly, the experience/innocence antithesis becomes even more suggestive as a reflection *after* the voyage is completed: qualifying the 'positive' value of experience, it also reduces the 'negative' element of an illusion. One implication of the antithesis, then, is a subtle modification of the importance, or usefulness, of the insight gained by the narrator through the trying experience of the voyage. The conclusion of such a reading could be to regard this antithesis as contributing to the novella's scepticism.

The final observation to be made on Chapter 3 builds on the question the narrator asks Burns by way of replying to another one already put to him: 'What's the good of letting go our hold of the ground only to drift, Mr. Burns?' (75). The dramatic irony observable in this question is established through the invitation to the reader to compare the view implied in it with the narrator's earlier impulse-like act of signing off his ship. But the question has thematic reverberations beyond such a superficial, though, effective, irony. As Daleski convincingly argues, the temptation to let go is one with which several of Conrad's main characters are confronted. For Daleski, the temptation is related to the four variations of loss of self that he finds in Conrad's fiction. It is the third variation which is relevant here, 'nullity or vacancy, the loss of self that is a concomitant of spiritual disintegration'.[7] Such 'nullity'

---

[7] C W D 20.

would seem fitting as a description of the narrator's state of mind during and after the act of signing off his previous ship. In contrast, the active response to the unexpected possibility of a command serves to counteract the threat of dispossession.

III

At the beginning of Chapter 4 there is a description of setting and scenery which not only identifies but unifies some of the narrative characteristics of the novella: 'It was impossible to distinguish land from water in the enigmatical tranquillity of the immense forces of the world. A sudden impatience possessed me' (76). The passage can best be considered together with that of the approaching dawn on the following page:

> ... in the still streak of very bright pale orange light I saw the land profiled flatly as if cut out of black paper and seeming to float on the water as light as cork. But the rising sun turned it into mere dark vapour, a doubtful, massive shadow trembling in the hot glare. (77)

The descriptive force of this prose is probably apparent to any reader. But if we ask how it is made so forceful and visually intense, then the attendant difficulties of such a question indirectly pinpoint some of the novella's structural and thematic characteristics. It is, however, possible to isolate and comment specifically on constitutive elements of the passage. We then first note the importance of visual impressions. The narrator attempts to render, as accurately as possible, what he, during his 'endless vigilance' (76), sees from the vantage point of his ship: a fusion of land and water. A second, more technical comment is to emphasize the intensifying effect of the combination of simile and metaphor. For the narrator, the land becomes 'mere dark vapour, a doubtful, massive shadow trembling in the hot glare'. This powerful identification metaphor could be compared with that discussed in the chapter on *The Nigger of the 'Narcissus'*. Its immediacy not only results from a particularly suggestive combination of verbs (especially 'trembling'), nouns ('vapour... shadow... glare'), and adjectives ('dark... massive... hot'), but is also generated by the metaphor's convincing illustration of the narrator's state of mind as established at this stage of his narrative. The description justifies a specification of the rather vague term 'immediacy' by relating it, as was also done in the discussion of *The Nigger of the 'Narcissus'*, to the concepts of the lyric and memory, and to reduced attitudinal distance between Conrad as author and his personal narrator. The narrative quality of *The Shadow-Line* is more pervasively lyric than that of *The Nigger of the 'Narcissus'*, and especially as the lyricism is specifically related to intensified memory.

A concluding comment on this central metaphor would be to draw attention to its content, and particularly the thematic importance of 'shadow' if we relate it—as we are being invited to do—to the title of the novella. This link increases the thematic scope of *The Shadow-Line*, taking it beyond the specific test (however crucial and demanding) during one particular voyage and at a certain point in time, to the challenge of how to live at all. There is, as Captain Giles says, 'precious little rest in life for anybody' (132). This is precisely what the action, reflections, and sensations dramatized in *The Shadow-Line* have made the narrator see, by opening his eyes to the wider implications of the experience of his first command.

The narrator's 'immense relief of the thought: on board my ship! At sea! At sea!' (78) helps bridge the transition from the delay before departure to the approaching problems. Leaving 'that contaminated shore' (79) is accompanied by 'a momentary exultation of freedom' (78). Then, as the ship is being virtually becalmed, the narrator again, in extraordinary textual concentration, combines a sober review of the ship's situation with a striking portrayal of his state of mind as he now recalls it:

Two more days passed. We had advanced a little way—a very little way—into the larger space of the Gulf of Siam. Seizing eagerly upon the elation of the first command thrown into my lap, by the agency of Captain Giles, I had yet an uneasy feeling that such luck as this has got perhaps to be paid for in some way. I had held, professionally, a review of my chances. I was competent enough for that. At least, I thought so. I had a general sense of my preparedness which only a man pursuing a calling he loves can know. That feeling seemed to me the most natural thing in the world. As natural as breathing. I imagined I could not have lived without it. (83)

The narrator's honesty is remarkable here. Not only does he, with the inestimable advantage of hindsight at the time of narration, make an explicit statement on his earlier naïvety; he also relates his naïve state specifically to the possibility of professional incompetence.

The question of whether *The Shadow-Line* includes 'super-natural' elements or not was one that puzzled contemporary readers and critics, and provoked Conrad to comment on it in his 'Author's Note'. If we accept—as the text invites us to—that it has a certain colouring of the supernatural or inexplicable, then the question can be specified by asking what narrative method is employed to generate such a colouring. One constituent factor is the narrative trick of making the narrator a firmly outspoken opponent to any sort of supernatural explanation of the distress which confronts both captain and crew. This narrative strategy succeeds remarkably well: the reader is gradually, almost imperceptively, manipulated into thinking, if not of supernatural forces as the direct cause of their problems, then at least of the 'double fight' (85) against the adverse weather and against malaria as a particularly trying one. Moreover, the way in which the 'fight' is portrayed brings the reader close to accepting that such a period of great strain is likely to activate the human need for some sort of explanation of the problems. At this level the supernatural has a function which may seem obvious, but is not unimportant: it enhances the psychological subtlety and range of the text's characterization, thereby also widening its thematic scope. If, at a different critical level, we ask, for instance, whether Conrad himself 'believed' in the supernatural, or if we reject the presence in the text of this aspect by referring to Conrad's religious scepticism, then we move dangerously close to what Ian Watt has called a 'heterophoric' interpretation,[8] that is, an interpretation ascribing to the text another meaning than that observable in it.

The narrator, to resume, is gradually forced into seeing his first command as a fight 'against the evil powers of calms and pestilence' (88). The sea, which at first seemed the liberating salvation to all earthly problems, no longer gives any solace: 'The intense loneliness of the sea acted like poison on my brain' (92). Life, the narrator must learn, can be difficult and trying at sea too: 'I discovered that life could hold terrible moments' (96). The 'extract from the notes I wrote at the time' (97), a diary divided into two with the first extract as the more important, constitutes the most obvious narrative variation in *The Shadow-Line*. It is a modest variation; yet it is

---

[8] Ian Watt, 'Conrad Criticism and *The Nigger of the "Narcissus"* ', *Nineteenth-Century Fiction*, 12 (1958), 257–83.

precisely the cautious way in which it is introduced that makes it so persuasive. The most important gains can be indicated as follows. First, as the distance between narration and narrated disappears in the diary, a more immediately convincing graphic picture is rendered of the ship's situation at its most desperate:

All sense of time is lost in the monotony of expectation, of hope, and of desire—which is only one: Get the ship to the southward! Get the ship to the southward! The effect is curiously mechanical; the sun climbs and descends, the night swings over our heads as if somebody below the horizon were turning a crank... How many miles have I walked on the poop of that ship! A stubborn pilgrimage of sheer restlessness... (97)

This writing is exceptionally intense and suggestive for late Conrad. But the intensity, which is clearly related to the lyric as considered briefly above, must not be allowed to make us overlook a second point which, paradoxically, both modifies and extends the first. For the *increase* of narrative intensity is not very striking. The narrator's diary is characterized by a unity of tone, pacing, and voice with the surrounding narrative which establishes a reciprocal relationship between them and enhances the plausibility and suggestiveness of both. As a corollary to this second point it follows that the above observation concerning the narrative consequences of the narrator's hindsight—which we could call his concentrated effort at a sustained act of memory—needs to be nuanced. One could, of course, question the narrator's ability to perform, under such great strain, the kind of mental activity which the diary reflects. But if this appears unproblematic, as it probably does to most readers, part of the reason no doubt lies in the affinity between diary and surrounding text. The novella's commentators have not sufficiently stressed how close some of the statements of the diary are to the thematic core or centre of *The Shadow-Line*. In addition to the passage from the first extract already quoted, the thematic significance of its last three sentences must be emphasized:

There they are: stars, sun, sea, light, darkness, space, great waters; the formidable Work of the Seven Days, into which mankind seems to have blundered unbidden. Or else decoyed. Even as I have been decoyed into this awful, this death-haunted command . . . (97–8)

One should beware of too far-reaching generalizations based on such a short passage, but through its focus on basic facts objectively verifiable through the visual senses, through the combination of this focus with the use of the verbs 'blunder' and 'decoy', and finally through the connection suggested between 'mankind' and 'I', the passage demonstrates the nadir of the narrator's test-like experience. The closest counterpart in Conrad (thematically, not technically) is probably the authorial description in *Nostromo* of Decoud's isolation and growing despair on the Great Isabel in the hours preceding his suicide.

'Moral isolation', which is also part of the problem Decoud cannot cope with, is mentioned by way of introducing the second extract from the diary on page 106. This form of isolation, which in some respects resembles that underlying Razumov's writing activity in *Under Western Eyes*, establishes a partial explanation of the writing of the 'notes'. Presented as 'another sample', this second extract is actually a logical continuation of the first. More directly focused on the narrator's unbearable situation, it contains a reference to the personal changes resulting from the present ordeal: 'It seems to me that all my life before that momentous day is infinitely remote, a fading memory of light-hearted youth, something on the other side of a shadow' (106). The shadow metaphor is here given a clearer temporal dimension than in the passage discussed above. This brings it closer to the '-line' constituting the second half of the novella's title, and suggests an intimate thematic link between the test the narrator undergoes and the crossing of the shadow-line.

As the endings of both diary extracts are thematically poignant, that of the second one must also be briefly commented on. 'My first command. Now I understand that strange sense of insecurity in my past. I always suspected that I might be no good. And here is proof positive, I am shirking it, I am no good' (107). Though we are certainly not asked to accept this conclusion, it is interesting that the narrator should relate the word 'insecurity' to the inertia and moodiness so prevalent at the beginning of the novella. But there is another implication of the passage which is more important: the very fact that the narrator's self-criticism is, to say the least, unreasonable, further dramatizes the human need for explanation of that which we do not comprehend. In the reading suggested in this chapter, then, the narrator's unjustified self-criticism (his efforts as captain are nearly superhuman, and he is evidently highly regarded by his crew) provides an indirect warning against making too conclusive comments on the various references to the supernatural throughout *The Shadow-Line*.

If the main tenets of the point concerning the basic human need for explanation and understanding are granted, then it seems logical enough that the element of the supernatural becomes more noticeable as the combined strain of the calm and the malaria increases. The narrator eventually lapses 'into complete indifference' and is overwhelmed by a 'sense of finality' (108), combined with a strong impression of 'losing the notion of time' (105). In contrast to *The Nigger of the 'Narcissus'*, where James Wait presents a much more serious threat to the ship's community than Burns does in *The Shadow-Line*, the threat is here essentially external. The fight to survive takes the form of a sustained struggle against elemental forces—both captain and crew tend to personify in order to understand them and thereby to withstand the imminent danger of extinction. They are all yoked together by external need. The captain has a supremely competent assistant in Ransome,[9] but the alliance between captain and crew (especially as described on page 109) is also very strong, and much more important for the main thematic effect of the tale as a whole than the incorporated account of Burns's relationship with the late captain.

Surprisingly but effectively, the turn for the better in Chapter 6 comes with Burns's hysterical laugh. It proves to bring him back on to the road to recovery and is accompanied by a most welcome breeze. 'The barrier of awful stillness which had encompassed us for so many days as though we had been accursed was broken. I felt that' (121). As the ship at last returns to port, and as the narrator gets the opportunity of a final talk to Captain Giles, the novella takes on a distinctly symmetrical structure, with an appropriately economical ending. At a superficial level the symmetry seems circular, but the circle drawn by the ship's movement marks the setting of the test which makes the narrator change decisively in the course of his narrative.

The dominance of the narrator in *The Shadow-Line* is striking. He is not only the novella's one and only narrator, but also its predominant protagonist, the ship's responsible captain, and the only healthy man on board. As a consequence of the direct, relatively uncomplicated personal narrative the various qualities and functions

9 Cf. Cedric Watts's short but illuminating section on *The Shadow-Line* in *The Deceptive Text*, which includes perceptive observations on Ransome: 'Ransome is given a strongly symbolic and Christ-like quality' (93). See Matthew 20: 28 and Mark 10: 45.

of the narrator are fused; hence it becomes impossible to isolate the various constituent elements of the narrative in order to comment separately on them. *The Shadow-Line* demonstrates how easily analysis of narrative may blend into character analysis. There is a sense, though, in which such a shift of emphasis or interest from narrator to character testifies to a successful narrative method: the technical problems of narrative are much less conspicuous here than in *The Nigger of the 'Narcissus'*. In *The Shadow-Line* the two key terms are instead narrative simplicity and detached immediacy.

The novella is a remarkable fictional achievement for late Conrad. It justifies the adjective 'ultimate' employed in the sub-title of this chapter, but my use of this appreciative term is not intended to imply a corresponding justification in generalizing from this text to the narrative method of late Conrad in general. In spite of the interest of a late short story such as 'The Tale', *The Shadow-Line* is the most obvious exception to the overall deterioration of Conrad's fiction after *Under Western Eyes*. The question of why Conrad achieved such a narrative success with *The Shadow-Line* is not easily answered, and is further complicated if the novella is related to the lengthy, rather monotonous and not very exciting narratives which followed it (*The Arrow of Gold*, *The Rescue*, *The Rover*). However, if we ask *how* the narrative success of *The Shadow-Line* is attained (and this is a more central question in the present study), the interpretation presented here would suggest that this question be related to the pivotal function of the personal narrator and protagonist of the novella. The narrator is related to Giles through an initial mistrust which then develops into a profound respect; to the crew of his ship through a stable loyalty; to his ship through a loyalty that is also stable; to Burns through an opposition modified at the end; and to Ransome in an intricate manner which illuminates the sophisticated connections between the overt plot revolving round the narrator's trying first command and the covert, supernatural plot associated not only with Burns's superstition and Ransome's Christ-like quality, but also with the peculiarly menacing and damaging influence emanating from the late captain.

To conclude, then, the principal characteristics of the personal narrator's discourse are these: honest presentation of early inertia and youthful impatience, (lyric) excitement intensified through an extraordinary vividness of memory, self-conscious reflection arising from the incidents and sense impressions with which the voyage confronts him, growing and then at last relieved tension, threatened self-possession, and a significant learning process.

9
Lord Jim:
Authorial Narrative as Diverse, Edited
Personal Narration

The narrative discourse of *Lord Jim* (1900) is exceptionally complex; it is indeed so complicated that no analysis of it can do it justice. Even the novel's story is not easily summarized; in spite of the marked difference between story and discourse, presentation of the former is greatly complicated by the characteristic complexity of the latter. To exemplify this point we might look critically at the summary Guerard gives of *Lord Jim*:

> The pilgrim-ship *Patna* strikes a derelict or other floating object at night, and her officers (believing she will sink quickly, and knowing there are not lifeboats enough) abandon her, leaving the pilgrims to drown in their sleep. Jim hesitates; and then, in spite of his romantic egoism and pride, impulsively jumps after the others. But the *Patna* does not sink. Marlow meets Jim at the court of inquiry: at this first of Jim's many efforts to rehabilitate himself in his own eyes and in the eyes of the world. He would like it believed that it was not he, the conscious man, who had jumped, yet can endure no reference to the incident. He wanders over the earth, generally eastward, pursued by guilt and shame. Marlow, sympathizing with Jim for various reasons, consults the entomologist and trader Stein, who sends Jim to Patusan—where he will be protected by isolation from the accusing world of white men. There Jim is a successful benevolent despot, and enjoys almost godlike power and prestige. His reign is ended, however, when he refuses to destroy the first intruding whites: 'Gentleman' Brown and his villainous pirate crew. The intruders massacre Jim's friends, including the son of the chief, and thereupon he surrenders his own life to the natives in atonement. He goes away from his native mistress Jewel for his pitiless wedding with a shadowy ideal of conduct.[1]

This elegant summary invites two critical comments. First, it omits significant material; in one sense the whole summary consists only of a selection, presented in chronological order, of some textual elements out of many. The inclusion of several of these elements is

---

[1] CN 129.

obvious, but some might have been substituted for others, and others again might have been added. Secondly, it is striking to what extent even a short summary of the action of *Lord Jim* tends to include elements that are not only textual, but also interpretative. Guerard's final sentence clearly moves towards interpretation; it is more obviously related to his overall analysis than to the summary it concludes. This observation could be used to extend the point Thomas C. Moser makes at the beginning of his fine introduction to the Norton Critical Edition of *Lord Jim*: the book is not only both an 'exotic adventure story' and a 'complexly wrought "art novel" ',[2] but it is also one in which these two characteristics are curiously intertwined.

It is a main conténtion of this chapter that generalizations about the thematic import of *Lord Jim* are often based on insufficient consideration of the intrinsic variation of its narrative method. This tendency is noticeable in several of the most influential interpretations of the novel.[3] Partly in order to counteract this tendency (but mainly because of my consistent focus on narrative functions, variations, and thematic effects) the chapter presents a relatively detailed analysis of the narrative method of *Lord Jim*. If, in the case of this particular text, most of my critical attention is given to the textual commentary on the novel's narrative method, this is partly because of the complexity of that method, partly a consequence of the criticism levelled at earlier interpretations of the text. In order to establish a basis for discussion I shall refer to some of the main points in Hillis Miller's thought-provoking and relevant chapter on *Lord Jim* in his *Fiction and Repetition*.[4]

---

[2] Thomas Moser, intro. to the Norton critical edn. of *Lord Jim* (New York: Norton, 1968), p. vi. This edition includes a number of the most important essays on the novel (359–484).

[3] See, for instance, *CN* 126–74; *C WD* 77–103; *CMP* 64–93; Cox, *Conrad: The Modern Imagination*, 19–44; Daniel R. Schwarz, *Conrad: Almayer's Folly to Under Western Eyes* (London: Macmillan, 1980), 76–94; Dorothy Van Ghent, *The English Novel: Form and Function* (New York: Harper & Row, 1961), orig. publ. 1953, 229–44; and Murray Krieger, *The Tragic Vision: Variations on a Theme in Literary Interpretation* (New York: Holt, Rinehart and Winston, 1960), 165–79. A detailed close reading of the novel is Jan Verleun, *Patna and Patusan Perspectives* (Groningen: Bouma's Boekhuis, 1979).

[4] Ch. 2 of *Fiction and Repetition*: '*Lord Jim*: Repetition as Subversion of Organic Form', 22–41. Cf. ch. 1 n. 22.

I

Miller emphasizes the importance of the self-interpretative elements in *Lord Jim*. Although interrelated, these elements work on different levels, and in part succeed one another. The primary interpreter is of course Marlow, but he is by no means the only one; and his interpretative endeavours are strongly influenced, indeed shaped, by the contributions of the narrators surrounding him. Building on Miller I suggest a division into five distinct yet related groups of interpreters in the novel.

1. The first group is constituted by Jim, especially in his long conversation with Marlow in the hotel room after the trial. As Miller notes, in these sections 'the reader can see Jim attempting to interpret his experience by putting it into words'.[5]

2. In the second group we have the contributions which the novel's minor characters make to an understanding of Jim. There are many of them; the quantity and diversity of their interpretative endeavours are two strong indications of the book's consistent focus on Jim. The understanding these characters show can be surprising; witness, for instance, the accuracy of Cornelius's description of Jim: 'He is like a little child' (378). And when they fail to understand, as Jewel does, additional evidence is adduced in support of the gradually strengthened impression of Jim as an enigma.

3. The interpreters in the third group would be such fascinating characters as Stein and the French lieutenant. For *Lord Jim*, the statements of the lieutenant are exceptionally unambiguous, but this is of course not to suggest that he is the one who understands Jim best. In the thematic web of the novel he functions basically as a contrastive character—simple in a way different from Jim, utterly dependable, an articulate version of the Malay helmsmen and Conradian heroes such as Singleton and Captain MacWhirr. Stein is a crucial but difficult case; paradoxically, the character who appears to understand Jim best is also enigmatic.

4. Marlow is the novel's principal interpreter. An investigation of his diverse functions is in itself a substantial venture, and one of the principal critical aims of this chapter. Miller interestingly finds that there is 'something suspect in Marlow's enterprise of

---

[5] Ibid. 32.

interpretation'.[6] This qualification is based on his reading of what he considers the most explicit formulation of the 'theme' of *Lord Jim*: Marlow's attempt (towards the end of Chapter 5) to explain why he concerns himself with Jim. As Miller interprets this section, Marlow has come to doubt the existence of a 'sovereign power enthroned in the fixed standard of conduct'.[7] If there is no such power, then the standard of conduct is without validity; if, however, Jim's act of desertion can be explained somehow, then it might still be possible to believe in the sovereign power. It is on this basis that Miller finds Marlow's interpretative activity suspect; and he goes on to argue that Marlow 'attempts to maintain his faith in the sovereign power in several contradictory ways':

(*a*) by stressing extenuating circumstances;
(*b*) by finding a fatal soft spot in Jim;
(*c*) by considering Jim 'the victim of dark powers within himself, powers which also secretly govern the universe outside'; and (via Stein)
(*d*) by finding 'the source of all Jim's trouble in his romanticism'.[8]

As the novel's repetitive pattern is gradually developed and confirmed, Marlow's attempts to understand Jim and explain his own interest in him prove increasingly futile: through this pattern the thematics of the novel is both developed and delimited. I shall return to the issue of narrative and thematic repetition by way of concluding the chapter.

5. An interpretative function is also performed by the omniscient authorial narrator of *Lord Jim*, though Miller rightly observes that he does not give the reader the 'sort of interpretative help provided by the narrator of *Middlemarch*'.[9] As many of *Lord Jim*'s commentators have noted, its personal narrative is surrounded by an authorial frame, but few critics before Miller have persuasively discussed the thematic implications of the fact that in this text authorial omniscience entails neither definitive information about nor conclusive evaluation of Jim.

---

[6] Ch. 2 of *Fiction and Repetition*: '*Lord Jim*: Repetition as Subversion of Organic Form', 29.
[7] Ibid. 28.
[8] Ibid. 29.
[9] Ibid. 32. George Eliot published *Middlemarch* in 1871–2.

As a possible sixth group of interpreters one might include Marlow's listeners or narratees, though I would hesitate to do so. These pensive auditors are virtually silent; their function is basically structural. One might perhaps see a thematic link between the comment on Marlow's subtlety and the French lieutenant's 'This, monsieur, is too fine for me—' (149), but the importance of such a point would easily be exaggerated. It seems probable, however, that as readers of the novel we are to some extent influenced by what we are told about Marlow's listeners; as I shall attempt to show, there is an advanced form of manipulation of readers' response in *Lord Jim*.

The term 'response' could be related to Guerard's discussion of the impact of a first reading of the novel.[10] Guerard is clearly right to suggest that this impact is exceptionally strong, but he appears to overlook the fact that it is also exceptionally varied, differing from reader to reader and depending on, among other things, his or her previous reading experience. As early reviews of *Lord Jim* show,[11] its contemporary readers were more puzzled by the complicated narrative method than modern readers are likely to be, especially if they are familiar with, for example, Faulkner's important modernist novel *Absalom, Absalom!* (1936), of which *Lord Jim* is frequently reminiscent. In the case of *Lord Jim*, then, it becomes particularly important to distinguish between response or first impression on the one hand and critical interpretation on the other. An interpretation of *Lord Jim*, which unavoidably involves systematization and selective ordering of the arguments employed, should be based on the best possible understanding of all the constitutive elements in the text; and then it would seem to be of minor importance whether one has read the book, say, three or four times. Tony Tanner's claim that he is working from 'a second reading'[12] is unconvincing. What can be stated unequivocally is that when one is writing about *Lord Jim* it seems impossible to work from a first reading; and this is certainly not attempted here, but at the same time the chapter does attempt not to forget or suppress initial responses to the novel.

[10] CN 154–5.
[11] Cf. the reviews of *Lord Jim* included in Sherry (ed.), *Conrad: The Critical Heritage*, 111–28.
[12] Tony Tanner, *Conrad: Lord Jim* (London: Edward Arnold, 1963), 16.

II

The structure of the textual commentary adheres to the tripartite division of the novel's narrative: with an omniscient narrator (chapters 1–4), with Marlow speaking (chapters 5–35), and with Marlow writing (chapters 36–45). It would seem that in a study of narrative method it becomes particularly important to consider the transitions between the three main parts; this applies above all to the transition from Chapter 4 to Chapter 5 and from Chapter 35 to Chapter 36. In addition to these most apparent narrative variations there are numerous additional modulations, especially in part two of the novel.

The first three paragraphs of *Lord Jim* are very characteristic of what Ian Watt calls 'the sylleptic quality of Conrad's narrative'.[13] This authorial opening, consistently focused on Jim, juxtaposes an initial presentation of Jim's appearance with a professional description of the duties of a water-clerk, and the connection between his incognito and the necessary hiding of 'a fact' (4). The whole section, but especially the third paragraph, is thus technically proleptic. As Watt notes, the time of the *in medias res* opening 'is not that of a specific action but of a phase in the appearance of the protagonist'.[14] One important effect of the mention of the unspecified fact which necessitates the continual retreat is that the reader's curiosity is aroused; we have here an early, and relatively simple, example of delayed decoding within part one. In this sense the mention of fact[15]—as problem and irrevocable event—functions structurally as constitutive element in the build-up of suspense which culminates in the description of the abandonment of the *Patna* at the end of Chapter 3. It also, obviously, anticipates the concerns of the inquiry.

As the narrative moves backward in time, however, we get a first indication of the novel's characteristic detours and deviations. For in the following paragraph the emphasis is not on the fact itself but on information about Jim's background and character that bears an important, though indirect, relation to the later 'fact', the jump which underlies the narrator's use of the adjective 'deplorable' (5).

---

[13] *CNC* 301.

[14] Ibid. 293.

[15] Tanner gives an enlightening discussion of 'fact' in the novel, see *Conrad: Lord Jim*, 18.

Overtly analeptic, the fourth paragraph connects Jim's origin to a parsonage, and continues as a generalization that includes elements of irony. One general observation to be made on the irony of *Lord Jim*, which is the least ironic of the four novels analysed in this study, is that the irony never seems to be directed at Jim himself: instead it is his father and the institution of the church that are subjected to ironic treatment here, although cautiously. There is an interesting similarity at this point between the attitudes to Jim of the authorial narrator and Marlow.

In the concluding passages describing Jim's education at sea some latent characteristics of his are revealed, such as his cleanliness and his tendency to dream. Miller finds that the omniscient narrator relinquishes his 'direct access to the hero's mind' early in the story.[16] It would be more accurate to say that while the authorial omniscience is pointed, the glimpses given of Jim's inner life are selective, the criterion of selection being the relevance of these glimpses to the later Marlow narrative. Thus the mention of Jim's *Conway* training (cf. 'The Secret Sharer') is indicative of an élitist education which enhances the gravity of his mistake; more broadly, his background is so described as to make his subsequent jump especially unexpected and disquieting. Reaffirming the strong emphasis on Jim, the training-ship episode at the end of the chapter not only stresses Jim's self-confidence and self-avowed 'avidity for adventure' (9), but also accentuates the irony implicit in the characterization by contrasting it with the challenge to which he fails to respond. Critics of *Lord Jim* have not sufficiently stressed the *twofold* prolepsis detectable in the training-ship episode: not just adumbrating Jim's jump from the *Patna* by revealing it as a form of repetitive action, it provides the reader with a crucial piece of background information which makes him or her more sceptical about Jim's defensive explanation of the jump. And, as this information is not shared by Marlow, it also makes the reader more critical of Marlow's sympathies and of the motivation for his narrative undertaking.

Early in Chapter 2, where the background-providing information about Jim is continued in sequence, there is an important characterization of him at the end of the first paragraph. The attitude and position of the authorial narrator are similar to those in

---

[16] Miller, *Fiction and Repetition*, 32.

Chapter 1: factual information on Jim is given authoritatively and with remarkable fullness of knowledge. But the characterization is more precise here in being more directly focused on what is to be Jim's basic problem or tragedy, the failure to pass the test. The crucial phrase is connected with the mention of Jim's appointment as first mate 'without ever having been tested by those events of the sea that show in the light of day the inner worth of a man' (10). As Daleski remarks, in the first of three observations, the essence of the test in Conrad 'is that it is always unexpected... In the Conradian universe... it is readiness, not ripeness, that is all'.[17] If we also accept Daleski's second point that in *Lord Jim* 'the idea of the test is explicitly formulated for the first time', then we are able to specify its first formulation even further by identifying it with the passage just quoted. However, once this is done Daleski's third point becomes dubious. For Daleski, the test has the same function in the action as Marlow's obscure allusiveness has in the narrative. But the precise, and uncompromising, authorial emphasis on the necessity of passing the test whenever it presents itself is very different from the tenor of Marlow's allusiveness, which tends to take the form of a search for extenuating circumstances. The principal function of the test as identified here is, rather, threefold: at the level of adventure story, it increases the suspense which culminates with the 'collision' dramatized in the subsequent chapter; at the level of *Lord Jim* as modernist psychological novel, it concisely identifies one of the most crucially constitutive elements in the novel's moral thematics; and finally it underscores the authority of the authorial narrator and indirectly characterizes him.

If the emphasis on the test early in Chapter 2 implies a necessary thematic specification, the gradually-established focus on the *Patna*'s voyage, with Jim aboard, constitutes a situation with the test present as imminent possibility, challenge, and threat. One of the many perceptive observations Watt makes on *Lord Jim* is that the narrative is here characterized by a 'pervasive atmosphere of ominous serenity'.[18] It is primarily this 'atmosphere' (which, inevitably, becomes more noticeable in later readings) that for Watt distinguishes the descriptive passages in Chapters 2 and 3 from those of the *Narcissus* in *The Nigger of the 'Narcissus'*. While

---

[17] C W D 81, cf. 80.
[18] C N C 271.

broadly agreeing with this comment, it would seem that the qualification Watt adds devalues the potentially very interesting comparison with correspondingly descriptive passages in the earlier novella. For certainly the point can be extended without the qualification being ignored. In my reading these descriptions of the *Patna*—particularly in the two last paragraphs of Chapter 2 and in the first and sixth paragraphs of Chapter 3—function not only as constitutive elements of the 'ominous serenity' preceding the 'collision', but also as descriptive interludes with a distinctly lyric quality.

Let us briefly consider the most essential constitutive elements of the lyric quality observable in these passages. The first paragraph, dwelling on the slow, almost painful, progress of the *Patna*, culminates with the last sentence:

The *Patna*, with a slight hiss, passed over that plain luminous and smooth, unrolled a black ribbon of smoke across the sky, left behind her on the water a white ribbon of foam that vanished at once, like the phantom of a track drawn upon a lifeless sea by the phantom of a steamer. (16)[19]

The simile employed here, comparing both the *Patna* and her track with a 'phantom', evokes the strong impression Conrad's fiction can give of life as terse, unreal, and strangely dream-like, but at the same time extremely fascinating. In the second paragraph there is a similar intensification of visual impression, from the stress on the repetitive rhythm of the slowly progressing voyage to the magnificent ending:

... and the ship, lonely under a wisp of smoke, held on her steadfast way black and smouldering in a luminous immensity, as if scorched by a flame flicked at her from a heaven without pity.

The nights descended on her like a benediction. (16)

The personification of the *Patna* as 'lonely under a wisp of smoke' establishes a fine basis for the ensuing similes, introduced by 'as if' and 'like'; and it also suggests a thematic link between day and night ('scorched' as opposed to 'benediction')—between trying daylight and peaceful darkness.[20]

---

[19] Moser has (p. 11 of his edn. of *Lord Jim*) a comma after 'plain', but I agree with John Batchelor that it is unlikely that Conrad actually used a comma here. Conrad's use of appended descriptive adjectives is highly productive in *Lord Jim*, and not excessive as in, for instance, 'The Lagoon' in *Tales of Unrest* (1898). See Batchelor, intro. to the World's Classics edn. of *Lord Jim* (Oxford: OUP, 1983), p. xxiv.

[20] The novel's highly suggestive light/dark imagery is considered by Miller; see *Fiction and Repetition*, 37–8.

The transition from the first to the second chapter is superb. If the two preceding paragraphs resemble each other structurally in the gradual intensification of their descriptive concerns, the first paragraph of Chapter 3 is a direct continuation of the descriptively climactic ending of Chapter 2. Yet there is a subtle limitation or narrowing-down of the descriptive focus here, not through direct mention of Jim (which comes in the next paragraph) but through the content of the imagery employed. More precisely, the shift comes with the verb 'seem' and with the 'as though' simile:

A marvellous stillness pervaded the world, and the stars, together with the serenity of their rays, seemed to shed upon the earth the assurance of everlasting security... The propeller turned without a check, as though its beat had been part of the scheme of a safe universe... (17)

One implication here, that human existence is fundamentally insecure and the universe unsafe, does not wholly remove from these paragraphs a sense of reassurance—or at least a peaceful rest in harmony with the surrounding elements. Both implications are present; neither seems to predominate. The lyric quality is essentially engendered by the intensity of the visual presentation. This intensity is related not only to the imagery we have considered, but also to a temporarily reduced attitudinal distance between Conrad and his authorial narrator.

Generally, the qualities of the authorial narrator which we have already identified (particularly the omniscience and the stress on factual information) are indicative of a very considerable distance between the narrator and the *Patna*. This point has been made by several critics. What the present interpretation emphasizes is that narrative distance, and especially that of attitude (in the authorial narrative, temporal and spatial distance remain unidentified), seem to vary in accordance with the changes between the different descriptive focuses. The attitudinal distance often decreases in the descriptive passages, whereas it appears to be more marked in the authorial narrator's authoritative characterizations of Jim. One of the most effective narrative variations in Chapter 3 is suggested by the way in which the descriptive passages modulate into an accurate rendering of Jim's thoughts and dreams; the illusory safety aboard the *Patna* at night activates his tendency to dream, which the narrator has underlined in the opening chapter.

The descriptive passages function not only as background for the authorial characterization of Jim, but also as textual instalments which carry their own thematic import. This point would appear to be strengthened by the fact that in Chapter 3, after the swing back to the revelation of Jim's thoughts, a fourth descriptive paragraph is added to those already commented on. The *Patna* continues her smooth movement, 'as though she had been a crowded planet speeding through the dark spaces of ether behind the swarm of suns, in the appalling and calm solitudes awaiting the breath of future creations' (21–2). If this image is more intellectual and less descriptively lyric than those considered above, the principal reason is to be sought in the proleptic implication that by leaving a ship one also, in fact, deserts 'a crowded planet'. The implicit criticism here affirms authorial distance from Jim, but it also reaffirms the movement towards identification with the *Patna* as ship and microcosm of mankind. The seriousness of the officers' desertion of their ship is underscored, indirectly but forcefully, through this description.

The subtly embedded proleptic elements noticeable in the descriptive passages are related to, and supplement, a more overt anticipation. For Jim, we are told, 'did not see the shadow of the coming event' (19). In later readings of the novel, when we know of the 'collision' and read the third chapter searching (more or less consciously) for an authorial explanation of his jump, we find that although no explicit explanation is given, the combination of the various proleptic elements and the characterization of Jim (which is also in a sense proleptic) at least makes us more hesitant as to his ability to act promptly and rightly when confronted with unexpected danger. The contrast between Jim and the other *Patna* officers (who are introduced on page 15) reduces but does not wholly remove this hesitancy.

The description of the moment of 'collision' is most interesting. Watt identifies two of its principal narrative characteristics, that 'we are really being given a replay of the event rather than a chronological continuation' and that the account of the 'collision' 'is really a case of decoding doubly delayed and doubly denied'.[21] The critical validity of these two points is unquestionable. Less convincing is the additional note that the 'collision' 'prepares us for the ultimately inexplicable mystery of how the occurrence affected the rest of Jim's life'.[22] Perhaps it does prepare us for what is surely to

[21] CNC 272.
[22] Ibid.

remain a mystery, but the most obvious reason why we never get to know what hit the *Patna* is that the identification of the object is of peripheral importance. Instead, this particular instance of delayed decoding essentially furthers a shift of emphasis from the factual to the psychological, and from the *Patna* to Jim. This is not to say that the questions, 'What had happened?... Had the earth been checked in her course?' (26) are unimportant, but their most obvious function is to reveal the officers' bewilderment. Providing an illustrative example of narrated monologue, the questions establish a link with Jim's irritation at the inquiry: 'They wanted facts. Facts! They demanded facts from him, as if facts could explain anything!' (29). Although the thematic importance of these examples of narrated monologue may be limited, they constitute an interesting variant on the authorial narrative in the first part, thus easing the transition from authorial overview to the intensely personal account Jim is to give Marlow in Chapter 7.

The fourth chapter is instrumental in establishing the transition from the authorial narrative to Marlow's spoken narrative. Within the chapter it is possible to identify three transitional stages. The first is anticipated by the instances of narrated monologue we have already noted, and is most clearly observable in the first paragraph of page 31. This paragraph consists of authorial reflection inserted into Jim's explanatory statement at the inquiry. But although technically authorial, these reflections are cautiously attuned to Jim's thought: 'This had not been a common affair, everything in it had been of the utmost importance, and fortunately he remembered everything. He wanted to go on talking for truth's sake, perhaps for his own sake also...' (31). The effect of this personal modulation of authorial narrative is twofold: it not only foreshadows Marlow's narrative and makes the reader more favourably disposed towards it, but also suggests a subtle change in the authorial narrator's own attitude to Jim. If previously factually informative and somewhat critical of Jim, he is now more eager to understand him.

The second stage in the transition from authorial to personal narrative is more overtly technical, and centred on the visual exchange between Marlow and Jim at one particular point of the inquiry:

He met the eyes of the white man. The glance directed at him was not the fascinated stare of the others. It was an act of intelligent volition. Jim between two

questions forgot himself so far as to find leisure for a thought. This fellow—
ran the thought—looks at me as though he could see somebody or something past my shoulder. (32–3)

Technically, the most original thing about this introduction of
Marlow is that the authorial narrator adopts Jim's perspective. His
ominscience, which enables him to do so, has a very obvious
narrative function here. Thus the transition from authorial to
personal narrative is not only brought one step closer, but both Jim
and Marlow are presented as characters observed and described by
the omniscient authorial narrator. This emphasis on the two as
characters is reaffirmed by the following suggestion of mutual,
intuitive understanding: 'That man there seemed to be aware of his
hopeless difficulty' (33).

The third and final stage is represented by the authorial commentary which constitutes the last two paragraphs of Chapter 4:

And later on, many times, in distant parts of the world, Marlow showed
himself willing to remember Jim, to remember him at length, in detail and
audibly.

Perhaps it would be after dinner, on a verandah draped in motionless
foliage and crowned with flowers, in the deep dusk speckled by fiery
cigar-ends. The elongated bulk of each cane-chair harboured a silent
listener. Now and then a small red glow would move abruptly, and
expanding light up the fingers of a languid hand, part of a face in profound
repose, or flash a crimson gleam into a pair of pensive eyes overshadowed
by a fragment of an unruffled forehead; and with the very first word uttered
Marlow's body, extended at rest in the seat, would become very still, as
though his spirit had winged its way back into the lapse of time and were
speaking through his lips from the past. (33)

Critical comment on the narrative method of this crucially important passage might usefully be divided into two, according to
whether one considers the narrative implications of the information
the passage gives, or instead describes the narrative characteristics
of the passage itself. Such a grouping broadly corresponds to the
main concerns of the two paragraphs, for if the second establishes
the narrative setting of Marlow's spoken narrative, the preceding
short one compresses a wealth of highly relevant narrative information, which could be systematized as follows:

1. 'later on... ' As one of the chief characteristics of narrative
fiction, temporal distance is a particularly important device in *Lord*

Jim since it is exploited by Conrad not only to establish, and retain, a strong narrative focus on Jim, but also to draw our attention to certain significant and more general problems extractable from Jim's life experiences. Temporal distance as observable here serves to strengthen the novel's characteristic combination of the two genres already mentioned; it not only presents a dramatic (and in one sense increasingly melodramatic) life story, but combines it with reflection on how and why it all came to happen as it did. The substantial narrative distance also establishes a partial explanation of Marlow's tendency to jump backward and forward in time rather than rendering a strictly chronological account; his narrative is often associative, centred on essentials, and engaged in a sustained attempt to form some sort of coherent picture of Jim. The structure of this search for meaning is in part conditioned by the temporal distance between the time of narration and the crucial incidents of Jim's life.

2. 'many times... ' The problem of repetition in *Lord Jim* is very basic and subjected to more extended discussion below. The most immediate implication is that the telling of the story is still going on. Although there is no reason to believe that the content of Marlow's story varies according to, for instance, how many times he has told it and what kind of audience he has, the continuing retelling makes the structure of the novel even more open.

3. 'distant parts of the world... ' Spatial distance is also emphasized several times later in the novel; and it is connected with both Marlow and Jim. In the case of Marlow, spatial or geographical mobility serves mainly as a technical device: it enables him to track Jim down in his continual retreat. One more obvious thematic implication of the spatial distance between Jim and Marlow is that it does not change anything. For Marlow Jim is 'one of us' (43, 93, 106): the relevance and significance of the tale are enhanced by Marlow's insistence that Jim's problem is general and present everywhere. Brierly's suicide most explicitly establishes the authority of Marlow's views here. As regards Jim himself it is primarily the great distance to England and to his family which is emphasized.

4. 'Marlow... ' Investigation of Marlow's diverse narrative functions in *Lord Jim* is necessarily a major aim of this chapter, as substantiated below. As the narrator of the story about Jim to the audience on the verandah, and as author of the concluding, though not conclusive, letter to 'the privileged man' (337), Marlow is a

peculiarly complex mixture: he is an intelligent and curious sailor, an experienced human being who has a reflective bent and nurtures pilosophical interests, an investigator of Jim's case and yet one who becomes deeply involved in it. The functions of Marlow in *Lord Jim* are much more complex than in 'Youth', but in important ways comparable with those in 'Heart of Darkness'. As regards the introduction of Marlow here, it might briefly be commented on by qualifying Berthoud's point that in *Lord Jim* Conrad 'shifts the emphasis from the narrator to the protagonist' and that 'a structural alteration of this sort entails a corresponding thematic change'.[23] If the last part of the point supports this study's postulation of a close relationship of structure and thematics in Conrad, the first observation is certainly only valid in relative terms: the careful introduction of Marlow anticipates the centrality of his position both as narrator and as character. Moreover, it follows from the complexity of *Lord Jim* that the importance attached to Marlow will partly depend on what aspect of the novel is considered—and yet the figure of Marlow looms large in most of the studies of *Lord Jim*.

5. 'remember [Jim] at length, in detail... ' We get here an early warning that Marlow's account will be long in the telling. The story of Jim's life is a complex and bewildering one, and one, moreover, about which Marlow has been able to gather a lot of information. Considering why *Lord Jim*, originally planned as a short story, expanded into such a long novel, one hesitates between different explanatory theories. Watt finds that 'Conrad's scepticism also leads him to present and explore with exceptional thoroughness whatever pieces of evidence are available, however fragmentary or ambiguous, which may provide clues to understanding what the characters do and are'.[24] This point is carefully phrased and quite persuasive, but it is also indicative of Watt's tendency to relate the narrative and structural characteristics of Conrad's fiction to his ideas, his ideology, and his intentions. There is probably some relation between Conrad's scepticism and the narrative method of *Lord Jim*, but the narrative's 'thoroughness' and also, by implication, its textual expansion, are clearly dependent on several factors. Another explanation of the great length is that it seems to have been difficult for Conrad to 'leave' a method if he had found it to be a

---

[23] *CMP* 65.
[24] *CNC* 269.

productive one. In an obvious sense the enumeration of narrative voices, which are more easily included once the device of Marlow as personal narrator is adopted, increases textual quantity. And again, even if one grants a connection between Conrad's scepticism and the need for thematic diversification which *Lord Jim* evinces, it might be argued that in this novel the scepticism is to some extent balanced, or counteracted, by Marlow's insistent effort to understand Jim, and if possible to exonerate him.

6. 'audibly... ' It is one of the novel's narrative inconsistencies that the stylistic features of Marlow's spoken and written narrative are less dissimilar than one would expect; generally, large sections of the narrative in Chapters 5 to 35 seem written rather than spoken. Randall Craig claims that one reason why the oral tradition appealed to Conrad was 'its conventional lack of concern with factual information'.[25] But surely neither facts nor information are unimportant in *Lord Jim*. Instead Marlow's narrative is characterized by his dissatisfaction with, and attempt to move beyond, the kind of fact aimed at by the inquiry. Marlow's attention is rather directed towards what Daleski aptly terms 'hidden fact'.[26] One principal function of his oral narrative is to obtain, and present, a diversification of the facts given by the authorial narrator in Chapter 4.

If the short paragraph briefly discussed here pinpoints narrative and thematic problems that reverberate throughout *Lord Jim*, the next one—the authorial narrator's last before Marlow takes over—specifies 5 and 6 and suggestively indicates the narrative setting of the oral account that follows. The setting is difficult to comment on critically since so much of its significance depends on the subtly-contrived evocation of atmosphere. The paragraph establishes a dreamy quality very reminiscent of the opening chapters of Faulkner's *Absalom, Absalom!*; this quality of dream or musing reflection underlies, as in Faulkner's novel, the whole narrative and is intimately related to Marlow's associative narration and to the frequent shifts between different levels of time. However, in spite of the importance attached to setting, the paragraph also includes an authorial characterization of Marlow. As the characterization, in the extended simile which concludes the chapter, portrays Marlow as a 'spirit' freed from the temporal restrictions of ordinary life, one

[25] Randall Craig, 'Swapping Yarns: The Oral Mode of *Lord Jim*', *Conradiana*, 13 (1981), 183.
[26] *CWD* 79.

could possibly interpret this simile as an instance of authorial vouching for Marlow's narrative authority, but such an interpretation would have to be strongly qualified. The two concluding paragraphs of part one do, however, suggest that the relationship between the authorial narrator and Marlow is particularly intimate.

In his useful study of *Lord Jim*, Tanner finds that 'having given us this much Conrad the author leaves the book'.[27] This statement is not only imprecise; it is clearly wrong, because Conrad is of course the author of Marlow's narrative as well as of Chapters 1 to 3, and also because, as we have seen, the novel's opening authorial narrative is more diversified than earlier critics have noted. One could argue that the authorial narrator is closer to Conrad than Marlow is, but then one would have to add that the novel's authorial narrator is a very flexible device. Still, this interpretation concedes one implication of Tanner's statement. For although it insists on a distinction (and not only a theoretical one) between Conrad and his authorial narrator, the discussion of the descriptive interludes suggests that the distance between author and narrator varies; and the strong sense of intensified memory in these sections—combined with the use of such poetic devices as repetition, simile, and metaphorical contrast between light and dark indicates that attitudinal distance may temporarily decrease. Other commentators on the narrative of *Lord Jim* have found that the authorial narrator reveals an attitude and professional knowledge which suggest that he is a sailor. But clearly his authority is not limited to matters of the sea; it also includes comments on basic aspects of Jim's personality. That the narrator does reveal intimate knowledge of life at sea tells more about Jim's experiences than his own, for his narrative contains very few (if any) suggestions of limited knowledge. Another matter is that his maritime knowledge eases the transition between his views and those of the experienced sailor Marlow.

If the basic narrative function of the authorial narrative is to establish a frame around Marlow's narratives, its principal thematic function is suggested by the way in which it introduces and anticipates the basic concerns of *Lord Jim* as a whole. The authorial narrative does not, as John Batchelor finds, present Jim in a different light,[28] but it introduces the reader to him and provides

---

[27] Tanner, *Conrad: Lord Jim*, 23.
[28] Batchelor, intro. to the World's Classics edn. of *Lord Jim*, p. xix.

essential information exceeding even that possessed by Marlow. Though not sceptical of the personal narrative it introduces, the authorial narrative thus makes the reader aware of the limitations of Marlow's knowledge of Jim and, by implication, cautiously suggests the limitations inherent in Marlow's attempts to understand him.

III

The authorial narrative link provided by 'he would say' in the opening line of Chapter 5 seems to suggest that the narrative is to remain authorial, and in a strictly technical sense it does, since all of Marlow's account is given in inverted commas—reported by the authorial narrator.[29] Nevertheless, in the textual practice of the novel Marlow's account clearly takes the form of a personal narrative, and the more so as he not only relates the story of his own encounters and talks with Jim, but also draws heavily on information from others.

An implication to be found in Dorothy Van Ghent's discussion of *Lord Jim* is that Marlow is rightly introduced at the stage which marks the starting-point of 'the processes of judgment'.[30] But surely Marlow feels no strong need to 'judge' Jim. To begin with he is, at most, interested; the pacing of his opening narrative seems deliberately hesitant. The slow narrative movement of Chapters 5 and 6 serves to explain how and why this interest arose; and it also establishes some narrative authority on Marlow's part. As Watt notes, reading the opening of Chapter 5 we cannot even be sure that Marlow is ever to see Jim again, 'since Marlow's narrative begins by taking up various events before the inquiry—first the sight of the four officers of the *Patna* arriving on the quay, then the Captain's grotesquely precipitate flight, and finally Marlow's conversation with the *Patna*'s chief engineer'.[31] The larger thematic implications of Marlow's conversation with the engineer are convincingly expounded by Watt. Little can be added to this discussion, whose critical value is further enhanced by Watt's application of two

---

29 Cf. Franz Stanzel, *A Theory of Narrative*, 79–110, esp. 104–6.
30 Van Ghent, *The English Novel*, 237.
31 *CNC* 273.

helpful narrative terms. 'Symbolic deciphering' suggests, unlike the more mechanical device of delayed decoding, the tenuous process of making out a message that is inherently difficult to read. 'Thematic apposition', which Watt sees as 'perhaps the most characteristic feature of Conrad's mature narrative technique',[32] is intimately connected with Marlow's associative narrative and with the juxtaposition of thematically related scenes.

Before the engineer's account, however, Marlow makes a quite explicit statement on the subjectivity inherent in his narrative: 'All this happened in much less time than it takes to tell, since I am trying to interpret for you into slow speech the instantaneous effect of visual impressions' (48). This subjectivity adds a new dimension to the novel, and one that is closely linked to the employment of personal narrative. Moreover, implicit in Marlow's attempts 'to interpret' there is an invitation both to his narratees and to the reader to join him in the attempt to understand the enigmatic Jim. At the same time, but at a more metafictional level, the quoted extract might be seen as revealing some of Conrad's reflection on his own medium—language—and its inherent limitations.

By way of introducing the engineer's account Marlow reflects on his attitude to Jim, and his whole narrative project, before their first talk. Great temporal distance, not only from the meeting with the engineer but from Jim's story at large, establishes the necessary overview and clarification (clarification, that is, in the sense of presenting Jim as problem, not understanding him) requisite for the meditative, rather resigned pondering of the passage. Marlow himself comments explicitly on the temporal distance when he says, towards the end of his reflections, that 'the only thing that at this distance of time strikes me as miraculous is the extent of my imbecility' (51). As Marlow's thoughts here are very relevant for both the narrative method and the thematics of *Lord Jim*, it is necessary to give the whole central section of the passage.

'Why I longed to go grubbing into the deplorable details of an occurrence which, after all, concerned me no more than as a member of an obscure body of men held together by a community of inglorious toil and by fidelity to a certain standard of conduct, I can't explain. You may call it an unhealthy curiosity if you like; but I have a distinct notion I wished to find something. Perhaps, unconsciously, I hoped I would find that something,

---

[32] Ibid. 285, cf. 276.

some profound and redeeming cause, some merciful explanation, some convincing shadow of an excuse. I see well enough now that I hoped for the impossible—for the laying of what is the most obstinate ghost of man's creation, of the uneasy doubt uprising like a mist, secret and gnawing like a worm, and more chilling than the certitude of death—the doubt of the sovereign power enthroned in a fixed standard of conduct.' (50)

With regard to narrative method, the most revealing thing about the passage is Marlow's use of words such as 'unhealthy curiosity... find... redeeming cause... merciful explanation... excuse' to offer a partial explanation of his interest in Jim. There are two immediate effects of these words as used in the passage. First, they reaffirm the tentative observation Marlow has already made earlier in the chapter—that his reasons for being intrigued by Jim's case are obscure. But more interestingly, a relation is suggested between obscurity at the level of narrative motivation and obscurity in Jim's actions and behaviour. Marlow's curiosity is increased by Jim's tendency to surprise him, and as this happens while he continues to feel an unexpectedly strong affinity with Jim, his interest is enhanced by his inability to understand it. It is best described as fascination—not only with Jim's case in a limited sense but also with its implications, including those which come worryingly close to Marlow himself.

Marlow's narrative project in *Lord Jim* is in a way very similar to that of Marlow in 'Heart of Darkness': in both texts, narrative motivation is augmented by the unconscious ('Perhaps, unconsciously, I hoped I would find that something') impression that the narrator is revealing a thematics which tends to absorb himself. The impression also intensifies the narrative by making its implications more profound, not only for Marlow but for the reader as well. As formulated in this key passage both narrative motivation and the thematics generated through it would appear to revolve around the word 'doubt'—'the doubt of the sovereign power enthroned in a fixed standard of conduct'. Miller's view of this statement as the most explicit formulation of the 'theme' in *Lord Jim* has much to recommend it,[33] though it is critically dubious to generalize so strongly from just one passage from a long and complex literary text. As briefly noted already, Miller refers to the passage by way of establishing his view of Marlow's narrative project as suspect. We shall see below that this view is partly unconvincing: at this stage I

[33] Miller, *Fiction and Repetition*, 26–9.

merely restate the close relation of 'doubt' as used here to a pressing sense of profundity—a sensation shared (more or less consciously) by Conrad, Marlow, Marlow's narratees, Jim, and the reader. Although Miller is right to note that 'Marlow's aim (or Conrad 's) seems clear: to find some explanation for Jim's action which will make it possible still to believe in the sovereign power,'[34] the doubt which not only motivates Marlow's narrative but also underlies all of it would appear to modify the aim by introducing a pervasive scepticism as to whether it can be attained.

It is interesting that Miller's interpretation of this passage is possible only if it is seen as a thematic statement on *Lord Jim* as a whole. If, on the other hand, one relates it more closely to the succeeding talk with the engineer, then his reading becomes less convincing. When Watt finds that 'the hospital scene must offer Marlow some slight degree of reassurance, since although the fixed standard of conduct has hardly exhibited a sovereign power, it has, in one instance at least, not been violated with impunity',[35] he implicitly criticizes or at least modifies Miller's reading. As contrastive interpretations of the same passage, these two authoritative views pinpoint one of the central interpretative problems of *Lord Jim*.

By the opening of Chapter 6 Marlow's personal narrative seems firmly established. However, it contains attempts to increase his authority further, for instance through the reference to 'human interest'—which implies that the other attendants of the inquiry are also intrigued by Jim's case, and would perhaps understand it in much the same way as Marlow does. 'Whether they knew it or not, the interest that drew them there was purely psychological' (56); contrary to the 'superficial how' of the inquiry itself, their interest is in 'the fundamental why... of this affair'. It is characteristic of the novel's narrative method that even this distinction, which is initially presented as obvious and which is reaffirmed by Jim's irritation with the inquiry's insistence on 'Facts!' (29), is modified—implicitly through Marlow's sympathizing interest, but more immediately and dramatically through the incorporated account of Captain Brierly, who, as assessor at the inquiry, should be exclusively concerned with the *how*, and yet by committing suicide shortly

[34] Ibid. 28.
[35] CNC 275.

afterwards reveals a striking inability to face the 'fundamental why' behind Jim's case.

Much of the thematic impact of the intercalated Brierly episode depends on its tripartite narrative structure. First Marlow gives a summary introductory account of Brierly's unparalleled professional career. Towards the end comes Marlow's very surprising and effective laconic statement: 'He committed suicide very soon after' (58). This information inevitably makes the reader pay much closer attention to the second part, the story presented to Marlow as narratee by Brierly's mate, Jones, of the events preceding the suicide. As narrator, Jones is accurate and reliable; as character he is rather naïve. This naïvety is highly functional thematically since it suggests that one does not need the kind of subtlety and wisdom possessed by Marlow to be mystified by the effects of Jim's jump. When Jones asks, 'Why did he commit the rash act, Captain Marlow—can you think?' (64), it sounds like a minor narrator's variant of the big question about Jim raised not only by Marlow but by the whole novel.

Jones's account, we are informed towards the end of it, is both spatially and temporally removed from the scene of the inquiry—it takes place in a ship 'more than two years afterwards' (64). The obvious gain from this temporal inversion is, as Watt notes, that 'forewarned by our detailed knowledge of Brierly's later suicide, we are alerted to whatever may be diagnostic in his behaviour now',[36] that is, in the dialogue between Marlow and Brierly which constitutes the third part of the episode. Brierly's words here, emphasizing a sailor's need for 'dignity' and 'decency' (67–8), blend into Marlow's reflections, which are coloured by the information later added by Jones. The conclusion of the episode not only emphasizes the necessity of temporal distance for the kind of thematic pressure it demonstrates,[37] but also offers an indirect comment on the mystery of Jim by leaving Brierly's suicide partly unexplained.

More generally, the best description of the narrative method of the chapters leading up to Marlow's long talk with Jim in the hotel may be the indirectness which follows from the apposition of thematically related scenes. The sequence of episodes just considered is not, however, as 'purely thematic' as Watt finds. It is true that

---

[36] CNC 277.
[37] Cf. ibid. 280.

there is no apparent narrative connection between the hospital scene and the Brierly episode. Still, the main reason why their apposition seems plausible is to be sought not only in the indirect relation of both to Jim's case, but in Conrad's success in manipulating the reader into tacit acceptance of Marlow's associative narrative method. Part of the success is dependent on the application of the oral mode of narration and on the great temporal distance; both these narrative devices make thematic apposition more likely, and thus easier to accept.

The temporal distance is emphasized again at the end of the Brierly episode. Then the narrative loops back to the inquiry and establishes a connection with the first visual exchange between Marlow and Jim which has already been described from authorial perspective. One effect of this bringing together of authorial and personal narrative (apart from the clarifying one of leading us to recognize an occurrence already described) is that the first two main narrative modes of *Lord Jim* become more obviously related, and the importance of the authorial opening's introductory function is reasserted. Another effect is to strengthen the reader's impression of Marlow's narrative as not only indirect, but also exceptionally elaborate and slow-moving: we seem to be back where we were at the end of Chapter 4.

The return to the inquiry serves to introduce the 'wretched cur' (70) incident in which Jim mistakenly imagines he is being rebuked by Marlow, and which establishes the basis for Jim's ensuing narrative in Chapters 7 to 12. Conrad's sophisticated use of symbolic deciphering here has been exhaustively discussed by Watt and need not detain us.[38] At the end of the incident Marlow is more confused than ever:

'I don't pretend I understood him. The views he let me have of himself were like those glimpses through the shifting rents in a thick fog—bits of vivid and vanishing detail, giving no connected idea of the general aspect of a country. They fed one's curiosity without satisfying it; they were no good for purposes of orientation. Upon the whole he was misleading.' (76)

These reflections are consonant with the earlier ones on Jim, and summarize Marlow's attitude to the whole problem. They also blend into his introductory reflections in the following chapter,

---

[38] Ibid. 283–4.

where he becomes Jim's confidant and much more directly involved in his case. In an important sense the extended dialogue between Marlow and Jim in the hotel room amounts to a private trial with the focus on *why*. At the same time, Chapters 7 to 12 constitute Jim's narrative to Marlow as narratee about *his* experience of the abandonment. It is, however, difficult if not impossible to discuss Jim's narrative as such, not only because of the blurred transitions between Jim's direct account and Marlow's indirect one, but also because Marlow repeatedly intervenes, supports, questions, and generalizes upon Jim's story.

Jim's narrative, to the extent that it can be isolated from Marlow's report of it, is characterized by an intense personal involvement: it is a fervent, desperate attempt to explain what the inquiry did not allow him to. It gives a strong impression of re-experience—we get the protagonist's version of the authorial narrator's earlier description of the abandonment of the *Patna* and the surrounding events. The culmination of Jim's narrative comes in Chapter 9, with the painfully tentative restatement of the jump: 'I had jumped... It seems' (111).

Marlow's narrative function in these chapters is exceptionally diverse, and four points must be made on it. First, although the whole section is coloured by Marlow's narration, he also performs a necessary function as narratee here. It is his ability and willingness to listen which spark Jim's narrative off in the first place; as it proceeds Marlow's sympathy for Jim increases and so does his respect for him. At times the sympathy verges on active defence: 'What a persistence of readiness!... And the endurance is undeniable, too' (122). The attempts to understand are rendered through narrative variations such as the narrated monologue on page 86: 'They *were* dead! Nothing could save them!' This exclamation could well have been Jim's; that it is uttered by Marlow indicates the extent to which he is able, and willing, to participate in Jim's painful reconstruction. Thus one question prompted by the narrative is whether Marlow's sympathy for Jim is consistent with his earlier attitude. The answer would seem to be that it is, since sympathy and understanding are balanced by what I suggest in my second point: the repetitive emphasis on distance between the two, coupled with Marlow's outspoken criticism of Jim. There are several references to this distance, which is predominantly attitudinal here. It is indicated, for instance, in Marlow's questioning ('How much more did you want?') of Jim's view that 'there was not the thickness of a sheet of paper between the right and wrong of this affair' (130). In the novel's sophisticated metaphorical pattern—proceeding further from the paragraph on page 76 already quoted—the variation of distance is connected with the metaphors of fog and mist. In Chapter 10 Marlow speaks of 'one of those bizarre and exciting glimpses through the fog' (114); in Chapter 11 the metaphor of mist is evoked twice, and again at the beginning of Chapter 12. Marlow is certainly fascinated, and there are moments of understanding, but on the whole his attitude is still ambivalent and hesitant.

Thirdly, Marlow's rendering of Jim's narrative is characterized by his tendency to add his own comments and to generalize upon the information from Jim, and by his gradually changing impression of him. Examples of this tendency abound, to the extent that Jim's narrative becomes virtually inseparable from Marlow's, except for the passages given in inverted commas. Marlow himself describes it as 'disjointed' (113), which may imply that he has edited it. The comments merge with the generalizing reflections, but interestingly both include elements of sympathy as well as distance. All three narrative characteristics identified so far are observable in this passage:

'His clear blue eyes turned to me with a piteous stare, and looking at him standing before me, dumb-founded and hurt, I was oppressed by a sad sense of resigned wisdom, mingled with the amused and profound pity of an old man helpless before a childish disaster.' (111)

Fourthly, there are some noteworthy references to the narrative setting (and thus by implication also to the authorial frame) in these chapters. Both in Chapter 8 and Chapter 9 Jim is referred to as 'one of us' (93, 106); Marlow attempts to strengthen the sense of professional alliance or kinship between narrator/narratees and protagonist. Additionally, two authorial insertions should be noted:

Marlow paused to put new life into his expiring cheroot, seemed to forget all about the story, and abruptly began again. (93–4)

He paused again to wait for an encouraging remark perhaps, but nobody spoke; only the host, as if reluctantly performing a duty, murmured—
    'You are so subtle, Marlow.' (94)

It is telling that this rare listener's comment on Marlow's story should provoke him into stressing his difference from Jim. But the main function of the authorial insertions is to remind the reader of the narrative setting, and to confirm that the oral narrative convention is still being adhered to—the authorial narrator is reticent but not totally absent. Brief as it is, the narratee's comment suggests agreement with Marlow's view of Jim and his problems. The implication is that the reader is being invited to take a similarly appreciative view of Marlow'a narrative.

As Jim's narrative ends, Marlow is 'overcome by a profound and hopeless fatigue' (132), which extends into Chapter 12 and colours the mixture of information and reflection preceding the proleptic episode constituted by his conversation with the French lieutenant. The episode is incorporated into the narrative in a manner which offers a good illustration of how thematic apposition may work in the novel:

' "*Fort intrigués par ce cadavre*," as I was informed a long time after by an elderly French lieutenant whom I came across one afternoon in Sydney, by the merest chance, in a sort of café, and who remembered the affair perfectly.' (137)

As one of the French officers who boarded the abandoned *Patna*, not only has the lieutenant come on board the ship Jim left and stayed there for thirty hours while it was being towed to harbour, but he has done so without the slightest hesitation and as the most obvious exercise of duty. The apposition at first seems purely informative, but then becomes more thematic as the conversation is focused on the key words 'fear' and 'honour' (146, 148). Marlow's earlier note on the 'extraordinary power' (137) of Jim's case bears an important relation to the thematic pressure, and is supplemented by very similar reflections on page 151. If the lieutenant's narrative is easier to single out for explicit commentary than Jim's, the most obvious reason is that Marlow's relationship with the officer is much shorter and less problematic. The lieutenant's function as narrator, however, is not easily distinguishable from that as character; in both capacities he is utterly dependable and severely factual.

The French lieutenant episode is arguably the most successful in the whole novel. The way in which his story is broken up and interposed between Marlow's commentary is peculiarly effective; and so is the insertion of French words, both as stylistic variation and in underlying the key notions of the lieutenant's account. His different perspective throws more light on Jim,[39] but not without emphasizing how strange and difficult (*'impossible de comprendre'* (138)) the case is, 'so that (*de sorte que*) there are many things in this incident of my life (*dans cet épisode de ma vie*) which have remained obscure' (142). The lieutenant is not a MacWhirr who seems unaware of the threat of fear ('Given a certain combination of circumstances, fear is sure to come', he says (146)), but his ability to resist it is at once greater and more unproblematic than Jim's; it is also more closely connected with the concept of honour. Although it seems an exaggeration to suggest, as Berthoud does, that the lieutenant is Jim's 'complete antithesis',[40] the two are unquestionably presented as contrastive characters; and one important thematic effect of this contrast is to emphasize the gravity of Jim's mistake. R. A. Gekoski finds that Marlow's defence of Jim makes him too unappreciative of the common sense of the French lieutenant.[41] This point becomes more persuasive if it is incorporated into one made by Guerard, that Marlow 'clearly diverges from Conrad' in this section.[42] Generally the attitudinal distance between Conrad and Marlow is not easily pinpointed in *Lord Jim*, but here it seems as though the moral integrity and impressive posture of the lieutenant provoke Marlow into a more active defence of Jim, particularly in the remark, 'but couldn't [the honour] reduce itself to not being found out?' (149). However, as this is a provoked riposte one should beware of generalizing upon it, or indeed upon the episode as a whole, to the extent Gekoski does. To proceed from his point would be to imply that the lieutenant is closer to Conrad than Marlow is in this section, which would be a dubious reading not only because of the general reliability and centrality of Marlow as narrator, but also because the moral position of Conrad—to the extent that it can be abstracted from the thematic web of a complicated text—is more ambiguous and certainly more complex than that of the lieutenant.

The proleptic French lieutenant episode is followed by various inserted accounts of Jim's difficulties in the period subsequent to the hotel conversation. The narrative variation of these chapters

---

[39] Cf. Van Ghent, *The English Novel*, 242.
[40] *C M P* 67.
[41] R. A. Gekoski, *Conrad: The Moral World of the Novelist* (London: Elek Books, 1978), 102.
[42] *C N* 157.

(13–19) confirms the importance of thematic apposition as a chief constituent of the narrative method of *Lord Jim*. Though not unimportant, the narrative modulations are minor ones and cannot be commented on in detail, yet four points should be made. First, we note the temporal transition back to the hotel conversation: this transition offers a good illustration of Marlow's associative method. Part of the reason why the 'looping method', to apply Warren Beach's term,[43] works well here is suggested by the way in which the temporal shift is directly related to Marlow's reflective, musing thought. Furthermore, the references to the narrative setting just after the shift serve as a partial explanation of it by reasserting that continued focus on Jim is the guiding principle for Marlow's thought pattern. And the reference is not a mechanical and isolated one; it blends into reflections revealing a certain scepticism on Marlow's part about the underlying reasons for his interest in Jim. The significance of the reflections is enhanced by their position in the text, after the French lieutenant episode.

Secondly, it is a shared characteristic of these episodes, and especially of that of Chester and Robinson, that our initial impression of irrelevance gives way to appraisal of additional insight into Jim's case from a new and unexpected angle. Chester's dismissive verdict on Jim, for example, 'He's no good, is he?' (166), has a touch of brutal truth in it; more indirectly, his simplified perception of Jim makes us more appreciative of Marlow's hesitant evaluations.

Thirdly, if the incorporation of narrative *writing* into Marlow's oral narrative in Chapter 18 is seen as anticipating the narrative method of part three, then the integration of oral and written modes in *Lord Jim* would appear strengthened. What is most striking about the use of the three letters—the two from Marlow's friend and Jim's explanatory letter—is the way in which the writing is attuned to Marlow's oral narrative.

And finally, we must note how Marlow begins Chapter 19, the chapter which serves as an introduction to Stein:

'I have told you these two episodes at length to show his manner of dealing with himself under the new conditions of his life. There were many others of the sort, more than I could count on the fingers of my two hands.' (197)

---

[43] Beach, *The Twentieth-Century Novel*, 363–4.

The passage invites two comments, which also apply more generally to the narrative pattern of *Lord Jim* as a whole. It establishes, first, a partial motivation for the novel's textual expansion: the episodes are told 'at length' because Marlow—with Jim as his determining focus of characterization—has judged it necessary to do so. Most readers would probably agree that these episodes offer intrinsic justification for their inclusion. The second comment starts from the implication that Marlow has selected just a few episodes out of many for narrative presentation. Not only epitomizing Marlow's crucial function as narrator, this stress on narrative selection from a larger and more indeterminate fund makes the structure of the novel even more open. A possible connection is suggested between the selective presentation and the indication of repetitive narration.

Marlow's introduction to Stein is not only more detailed and prolonged than his previous ones. Giving an evocative description of the spacious, gloomy rooms of his secluded house, it establishes a sense of detachment and dream—it promotes, indeed, an aura of mystery which comes to surround Stein as well as Jim. Paradoxically, Stein, who is regarded by Marlow as the person most eminently capable of understanding and possibly of helping Jim, is himself strangely distant and enigmatic, for Marlow and by implication for the reader. To support this observation, which further increases Marlow's qualities as reflective, doubting narrator and the ambiguity of *Lord Jim* as hesitant, modernist text, I wish to draw attention to the opacity or basic uncertainty implicit in Stein's diagnosis of Jim as 'romantic' (212), and to the apparent self-contradiction in Stein's advice (214–15).

As soon as Stein has described Jim as romantic, Marlow admits that he is 'quite startled to find how simple it was' (212). Both in common usage and as a literary term, however, the word 'romantic' is far from simple; indeed, it is one of the most ambiguous we have.[44] It would seem, therefore, that the meaning of 'romantic' as used by Stein would have to be delimited somehow. In one of the most useful essays on *Lord Jim*, Zdzisław Najder, referring to G.Pigna's theories about honour, relates 'romantic' to 'an exalted sense of responsibility'.[45] For Najder, the essence of the psychological problem

---

[44] Cf. *OED*.
[45] Zdzisław Najder, '*Lord Jim*: A Romantic Tragedy of Honor', *Conradiana*, 1 (1969), 3.

propounded in *Lord Jim* is 'the conflict between the notions and ideas an individual holds and reality'.[46] If Jim's 'notions and ideas' are understood not only as romantic, but also as indicative of his sense of honour and responsibility, then the term becomes more obviously integrated into the novel's thematic structure, not least through the link which is established with the earlier pronounce-ments of the French lieutenant. Furthermore, 'an exalted sense of responsibility' would seem to be related to what is for Jim a brutal 'reality'—witness Jim's very different reaction from that of his fellow officers after their common desertion of the *Patna*.

Stein's advice consists of two constitutive elements: 'in the destructive element immerse' (214) and 'to follow the dream— and so—*ewig—usque ad finem . . .*' (215). The apparent self-contradiction here emerges from Stein's earlier association of a 'destructive element' with the reality of life on the one hand, and the common association of 'dream' with romantic imagination on the other. As Najder notes, imagination and dream are opposed, but not inconsistently since Stein has previously used 'dream' as synony-mous with reality: 'A man that is born falls into a dream like a man who falls into the sea.' (214). This is of course a generalizing remark, but one through which Stein reveals a surprisingly strong kinship between himself and Jim. His understanding of Jim is intuitive, expressed in a terminology which for Marlow remains largely impenetrable and puzzling.

C. B. Cox is obviously right to stress that Stein is not a spokes-man for Conrad.[47] But such a rather self-evident point should not make us underestimate his thematic importance; Daleski, for instance, unconvincingly observes that Stein is 'important structur-ally [but not] thematically'.[48] It is true that the Sein interview occurs at the structural centre of *Lord Jim*: Stein is sought out by Marlow in a final attempt to find a genuine solution to Jim's problem, and the interview immediately promotes the Patusan venture which consti-tutes the second half of the novel. Stein rapidly becomes a very important character, who, unlike the French lieutenant, is to remain with the novel's cast until the end; and chronologically, as Watt notes, 'it is the only scene since Marlow and Jim first met when story and narrative time are fully coordinate'.[49] The full thematic

---

[46] Ibid. 5.
[47] Cox, *Conrad: The Modern Imagination*, 37.
[48] *CWD* 95.   [49] *CNC* 305.

significance of this most important of Marlow's interrogations cannot be explored here, but some of the implications have already been hinted at in our brief discussion of Stein's vocabulary. What needs to be stressed is that the whole Stein interview is steeped in ambiguity. It is noteworthy how tentative and elusive Stein's words are, and how Marlow is confused, if not misled, by Stein's musing reflections. Miller finds that Stein 'appears to be either an unreliable narrator or a trustworthy commentator, depending on one's judgment of his life and personality'.[50] But these two alternative readings of Stein's function are not equally well supported in the novel. Miller's point is in fact dubious, since Stein is not—in contrast to the French lieutenant, with whom many critics have compared him—a narrator. One of the few observations that can unequivocally be made on Stein is that he is presented as a character who becomes a 'trustworthy commentator' only to the extent he is able to impose valid generalizations on the information about Jim provided for him by Marlow.

If Marlow is impressed by Stein's personality and reflections, he is also left bewildered and confused; this confusion is observable in the generalizations Stein provokes him to make. There can be no doubt that, seen as thoughts following Stein's diagnosis and advice, these reflections are distinctly anticlimactic, as in the romantic phraseology which permeates this sentence: 'we had approached nearer to absolute Truth, which, like Beauty itself, floats elusive, obscure, half submerged, in the silent still waters of mystery' (216). Yet in a different sense these reflections reveal much: not only showing how little Marlow has understood of Jim (or Stein) and thus further stressing the enigmatic nature of the set of problems surrounding the novel's protagonist, they also increase the textual prominence of Marlow both as narrator and as character. Marlow doubts 'Jim's existence' (216) and yet he is struck by his 'imperishable reality'. This problematic contradiction indicates Marlow's characteristically suspended position between conflicting forms of repetition, a position to be discussed shortly.

Stein's remedy for Jim is Patusan, and the action set there constitutes the second half of the novel. Chapter 21, which opens with a short authorial break reminding the reader that the oral narrative situation is still being adhered to, introduces a long series of

---

[50] Miller, *Fiction and Repetition*, 33.

chapters which recount Jim's rise and fall in the setting provided by Stein. As the narrative method of these chapters is simpler and less varied than in the first part, the textual commentary on the sequence can be correspondingly brief. What follows is mainly centred on problems that critics have tended to overlook or treat too lightly.

Chapter 21 includes two important modifications of the reflections Marlow is led to make after the Stein interview. First, in a manner reminiscent of the language teacher in *Under Western Eyes*, he disclaims any capacity for imagination: 'As to me, I have no imagination (I would be more certain about him today, if I had)' (223). One effect of this disclaimer may be to increase narrative reliability; yet it is typical of Marlow's doubting self-reflection that he himself qualifies the possible advantage resulting from this missing quality. His narrative consciousness is further strenghened by the next modification:

'I am telling you so much about my own instinctive feelings and bemused reflections because there remains so little to be told of him. He existed for me, and after all it is only through me that he exists for you.' (224)

It is tempting to read this passage as an indication of Marlow's thematic significance in *Lord Jim*, a significance which results from his crucial narrative function, but which gradually takes on a more independently thematic dimension which again makes the novel more modernist—tentative, searching, remarkably metafictional. As Watt notes, the proleptic elements of Chapter 21 are exceptional for this sequence, and are based on information Marlow gets from Jim when he visits Patusan nearly three years later. The narrative of Chapters 25–33 takes the form of an extended analepsis, continued in sequence up to the authorial break at the beginning of Chapter 34.

The first part of this narrative in particular is possible only because Marlow has first been listening to Jim. However, Jim's dramatic, pointed story of how he overcame the immense early challenges and problems in Patusan is much more attuned to Marlow's own narrative idiom than Jim's intense self-examination in the hotel conversation. Our picture of Jim's narrative is blurred here by Marlow's interposed, explanatory remarks and the relatively unproblematic focus on the action itself, rather than, as in the hotel conversation, on the protagonist's experience of the action. One striking tendency of the remarks is to establish a picture of

Patusan as appearing, in Watt's expression, 'in a soft pink glow behind a gauze curtain'.[51] Marlow, with his general predilection for literary terms, evokes words like 'legend' (266) and 'this amazing Jim-myth' (280) to describe Patusan and Jim's rule there. Such descriptions not only strengthen the suggestions of mystery surrounding Jim's character, but also reaffirm Marlow's reflective attitude towards the narrative he presents.

With 'the story of his love' (275) in Chapter 28, an additional focus is established which entails a sort of new start. Although, for all its magazine-like romanticism, the love story is better integrated into the thematic patterns of *Lord Jim* than seems to be the case at first, there is no reason to disagree with the critics who point out that the narrative deteriorates from the searching method and the probing moral cross-examinations of the first part to the simplistic, at times melodramatic, action-oriented account of the second. But two minor qualifications can be made. First, there are qualitative differences also within the Patusan narrative. The longish and monotonous writing of Chapter 30, for instance, is distinctly inferior to that of some other chapters (such as 34); and this in spite of the fact that Marlow attempts to justify the excessive length of the previous chapter in the opening of Chapter 31. Secondly, Marlow's reflections and doubts are not entirely absent from this sequence either; compare such observations as 'All this, as I've warned you, gets dwarfed in the telling' (272) and 'To tell this story is by no means so easy as it should be—were the ordinary standpoint adequate' (275). But it must be granted that the reflections seem more conspicuously superimposed and less successfully integrated than in the first half of the novel.

IV

At the beginning of Chapter 36 the oral narrative situation with Marlow as narrator to his pensive, almost silent verandah audience dissolves: 'Each of them seemed to carry away his own impression, to carry it away with him like a secret' (337). There is a twofold implication of this authorial comment on Marlow's narratees. First, we seem invited to regard their patience (Marlow's narrative has

---

[51] CNC 309.

been very long) and absence of objections as an indication that they are deeply moved by Marlow's tale and inclined both to accept its content and to assent to his accompanying reflections and interpretations. But as a corollary to this tacit invitation, there is the authorial suggestion that the impressions of the story vary, as do, one would assume, their interpretations. This suggestion does not exactly contradict the first implication, but it modifies it by reducing further the stability of the thematics generated by the narrative structure. The implication also embeds some subtly presented guidelines for the reader's response; the authorial narrator seems to be saying that it is impossible to get a complete impression of Jim or to understand him fully.

With regard to narrative method, an important feature is that the authorial narrator of the novel's opening is reintroduced at this point. Some readers and critics would say that his reappearance is belated, or at least that the oral narrative situation is becoming strained because of its length and the wealth of material it contains.[52] If part of the function of the authorial narrator is to modify Marlow's personal account (there is no indication of his contradicting it), this is done only implicitly, by reminding the reader that the novel contains a narrative instance supervening, and more knowledgeable than, its principal personal narrator. However, the omniscience of the authorial narrator is much less pointed now than it was in the early, pre-Marlow descriptions of Jim. The authorial narrator's function here is essentially an editorial one: he introduces the reader to 'the privileged man' (337) and outlines the contents of the packet this anonymous character has received from Marlow. The introductory description (in the second and third paragraphs) of this recipient of the concluding, though certainly not conclusive, information about Jim is very suggestive. In spite of obvious differences, both character and setting call Stein strikingly to mind. The resigned wisdom of the anonymous character is vividly evoked, and intensified through narrated monologue ('The hour was striking! No more! No more!—' (338)), while the imagery reveals some constituent aspects of his past experience ('and his glance could travel afar beyond the clear panes of glass, as though he were looking out of the lantern of a lighthouse' (337)). This portrayal of the 'privileged man' substantiates the narrative's subtle manipulation of the reader's response—as

---

[52] Cf. Conrad's claims to the contrary in his 'Author's Note' to the novel, p. vii.

readers we are being asked to be as wise and nuanced in our response to the story as he is supposed to be.

Before discussing Marlow's written narrative it is necessary to make a few observations on the three other constitutive parts of the packet. There is, first, the brief mention of Jim's attempt at a letter to his father, from 'The Fort, Patusan' (340). Marlow's explanation of why this letter was never sent indicates that his importance as narrator is not severely reduced by the reintroduction of the authorial narrator. Attention is drawn to his personal and necessarily limited perspective, but basically he retains his key function as commentator and interpreter. The comment on the letter is consistent enough with Marlow's earlier reflections, '[Jim] was overwhelmed by the inexplicable; he was overwhelmed by his own personality' (341). In one sense Suresh Raval is right to assert that even such a negating or negative explanation is indicative of some sort of narrative authority, a 'contingent authority' which he usefully distinguishes from an 'absolute' one.[53] However, to be tenable as a descriptive term for Marlow's narrative function, 'contingent authority' must be adjusted to accommodate his epistemological uncertainty, which Raval tends to underestimate.

Secondly, the packet contains 'a very old letter' (341) to Jim from his father. The fact that this letter is from the time before Jim joined the *Patna* strengthens the novel's narrative focus on Jim, and also increases the thematic links between the *Patna* and Patusan. Claiming that the letter contains nothing 'except just affection' (341), Marlow is surprisingly quick to dismiss it, and refrains from giving it in full as one would perhaps expect him to do. For Mary Sullivan, Marlow's narration here is an example of *paralipsis*, 'a deliberate passing over with brief mention so as to emphasize the importance of what is omitted; feigning to pass it by and thereby stressing it'.[54] It is true that the narrative here provokes us to inquire, with Sullivan, about Marlow's reason for dismissing the letter. But if we go on to regard the dismissal as indicative of its importance, then we refuse to accept Marlow's explanation, and it is doubtful whether we are in a position to do so here.

---

[53] Suresh Raval, 'Narrative and Authority in *Lord Jim*: Conrad's Art of Failure,' *ELH* 48 (1981), 398. Cf. his illuminating ch. on this novel in *The Art of Failure*, 45–72.

[54] Mary Sullivan, 'Conrad's Paralipses in the Narration of *Lord Jim*', *Conradiana*, 10 (1978), 124.

A different matter is that Marlow's explanatory letter, which is the third enclosure, reveals the characteristic mixture of self-assurance and doubt concerning the legitimacy and adequacy of his presentation:

'My information was fragmentary, but I've fitted the pieces together, and there is enough of them to make an intelligible picture. I wonder how he would have related it himself. He has confided so much in me that at times it seems as though he must come in presently and tell the story in his own words...' (343)

This reflective comment reaffirms the picture of Marlow as investigator, but it also contains the suggestion of personal colouring (through Jim) of the written material, and by implication possibly of all of Marlow's narrative.

The explanatory letter includes Chapter 37, which abruptly introduces Brown and, in an analepsis extending over some pages, recounts Marlow's unexpected encounter with Jewel at Stein's house. Her despairing accusations against Jim and white men in general ('He has left me... you always leave us—for your own ends' (348)) ironically echo Jim's earlier unannounced departures from his former employers. However, the main effect of her outbursts, and Stein's attempt to comfort her, is to mystify the reader and to create suspense as to what can have happened to upset the apparent stability of Jim's Patusan rule.

With the opening of Chapter 38, Marlow's final written narrative starts by outlining Brown's background, and goes on to give a rather condensed and predominantly chronological account of the dramatic incidents that end with Jim's death and Jewel's grief. One remarkable aspect of the narrative method of this section is that Marlow claims to have derived the information directly from the dying Brown:

'I am sorry that I can't give you this part of the story, which of course I have mainly from Brown, in Brown's own words. There was in the broken, violent speech of that man, unveiling before me his thoughts with the very hand of Death upon his throat, an undisguised ruthlessness of purpose...' (369–70)

It is of course most unlikely that a dying person should be able to provide Marlow with such a wealth of detailed information—some of which is surprisingly neutral as well. Yet this artificiality is after all just an additional one, following, for instance, the unlikelihood of Marlow's encounters with some of his informants (such as the French lieutenant) and the unnatural length of the oral narrative. As reported by Marlow, Brown's narration seems to have been peculiarly intense; and this quality is not wholly eliminated by Marlow's editing comments and additions. Brown's psychopathic hatred is convincingly rendered; and the indirect self-characterization which filters through Brown's information also adds credence to Marlow's view of him. Thus the question of Marlow's ambivalent attitude to his sources is focused on once again. On the one hand, he seems to regard it as a strength of his narrative that the information comes from a main character. On the other hand, he makes reservations, almost excuses, regarding the biased and subjective account this fact results in: 'It is impossible to say how much he lied to Jim then, how much he lied to me now—and to himself always. Vanity plays lurid tricks with our memory, and the truth of every passion wants some pretence to make it live' (383). The last part of the quotation is particularly interesting, since its implications seem not to be limited to this sequence, but also to extend to the other parts of Marlow's narrative. This particular sentence, then, gives a more distinctly thematic dimension to the problem of narrative reliability.

The vividness of the portrayal of Brown is balanced by Marlow's understandable need to distance himself from him. Even such distancing manoeuvres, however, appear suffused with Marlow's doubting scepticism, as in the thoughts he expresses on hearing of Brown's brutally calculated murder of Jim's men:

'Thus Brown balanced his account with the evil fortune. Notice that even in this awful outbreak there is a superiority as of a man who carries right—the abstract thing—within the envelope of his common desires. It was not a vulgar and treacherous massacre; it was a lesson, a retribution—a demonstration of some obscure and awful attribute of our nature which, I am afraid, is not so very far under the surface as we like to think.' (404)

In spite of the theoretical reservations one can voice against comparison of Marlow's various functions in different Conrad texts, it is tempting to emphasize (building on Chapter 2 above) the resemblance which the conclusion of this passage bears to Marlow's reflections in 'Heart of Darkness'. It is certainly true, as Berthoud notes,[55] that in relation to 'Heart of Darkness' there is a shift from

[55] *CMP* 65.

the narrator to the protagonist in *Lord Jim*, and that Marlow's scepticism and disillusionment in 'Heart of Darkness' make a stronger impression because both follow more directly and unavoidably from his own painful experience. At the same time, the Marlow of *Lord Jim* is also an experienced and shrewd person. Moreover, in several of his reflections he goes far to identify himself with Jim, and even, as here, with the dark sides of human nature that underlie the atrocities of such a character as Brown. Generally, Marlow's combined functions as narrator and character are difficult to keep separate in *Lord Jim*, but in this quotation his disillusionment as character and human being is forcefully presented.

In the last chapter of the novel two aspects of Marlow's narrative function must be emphasized. First, through the widening of the narrative perspective the Patusan episode is brought into closer relation to the first part of the novel. Again, Marlow not only writes about the almost ritualistic execution of Jim by Doramin; he also adds comments that are clearly interpretative and that move far beyond the information Brown can possibly have given him. These interpretative thoughts, however, are not only more directly centred on Jim than previously; they are also fittingly conclusive for a last chapter. Jim's recognition of his defeat is well rendered, through a subtly sliding narrative movement which concisely brings together his adult life, slanting from direct narrative statement into narrated monologue:

'Then Jim understood. He had retreated from one world, for a small matter of an impulsive jump, and now the other, the work of his own hands, had fallen in ruins upon his head. It was not safe for his servant to go out amongst his own people!' (408)

It must added, though, that in this chapter too the quality of the prose is uneven. There are other passages which unnecessarily add to the melodrama of the ending, such as 'She sobbed on his shoulder. The sky over Patusan was blood-red, immense, streaming like an open vein' (413).

The second aspect to be stressed revolves around the final three paragraphs of the novel. It is striking how Marlow, through his questions and final reflections, manages to make the ending much more open than it would have been had it ended with the terse account of the execution itself. Returning to his sense of kinship with Jim, and to the privileged reader, Marlow's last reflections bring together his earlier contradictions and doubts; and the fact that they are not followed by any framing authorial remarks adds to Marlow's textual authority.

In an analysis of such an exceptionally complex literary text as *Lord Jim*, the distinction between critical commentary and interpretation becomes blurred indeed. The textual commentary presented here goes far to justify a sceptical attitude towards short, and often overtly thematic, interpretations of the novel: such critical contributions tend to simplify the book's thematics because its narrative is improperly considered. Once this criticism is made, however, it becomes the more difficult to conclude this chapter. Moreover, as Miller observes, 'When *Lord Jim* is approached from the perspective of its narrative structure and its design of recurrent images it reveals itself to be not less but more problematic, more inscrutable, like Jim himself.'[56] There is, then, a twofold sense in which a concluding statement about *Lord Jim* is complicated: the novel's narrative method needs to be carefully considered, but the more closely the text is studied the more problematic it seems. There is also a theoretical and hermeneutic issue involved here: it is debatable to what extent a short conclusion (and conclusions have to be short) can do justice to the wide range of narrative functions and variations observable in Conrad's fiction.

Still, I shall suggest three concluding comments on the narrative method of *Lord Jim*. First, we return to Miller's notion of Marlow's narrative project in *Lord Jim* as suspect, revolving round the word 'doubt'—'the doubt of the sovereign power enthroned in a fixed standard of conduct'. There is certainly a sense in which Marlow's narrative project is suspect—and not only for Marlow himself but by implication for the reader too. However, Marlow's doubt is not stable or constant; on the contrary, it gradually increases. The harder Marlow attempts to understand Jim, the more enigmatic Jim appears. As the understanding of Jim's motives and action is closely related to Marlow's ideas of origin, direction, coherence, and 'sovereign power', the novel's gradual revelation of the impossibility of understanding these motives and actions serves not only to increase its scepticism, but furthers also a radical change in Marlow's existential orientation, epistemology, and personal convictions.

---

[56] Miller, *Fiction and Repetition*, 31.

In order to specify this change, Miller's notion of Marlow's narrative project as suspect needs to be combined with his distinction between two forms of repetition in narrative fiction. As briefly mentioned in the Introduction to this book, this distinction refers to two more thematic, complex forms of repetition. Building on Gilles Deleuze, Miller differentiates between a 'Platonic' form of repetition which is relatively simple, based on an archetypal model and presupposing a fundamental 'ground' and identity, and a 'Nietzschean' mode of repetition which is more disillusioned in assuming that no such ground exists, but that each thing is in fact unique, intrinsically different from every other thing.[57] There is a certain affinity, then, between the belief in, or need for, 'the sovereign power' and the first form of repetition. One of the most intriguing aspects of the narrative and thematic developmet of *Lord Jim* is that Marlow's interest in Jim seems correlated with a loss of belief in the sovereign power: having been, at the outset of his narrative, suspended between the first and second forms of repetition (and probably closer to the first), he is gradually forced—as a result of the conclusions he has to draw because of his involvement in Jim's case—into a position broadly conforming to the second form of repetition.

I would suggest that Miller's understanding of *Lord Jim* as an interesting literary manifestation of the second form of repetition may usefully be specified by way of reference to Marlow's combined function as narrator and character. Much of Marlow's compelling force as a narrator derives from his movement—a movement necessitated or provoked by the narrative he presents and the

---

[57] Cf. ch. 1 n. 22. In Gilles Deleuze's *Logique du sens* (Paris: Les Éditions de Minuit, 1969), two alternative theories of repetition are set against each other by way of opposing Nietzsche's concept of repetition to that of Plato: 'Let us consider two formulations: "only that which resembles itself differs", "only differences resemble one another" ["*seul ce qui se ressemble diffère*", "*seules les différences se ressemblent*"]. It is a question of two readings of the world in the sense that one asks us to think of difference on the basis of pre-established similitude or identity, while the other invites us on the contrary to think of similitude and even identity as the product of a fundamental disparity [*d'une disparité de fond*]. The first exactly defines the world of copies or of representations; it establishes the world as icon. The second, against the first, defines the world of simulacra. It presents the world itself as phantasm.' *Logique du sens*, 302; Miller's translation, *Fiction and Repetition*, 5–6. For a more extended presentation and application of the two forms of repetition, see my 'Repetition and Narrative Method: Hardy, Conrad, Faulkner', in Jeremy Hawthorn (ed.), *Narrative: From Malory to Motion Pictures* (London: Edward Arnold, 1985), 116–31.

interest in Jim which it documents—from the first to the second form of repetition. As Marlow's doubt of Jim's belief in the sovereign power is related to his own, the thematic association of this shared doubt with the possibility (or threat) of loss of ground, direction, and coherence not only enhances the complexity of Jim as a character, but also makes the relationship between main narrator and main character more compelling and unpredictable. It is important to recognize the extent to which this exceptionally productive thematic association is dependent not only on the characteristics and modulations of Marlow's activity as a narrator, but also on the way in which his narrative is related to both the surrounding authorial narrative and his pensive narratees.

The second concluding point is closely connected with the first. Although there are several ways in which a strong scepticism permeates *Lord Jim*, this thematic aspect should not make us overlook or denigrate (as some critics have tended to do) the 'simpler' or more 'positive' elements of the thematics of the novel. What is essential here is to emphasize the value of human friendship as dramatized in *Lord Jim*. Now it could certainly be argued that Marlow's interest in, if not obsession with, Jim is the factor which initiated his process of disillusionment. As in 'Heart of Darkness', increased insight and understanding are here too connected with a pervasive scepticism and resignation of the kind which the second form of repetition may imply. Yet these fundamental, existential problems augment the value, even the necessity, of friendship. The reasons for this are obvious enough—few would dispute that friendship is one of the most unproblematically positive assets of human existence. Conrad's fiction, however, also suggests more specific reasons for the human need for friendship. Part of its great importance is suggested by the way in which friendship is linked to human activity in Conrad. A related reason why it is so essential is that it can serve as a means of withstanding the constant threat of moral and existential isolation. Friendship is a variant on the human contact Conradian characters need in order not to succumb to the pressures of alienation, which in the author's major works is repeatedly portrayed as external and objectively present. Especially if prone to intellectual scepticism, Conrad's characters cannot cope with this alienation unless they are part of some form of human community. The most obvious example here is, as we shall see in the next chapter, the authorial description of Decoud as he approaches his suicide off the Great Isabel, but for Jim too the contact and friendship with Marlow are very precious, and perhaps most clearly evinced in their hotel conversation. Although I agree with Berthoud that Marlow's function as a character is less significant in *Lord Jim* than in 'Heart of Darkness', still he is, in the sense described here, crucially important for at least two of the most essential aspects of the thematics of *Lord Jim*: the movement towards the second form of repetition on the one hand, and, in part to counteract this movement, the importance of friendship on the other. Paradoxically, the inexplicable friendship with Jim which initiates Marlow's slanting movement towards the second form of repetition becomes particularly important as a means of withstanding the (possibly disastrous) personal consequences of this movement. At the same time, the friendship of two main characters whose existential and epistemological orientation approach the second form of repetition could be seen as accentuating the tragic dimension of the novel.

This penultimate observation blends into the third concluding comment to be made. Arguably, the narrative and thematic centrality of Marlow in *Lord Jim* is reinforced by the authorial frame in which his narrative is placed. It seems appropriate that the novel ends with Marlow's last reflections. They are focused on both the aspects stressed here: his sense of kinship with Jim and his far-reaching doubts. *Lord Jim* does not exhibit the kind of overt contrast observable between the first and second narrators in 'Heart of Darkness'. In *Lord Jim* Marlow's narrative is presented and edited by an authorial narrator, but the fact that this apparently omniscient narrator largely refrains from imposing evaluative judgements on Marlow can be interpreted as another indication of the narrative and thematic authority of Marlow as a personal narrator with an original and productive authorial function.

10

Nostromo:
Panoramic, All-Inclusive Authorial
Narrative

Though in rather different ways, the narrative complexity of
Nostromo (1904) is as exceptional as that of *Lord Jim*. The sheer
size the novel—the number of important characters, the long time
period covered, the significance of setting and history, the complicated political environment and changes, and the wide range of
thematic preoccupation—all this not only makes the task of anything approaching an exhaustive interpretation appear impossible,
but also complicates the choice of prefatory observations and makes
the problem of critical selection and angle a difficult one. When
J. A. Verleun, in his book on the *minor* characters in *Nostromo*,
justifies his 320-page study by noting, in his preface, that his aim
'has been to show that the major characters of *Nostromo* cannot be
fully understood without detailed analysis of the minor characters',[1]
then one begins to wonder about the scope of criticism, but in one
sense he is certainly right.

It follows that a problem for any critic discussing the narrative
method of *Nostromo* is where to begin; a related problem is what to
include, and how to grade and evaluate the different narrative
devices and functions in relation to one another. A first impression
is that the thematic concern with narrative observable in *Lord Jim* is
absent from *Nostromo*. On the other hand, one of the peculiarities
of *Nostromo* is that first impressions are altered, even radically, as
rereading helps one towards a fuller understanding of the work. As
regards this Conrad text, too, it would seem that rereading is not
only advantageous, but necessary. To substantiate this claim one
might refer to the novel's opening, which on a first reading seems
long-drawn-out, strangely static, and to many so tedious that they
put the book down, but which on a second (and even on a third or
fourth) reading becomes increasingly interesting and impressive:

---

[1] J. A. Verleun, *The Stone Horse: A Study of the Function of the Minor Characters in Joseph Conrad's Nostromo* (Groningen: Bouma's Boekhuis, 1978), p. xii.

anticipatory, dense, suggestive, in short masterly. The higher appreciation which rereading furthers is, to specify the point, dependent on our gradual realization that the book's narrative method is not only more sophisticated, but also more productive than at first sight.

Because, as already indicated, the complexity of *Nostromo* is of a different kind from that of *Lord Jim*, the structure of this chapter is somewhat different from that of the preceding one. We have seen that in *Lord Jim* there is a wide-ranging intrinsic narrative variation, particularly of perspective and voice, both of which are intimately related to the key function of Marlow as unifying and editing narrative device. In *Nostromo* the formal narrative variations are less remarkable, since they are all subsumed under the all-inclusive, omniscient voice of the text's authorial narrator. This is not to suggest that the variations of the book's narrative method are unimportant, but they do not seem to necessitate the kind of detailed commentary required by *Lord Jim*. On the other hand, *Nostromo* throws the spotlight on complex problems which in one sense may appear obviously thematic, but which, this chapter argues, bear an important, though more indirect, relation to narrative method. In the light of the above introductory comments it is not surprising that several of the most influential studies of the novel have tended to concentrate on its very interesting thematics.[2] Although my contribution is intended as a supplement, and partly also as a corrective, to these studies, it must be remembered that this study is sceptical about discussions of narrative that become exclusively or narrowly technical. As my critical concern is instead to employ the narrative variations identified in the text as a basis for thematic generalizations, including observations on the intriguing relationship between narrative method and thematics in Conrad, the following tripartite structure of this chapter on *Nostromo* can be proposed.

First, the chapter provides a relatively brief commentary on the narrative method of the novel. The combination of the commentary's shortness and the novel's complexity unavoidably entails

---

[2] See *CN* 175–217; *CWD* 113–43; *CMP* 94–130; Avrom Fleishman, *Conrad's Politics: Community and Anarchy in the Fiction of Joseph Conrad* (Baltimore: Johns Hopkins University Press, 1967), 161–84; and Juliet McLauchlan, *Conrad: Nostromo* (London: Edward Arnold, 1969). An exceptionally perceptive thematically-oriented essay is Joyce Carol Oates, ' "The Immense Indifference of Things": The Tragedy of Conrad's *Nostromo*', *Novel*, 9 (1975), 5–22.

simplifications and omissions: an exhaustive commentary would require its own full-length study (cf. the above reference to Verleun). The commentary attempts to focus on observations and points which, in addition to their own narrative and thematic import, serve to constitute the critical basis for the chapter's following two parts. If the comments on Decoud are more detailed than those on the other main characters, this is ascribable to the crucial function Decoud performs not only as character, but also as a narrative device which serves to modify and extend the authorial narrative of the novel. The second part then lists and briefly discusses narrative characteristics and problems of *Nostromo*. Finally, I shall relate my observations and tentative conclusions to some of the most interesting thematic generalizations which have been made about the novel: this critical comparison will make it possible to specify the conclusions of the chapter.

I

Setting is exeptionally important in *Nostromo*: it might be suggested that in spite of the large number of important characters the protagonist proper is the town of Sulaco, with its historical characteristics and changes.[3] This emphasis on setting is especially striking in the opening chapter, which begins by giving a broad description of the area, then gradually 'zooming in' on Sulaco as setting of the subsequent action. However, this narrowing of perspective is not obvious until in Chapter 2; the first chapter is a general, panoramic introduction to Costaguana.

The novel's slow, extremely detailed opening has been much criticized;[4] and it is certainly confusing, even trying, on a first reading. If we are unaware of the principal issues the novel explores then we cannot see how relevant and well-calculated the opening description is. We are unable, for instance, to note how fitting it is that the first chapter should be unspecified temporally. In actual

---

[3] Going even further, Arnold Bennett, writing to Conrad about *Nostromo* in 1912, underlined the abiding presence of the mountain of Higuerota: 'the said mountain [is] the principal personage in the story'. Here quoted from Edward Said, *Beginnings: Intention and Method* (New York: Basic Books, 1975), 123. Cf. my comments on Higuerota below.

[4] See, for instance, *CN* 211–15.

fact, this lack of temporal specification accords with the novel's description of human beings as curiously vulnerable, only partly and insufficiently able to understand themselves, and with a corresponding want of control over the consequences of their own actions. Neither can we, on a first reading, appreciate the prolepsis about later thematic concerns of the novel which the opening incorporates. For in Chapter 1 the authorial narrator already anticipates, in his omniscience and inclination towards generalization (two important characteristics of his already observable here), some of the novel's major emphases. On page 7, for instance, we are told about the 'blind darkness' of the gulf. Rereading the opening, these words make us think of Nostromo and Decoud with the silver in the lighter, passing 'out between almost invisible headlands into the still deeper darkness of the gulf' (261). Furthermore, what we hear about tragedies in past searches for treasure serves as an ominous prolepsis of the effect of the silver mine on the inhabitants of Sulaco; more specifically, the 'fatal spell' of the 'success' (5) of American adventurers inevitably makes us think of the fate of Nostromo.

Although the beginning of *Nostromo* is overtly panoramic, and presented through the authoritative, all-embracing voice of the omniscient authorial narrator, human beings are conspicuously absent from the book's opening descriptions. The focus on Sulaco in Chapter 2, however, is correlated with the introduction of Captain Mitchell. It is structurally significant that Mitchell is the first character we encounter; the form of his recollections here is similar to that in Chapter 10 of Part Third. Mitchell's frequent use of the epithet 'sir' serves to characterize this form—simplifying and naïvely boasting recollections which nevertheless contain useful information. It is at this stage of the narrative that the dictator Ribiera's pathetic arrival in Sulaco is mentioned for the first time. This incident is later referred to on several occasions and functions as a reference point in the temporal period within which the main action of the novel takes place. It is here, too, that one of the first examples of authorial irony occurs, in the added sub-clause: 'where the military band plays sometimes in the evenings between the revolutions' (11). Overall, the function of irony is extremely complex in *Nostromo*; and a second reading discloses many more ironies than are initially detected. For example, when Mitchell somewhat later informs his visitor that 'This Nostromo, sir, a man absolutely

above reproach, became the terror of all the thieves in the town'
(13), this is naturally first read as a piece of factual information
about a character obviously admired by Mitchell. The ironic implications are only appreciated when we learn that Nostromo's own
theft brings terror upon himself. Mitchell's casual conversation
conceals ironic prefigurations of the novel's ending.

From this point on, the narrative, instead of progressing forward
in time in the conventional manner, spirals backward, providing a
wealth of information about past events, until in Chapter 8 we are
told more about the nature of Ribiera's position. On a first and even
a second reading, this backward narrative movement is confusing
indeed. Only gradually, and on a first reading belatedly, do we
realize how closely Ribiera's humiliating defeat is related to the
complex evolution of action in *Nostromo*. The establishment of his
puppet dictatorship depends on the support of Charles Gould. As
Cedric Watts's helpful chronology of the novel's central events
suggests,[5] its beginning can be set at May 1888. As administrator of
the rich San Tomé silver mine, Gould uses its wealth to manipulate
the state apparatus of Costaguana in his own interests and the
interests of the foreign capital invested in the mine, notably that of
the American millionaire Holroyd. Ribiera's defeat, however, is the
result of an unpredicted consequence: as his dictatorship implies a
pledge to serve the cause of the mine, it engenders another revolution in Costaguana. Less than a year after his inauguration, Ribiera
is defeated by General Montero and flees to Sulaco where, on his
arrival, he is rescued from Montero's supporters by Nostromo and
the railwaymen he leads. Thus Ribiera's defeat is correlated with
the beginning of a war of separation which, after a turbulent period
within which most of the dramatic action of the novel takes place,
results in the emergence of the independent state of Sulaco.

It must be stressed that such a crude outline does not pretend to
summarize the action of *Nostromo*; it merely indicates its main
pattern or direction and relates it to the fate of a minor character,
Ribiera. The essential point to make at this stage of our discussion is
that even this main pattern is distorted in Part First. The effect is
paradoxical because, as already indicated, the detailed scenic
descriptions early in 'The Silver of the Mine' become much more
suggestive when read in the light of the total action the novel

---

[5] Cedric Watts, *A Preface to Conrad* (London: Longman 1982), 162–3.

dramatizes. Important aspects of this action are more systematically prefigured and foregrounded here than in more conventional narratives with less chronological distortion.

This observation applies in particular to the analeptic narrative movement of Chapters 2 to 8. Watts suggests four reasons for this extended 'deviousness' of the novel; and they are all so relevant to an analysis of narrative method that I shall list them and comment briefly on them. First, Watts observes that 'this technique gives an unusual plausibility to the fictional historical events [which thereby acquire] a stereoscopic quality'.[6] The textual evidence supporting this point is convincing enough: much later in the novel (in Chapter 7 of Part Second) Decoud writes to his sister that 'You should also have learned from the cable that the missing President, Ribiera, who had disappeared after the battle of Sta. Marta, has turned up here in Sulaco by one of those strange coincidences that are almost incredible' (224).

Secondly, Watts points out that the long, analeptic detour of the text gives some of its ironies 'a radical and tentacular quality'.[7] Reading about Ribiera's inaugural banquet in Chapter 5, for instance, we can appreciate the irony which arises from the contrast between the imposing posture of the 'President-Dictator' (34, 35) here and his humiliating arrival (which we already know of) in Sulaco the following year. To rephrase Watts's observation: an early prolepsis enables the reader to estimate rightly the irony embedded in an extended analepsis.

Thirdly, as Jocelyn Baines has noted and other commentators seconded,[8] the analepsis suggests both that history is cyclical or repetitive and that history displays a steady evolution which cannot be halted. The second suggestion is clearly related to another which presents itself forcefully, and which Watts phrases thus: 'in the long run the success of men's schemes depends on the compatibility of those schemes with international economic forces'.[9] Yet it tells us something about the sceptical and paradoxical qualities of the novel that even this suggestion, which receives a great deal of textual support from the alliance of Mr Gould and Holroyd and the

[6] Ibid. 152.

[7] Ibid.

[8] Jocelyn Baines, *Joseph Conrad: A Critical Biography* (Harmondsworth: Penguin, 1971), orig. publ. 1960, 358–63.

[9] Watts, *Preface*, 147.

enormous influence and power of the silver mine, is strongly qualified, if not withdrawn, at the end of the narrative. Part of the qualification is prefigured in the explicit characterization the authorial narrator gives of Holroyd. As so often, the characterization takes the form of a quotation followed by an authorial comment:

'We shall run the world's business whether the world likes it or not. The world can't help it—and neither can we, I guess.'

By this he meant to express his faith in destiny in words suitable to his intelligence, which was unskilled in the presentation of general ideas. His intelligence was nourished on facts; and Charles Gould, whose imagination had been permanently affected by the one great fact of a silver mine, had no objection to this theory of the world's future. (77)

Even on a first reading we notice the relatively light, humorous irony of this passage. Yet when rereading it we realize that it also contains more serious and sombre implications. Although it could be argued that the mine proves to have a more damaging influence on the novel's characters (particularly Mr Gould and Nostromo) than on Sulaco, still there is no doubt that its total impact on the town is not only immense, but also partly detrimental; and neither can we doubt, on the basis of the passage just quoted, that Holroyd's ability to foresee these effects is poor indeed. Limited ability is here virtually indistinguishable from lack of human care: the overriding motive of profit-making is basically simple, and disturbing side-effects can all too easily be toned down or rationalized. A related implication is that Holroyd's simplicity is closely connected with his efficiency as a capitalist; moreover, this kind of simplicity does not, the narrative of *Nostromo* shows, preclude the possibility of understanding people well enough to use, or misuse, them. This last implication becomes clearer later in the chapter, in an authorial comment which modulates towards narrated monologue: '[Holroyd] was not running a great enterprise there; no mere railway board or industrial corporation. He was running a man!' (81).

Let us return to Watts's four reasons for the narrative obliquity of Part First. He finally points out that the various time-shifts are valuable '*as resistances to be overcome*',[10] and that they spark off, or at least encourage, constructive moral and political thought.

---

[10] Ibid. 153.

There is much to be said for this view of the time-shifts in the novel, and rereading supports it. My only doubt centres on the content or essence of the novel's ultimate 'vision':[11] is it not perhaps too sceptical and disillusioned to be constructive? Does not the reader's movement towards a full understanding of *Nostromo* seem to be correlated with one towards resignation, at a deep and general level? These two questions, both in part prompted by narrative analysis, are one way of specifying an important aspect of the novel's thematics.

The repeated references to Nostromo early in the novel lead the reader to infer that he must be one of its main characters. In the opening of Chapter 4 he is described by the authorial narrator directly, and here the narrator's omniscience is indicated through the use of quoted monologue: ' "If I see smoke rising over there," he thought to himself, "they are lost" ' (22). However, the most remarkable paragraph of this chapter does not deal with Nostromo but is related to a minor character, Giorgio, who witnesses a battle of the riot. This passage is so central to the authorial narrative method of *Nostromo* that it deserves to be quoted in full and considered more closely:

On this memorable day of the riot his arms were not folded on his chest. His hand grasped the barrel of the gun grounded on the threshold; he did not look up once at the white dome of Higuerota, whose cool purity seemed to hold itself aloof from a hot earth. His eyes examined the plain curiously. Tall trails of dust subsided here and there. In a speckless sky the sun hung clear and blinding. Knots of men ran headlong; others made a stand; and the irregular rattle of firearms came rippling to his ears in the fiery, still air. Single figures on foot raced desperately. Horsemen galloped towards each other, wheeled round together, separated at speed. Giorgio saw one fall, rider and horse disappearing as if they had galloped into a chasm, and the movements of the animated scene were like the passages of a violent game played upon the plain by dwarfs mounted and on foot, yelling with tiny throats, under the mountain that seemed a colossal embodiment of silence. Never before had Giorgio seen this bit of plain so full of active life; his gaze could not take in all its details at once; he shaded his eyes with his hand, till suddenly the thundering of many hoofs near by startled him. (26–7)

The passage is not only exceptionally dense and evocative; its narrative devices are also combined in a manner which complicates

[11] Watts, *Preface*, 153.

systematic critical commentary upon it. Still, the following four observations can be made. First, although related to Giorgio, the voice and panoramic perspective of the authorial narrator are very noticeable in this generalized description of war. This is not to suggest that the personal colouring is unimportant; on the contrary, it enhances both the visual intensity and the thematic suggestiveness of the description. Giorgio's 'eyes examined the plain curiously... his gaze could not take in all its details at once'. The description is made more reverberant thematically through the implication that Giorgio is surprised, bewildered, even frightened, by the sight exposed to him. He might have participated in the battle himself; seen from afar it makes an astonishingly different impression on him.

Secondly, there is an interesting approximation of authorial and personal perspective in the passage. At first Giorgio's eyes are fixed on the plain: 'he did not look up once at the white dome of Higuerota, whose cool purity seemed to hold itself aloof from a hot earth'. However, in the second reference to Higuerota—'the mountain that seemed a colossal embodiment of silence'—the two perspectives appear closer, though they do not coalesce. It is as though the authorial narrator is attempting, using the opportunity provided by Giorgio's temporary detachment from the violent activities of the riot, to give him a sense of the absurdity and futility of war.

Thirdly, the predominant image in this passage provides perhaps the best example in the Conrad canon of the narrative device the Russian formalists labelled 'defamiliarization'. According to Victor Shklovsky, the process of defamiliarization consists of making something familar appear unfamiliar and strange through the combination of selected linguistic and narrative devices.[12] For Giorgio, like most inhabitants of Costaguana, war is all too familiar. But from this particular vantage point 'the movements of the animated scene were like the passages of a violent game played upon the plain by dwarfs mounted and on foot, yelling with tiny throats'. Giorgio's spatial distance from the fighting activities, combined with the large plain and, especially, the enormous Higuerota, make the battle look like 'a violent game played... by dwarfs': through this metaphoric

---

[12] See Victor Shklovsky, 'Art as Technique', in Lemon and Reis (eds.), *Russian Formalist Criticism*, 13 and *passim*. A great number of Conrad's narrative devices and variations have a defamiliarizing effect.

substitution the absurdity of the killing is accentuated, for Giorgio and by implication for the reader too. The contrast between the activity on the plain and the silent Higuerota contributes decisively to the defamiliarizing effect.

Higuerota can be interpreted both as a metaphor and as a symbol. If we, following Umberto Eco, look in the 'encyclopedia' constituted by this passage 'for some other sememe that possibly shares some of the focused properties of the first sememe(s) while displaying other, *interestingly different* properties',[13] we notice that the first, 'metaphorizing sememe' ('vehicle') is in itself complex, constituted by the elements 'colossal embodiment' and 'silence'. Although Higuerota as a new sememe shares some of the properties of the first sememes, it is sufficiently different from them to ensure its candidature 'for the role of metaphorized sememe (*tenor*)'.[14] Interestingly, however, as we consider the properties of Higuerota as metaphorized sememe, the complexity of the metaphorizing sememes not only serves to make the new sememe more complex, but also accentuates the metaphor's symbolic implications. As a symbol Higuerota not only represents—in a manner partly comparable to the sea in Conrad's fiction—stable, awesome, and majestic nature. It can also, as Edward Said puts it, be seen as symbolizing Conrad's 'desperate search in his personal life for Higuerota's positive qualities of consistency, power, and unity'.[15] Such a symbolic reading is related to a shift of critical emphasis, from textual commentary on narrative to more thematic interpretation. As Eco says, 'The symbolic mode is thus not only a mode of producing a text, but also a mode for interpreting every text— through a pragmatic decision: "I want to interpret this text symbolically." '[16] However, though there is much to be said for this view of the symbol as 'a modality of textual *use*',[17] it should be noted that the symbolic implications of some of the central metaphors of *Nostromo* (such as the strangely anthropomorphic Higuerota and, even more obviously, the silver and the mine) are indicated very

---

13 Eco, *Semiotics and the Philosophy of Language*, 123. 'Sememe' is the term Eco usefully substitutes for the more traditional 'tenor' and 'vehicle'. Cf. ch. 6 n. 4.
14 Ibid.
15 Said, *Beginnings*, 123. There are two helpful reviews of Said's important study (by Hillis Miller and Hayden White) in *Diacritics*, 6 (1976), 2–13.
16 Eco, *Semiotics and the Philosophy of Language*, 163.
17 Ibid.

clearly through the narrative method of the novel. This is done partly through repetition, partly through the application of the metaphors to the main thematic focuses as they are developed, and ironically modified, in the course of the narrative.

The final comment to be made on this passage concerns the noun 'details': Giorgio's 'gaze could not take in all [the plain's] details at once'. Like most of the characters in the novel, Giorgio is confused by the wealth of fragmented details of the life into which he is thrown, but at this point his distance from the activities makes him more aware of his confusion than he normally is. More indirectly, 'details' as used here also indicate an aspect of the method of the panoramic, chronologically distorted narrative in Part First: the reader's ability to understand Giorgio's confusion is enhanced by his or her own bewilderment by the wealth of detail in the novel's dramatized presentation of a country's history.

Although the narrative structure of this passage is particularly dense, narrative and thematic complexity can still be seen as a characteristic of *Nostromo* as a whole; and this exceptional textual complexity necessitates critical selection of the aspects of narrative to be commented on. One important narrative aspect established in Part First is that the authorial narrator frequently comments on the action and characters he presents. An example occurs early in Chapter 6: 'The inference was true. Its deeper meaning was hidden from their simple intelligence' (45). This authorial remark indicates how different levels of insight are combined in *Nostromo*. The explicit, almost crude character of the comment is not untypical of the novel's authorial narrator. Throughout the book there is a marked distance in insight and understanding between the narrator and the different characters (although the distance is certainly much less between the narrator and Decoud than between the narrator and, say, Mitchell). Characteristically, however, even though the narrator's omniscience is striking, the 'deeper meaning', though perhaps understood, is not necessarily explained.

Sometimes partial explanation may take the form of an authorial generalization. There are two illustrative examples on page 56: 'But man is a desperately conservative creature' and 'It is a failing common to mankind, whose views are tinged by prejudices'. Some critics of *Nostromo* tend to interpret such generalizations as narrative statements approaching Conrad's own views. This tendency applies, for instance, to a much-discussed authorial comment further on in Chapter 6: 'Action is consolatory. It is the enemy of thought and the friend of flattering illusions. Only in the conduct of our action can we find the sense of mastery over the Fates' (66). As a philosophical description of action this is, indeed, a remarkable authorial statement; and the contrast the novel presents between Decoud and the early Nostromo goes some way to confirm it. In general, however, critical commentary on this and other authorial generalizations has tended to isolate them too much from the narrative context in which they occur. The context of this particular generalization shows a clear relation to Mr Gould, who, in his full-time involvement with the mine (the sentence which follows the generalization reads: 'For his action, the mine was obviously the only field') is much more strongly exposed to 'flattering illusions' than his more detached, and wiser, wife. As a rule, Conrad's own position on the matters he explores in *Nostromo* is not easily ascertained. One critical possibility might be to regard this indeterminacy of authorial position as a weakness of the novel. This chapter suggests otherwise: it is part of the text's intrinsic consistency that it refuses to provide easy answers to the complex thematics it presents.

As further authorial generalizations and reflections follow on page 74, the narrator's scepticism becomes more evident. Although Mr and Mrs Gould are described as contrastive characters, we realize that not even Mrs Gould is immune to the 'contagious' (75) faith in the mine possessed by her husband. The analeptic narrative of Chapter 6 provides, in addition to the characterization of Holroyd already discussed, much of the necessary background information about the Goulds' early period in Europe, where Mr Gould, reacting to his father's experience, acquired 'a dramatic interest' (59) in mines, and where the idea of reopening the San Tomé silver mine first dawns upon him. Again, the authorial narrator indulges in a generalization whose implications (particularly that of resigned scepticism) require rereading to be properly appreciated. The generalization is focused on the 'vague idea of rehabilitation' which 'had presented itself to them at the instant when the woman's instinct of devotion and the man's instinct of activity receive from the strongest of illusions their most powerful impulse' (74). It must be added, though, that some of the implications are indicated in Chapter 7, which describes the Goulds' activities and unique social position in Sulaco. They are suggested partly through authorial irony, partly through Mrs Gould's growing doubts about the mining venture.

In the opening of the following chapter the authorial narrative situation, by now well established, apparently breaks down:

Those of us whom business or curiosity took to Sulaco in these years before the first advent of the railway can remember the steadying effect of the San Tomé mine upon the life of that remote province. The outward appearances had not changed then as they have changed since, as I am told... (95)

The phrase 'as I am told' indicates an abrupt, unexpected personal intrusion. There is a momentary identification of the authorial narrator as a visitor to Costaguana, from 'business or curiosity'. This personal intrusion, which resembles that in the second paragraph of Chapter 2 of *The Secret Agent*, is not often critically discussed. Watts suggests that one reason why the narrator takes care to identify himself may be 'partly psychological', that Conrad 'needs to don a mask, however transparent, in order to speak most eloquently'.[18] There is no doubt much to be said for such an explanation—particularly as it turns out that this is actually the only personal intrusion in the novel. Authorial narrative will prevail in *Nostromo*; and the identification of this 'I' comes to function as a sort of safeguard against the reader's possible tendency to identify the narrator with the author.

Still, the implications are complex. If, following Watts, we stress that this narrative variation is needed to enable Conrad to speak more freely and eloquently, then it should also be emphasized that the modulation helps Conrad to distinguish himself from the novel's authorial narrative voice—and this in spite of all the authorial generalizations and reflections which the text seems to support. Modifying Watts's psychological explanation, we might regard the personal intrusion as an illustration of Conrad's general need for distance from his fictional material. Moreover, although short, the information that the narrator has actually visited Costaguana strengthens the novel's emphasis on information and detailed description. It may, of course, also raise logical objections—how can a personal narrator be omniscient and so mobile? If, however, this is hardly a problem to most readers of *Nostromo*, part of the reason is suggested by the novel's extraordinary flexibility of

18 Watts, *Preface*, 146.

narrative, which remains predominantly authorial but with varying degrees and directions of personal colouring. With the exception of the first paragraph, then, the narrative of Chapter 8 exhibits the authorial characteristics to which we have by now become accustomed. Part of the structural importance of the chapter lies in the fact that it concludes the extended analepsis, and ends with yet another reference to Ribiera's appearance in Sulaco after his defeat. From this chapter on, narrative progression is more conventionally chronological, and the text more immediately understandable on a first reading.

The authorial narrative movement in the opening of Part Second, 'The Isabels', is again broadly descriptive—panoramic and informative in an inclusive sense. The central position and influence of the Goulds are abundantly confirmed. As Decoud is introduced in Chapter 3 we notice again how abrupt and authoritative the authorial evaluation can be: 'He imagined himself Parisian to the tips of his fingers. *But far from being that* [my emphasis] he was in danger of remaining a sort of nondescript dilettante all his life' (153). This example indicates both the authorial narrator's omniscience and his tendency to impose evaluative judgement even on one of the novel's most complex characters. As we read on, however, we realize that the description of Decoud is more nuanced than that of any other character in the novel. Part of Decoud's contribution to the conversations with Mrs Gould in Chapters 5 and 6 illustrates how Conrad uses the dialogue of the authorial narrative to attach an exceptional authority and interest to Decoud as a character. Consider, for instance, this statement:

'No, but just imagine our forefathers in morions and corselets drawn up outside this gate, and a band of adventurers just landed from their ships in the harbour there. Thieves, of course. Speculators, too. Their expeditions, each one, were the speculations of grave and reverend persons in England. That is history, as that absurd sailor Mitchell is always saying.'... 'It has always been the same. We are a wonderful people, but it has always been our fate to be'—he did not say 'robbed,' but added, after a pause— 'exploited!' (174)

Decoud here expounds his theory of the history of Latin America as one of continual economic exploitation. What is interesting about the narrative presentation of the theory is that it is not directly commented upon or modified by the authorial narrator. Thus

Decoud's views come to carry more weight, and could be interpreted as an acute comment on the functions and effects of the silver mine. This is a significant narrative variation: as the authorial narrator has earlier distanced himself from Decoud, he can now support his opinions indirectly by refraining from commenting on them. Moreover, as Decoud applies the adjective 'absurd' to what Mitchell says, an attitudinal connection is established with the authorial irony Mitchell has been exposed to earlier in the narrative. 'Absurd' is one possible word to describe Mitchell's pompously over-simplifying rhetoric. The important conversation in Chapter 6 establishes a corrective to the naïve optimism of Mitchell and the single-minded fanaticism of Mr Gould. We listen to two sceptics here: Mrs Gould's 'calmness of despair' (212) indicates that her doubts about the mine and its effect on Sulaco are growing; and these doubts are nourished by Decoud's more intellectual scepticism.

The narrative and thematic significance of Chapter 7 is inextricable from one particular narrative variation: Decoud's long letter to his sister. It seems apposite that the letter is presented at this point; and there are at least three reasons for its importance. First, it provides much relevant information in concentrated form. And there is a convincing implicit motivation for it: as an émigré in Paris, Decoud's sister is out of touch with recent developments in Sulaco/Costaguana. The information is particularly welcome on a first reading of *Nostromo*: I recall that my interest in the novel was greatly increased when I first came to the letter. Secondly, it functions well in the indirect characterization of Decoud. It reveals not only his insight, intelligence, and interest in the affairs of his country, but also, paradoxically, his disengagement from emotional involvement in them. Thirdly, the textual position of the letter is just right: it summarizes and analyses the main action of the novel just before its dramatic climax, the transport of the silver to the Great Isabel. A structural characteristic of the letter is that it is broken up into five different sections, interspersed with authorial commentary, and I shall comment briefly on each of them. My observations on the authorial insertions are incorporated into the discussion of the sections they introduce.

Section one (pp. 223–6). Decoud starts his letter with a question which indicates that his intellectual scepticism will be noticeable here too: 'Prepare our little circle in Paris for the birth of another South American Republic. One more or less, what does it matter?'

(223). He then goes on to outline the political situation, and here he mentions, to the reader's surprise, Ribiera's appearance in Sulaco 'by one of those strange coincidences that are almost incredible' (224). We are surprised not only because this particular incident has been referred to several times before (and as early as on page 11), but also because the repeated mention of it here, almost half-way through the text, makes us wonder at the novel's slowness of narrative progression. This is not to say that the link which section one establishes between Ribiera's arrival in Sulaco and Nostromo's activities there is not illuminating; in general, the letter contains several welcome references to important incidents and their interconnections.

Section two (pp. 226–9). After a short authorial insertion on page 226 Decoud continues his account of the critical situation in Sulaco, whose secession from Costaguana he has proposed the day before. Since the authorities (including Ribiera) escaped on the *Minerva*, the lightermen (led by Nostromo) have been able to resist the Monterist mob, and Decoud is writing his letter in relative security in the Casa Viola. The way in which this section relates the object of the riot to the silver serves to prefigure the thematic centrality of the silver in the following chapter.

Section three (pp. 229–31). The authorial introduction to this section of Decoud's letter is almost as long as the section itself, and it includes a characterization of Decoud which slants into authorial generalization. The authorial comment starts by emphasizing the isolation of Decoud, and the ominous silence and darkness surrounding this 'man with no faith in anything except the truth of his own sensations' (229). The generalization partly, though not wholly convincingly, explains why Decoud is composing such a long, reflective letter at this critical time of fighting for survival. But it has further implications as well:

It occurred to him that no one could understand him so well as his sister. In the most sceptical heart there lurks at such moments, when the chances of existence are involved, a desire to leave a correct impression of the feelings, like a light by which the action may be seen when personality is gone, gone where no light of investigation can ever reach the truth which every death takes out of the world. (230)

If this authorial statement is read as a prolepsis of Decoud's later suicide, then the combination of his letter and the authorial commentary attached to it could be seen as constituting his intellectual

testament. On later readings of *Nostromo* this interpretative possibility forcefully presents itself, thus enhancing the seriousness and
dramatic intensity of all the five sections. Moreover, the generalization interestingly relates 'action'—a key concept in the thematics of
the novel—not only to Decoud's thought but also to his 'feelings'. In
the suggestive simile of the generalization, Decoud's letter is his
attempt 'to leave a correct impression of the feelings'; these feelings are
then compared to 'a light', which may indicate an individual's contribution to the pattern of actions which characterizes human existence. Clearly, the understanding of action presented in *Nostromo*
cannot be accurately summarized. Still, if we connect this passage
with the description of Decoud's suicide, then its more positive
aspects would seem to include human company and friendship.
There is no doubt that Decoud's sister is a good and reliable friend of
his, but the possibility of meaningful and helpful human communion
is definitively eliminated by the obvious, brutal fact of spatial distance. 'I have the feeling of a great solitude around me,' Decoud
writes as he continues his letter; and he goes on to introduce a distinction between solitude and loneliness which could be related to, and
which supports, that I suggested in the chapter on 'The Secret Sharer'.
'But the solitude is also very real,' Decoud observes; 'the silence about
me is ominous.' And the words which conclude the section indicate
the effect the solitude has on him: 'I feel more lonely than ever'.

As used by Decoud here, solitude seems to signify a dimension of
human existence which, at one level, is relatively objective and external and, at another level, clearly existential. A possible connection
between the two levels is suggested by Decoud's epistemological
position; he has 'no faith in anything except the truth of his own sensations' (229). The existential aspect of his understanding of solitude
establishes a relation, albeit a problematic and indirect one, to the
adjective 'lonely' which he uses later on in the letter. Loneliness also
has an existential dimension, but here the authorial emphasis is
placed more firmly on Decoud's psychological experience of his isolated condition. The diversification of the motif of loneliness is not
only important in itself, but also a prolepsis of Decoud's solitude *and*
loneliness in the hours preceding his suicide off the Great Isabel.

Section four (pp. 231–44). The length of this section of Decoud's
letter is excessive, and it is distinctly less productive than the preceding one. Its predominant narrative variation is negative, in the sense
that the narrative characteristics of the letter apply less well here; and

the narrative method of this section seems instead to revert to that of
the novel's general, authorial narrative. This is another way of saying
that the effects associated with the most obvious formal variation
of the letter—Decoud's use of the first person, which gives the
impression of a personal narrative incorporated into the authorial
one—are less noticeable in section four than in those surrounding it.
It must be added, however, that the letter not only provides more
useful information about the political crisis in Sulaco, but also
specifies further how and why Decoud is so strongly involved in it.
Furthermore, the authorial introduction to the section indicates
that only a selection of Decoud's letter is actually presented as part
of *Nostromo*: 'Decoud gave up the point, and after writing steadily
for a while turned round again' (232). Thus the authorial narrator
has not only chosen to include the letter as a variant on, and supplement to, his own authorial narrative. He has also edited it; and the
omitted part provides an interesting instance of textual gap in a
Conrad work.

Section five (pp. 244–9). In this last section of Decoud's letter its
extraordinary honesty and intensity are reasserted. Decoud starts
by outlining the ensuing drama of the silver expedition across the
Golfo Plácido: 'I am not running away, you understand… I am
simply going away with that great treasure of silver which must be
saved at all costs.' He then goes on to expand his earlier characterizations of Mr and Mrs Gould and Nostromo. The quality of
these descriptions seems improved on rereading: we then realize how
accurate they are. The shift of focus from the Goulds to Nostromo
is rendered elegantly. Having presented the plan to remove the silver
from Sulaco and outlined the various missions of the participants in
the operation, Decoud continues:

'Nostromo's mission is to save the silver. The plan is to load it into the
largest of the Company's lighters, and send it across the gulf to a small port
out of Costaguana territory just on the other side the Azuera, where the first
northbound steamer will get orders to pick it up. The waters here are calm.
We shall slip away into the darkness of the gulf before the Esmeralda rebels
arrive…

The incorruptible Capataz de Cargadores is the man for that work; and I,
the man with a passion, but without a mission, I go with him to return—to
play my part in the farce to the end, and, if successful, to receive my reward,
which no one but Antonia can give me.' (245–6)

The passage is not only an effective prolepsis of the following drama in the lighter; it also implies a partial explanation of the narrowing of perspective from here on. The authorial narrative of *Nostromo* will remain omniscient and panoramic, but the thematic centrality of the desperate attempt to save the silver motivates a narrative modulation which implies an exceptionally stable authorial focus on this aspect of the novel's action in the last pages of Part Second. Furthermore, although Decoud's application of the adjective 'incorruptible' to Nostromo here is consistent enough with earlier descriptions of him, on later readings it inevitably attains an ominously proleptic quality, which is strengthened by the indications of a changed Nostromo towards the end of the chapter.

As Decoud ends his letter, then, we can conclude that it has not just summarized much of the main action of *Nostromo* up to this point, but also commented on it and revealed Decoud's pivotal position as a main character associated with most of the various cross-currents of action in the novel. Moreover, it has economically set the scene for the approaching drama of the silver expedition. As this gets under way later in the chapter, the forced coexistence and co-operation of Decoud and Nostromo are convincingly described:

[Nostromo] was already pushing against a pile with one of the heavy sweeps. Decoud did not move; the effect was that of being launched into space…
    The two men, unable to see each other, kept silent till the lighter, slipping before the fitful breeze, passed out between almost invisible headlands into the still deeper darkness of the gulf. (261)

The action gradually builds up to an impressive climax in Chapter 8; and the narrative function of suspense here should not be underestimated. Within the overall structure of the novel, the dramatic account of Nostromo and Decoud in the lighter becomes a sort of narrative-within-a-narrative; and there is a relative simplicity about the adventure which the reader of this demanding novel appreciates. It is not that the problems in Sulaco / Costaguana are now removed or controlled. Far from it; these basic socio-economic problems, which initiate much of the novel's dramatic action and which the silver in a way symbolizes, remain largely unresolved. However, once Decoud and Nostromo are isolated with the silver in the lighter, the complexities of *Nostromo* are, as it were, temporarily suspended, and its narrative attains an exceptional simplicity which, combined with the gradual increase of suspense, establishes a significant variation on the authorial narrative.

As in 'The Secret Sharer', Conrad's use of the suspense principle is integrated into his narrative method here. The authorial commentary in Chapter 8, for instance, has the gradual increase of suspense as one of its main purposes. When we are first told about the approaching steamer, carrying Sotillo's troops but no lights, it is 'as if that invisible vessel, whose position could not be precisely guessed, were making straight for the lighter' (277). The distinctly personal colouring of this authorial impression does not reduce its suspense-generating function; on the contrary, the self-imposed restriction on authorial knowledge serves to augment it. A related example of personal colouring is the use of narrated monologue on page 283: 'As Nostromo remarked, in answer to Decoud's regrets, it was too late!'

Shortly afterwards there is a shift of perspective from the lighter to the troop-carrying steamer. The narrative perspective temporarily approximates to that of Sotillo, who, considering his military and political objective, reveals an astounding ignorance of the present situation and recent changes in Sulaco. This indication of ignorance is one of many authorial suggestions that the characters are engaged in actions whose deeper causes, purposes, and consequences remain obscure to them. As the narrative shifts back to the lighter (290), the fateful collision is imminent. One function of the perspectival shift is to relate the reader's impression of suspense more clearly to a notion of danger. Another function is to bring our attention back to the problems ashore and to connect them with the venture in which Nostromo and Decoud are engaged; thus the frame of action is again widened. As a result of the flexibility and mobility of the authorial narrative, the shift can easily be made.

In the immediate aftermath of the collision Nostromo and Decoud are, in spite of their co-operation in the lighter, strangely separated from each other:

Each of them was as if utterly alone with his task. It did not occur to them to speak. There was nothing in common between them but the knowledge that the damaged lighter must be slowly but surely sinking. In that knowledge, which was like the crucial test of their desires, they seemed to have become completely estranged, as if they had discovered in the very shock of the collision that the loss of the lighter would not mean the same thing to them both. This common danger brought their differences in aim, in view, in character, and in position, into absolute prominence in the private vision of each. (295)

This passage is a good illustration of the authorial narrator's mixture of information and reflection. A variant on authorial reflection here is that it does not, in spite of the modification suggested by 'seemed', appear to be related to a personal perspective, but neither is it as generalized as several other authorial comments. During their frantic attempt to save and hide the silver Decoud voices his doubts about Nostromo's incorruptible quality; these doubts confirm the proleptic function of the last section of his letter. We are told Nostromo detects 'the ironic tone' (301) in Decoud's bitter comments on the silver; left with it on the beach of the Great Isabel, the latter is 'solitary... like a man in a dream' (301). The contrast between the two characters is stengthened towards the end of the chapter, but on page 302 the loneliness motif is extended to include both of them. When Nostromo swims ashore, Decoud remains on the island; and we have to turn many pages before reading about him again. The withholding of information about his fate on the Great Isabel is one constituent element of the suspense of the novel.

The opening of Part Third, 'The Lighthouse', continues the main action in sequence as from the departure of Nostromo and Decoud with the lighter, but it presents an analepsis as from the ending of Part Second. The authorial narrative at the beginning of Part Third is relatively monotonous; and it is hard to avoid a sense of anticlimax after the effectively dramatic account of the silver expedition. Chapter 2 provides an example of the subtlety of time-shifts in *Nostromo*. When we first meet Mitchell in this chapter he is 'pacing the wharf' (323) and waiting for news about Sotillo; on the same page, however, we read about what he 'used to confess afterwards'. What is impossible to know on a first reading is that 'afterwards' is in fact seven years later: Mitchell is taken captive by Sotillo on 4 May 1890; not until 1897 does he take the visitor on a tour of Sulaco.[19] On a first reading the two different planes of time appear virtually indistinguishable—one temporal plane blends into the other in a manner reminiscent of the fiction of Faulkner or Claude Simon. The references to Mitchell early in Chapter 2 anticipate his 1897 orientation; and the accompanying authorial commentary warns us that his views may be dubious. For instance, Mitchell's recollections here are interrupted by the authorial narrator's evaluative 'In this Captain Mitchell was right' (326), which implies that he is not infrequently wrong. There are, in fact, severe limitations to his knowledge; and the

---

[19] Cf. Watts, *Preface*, 163, 161.

narrator ironically comments: '[Mitchell] did some hard but not very extensive thinking' (338). These reservations about Mitchell's authority make us more sceptical about his wordy account addressed to the visitor in Chapter 10.

In Chapter 3 Mitchell and Monygham are held and interrogated by Sotillo, whose 'moral stupidity' (350) is exposed to the narrator's irony. The Goulds are relatively absent in several chapters, but in Chapter 4 the narrator again turns his attention directly to Mr Gould, who, it is said, 'unlike Decoud... could not play lightly a part in a tragic farce' (364). At this stage of the narrative the authorial narrator's judgement of Mr Gould is more precise and unqualified: 'the Gould Concession had insidiously corrupted' him. But the judgement does not imply that no attempt is made to understand Mr Gould: 'To him, *as to all of us* [my emphasis] the compromises with his conscience appeared uglier than ever in the light of failure' (364). The general truth of such an authorial observation is striking, and the plausibility and human relevance of the narrative are futher increased. Supporting Decoud's earlier analysis, the ending of this chapter confirms Mrs Gould's estrangement from her husband: 'Mrs Gould watched his abstraction with dread... A man haunted by a fixed idea is insane. He is dangerous even if that idea is an idea of justice; for may he not bring the heaven down pitilessly upon a loved head?' (379). As the slanting movement towards narrated monologue indicates, distinctions are blurred between Mrs Gould's reflections and those of the authorial narrator; the more she learns, the more resigned and disillusioned she becomes. Earlier in the novel we have been told about her gentle irony; now we read that Mr Gould 'had no ironic eye. He was not amused at the absurdities that prevail in this world' (378).

As the wealth and far-reaching influence of the mine are subjected to further authorial treatment in Chapter 7, the economic corruption which accompanies it is described ironically through a series of brief statements. The mine is not only 'a serious asset' in the economy of Sulaco, but 'in the private budgets of many officials as well. It was traditional. It was known. It was said. It was credible. Every Minister of Interior drew a salary from the San Tomé mine' (402–3). The political involvement of Mr Gould becomes more and more unavoidable; and there are hints of his plans for tampering with Don Pépé, who is characterized in the preceding chapter. Gould is trapped; and his earlier insistence on some vague neutrality seems increasingly ridiculous. The ending of the chapter, which describes how Nostromo awakens 'from a fourteen hours' sleep (411), reveals his change of personality:

Handsome, robust, and supple, he threw back his head, flung his arms open, and stretched himself with a slow twist of the waist and a leisurely growling yawn of white teeth, as natural and free from evil in the moment of waking as a magnificent and unconscious wild beast. Then, in the suddenly steadied glance fixed upon nothing from under a thoughtful frown, appeared the man. (411–2)

Earlier in the novel the unparalleled prestige Nostromo enjoys as chief of the dockworkers is related to his courage, his romantic pride, and his intuitive ability to find the right course of action whenever necessary. As late as during the trying experience in the lighter, Nostromo and Decoud are presented as contrastive characters, with the latter as the more reflective. The difference between them is, however, less absolute than earlier in the narrative. It is Nostromo who is undergoing a change of character; and it is a change which is related to his involvement with the silver. Anticipating the following chapter, this ending presents Nostromo as suspended between the earlier, unproblematic state as 'a magnificent and unconscious wild beast' and the new 'man' who, corrupted by the silver, is confronting an immense problem to which he eventually succumbs.

Chapter 8 retains the narrative focus on Nostromo's actions after leaving Decoud, about whom, however, we hear nothing. As the changes in Nostromo's personality are detailed he emerges as a more complex and more interesting character—capable of new insights, burdened with new problems. The authorial narrative is more directly centred on Nostromo in this chapter than earlier in the book. An example is this direct characterization: 'He was simple. He was as ready to become the prey of any belief, superstition, or desire as a child' (417). The stress on his simplicity does not remove the impression of a changed Nostromo, more reflective and uncertain in 'his profound isolation' (422).

Cedric Watts rightly relates the narrative mobility of *Nostromo* to that between different informants.[20] We have seen that Decoud's letter is an important source of information which supplements that of the authorial narrator. As informant Mitchell is very different from

---

[20] Watts, *Preface*, 145.

Decoud. Although there is a temporal lapse of seven years between the two accounts, it is clear that the two characters give conflicting interpretations of the historical events with which the novel is concerned: though confusing, this disparity contributes to the thematic richness, complexity, and persuasiveness of *Nostromo*. It substantiates the novel's sustained suggestion that as history is made by human beings and the complicated materialist forces they activate, it follows that their understanding of history will vary in accordance with their dissimilar perspectives, levels of insight, and degrees of personal involvement. If Decoud's written reflections are coloured by his pervasive scepticism, Mitchell's account is distinguished by an untroubled, naïvely self-confident optimism.

A structural similarity between the two extended pieces of information is that of narratee: like Decoud's sister, the visitor to the Sulaco of 1897 is ignorant of the recent historical changes; and this provides the opportunity for a clearer, more concise account. It is true that the reader, too, may be bewildered by the wealth of names and events referred to by the garrulous Mitchell. There is even an indirect suggestion of such a similarity in the text: as the visitor is 'stunned and as it were annihilated mentally by a sudden surfeit of sights, sounds, names, facts, and complicated information imperfectly apprehended' (486–7), so the reader of *Nostromo* is hard put to it to understand the all-inclusive action and characterization which the novel presents. If the reader is, after all, in a far better position to understand the essential information Mitchell provides than his 'privileged captive' (475), this is due to its close relation to occurrences already dramatized. As a result some bits of the complex picture the novel has been drawing fall into place; we understand more, if still far from all.

It dawns on us, for instance, that Mr Gould must have managed to retain control of the mine during the 1890 riot; and that the importance of the mine is now, in 1897, as crucial as ever. Not all the information is conclusive, however. We learn that Decoud is dead, but we wonder how he died—and we have to wait until the last part of the chapter to find out. Mitchell does not, of course, wholly escape the irony of the authorial narrator, but the irony is relatively mild in this section, which generally has a lighter tone and is more humorous than what we have come to expect. Numerous passages qualify as possible illustrations; consider, for instance, this one:

And all day Captain Mitchell would talk like this to his more or less willing victim—
'The Plaza. I call it magnificent. Twice the area of Trafalgar Square.' (476)

In addition to the useful information provided, the humorous irony in the section is a welcome contrast not only to the novel's general seriousness, but also to the deep scepticism prevailing in the description of Decoud's suicide which follows.

The narrative dramatization of Decoud's last days on the Great Isabel constitutes one of the most significant passages in the Conrad canon. The narrative achieves an exceptional seriousness and intensity here. It is telling that authorial irony is virtually absent from the section. Concomitantly, as the combination of absence of irony and authorial detachment establishes an impression of authorial sympathy for Decoud, the attitudinal distance between the latter and the authorial narrator is temporarily reduced. This goes some way to explain the intensity of the description, which embodies essential constitutive aspects of Conrad's sceptical existentialism. One reason why the section becomes so suggestive and convincing lies in the manner in which it has been prepared for. The narrative device of delayed presentation forms part of this preparation: like Nostromo, the reader has long been wondering what happened to Decoud. Mitchell's casual reference to his death does, it is true, give away the eventual fact or outcome, but Mitchell is ignorant of the cause: therefore our curiosity is increased rather than satisfied. At the same time it would seem that one reason why the passage can be delayed for so long, and still retain its impact, must be sought in the great interest in Decoud which has been established through the earlier authorial characterizations of him and through his letter.

The authorial narrator re-introduces the reader to Decoud by making a categorical statement which presupposes omniscience: 'But the truth was that he died from solitude, the enemy known but to few on this earth, and whom only the simplest of us are fit to withstand' (496). As this explanation, which in one sense seems inadequate, is given at once, the reader is encouraged to read the following description of Decoud's last days as an intensified dramatization of the effects of solitude on a character unable to bear it. Not only diversifying Decoud's self-portrayal in the letter to his sister, the description also incorporates powerful generalizations which, while related to Decoud's own reflections both in the letter and elsewhere earlier in

the narrative, proceed from the authorial narrator's understanding
of the total action presented in the text:

> Solitude from mere outward condition of existence becomes very swiftly a
> state of soul in which the affectations of irony and scepticism have no place.
> It takes possession of the mind, and drives forth the thought into the exile of
> utter unbelief. After three days of waiting for the sight of some human face,
> Decoud caught himself entertaining a doubt of his own individuality. It had
> merged into the world of cloud and water, of natural forces and forms of
> nature. In our activity alone do we find the sustaining illusion of an
> independent existence as against the whole scheme of things of which we
> form a helpless part. (497)

The last sentence of the quotation is one of the best-known and
most important generalizing reflections in Conrad; and we shall
consider it in a moment. But first it must be noted that the whole
description of Decoud's movement towards suicide has a strictly
chronological, and in one sense logical, progression which gives it a
quality of ominous finality and inevitability. The 'doubt of his own
individuality' starts tormenting Decoud 'after three days'; 'On the
fifth day an immense melancholy descended upon him palpably'
(497); after seven days 'both his intelligence and his passion were
swallowed up easily in this great unbroken solitude of waiting
without faith... He beheld the universe as a succession of incomprehensible images' (498); and 'On the tenth day... the solitude
appeared like a great void, and the silence of the gulf like a tense,
thin cord to which he hung suspended by both hands, without fear,
without surprise, without any sort of emotion whatever' (498).

There is a characteristic combination of authorial distance and
sympathy in this description. Narrative distance is indicated not
only by its prevailing omniscience, but also through the narrator's
ability, and readiness, to generalize about mankind on the basis of
the insoluble problems confronted by Decoud. Narrative sympathy
is indicated partly by the remarkable intensity of the description and
the absence of irony, partly by the similarity between some of the
narrator's comments and Decoud's own views as expressed earlier
in the narrative. The best illustration of this interesting affinity is
provided by the last quotation. In the discussion of section three of
Decoud's letter we noted the link established between 'solitude' and
'silence'; this connection is confirmed by the authorial narrator here.
Furthermore, the narrator's use of 'solitude' seems concordant with

my understanding of the concept in the interpretation of the letter: the image 'like a great void' suggests both its external and existential dimensions. 'Void', 'silence', and 'cord' function here as three reverberant images that not only signify and intensify Decoud's absolute isolation, but also suggest how it engenders an unbearable feeling of loneliness associated with an increasing sense of unreality. In the terse account of the actual suicide, distance between the narrator and Decoud again seems to increase, and irony reappears, but it is immediately qualified: 'the brilliant Don Martin Decoud, weighted by the bars of San Tomé silver, disappeared without a trace, swallowed up in the immense indifference of things' (501).

If we now return to the last sentence in the extended quotation from page 497, it seems obvious that in a consideration of the complex thematics of *Nostromo* this generalization would have to be given close attention. But it would also have to be related to, and critically compared with, the surrounding context and the whole text. We note the use of the plural form of personal pronouns; this gives a quality at once personal and generalizing to the authorial comment. However, a more important reason why the statement is so powerful is suggested by the way in which the personal element is integrated with the broad narrative movement of the text: the generalization is provoked by the whole set of complex historical processes *Nostromo* dramatizes. Although this does not wholly eliminate the explicit character of the generalization, it makes it more convincing and understandable. A related effect is that the statement presents a subtle manipulation of the reader's response— not only to the passage, but to the text as a whole—and influences his or her interpretation of the novel. It is certainly true that the authorial description of Decoud's death constitutes, in Watts's phrase, a 'thematic nexus',[21] but it should be noted that although Decoud may seem to come close to Conrad in this passage, and although the authorial reflections related to Decoud carry exceptional weight and indicate great seriousness and relevance, he is but one of several important characters in the novel; and in some ways he is portrayed as exceptional rather than as typical.

The last three chapters of *Nostromo* are often criticized. Certainly there is a decrease of narrative intensity at the end, which becomes somewhat melodramatic. Chapter 11, where we return to

21 Watts, *Preface*, 156.

a description of an apparently prospering Sulaco, includes an important dialogue between Mrs Gould and Monygham. In their talk there are further indications of Mrs Gould's growing understanding and resignation; and Monygham pronounces: 'There is no peace and no rest in the development of material interests' (511). The assertion is not modified by the narrator; and as the conversation continues Mrs Gould comes close to accepting it. The penultimate chapter is a continuation in sequence as from the end of Chapter 10—at last we return to Nostromo, who, 'growing rich very slowly', has 'lost his peace; the genuineness of all his qualities was destroyed. He felt it himself, and often cursed the silver of San Tomé' (523). His confession to Giselle does not help: 'He had not regained his freedom' (542).

In the last chapter the melodramatic jealousy motif is strengthened in the account of Linda's love for Nostromo. The description of how Nostromo is shot is connected with a reference to Decoud's disillusioned view of existence, 'beholding life like a succession of senseless images' (553). An effective narrative tactic here is to make the dying Nostromo wish to see Mrs Gould. Bringing together two of the novel's most important characters at the very end of the narrative, this meeting provides Conrad with the opportunity to make his authorial narrator emphasize Mrs Gould's bitterness and loneliness ('as solitary as any human being had ever been, perhaps, on this earth' (555)) and Nostromo's suffering despair ('and the Capataz de Cargadores died without a word or moan after an hour of immobility, broken by short shudders testifying to the most atrocious sufferings' (563)).

The concluding paragraph of the novel has a remarkable resonance. The narrative focus on Nostromo is retained, but at the same time the perspective is widened through a description of scenery which recalls the novel's opening; and the paragraph incorporates a highly significant image as the line of the horizon is 'overhung by a big white cloud shining like a mass of solid silver' (566).

II

As we now proceed to discuss briefly the most important narrative characteristics and variations in *Nostromo*, some introductory qualifications must be made. First, if this commentary on the novel's narrative method has, necessarily, been far from exhaustive, the following observations are also selective and do but partial justice to the narrative sophistication and thematic range of this exceptionally complex text. This is, however, a general problem which in one form on another is bound to confront any critic of Conrad's fiction: certain simplifications and distortions follow not just from the need to keep the discussion within manageable length, but also from the problematic relationship between systematized, critical discourse and the characteristic fusion of different narrative strategies and complex thematic effects in Conrad. Secondly, if some of the points below seem to approach, or revert to, comments I have already made on the narrative, it must be remembered that after all they are based, to a greater extent than the observations from which they proceed, on a critical understanding of the whole text. But the methodological and hermeneutic problem which surfaces here should not be suppressed: as the initial, consecutive commentary will inevitably tend to emphasize those narrative elements that can provide a basis for more general discussion, so the critic's general idea of the work—and Conrad, and the novel as a genre—will necessarily influence both his or her approach to the text and the initial response to it.[22] A related problem is that although the choice of critical focus and methodology is a prerequisite for critical disourse, they can both entail a certain reductiveness in relation to the complexity of Conrad's fiction, especially as constituted by the four novels analysed in this study.

1. The interplay of spatial and temporal dimensions of narrative

When, for instance, we note that the narrative of the opening of Part First of Nostromo is exceptionally slow, this observation is related to a particular form of reader's expectation and response: Nostromo

---

[22] More than most novels, Nostromo draws attention to problems discussed in theological, philosophical, and literary hermeneutics. Two lucid and mutually supplementary surveys of the main issues are David C. Hoy, The Critical Circle: Literature, History, and Philosophical Hermeneutics (Berkeley: University of California Press, 1978), and Anthony C. Thiselton, The Two Horizons: New Testament Hermeneutics and Philosophical Description with Special Reference to Heidegger, Bultmann, Gadamer, and Wittgenstein (Exeter: Paternoster Press, 1980).

does not seem to have the kind of narrative progression we expect from a novel. Daleski finds that the reader is forced, partly as a result of this response, to 'register his confusion as a mark of his own inadequacy'.[23] It is no doubt true that this problem is closely related to that of reading, but it is also a narrative feature which enhances the spatial dimension of the novel. As the detailed description of Costaguana and Sulaco evolves, the momentum of the narrative slackens and its approximates to what Genette calls a descriptive 'pause';[24] this pause then functions as a foil to the action throughout the narrative. One problem in Part First is that much of its information is more meaningful and relevant to the plot of the novel than it at first seems. It contains proleptic and explanatory elements which can neither be noticed nor appreciated on a first reading. Rereading the opening chapters we realize that surprisingly much in 'The Silver of the Mine' has a bearing on the subsequent main action; thus the narrative economy of *Nostromo* cannot be fully discovered at first.

It is most important that there is, in spite of the reader's initial impression to the contrary, a decisive development of action in *Nostromo*: not only does much of the novel's suspense depend on it, but the progressing action is also integrated into the gradual expansion and diversification of its thematics. The function of the time-shifts and the extended analepsis in Part First is not to impede the temporal progression of action, but rather to draw the reader's attention to particular aspects of it, to indicate connections which might otherwise have been overlooked, and to make the fictional historical events more plausible. Moreover, as the sense that history is cyclical is played against the understanding of history as displaying a continuous evolution, both narrative tension and thematic complexity increase. Arguably, then, the time-shifts accentuate both the spatial and the temporal dimensions of the novel's narrative. In Part First in particular, the chronological distortion and the emphasis on setting reinforce the sense of the fictional text as stabilized, linguistically fixed, form. However, as we begin to realize how the various time-shifts are related to one another and to the temporal progression which the novel after all displays, our appreciation of this progression is paradoxically enhanced by its

---

[23] *CWD* 116.
[24] Cf. *ND* 95.

apparent absence. A further paradox—and one which indicates the interrelationship of narrative and thematics in the novel—is that aspects of its scepticism seem to confirm the emphasis on spatial form in Part First: as the scenery remains static and unchanged, so the ending of the novel implies that the human condition of the inhabitants of Sulaco has not undergone any significant or lasting improvement.

The time-shifts are closely connected with Conrad's sophisticated use of authorial narrative in *Nostromo*. They are an integral part of his narrative method and repeatedly provide contrasting viewpoints that are essential in order to understand the text. The time-shifts not only further the temporal mobility of the novel, but also serve as constituent aspects of a wide-ranging analogical mobility which, as Watts notes, 'generates many ironies',[25] and which is often correlated with the suggestive use of contrasts. Numerous characters and passages are interlinked, often in surprising ways, and the effect is frequently ironic and paradoxical. For example, Decoud's suicide occurs in 1890, but as we read about it just after Mitchell's 1897 account, the pervasive scepticism and gloom of the section confirm and increase our reservations about Mitchell's boastful talking.

2. *Story and plot*

As Watts's useful and accurate chronology of the central events in *Nostromo* shows, it is possible to construct a surprisingly specific and internally consistent story on the basis of its bewildering and complicated plot. The complications of this plot are obviously related to the text's narrative mobility, which is again linked to the diverse functions of the authorial narrator. The narrative of *Nostromo* presents massive evidence in support of Ricoeur's emphasis on the dynamic, shaping function of plot.[26] It unfolds slowly and with a wealth of detail through the many informants the authorial narrator employs in his service, and whose different perspectives enrich both his voice and his own omniscient, all-inclusive, and often ironic perspective.

If, following Peter Brooks, we ask where in Barthes's *S/Z* we find

[25] Watts, *Preface*, 146.
[26] See ch. 1 n. 17.

a notion approximating to 'plot', the above commentary on the narrative of *Nostromo* would seem to suggest agreement with Brooks's focus on Barthes's *proairetic* and *hermeneutic* codes, that is the code of actions ('Voice of the Empirical') and the code of enigmas and answers ('Voice of Truth').[27] As Brooks ably summarizes Barthes's understanding of the code of actions, it 'concerns the logic of actions, how their completion can be derived from their initiation, how they form sequences'.[28] As my critical comments have indicated, both these two aspects of action (as summarized by Brooks) are not only observable in *Nostromo*: they are very characteristic of the novel's action as Conrad presents it. The best example of completion of an initiated action is perhaps that associated with the silver mine. As so often in Conrad, this aspect of action is multi-faceted, and is played out at different levels which supplement and ironically modify one another. Two of the levels are interrelated as Mr Gould (in Chapter 6 of Part First) comments on the function of the mine: 'I pin my faith to material interests. Only let the material interests once get a firm footing, and they are bound to impose the conditions on which alone they can continue to exist' (84). At one level, the enormous influence of the mine on the development of Sulaco could be seen as verifying Mr Gould's statement. Yet at the level of characterization, the 'conditions' imposed by the mine lead to Gould's personal disintegration—they make him a single-minded fanatic and estrange him from his beloved wife.

The novel's dramatization of Mr Gould's change of character could also be seen as a sequence of its action. The logic of this sequence, which for Barthes is a second characteristic of the proairetic code, is illustrated by another which follows it: as Mr Gould's involvement with the mine destroys his humanity, so it results in Mrs Gould's disillusionment and influences her contributions to the important conversations with Decoud (in Chapter 6 of Part Second) and Nostromo (in Chapter 13 of Part Third). One narrative characteristic of *Nostromo* is that the numerous time-shifts and changes in authorial focus make the reader more conscious of the function of the novel's sequences as thematic apposition: they both concatenate the various facets of action in the novel and enrich its thematics by indicating and exploring this action from a variety of temporal planes and personal angles.

---

[27] Brooks, *Reading for the Plot*, 18; cf. Barthes, *S/Z*, 26 and *passim*.
[28] Brooks, *Reading for the Plot*, 18.

Building on Barthes, Brooks thinks of plot as 'an "overcoding" of the proairetic by the hermeneutic, the latter structuring the discrete elements of the former into larger interpretive wholes, working out their play of meaning and significance'.[29] Barthes's hermeneutic code concerns the questions and answers that structure a narrative, their suspense, partial unveiling (through, for instance, delayed decoding), and, possibly, eventual resolution. The relevance of all these concerns to *Nostromo* is suggested by my textual commentary, which goes far to confirm the critical usefulness of Brooks's understanding and application of the concept of plot. Although, in the critical practice of this study, aspects of Barthes's hermeneutic code would seem to transcend the textual level and merge with problems of reading and interpretation, *Nostromo* demonstrates how problematic the distinction between textual characteristics and interpretation can be in practical criticism. For instance, many of my points about the narrative functions and effects in *Nostromo* necessitate careful rereading; and such a process of rereading involves a noticeable, if not substantial, interpretative element. This is another way of saying that the novel's narrative method presupposes a rereading which not only substantiates its plot, but also makes this plot denser, more interesting and more internally consistent. Hence the 'dynamic notion of structuration'[30] which Brooks advocates receives a great deal of support from the fictional universe constituted by Conrad's narrative in *Nostromo*.

3. The omniscient authorial narrator

Considering his position in the text as a whole, the authorial narrator in *Nostromo* is omniscient and detached—removed from the novel's action and yet with a complete overview of it. The only instance where this position is directly contradicted in the narrative is, as we have seen, the opening of Chapter 8 of Part First. Here a personal 'I' intrudes, but this 'I'—which, as it were, appears just in order to disappear—is not identified; and the principal function of the narrator in *Nostromo* is clearly authorial.

However, this authorial function is complex, and linked to other narrative devices such as irony and variations of distance. Part of this complexity is indicated by C. B. Cox as he observes that, in *Nostromo*,

---

[29] Ibid.
[30] Ibid.

There is no Marlow through whose narration we see the events. The anonymous story-teller of *Nostromo* has no identity; we know that this person visited Sulaco on occasions, but we are not given any information about his character, not even his age. Yet he makes quite firm moral judgments on certain occasions, judgments which may not seem validated either by the events or by his choice of imagery.[31]

This observation seems valid as far as it goes, but the view of the authorial narrator as a 'person' becomes problematic when we consider his omniscience, his mobility, his authority, and his distance from his characters. It would be more accurate to say that the narrative, though technically authorial, is given various forms or degrees of personal colouring—not least in some of the important generalizations we have been considering.

One obvious but important point to make about the authorial narrator is to emphasize the indeterminacy of his position in relation to the characters and events he describes. Paul Goetsch considers the attitude of the authorial narrator as both conservative and ironic, and finds that it is contrasted with Decoud's scepticism and with Mitchell's more positive approach.[32] This observation is dubious for two reasons. First, though it is certainly true that the narrator is often ironic it does not follow that he is 'conservative': his ideological or political position cannot be determined in the way we can ascertain that of, say, the language teacher in *Under Western Eyes*; and the main reason for this indeterminacy is suggested by his complex function as authorial narrator. Secondly, although the narrator is often ironic we have seen that his use of irony varies more in relation to Decoud, to whom he may come quite close, than to Mitchell, by whom he seems faintly amused.

It may be helpful to distinguish between the structural and thematic function of the authorial narrator. Structurally, the overview and general omniscience of the narrator are a means by which the many different threads of the complex narrative can be tied together. Without this device, which has a unifying function structurally, the transitions between different time-shifts and thematic emphases would not only have been more abrupt and distracting, but technically much more conspicuous. The essential point to

---

31 Cox, *Conrad: The Modern Imagination*, 76–7.
32 Paul Goetsch, 'Joseph Conrad: *Nostromo*', in Horst Oppel (ed.), *Der moderne englische Roman: Interpretationen* (Berlin: Erich Schmidt, 1971), 52.

make here is that whereas the narrative variation of *Lord Jim* serves to explore a twofold problem, not just an understanding of Jim but also an understanding of how various narrators and characters attempt to understand him, the all-inclusive authorial narrative of *Nostromo* is more unambiguously directed towards a dramatized presentation, and possible understanding, of a whole country undergoing a historical transformation. To say that the authorial narrator has a unifying structural function is not to claim that *Nostromo* is a unified or wholly coherent text, but to suggest that it would have appeared more distorted and fragmentary without the authorial narrator's overview. This overview and omniscience do not, however, imply exhaustive explanation: in *Nostromo* Conrad achieves a successful balance between incomprehensible fragmentation and over-simplified presentation.

To stress the thematic function of the narrator is to draw attention to the following narrative characteristic of his: transitions are blurred between his structural function and the information he provides on the one hand, and the views and attitudes be embodies on the other. Selective aspects of the latter quality, which may appear personal in spite of the general absence of personal identification, are indicated in the following paragraphs on his relation to Conrad and the novel's four most important characters.

The narrator's relation to Conrad is not ascertained without difficulty. That there is a relation is evident, but then it is also evident that it is an indirect and complicated one. The scepticism and ironic stance of the authorial narrator may be shared by Conrad, but not necessarily, and not always. It is also difficult to say what is *the* view of the narrator, even on a given issue or problem, because of the personal colouring of his opinions. It is one of the paradoxes of *Nostromo* that although the narrator is removed and detached from the lives and the action he presents in dramatized form, he remains heavily involved: part of his scepticism seems indeed to result from the action and fates he so convincingly describes. If there are no lyric interludes in *Nostromo* where the attitudinal distance between Conrad and the authorial narrator seems markedly reduced, part of the reason is suggested by the complicating and distancing effect of the authorial irony which pervades the novel. At the same time, *Nostromo* demonstrates that authorial narrative can be intensified while narrative distance is retained. The absence of the lyric aspect from the authorial description of Decoud's last days on the Great Isabel makes its narrative intensity and eidetic quality even more remarkable.

The relation of the narrator to Nostromo is unstable, indicative of an attitude which at first may seem inconsistent since it oscillates between apparent praise (in which, however, irony can by embedded) and obvious irony (as on page 531: 'A sudden dread came upon the fearless and incorruptible Nostromo'). Although there is no single predominant character in *Nostromo*, one could make a case for Nostromo as its protagonist: his crucial position in the action, his intrepidity, corruption, and tragic fate are among the most central concerns of the novel; and its title is (as usual with Conrad) well chosen. The fact that even Nostromo is viewed ironically strengthens the detachment of the authorial narrator, but it does not remove the tragic dimension of Nostromo's life.

The narrator's relation to Decoud is particularly interesting. Decoud is the novel's most intriguing character; and we have seen that he also performs crucial narrative functions. R. A. Gekoski finds that 'There are, in fact, times in *Nostromo* when the voice of the omniscient narrator is virtually indistinguishable from that of Decoud. Conversely, there are also times when Decoud's voice is unmistakably Conradian in tone and content.'[33] It does, indeed, seem clear that no character is closer to the authorial narrator than Decoud, and this in spite of the fact that he too may be the target of authorial irony. His relation to Conrad, however, is much more indeterminate. Decoud's authority is established most clearly in Chapters 6 and 7 of Part First and in the letter to his sister. The corroborative authorial comment on his characterization of Mr Gould as 'an idealist' (214) indicates some of this authority. It is consistent with the intelligence and reliability of Decoud that he is the first who—influenced by this general scepticism but, as it turns out, quite rightly—questions the commonly-held view of Nostromo as 'incorruptible'. Structurally a prolepsis, this suspicion of Decoud's is an authorial indication not only of his shrewdness, but also of the scepticism which, pervading the whole novel, contributes essentially to its thematics. There is a curious sense in which the combination of detachment and involvement in the narrator's attitude seems reflected, and heightened, in the character of Decoud. As his sceptical position encourages detachment and reflection, so his

---

[33] Gekoski, *Conrad*, 133. Cf. Watts, *Preface*, 154.

intense passion for Antonia and, in spite of his claims to the contrary, Sulaco, make him play a key role in the secession of the town from Costaguana.

The narrator's relation to Mrs Gould is also of great interest. There can be no doubt that Mrs Gould is the most intelligent and most fully individualized of Conrad's female characters. Yet she too remains at a certain distance from the authorial narrator; some of the community's respect for the First Lady of Sulaco seems strangely reflected in his attitude to her. But the relation is not static: the narrator moves closer to Mrs Gould in the conversation between her and Nostromo at the very end of the novel. There is a curious similarity between the authorial narrator and Mrs Gould in that they are both exceptionally well informed (to the extent, that is, that the narrator's omniscient knowledge can be compared with that of one of the characters he describes) and at the same time peculiarly removed from the main action. As Edward Said notes in his long section on *Nostromo* in *Beginnings*, 'Only Mrs. Gould knows Sulaco for what it is, but she can never make her knowledge effective.'[34] It is very much part of the novel's scepticism that those who understand best, and know most, about the the real long-term needs of the people, are not in a position to influence the historical development significantly. Mrs Gould undergoes a dramatic process of learning in the course of the novel. Given her centrality as a character, it tells much about the thematic thrust of the work that this painful learning process of hers leads ultimately to disillusionment and resignation.

The narrator's relation to Mr Gould changes in inverse ratio to his relation to Mrs Gould. It is as though the narrator, too, is estranged from Mr Gould, who is treated with some authorial sympathy early in the narrative. Towards the end of the novel the distance between the narrator and Mr Gould is very substantial, but both his relative complexity as a character and the seriousness of the problem dramatized through his regressive development are indicated by the absence of stable, ridiculing irony in the authorial descriptions of him. There is a distinctly tragic dimension in the development of all the four main characters briefly considered here. This element of tragedy is strengthened by the way in which the characters' lives are integrated with, and partly determined by, the

[34] Said, *Beginnings*, 108.

action of the novel—an action 'enlarging individual into national tragedy'.[35]

Although the authorial narrator's relation to other characters is also of interest (Monygham in particular attains a special authority towards the end of the book), we must now proceed to comment on five other important characteristics and functions of his: generalizations, scepticism, defamiliarization, distance, and irony.

The narrator's generalizing tendency is striking throughout. We have noted examples of such generalizations, many of which incorporate elements of scepticism and irony. Structurally, the generalizations often have a unifying function since they make the reader think of other aspects of, or incidents in, the narrative. Broadly, generalized observations are of mixed quality in Conrad. Although this point could be made about *Nostromo* too, several of the authorial statements and reflections here belong among the most searching in the Conrad canon.

The pervasive scepticism of the authorial narrator is partly indicated through his generalizations, but it is also noticeable elsewhere in his narrative. We have considered instances of this inclination of the narrator. Examples abound, and are often related to his descriptions of the different characters. The scepticism may become explicit to the extent that the word actually occurs in the text, cf. 'The popular mind is incapable of scepticism' (420).

If, however, scepticism can be seen as one of the most characteristic attitudinal features of the authorial narrator, and hence as an importance constituent aspect of the novel's thematics, more difficult problems arise if we probe into the relation of scepticism as presented in this fictional text and other thematic elements such as disillusionment, resignation, gloom, and pessimism. If this study of Conrad's narrative method suggests that it may be less critically dubious to say something about Conrad's scepticism than about his possible pessimism, this is because of the interesting affinity between scepticism and the epistemological uncertainty of several of Conrad's personal narrators. The application of philosophical terminology to an analysis of narrative method is certainly a complicated manoeuvre in itself, and the levels of linguistic precision will necessarily vary (as philosophical concepts both scepticism, pessimism, and epistemology have long histories and many nuances

[35] *CMP* 126.

of meaning). Furthermore, even though the epistemological uncertainty of the personal narrator in 'The Tale', for instance, might be related to Conrad's scepticism, it surely does not follow that the pervading scepticism of *Nostromo* must be connected with problems of epistemological orientation on the part of the authorial narrator. Still, the possibility of making this point about Decoud, combined with the affinity of his sceptical attitude and that of the narrator, suggests that one way of offering a partial explanation of the authorial narrator's scepticism is to connect it with a position often held by sceptics from Aenesidemus on: his recognition of the fact that there is something there to be known which he is not in a position to know.[36] In the context of my discussion this 'something' could be rephrased as two questions. Given the strong sense of inevitability of the action of the novel, is there no possible alternative course? If the novel suggests, as Jeremy Hawthorn argues, that 'although, fundamentally, it is material interests not ideas that effect historical change, material interests effect this change through ideas',[37] could not then these ideas (as expressed through the naïve idealism of Mr Gould and Holroyd) be altered or morally improved, for instance through the influence of Mrs Gould? The legitimacy of such questions would appear strengthened by the notion present in many of Conrad's texts that man is free to act, but their relevance seems reduced at the end of *Nostromo*, where even the possibility of the 'something' the sceptic allows for is questioned. Here the novel's lurking doubt about the existence of a more positive alternative, however difficult to realize, becomes stronger. Nourished by the effects of the silver and the mine on the characters described, the doubt is associated with the movement of the narrative towards resignation and pessimism.

At the more technical level, we have seen that the authorial narrator productively applies the device of defamiliarization, as in the description of Giorgio as witness of a battle. This is not, however, the only instance where this narrative variation is observable. There is an interesting sense in which both the time-shifts and the analogical mobility of the narrative have a defamiliarizing effect: they make us more critical spectators of the

---

[36] See Julia Annas and Jonathan Barnes, *The Modes of Scepticism: Ancient Texts and Modern Interpretations* (Cambridge: CUP, 1985).

[37] Hawthorn, *Conrad: Language and Fictional Self-Consciousness*, 60.

events described and enhance our awareness of the various inconsistencies of human behaviour.

I have already commented on aspects of the authorial narrator's relation to Conrad on the one hand and to the main characters on the other; and as used in this study the meaning of 'distance' frequently approximates to that of 'relation'. The narrator is often greatly distanced from his characters; and this narrative characteristic is closely connected with his omniscient, all-inclusive, and panoramic narrative. Still, attitudinal distance does vary; and this variation is, as we have seen, related to the characteristic flexibility and mobility of the authorial narrative. It is also closely related to, though not determined by, the text's sophisticated use of irony.

As D. C. Muecke defines irony in *The Compass of Irony* it can be seen as a 'two-storey phenomenon',[38] the lower level being that of the victim(s) and the upper level that of the ironist. The main ironist of *Nostromo* is of course the authorial narrator, but the conscious use of irony which both Decoud and Mrs Gould habitually make in their personal discourse is one indication of the relative proximity of these two characters and the narrator. This proximity indicates that the device of irony works at varying levels in the course of the narrative; Decoud's and Mrs Gould's uses of irony serve (in addition to the irony of less important characters such as Monygham and Father Corbelàn) as personal extensions of the authorial narrator's own, wide-ranging ironic voice. A further complication is that the ironic effects are also dependent on how well the reader knows the text: with improved textual knowledge, ironies multiply. The various functions of irony in *Nostromo* may be exemplified as follows:

1. Irony can be indicated in titles, both of persons ('President-Dictator' and 'Cardinal-Archbishop') or of a book (*Fifty Years of Misrule*). It can also be brought out in a quotation such as that from the preface to *Fifty Years of Misrule*, where Costaguana's 'honourable place in the comity of civilized nations' (140) is described.

2. Irony may be suggested by an unexpected, often comic, word constellation such as 'But Don Vincente, a doctor of philosophy from the Cordova University, seemed to have an exaggerated respect for military ability' (144).

---

[38] Muecke, *The Compass of Irony*, 19.

3. It can vary between the authorial narrator's intended irony, e.g., 'The inference was true. Its deeper meaning was hidden from their simple intelligence' (45) or 'Captain Mitchell, feeling more and more in the thick of history' (136), and irony of which the characters (especially Decoud and Mrs Gould) are conscious, e.g., 'Decoud murmured to him ironically: "Those gentlemen talk about their gods" ' (199) and 'Agreeing ironically, [Mrs Gould] assured him that certainly not—nothing ever happened in Sulaco' (36).

4. The novel also has examples of what could be called dramatic irony, as in the authorial comment: 'Probably neither the priest nor the bandit saw the irony of it' (353). This variant does not rest upon any character's (or the narrator's) ironic intention, but it is related to the narrator's omniscience and scepticism.

5. Irony can be associated with images, metaphors, and symbols. This sort of irony has a modifying, more resigned effect. Consider the use of the adjective 'magnificent' in this example: 'The light in the room went out, and weighted with silver, the magnificent Capataz clasped her round her white neck in the darkness of the gulf as a drowning man clutches at a straw' (545).

One indication of the range of irony in *Nostromo* is that sometimes it may be hard to decide whether a passage actually contains irony or not, as in Mrs Gould's words to Sir John: 'And yet even here there are simple and picturesque things that one would like to preserve' (120). Certainly the remark points to Mrs Gould's early naïvety and humanistic idealism, which, though of a different kind from that of her husband, could be seen as vulnerable to the ironic authorial attitude in the broader context of the novel. However, such an impression is counteracted by the circumstance that, at this stage of the narrative, Mrs Gould is one of the very few characters to be sceptical about the effects the mine has on Costaguana. The possibility of irony seems to be suggested and withdrawn virtually at the same time.

A main reason why Conrad's use of irony in *Nostromo* is so flexible and rewarding is that it is better integrated into his narrative method than in any other of this works, with the possible exception of *The Secret Agent*. The sombre subject matter of the novel provides, in combination with the characters' limited understanding of the actions in which they are engaged, internal justification of the authorial narrator's wide-ranging use of this distancing device. However, its various functions are not necessarily indicative, as Goetsch seems to think, of authorial scorn or lack of care. Irony could rather be seen as a means of achieving, and keeping, an attitudinal distance which the authorial narrator needs in order to retain a concentrated focus on the vast and distressing thematics the novel explores. Thus in *Nostromo* irony becomes a paradoxical indication of authorial seriousness and involvement.

4. *Decoud's letter*

In his justly famous introduction to the 1951 Modern Library edition of *Nostromo*, Robert Penn Warren places Decoud's letter 'at the very center of the book'.[39] It is paradoxical, but ultimately convincing, that the situation in Sulaco can be described precisely only to a person (not even a fictional character) in another continent. In the letter Decoud the adept journalist reveals himself by providing an accurate and (for *Nostromo*) exceptionally lucid account of the present situation in Sulaco. The reader is surprised how much action there really is in the novel and how interrelated, progressive, and internally consistent it is. The narrative variation of Decoud's letter is one of the major successes of Conrad's narrative method in *Nostromo*. It provides the opportunity to incorporate a personal account into the authorial narrative: this account brings Sulaco and its inhabitants much closer to the reader; it makes Conrad's fictional universe in *Nostromo* more real and more immediately convincing. Moreover, the letter not only presents a remarkable, even moving, characterization of an exceptionally intelligent and perceptive character, but also highlights and intensifies several of the novel's main thematic concerns through this characterization. Finally, it may be noted that as the recipient of the letter, Decoud's sister performs an interestingly combined function as narratee and reader here. The structural elimination of the possibility of response from the narratee confirms Decoud's isolation; it may also make the letter more reliable as a narrative document.

[39] Penn Warren, 'On *Nostromo*', intro. to the Modern Library edn. of *Nostromo*, (New York, 1951); rpt. in Stallman (ed.), *Conrad: A Symposium*, 222.

5. Mitchell's account

Regardless of the great personal difference between Decoud and Mitchell there are, as argued above, structural similarities between Decoud's 1890 letter and Mitchell's 1897 account addressed to the unnamed visitor to Sulaco. Here, too, the occasion provides an intrinsic justification of the narrative variation: the visitor from abroad is uninformed about the events that have taken place in the country, and understands less than the reader does in the light of earlier action. Mitchell's account constitutes a narrative variation, with one of the novel's characters functioning as personal narrator within the all-embracing authorial framework of the book, and with a directly addressed narratee ('All the great world of Sulaco here, sir' (481)). If it is necessary to stress that the similarity between Decoud's letter and Mitchell's boasting, simplifying, and rather uncomprehending résumé is essentially structural, this is because some critics of the novel exaggerate the thematic affinity not only between Decoud the reflective writer and Mitchell the naïve speaker, but even between Mitchell and the authorial narrator. Torsten Pettersson, for instance, finds that 'the parallel between the narrator's associative shifts and Mitchell's desultory account of memorable events suggests that the history of Costaguana unfolded before us is similarly steeped in the personality of its historian'.[40] But certainly the narrator's sophisticated temporal and spatial shifts of focus would seem to constitute a contrast, rather than a 'parallel' (a difficult term for a critic of Conrad), to the simplified personal version given by one of the characters whom the omniscient narrator not only describes but also, we suspect, secretly resents.

6. Images, metaphors, and symbols

Especially in his generalizations, the authorial narrator tends to employ images introduced by 'as though' or, more often, 'like.' Although the images are not all equally effective, their implications are generally significant, and not seldom unpleasant. Broadly, the imagery of Nostromo is in keeping with, and helps to constitute, the scepticism of the novel. Though formulated by the narrator and

---

[40] Pettersson, Consciousness and Time, 125.

apparently provoked by his omniscience, the images are often related to a personal perspective. We have considered one of the book's most resonant images, the authorial passage which describes Giorgio as witness of the battle on the plain below Higuerota. Important characteristics of the novel's imagery are observable here: starting from a personal anchor-point, the authorial narrator associatively presents a panoramic overview which includes absurdist elements and incorporates a powerful metaphor, Higuerota, whose clearly symbolic implications are engendered and strengthened not only by the narrative context of *Nostromo* but also, as we have noted in connection with the references to Eco and Said, by the affinity between the qualities ascribed to the mountain and major thematic concerns in Conrad's fiction generally.

If we compare the imagery of this passage with that in section three of Decoud's letter, we note that the imagery in the letter is more reflective and intellectual. Yet as a generalizing characterization of Decoud as representative of a particular combination of human qualities (whose lack of internal consistency confirms the irrational element in the actions of human beings), the image is both convincing and suggestive. Formulating a partial, authorial explanation of Decoud's seemingly self-contradictory activities as sceptical, detached journalist and involved activist, the image combines emphasis on his loneliness with a cautious warning not to be misled into regarding Decoud's position as entirely untypical.

We have seen that Higuerota can be interpreted both as a metaphor and as a symbol. This point can be extended to include two other important metaphors in the novel, the silver and the mine. Here the symbolic dimension is even more apparent than in the case of Higuerota; indeed, the fusion of the silver and the mine could be seen as the most significant symbol of *Nostromo*. As with any symbol proper, its meanings and implications are not easily indicated: its suggestiveness prevents explicitness. Still, the implications of the silver symbol are sombre. It brings about estrangement (Mr and Mrs Gould), corruption (Sulaco officials and politicians, and Nostromo), loneliness (Decoud, Nostromo, Mr and Mrs Gould), disillusionment (Nostromo and Mrs Gould). Interestingly, there is one instance where the silver is actually described as a symbol in the text. On the evening of the riot, with the Europeans gathering round Mr Gould, it is to the narrator 'as if the silver of the mine had been the emblem of a common cause, the symbol of the supreme importance of material interests' (260). This seems an authorial indication that although the silver symbol can be connected with a wide range of meanings, its essence revolves round the 'material interests' that manifest themselves in *Nostromo*.

7. *The motif of loneliness*

Most of the characters in *Nostromo* are described as lonely, but sometimes the motif becomes especially prominent and is given particular thematic significance. This happens, for instance, in the description of the transport of the silver to the Great Isabel, but most of all in that of Decoud's absolute solitude on the island. It is helpful to distinguish between solitude as a more external, existential quality and loneliness as a more subjective, psychological one: the surrounding static solitude engenders a pressing loneliness which becomes unbearable. For Decoud, that is; an implication of the exceptionally intense authorial narrative here is that a less intelligent and less consistent character might have survived, but then he or she would probably not have confronted the problem in the way Decoud does. The combination of reflective intellect and human isolation is extremely dangerous for a Conrad character. One indication of the centrality of the loneliness motif in *Nostromo* is that it is applied to all the four most important characters in the novel—Decoud, Nostromo, Mr and Mrs Gould. When, at the very end, Mrs Gould is seen by the authorial narrator—and there is no indication that his general omniscience is not at work here too—as 'as solitary as any human being had ever been' (555), we are given a pessimistic concluding statement on the state of mind of the character in the novel who cares most for human company and meaningful human relationships.

III

Both the textual commentary and the systematized critical observations above suggest that the authorial narrative of *Nostromo* has an extraordinary range and flexibility. The best indication of this range is perhaps provided by the narrative device of irony as it functions as integral part of the narrative method of the novel: irony serves both as a means of achieving diversified characterization and as an authorial attitude necessitated by the novel's thematic concerns and disillusioned insights. The authorial narrator employs various forms of ironic modulation both by way of characterization and in order to introduce and develop essential aspects of the content of the novel. These aspects are diverse: they include moral issues such as personal integrity and depravity as well as socioeconomic questions such as economic exploitation and the relationship of power and influence.

The main point implied in the distinction between irony as a means of characterization and as authorial attitude may be specified and developed via a short discussion of Fredric Jameson's presentation of a threefold ideological interference in *Nostromo*. The interpretation Jameson gives of the novel in *The Political Unconscious* is one of the most interesting and consciously ideological that we have.[41] In the words of Jacques Berthoud, whose critique of Jameson's study is as stimulating as the book itself, Jameson reads *Nostromo*

as a novel in which real history is allowed to declare itself. This allegedly happens less because Conrad has learnt something since writing *Lord Jim* than because in the new novel narrative conventions are enlarged to include the collective, and the conditions favouring strategies of containment are thereby largely removed.[42]

For Jameson, this enlargement of narrative conventions makes *Nostromo* a more interesting, and also, in the critical context of *The Political Unconscious*, a more relevant work than *Lord Jim*. In order to comment critically on the threefold ideological interference he sees in the former novel I first give a summarized presentation of the basic, tripartite distinction he expounds.

First, at the most general level we have, Jameson says, 'the classic "Anglo" picture of a Latin "race," lazy, shiftless, and the like, to which political order and economic progress must be "brought" from the outside'.[43] Although Jameson emphasizes that this attitude is more complex than 'simple racism', it seems to incorporate racist elements.

[41] Fredric Jameson, 'Romance and Reification: Plot Construction and Ideological Closure in Joseph Conrad', ch. 5 of his *The Political Unconscious: Narrative as a Socially Symbolic Act* (London: Methuen, 1981), 206–80.

[42] Jacques Berthoud, 'Narrative and Ideology: A Critique of Fredric Jameson's *The Political Unconscious*', in Jeremy Hawthorn (ed.), *Narrative*, 113–14.

[43] Jameson, *The Political Unconscious*, 270.

At the second level Jameson locates 'Conrad's political reflections and attitudes proper'.[44] As the complicated action in the early chapters of Nostromo slowly unfolds, these attitudes enable the reader to identify '[Conrad's] positive figures among the locals—the so-called Blancos—with the aristocratic party, and... the evil Monteros with the mestizos'. Yet Jameson does not consider Nostromo as a political novel in the sense in which a full confrontation of the two opposed sides could be realized. Rather, 'Conrad's own political attitudes are presupposed, and rhetorically reinforced by ethical and melodramatic markers (the Blancos are good, the Monteristas evil).'[45]

The third and deepest ideological level is for Jameson the theory of ressentiment, which in this particular case means that the 'bad' or 'evil' characters of the novel 'are described, and their motives explained, in terms that are the commonplaces of all the great counterrevolutionary nineteenth-century historians'.[46] The ideologeme of ressentiment is one of the key concepts in The Political Unconscious; and Jameson sees Nietzsche as its first main theorist. The far-reaching implications of this complex term cannot be considered here, but it must be stressed that Jameson's concluding assessment of Nostromo is more nuanced and appreciative than this very short (and, unavoidably, simplifying) presentation of the three ideological levels may seem to indicate.

If related to the above analysis of the novel's narrative method, and more specifically to the distinction introduced between two supplementary functions of irony detectable in it, Jameson's tripartite, ideological diversification provokes the following two critical comments, which are most obviously connected with his first two levels.

First, if there are racist elements in the novel that help constitute the first ideological level Jameson identifies, it is—on the basis of the narrative analysis presented here—doubtful whether an attitude incorporating such elements can be attributed to the authorial narrator, and even less to Conrad. One could, possibly, say that the text introduces racist or nationally biased elements in order to

---

[44] Ibid.
[45] Ibid.
[46] Ibid. 270–1. Cf. Hayden White, Metahistory: The Historical Imagination in Nineteenth-Century Europe (Baltimore: Johns Hopkins University Press, 1973), and Jameson's review of this magisterial study in Diacritics, 6 (1976), 2–9.

criticize or eliminate them, but that would imply a theoretically dubious understanding of the term 'ideology' (and one, moreover, which is contrary to Jameson's consistent use of the concept). My reading, it will be recalled, stresses the flexibility and range of the authorial narrator's voice. It is a voice which, supplementing its own panoramic and diversified perspective with that of various characters, records and transmits an enormous and bewildering wealth of fictional information. But this information does not serve as a basis for ill-conceived, racist attitudes; and to the extent that the narrative presents *characters* whose pronouncements testify to such attitudes, these characters rarely escape some variant of the novel's wide-ranging irony. Mitchell's account provides an obvious, but illustrative, example. Employing my broad distinction between two forms of irony, the first form (the one directly related to the novel's characterization) is the more relevant here.

The other form, however—and we now proceed to the second comment on Jameson's ideological stratification of *Nostromo*—is a variant of irony that makes it extremely difficult to identify 'Conrad's political reflections and attitudes proper' in the novel. As my interpretation relates this form of irony to a resigned and disillusioned authorial attitude which permeates the whole text, I must dissent from Jameson's exposition of Conrad's attitude as one which, consciously or unconsciously, distinguishes between 'positive' and 'negative' characters in the novel. It is true that we hear more about the 'aristocratic' party than the mestizos, but both parties are criticized—at least in the sense of being subjected, indirectly but forcibly, to authorial irony. There is an additional problem involved here. Jameson laudably resists the rough and ready contrasts of Greimasian structuralism: the comments on the dynamic aspects of narrative fiction belong among the most instructive in *The Political Unconscious*, and suggest an interesting affinity with Brooks's understanding of plot. Still, the distinction between positive and negative characters in *Nostromo* implies a problematic simplification of one of the most basic problems the novel dramatizes: how human beings change under the pressure of varying, predominantly external and material, circumstances. Nostromo's change—from 'unconscious wild beast' to 'man' (412)—is a case in point.

If this cursory criticism of the ideological diversification Jameson imposes upon the narrative of *Nostromo* draws some support from the analysis of narrative method presented in this chapter, the relevance and argumentative force of such evidence are an indication not only of the thematic implications of the narrative method observable in a Conrad text, but also of certain limitations to such implications. Although Jameson's discussion of *Nostromo* (and also of *Lord Jim*, the other Conrad novel he considers) contains a number of valuable insights, several of his generalizations about the novel become less convincing if critically related to the narrative complexity of the fictional text they refer to. This is not to suggest that there is no ideological structure in Conrad's fiction, but the kind of tripartite ideological 'interference' suggested by Jameson does not, on the basis of this analysis of the novel's narrative method, appear wholly persuasive.

If we now go on from *The Political Unconscious* to comment briefly on Edward Said's discussion of *Nostromo* in *Beginnings*, we notice that although his and Jameson's considerations are tangential and supplementary in various ways, Said is less concerned with the ideological and political issues of the novel, and more with fundamental philosophical (in part epistemological) questions such as beginning, change, and the human need or desire to leave some sort of record behind (cf. Decoud's letter). Thus Said's thematic discussion of *Nostromo* specifies and extends some of the thematic implications and effects of narrative method that we have noted.

For Said, *Nostromo* 'is masquerading as an ordinary political or historical novel. The real action, on the other hand, is psychological and concerns man's overambitious intention to author his own world because the world as he finds it is somehow intolerable: this action underlies the historical and political events in *Nostromo*. The horror occurs in the gradual, prolonged discovery that the world created by one man is just as intolerable as the world he has superseded.'[47]

This very interesting view of the novel could be related to several of my points about the text's narrative method and the thematics it engenders. On the level of characterization, for instance, Said's notion of the novel's dramatization of man's 'overambitious intention to author his own world' applies particularly well to Mr Gould and Nostromo, but the notion is also suggestive if associated with Decoud. And as far as the effects of this 'overambitious intention'

[47] Said, *Beginnings*, 118.

are concerned, there is an interesting sense in which they seem to be connected, albeit indirectly, with the authorial narrator's omniscient perspective, his peculiarly mixed attitude (involving both irony and sympathy), and his attitudinal movement towards resignation. On the basis of my interpretation it seems, however, doubtful if the two basic thematic dimensions Said identifies in *Nostromo*, the political/historical and the psychological, are mutually exclusive. It is probably more accurate to say that the all-inclusive authorial narrative not only incorporates both these aspects, but also explores each of them and demonstrates how interrelated and interdependent they are.

If Jameson's ideological concerns sometimes make him pay insufficient attention to the diverse narrative method of *Nostromo*, Said's emphasis on the novel's psychological aspects occasionally entails comparable critical effects. To exemplify this criticism we might consider his point about Conrad's 'excessive use of appositional phrases',[48] particularly in the characterization of Nostromo. Surely these phrases have an important function: they help characterize Nostromo as strong, courageous, and unreflective. Applying Miller's distinction between two forms of repetition to this novel, we could say that such appositional phrases serve, combined with other narrative devices, to constitute Nostromo's position as a major representative of the first form of repetition: in the first part of *Nostromo* the world has an unproblematic origin and coherence for him. However, as Nostromo gets inextricably involved in the hopes, anxiety, and disillusionment associated with the silver—as, in the terminology of the novel, corruption is extended to include and absorb the hero—his role as a main representative of the first form of repetition becomes less evident. This change is related to the increasingly pessimistic thematic implications revealed by means of the narrative.

On balance, however, the distinction between two forms of repetition seems less critically rewarding when applied to *Nostromo* than to *Lord Jim*. One reason for this is suggested by the larger scope of the former work—panoramically describing a whole country at a transitional point in its history. Conrad's flexible use of authorial narrative in order to give this exceptionally detailed, all-inclusive, and persuasive description constitutes one of his most

[48] Ibid. 127.

impressive fictional achievements. In the last analysis, it seems consistent with the complicated and wide-ranging thematics the novel explores that it should, essentially, ask questions rather than provide answers. Aspects of the authorial generalizations might be seen as suggesting partial answers to some of the questions and problems dramatized, but basically the authorial narrator's attitude to the events and characters he describes is one of wonder, fascination, even despair: this serious involvement is established along with his more technical detachment and becomes a paradoxical, convincing justification of the pervasive use of irony throughout the novel. Thus the reverberant questions asked by, and dramatized through, this text are intimately connected with the varying attitudinal position and complex narrative function of its authorial narrator.

11
The Secret Agent:
Ironic and Disillusioned Authorial
Narrative

At first sight the narrative method of Conrad's next novel, *The Secret Agent* (1907), seems very similar to that of *Nostromo*. Not only is the narrative of both novels authorial in a sophisticated and wide-ranging sense (we might even say a characteristically 'Conradian' sense, as these particular texts are major examples of Conrad's authorial narrative method). Additional points of resemblance include the pervasive and multi-faceted use of irony, which in both works is closely related to narrative effects and modulations, and also refer to similar, though hardly identical, fictional manifestations of Conrad's scepticism and political insights.

Yet this chapter hopes to demonstrate that Conrad's authorial method in *The Secret Agent* has a narrative rhythm and expressive thematics of its own. This is another way of suggesting that the narrative method of *The Secret Agent* is an enriching supplement to, rather than a mechanical echo of, that of *Nostromo*. As in the discussion of *Lord Jim*, I want to begin this chapter by presenting one possible summary of the action of *The Secret Agent*:

A seedy shop in Soho provides cover for Verloc, the secret agent, who is working as a spy for a foreign embassy and as informer for Chief Inspector Heat of Scotland Yard. His wife Winnie has married him chiefly to provide security for her simple-minded younger brother Stevie, and is ignorant of Verloc's spying activities. The foreign embassy is planning a series of outrages aimed at discrediting the revolutionary group which will be held responsible. The first target is the Greenwich Observatory and an unwilling Verloc is ordered to engineer the explosion. He uses the poor innocent Stevie as an accomplice, but the boy is blown to pieces while carrying the bomb. Winnie, stricken by her brother's death and outraged by Verloc's lack of remorse, kills him with a knife. Fleeing, she encounters the anarchist Ossipon who flirts with her and they plan to leave the country. But when he discovers Verloc's murder he steals her money and abandons her. Winnie, alone and in terror of the gallows, throws herself overboard from the Channel ferry.[1]

Like summaries of other Conrad texts (and not only Guerard's of *Lord Jim* but also those of 'An Outpost of Progress' and 'The Tale') this one is also only an outline. The summary simplifies and distorts *The Secret Agent* not only by presenting just a selection out of a large number of significant textual elements, but also by adding descriptive adjectives ('unwilling Verloc... poor innocent Stevie') which, though by no means improper or wrong, serve to blur the transition between summary and interpretation.

Furthermore, the summary includes no reference to the novel's most decisive and all-embracing narrative device, the authorial narrator. However, in one obvious sense this omission is consistent enough. For as a summary of action refers to the diegetic level of a fictional text, we cannot expect it to incorporate references to a narrator as clearly extradiegetic as that of *The Secret Agent*. Like the authorial narrator of *Nostromo*, this one too neither participates in the action he presents nor establishes contact with the characters he introduces and depicts. On the whole, he preserves a very considerable distance both from the events and from the characters engaged in these events. However, again in a manner reminiscent of *Nostromo*, this distance, which is not just attitudinal but also one of level and insight, increases rather than reduces the narrator's knowledge and flexibility. If, on balance, the authorial narrative appears less flexible and nuanced here than in the former novel, this may be due to differences in subject matter as well as in authorial attitude to the dramatized characters and events.

The purpose of this cursory comparison with *Nostromo* is not just introductory; I hope the affinities of the two works may suggest a reason why the structure of this chapter resembles that of the preceding one. Broadly, it is divided into two: I start with comments on selected aspects of the novel's narrative method, and then proceed to some more generalized observations on the authorial narrator and his relations to the most important characters.

---

[1] This summary condenses that given in the latest edition of Margaret Drabble (ed.), *The Oxford Companion to English Literature* (Oxford: OUP, 1985), 882.

I

On a first reading, the beginning of *The Secret Agent* seems to establish a narrative situation in which the narrator, though apparently authorial, keeps a rather low profile as far as evaluative judgements of the characters are concerned. This is not to imply that there is no authorial irony, for instance, observable in the first chapter, but it is striking how much denser, more proleptic and suggestive the opening of the novel becomes on rereading. Thus a critical comment such as this one by Christine Sizemore is hardly based on just one reading:

The Secret Agent opens seemingly inauspiciously with a description of Mr. Verloc's shop and a long list of its questionable, and carefully wrapped, wares. This description strikes the ironic tone and provides the appropriate squalid setting for a tale of intrigue. More importantly, it establishes an image pattern of boxes and containers which, as they are repeated in significant places throughout the novel, become potent symbols... Furthermore, the image of the box represents the structure of the novel itself, which is built around an empty space, the actual explosion that is never described.[2]

This is well said, but without reducing the structural and thematic significance of the 'square box' (3) it might be added that this is certainly not the only textual element in Chapter 1 which Conrad is to repeat and explore later on in the novel. There are aspects of Winnie's character, for instance, which are more immediately convincing on rereading. Indeed some of the authorial narrator's introductory comments on her then become clearly proleptic, for instance his mention of 'the provocation of her unfathomable reserve' (6). Moreover, the introductory observations on Verloc and Stevie are not just consonant with the action and characterizations later in the narrative. Additionally, there is an exceptional precision about them which on rereading not only suggests a number of more or less overt prolepses, but also serves as an early indication of the remarkable density of the authorial narrator's discourse. Several critics have noted that the authorial characterization of both Verloc and Winnie is focused on details which reappear later in the plot. This observation is valid enough, but it

---

[2] Christine W. Sizemore, ' "The Small Cardboard Box": A Symbol of the City and of Winnie Verloc in Conrad's *The Secret Agent*', *Modern Fiction Studies*, 24 (1978), 23.

might be extended to include not only the authorial narrator's characterizations of members of the Verloc family, but his own characteristics as narrator as well: omniscience and flexibility combined with distance and irony, a certain attitudinal rigidity connected with a tendency to generalize, a predilection for rather unpleasant imagery related to grim and quirky humour.

As all these characteristics of the authorial narrator apply to the novel as a whole, what needs to be emphasized is the surprising extent to which, on a second or third reading, they are already found to be present in Chapter 1. I cannot give examples of all these narrative characteristics here (this would require a detailed analysis of Chapter 1), but I should add that the way in which they are *combined* similarly prefigures what is to become an essential aspect of the novel's narrative method.

Consider, for example, this authorial comment on Verloc: 'He generally arrived in London (like the influenza) from the Continent, only he arrived unheralded by the Press' (6). What strikes us first here is the blend of irony and humour in the parenthetically inserted image. Additionally, however, the narrator's omniscience and overview are noticeable here too, constantly interrelating the various textual elements. Alluding to his anarchist activities, the comparison of Verloc and influenza establishes a more specific link with Vladimir (the First Secretary of the embassy) in Chapter 2, where the latter, in the conversation with Verloc, suggests that what is needed now is a 'cure' (25). Although striking, the narrator's omniscience here is not, as is often the case, used as a basis for authorial evaluation of Verloc. Rather, anticipating the next chapter, the authorial omniscience establishes a slanting movement into Vladimir's perspective. Similarly, although the word 'Press' at first comes across as a relatively simple indication of Verloc's need for anonymity, there is a nice irony in that information about two of the most dramatic deaths in the novel, those of Stevie and Winnie, is given via references to newspaper reports.

As we move on to Chapter 2, then, several of the most important constitutive aspects of the novel's authorial narrative method are introduced, and to some extent even confirmed. Because of this apparent stability of authorial narrative we are surprised when we reach the middle of the second paragraph:

But there was also about [Verloc] an indescribable air which no mechanic could have acquired in the practice of his handicraft however dishonestly exercised: the air common to men who live on the vices, the follies, or the baser fears of mankind; the air of moral nihilism common to keepers of gambling hells and disorderly houses; to private detectives and inquiry agents; to drink sellers and, I should say, to the sellers of invigorating electric belts and to the inventors of patent medicines. But of that last I am not sure, not having carried my investigations so far into the depths. For all I know, the expression of these last may be perfectly diabolic. I shouldn't be surprised. What I want to affirm is that Mr. Verloc's expression was by no means diabolic. (13)

That the narrator's description of Verloc should provoke some rather critical authorial generalizations is not alone cause for surprise here. For when we first encounter the sudden influx of first-person personal pronouns, the effect on us as readers is very similar to that created by the opening of Chapter 8 in Part First of *Nostromo*. Here too the authorial narrative situation seems to be breaking down: the repeated references to 'I' appear to signal a personal identification of the authorial narrator, particularly as the first-person pronouns introduce qualifications indicative of severe restrictions of authorial knowledge ('I am not sure... For all I know').

Most commentators on the novel have paid insufficient attention to this passage. That the passage is hard to explain enhances rather than reduces its critical interest, which is further augmented by the resemblance it bears to Chapter 8 of *Nostromo*. We might expect the narrative to turn personal here, that the narrator would go on to identify himself as a narrator-character on the diegetic level. Although such a shift would have been problematic (especially with regard to narrative omniscience), it would in a way have been more logical than the reversal to authorial narrative which actually takes place in the next paragraph. The authorial narrative here is indistinguishable from that we are accustomed to, and it remains uninterrupted for the rest of the novel.

Who, then, is this 'I' that suddenly and surprisingly appears just in order to disappear? To ask this question would be tantamount to probing the identity of the authorial narrator, for one thing which seems certain is that 'I' must refer to him. The association of the authorial narrator and 'him' here surely does not imply that the narrator must be a man; an authorial narrator is characterized not least by his disassociation from human gender and the personal limitations attached to both sexes. Still, the passage does add a personal flavour to the authorial narrative of *The Secret Agent*.

Although, as we read on, we may soon forget this paragraph, it points towards a certain limitation of authorial understanding—introducing a more subjective and less self-assured perspective. From this observation one might go on to suggest that Conrad, here as in the relevant *Nostromo* chapter, possibly wants to make some sort of formal reservation, repeating the first-person personal pronoun five times to emphasize that he, as author, is not to be confused with his authorial narrator. Although this may perhaps be the case, the intrusion of first-person pronouns seems rather awkward; and it probably does not make the narrative as a whole appear less authorial. Even so, it represents a notable narrative variation, and one whose significance is increased if related to the narrator's modified irony in the presentation of Stevie.

The remaining part of Chapter 2 is largely centred on Verloc's meeting with Vladimir. Their extended dialogue is instrumental in confirming essential constitutive aspects of the authorial narrative method of the novel, as well as of its thematics. Vladimir here gives Verloc the order which leads not only to the explosion, but also to the dramatic deaths of the three main members of the Verloc family. The function of the authorial narrator in this section can usefully be related to his descriptions of, and attitude to, Vladimir on the one hand and Verloc on the other. My first point is perhaps self-evident, but provides the basis required for further differentiation: the characterizations of both Vladimir and Verloc depend on the way in which authorial omniscience is combined with the narrator's attitudinal distance. However, possibilities remain for narrative modulations within this broader pattern.

At the beginning of the interview, authorial omniscience is pointed indeed. Verloc is described as 'in truth, startled and alarmed' (26); Vladimir 'formulated in his mind a series of disparaging remarks concerning Mr. Verloc's face and figure' (27). The phrase 'formulated in his mind' (an authorial pointer towards the linguistic structuring of a character's associative thoughts) precedes a long paragraph in which the narrative not only reports Vladimir's reflections on Verloc, but is coloured by them as well. This happens partly through the use of narrated monologue ('This fellow!'), partly through a momentary blending of authorial and personal irony—in the sense that Vladimir's ironic thoughts on Verloc seem to derive at least some support from the authorial narrator's authoritative reflections.

Some paragraphs further on, however, this narrative modulation is supplemented by another inclined to Verloc's perspective rather than Vladimir's:

And Mr. Vladimir developed his idea from on high, with scorn and condescension, displaying at the same time an amount of ignorance as to the real aims, thoughts, and methods of the revolutionary world which filled the silent Mr. Verloc with inward consternation. He confounded causes with effects more than was excusable... (29–30)

Clearly this passage cannot be considered in isolation, but must be related to Vladimir's whole presentation of his 'philosophy of bomb throwing' (32). What it indicates then is that the authorial narrator's attitude to both Vladimir and Verloc is more unstable and flexible than it seems to be to begin with: if he gradually becomes more sceptical of the views of the former, he establishes a closer relation to the latter by relating his authorial scepticism to that of Verloc. As a result of the attitudinal affinity thus established with Verloc's perspective, this passage diversifies the reader's view of Verloc; our respect for him grows somewhat and his complexity as character increases.

However, this kind of increased authorial distance from Vladimir does not imply that his views and evaluations are to be rejected altogether. Although in dissimilar ways, Vladimir's criticisms of the anarchists receive support from several quarters of the text. The authorial narrator, the action of the novel, and such a character as the Professor (who in a sense voices the strongest and most explicit criticism) all variously confirm the validity of Vladimir's association of anarchist activity with the Latin phrase he starts but does not finish, 'Vox et . . . [praeterea nihil]' (24).[3] Once this qualification has been made, then it can be suggested that the novel's authorial method is here made more sophisticated through modulations of authorial perspective. This perspective first approaches that of Vladimir, then that of Verloc, but still the characteristic combination of authorial omniscience, reticence, and irony is retained throughout the dialogue. This way of extending authorial perspective is noticeable in later chapters too, and can be seen as a slight but

---

[3] Jeanne Delbaere notes that the whole Latin phrase ('A voice and nothing else') comes from a story by Plutarch. See her *Notes on The Secret Agent* (Harlow: Longman, 1981), 17.

significant modification of the novel's pervasive authorial irony. It might be added that the use of narrated monologue also serves to modify authorial voice slightly here, but the perspectival modulations are the more important.

It is often pointed out that the presentation of the gathering of Verloc's anarchist friends in Chapter 3 verges on caricature. What is more seldom noted is that this impression of caricature is in part established through an uncompromising stability of authorial perspective in the first part of the chapter. Michaelis is the first character to be subjected to the narrator's irony, which is again combined with omniscience and pointed attitudinal distance. But the effect of narrated monologue is now rather different from that in the preceding chapter. In the description of Michaelis in particular, the use of this narrative variant seems essentially to underline authorial irony and distance rather than modifying it: 'He a pessimist! Preposterous! He cried out that the charge was outrageous. He was so far from pessimism that he saw already the end of all private property coming along logically, unavoidably, by the mere development of its inherent viciousness' (43).

If authorial distance is pointed in the early part of the chapter, this is not only because the anarchists are sardonically exposed here, but also because the last part of the chapter contains two of the most remarkable metaphors in the novel. The first is centred on Stevie's drawing of circles; and we shall turn to it later when discussing the authorial narrator's relation to Stevie. The second is focused on Verloc, but before considering it some remarks must be made on the authorial narrator's relation to Verloc at this stage of the narrative. Clearly Verloc is not as heavily caricatured as the anarchists Michaelis and Ossipon. But although our increased respect for Verloc (from the dialogue with Vladimir) may appear to be confirmed by his taciturnity, it may just as well seem reduced if we think of his function as double agent. Indeed, as the chapter develops Verloc is subjected to direct, almost crude, authorial irony on various occasions. Consider, for instance, this authorial comment: 'Mr. Verloc descended into the abyss of moral reflections' (52). The irony is evident enough, but its effect is changed somewhat as, half a page further on, it blends into the authorial contempt of this sentence: 'And Mr. Verloc, temperamentally identical with his associates, drew fine distinctions in his mind on the strength of insignificant differences' (53).

If we recall Muecke's definition of irony as a 'two-storey phenomenon', then the supreme insight of the ironist, situated at the upper
'storey' or level, is very striking here. The sentence also illustrates
how strongly the effects of authorial irony in this novel can depend
on authorial omniscience: had we doubted the validity of this
authorial assertion, the ironic effect would have been considerably
reduced. Moreover, the sentence is also a good illustration of the
way in which irony is related to, and established through, authorial
distance. Two variants of distance are interconnected here. The
first variant is clearly attitudinal in the sense that the authorial
narrator obviously approves neither of anarchy nor of anarchist
activity. Additionally, distance is also very marked as far as level of
insight is concerned. This is another way of stressing the productive
relationship between distance and irony in the novel: as irony is
established not least by means of authorial distance, so one effect of
the irony is to reinforce the reader's impression of the narrator's
need for distance from the characters described. And, in a complex
way, this need of the narrator's can be seen as reflecting Conrad's
need for distance from the fictional reality of *The Secret Agent*.

Some sentences further on, a further narrative variation is introduced which both modifies and complicates the function of the
authorial narrator. Proceeding in the same vein and voicing various
criticisms of the anarchists, the narrator then again focuses attention on Verloc: 'Lost for a whole minute in the abyss of meditation,
Mr. Verloc did not reach the depth of these abstract considerations.
Perhaps he was not able. In any case he had not the time' (53). One
possible explanation of this curious passage is to relate it to the
surprising personal intrusion in Chapter 2 that we have already
considered. As the words 'not sure' indicate a momentary limitation
of authorial knowledge in the former passage, so 'Perhaps' here
similarly signals a more hesitant authorial evaluation of Verloc.
However, the essential point to make about this passage is suggested by the authorial statement to which 'perhaps' refers: 'Mr.
Verloc did not reach the depth of these abstract considerations'.
What is problematic about this statement is that it takes the form of
an explicit authorial self-characterization of the narrator's 'abstract
considerations'. For there is a complicating personal element in this
kind of authorial self-description: although abstract and general, the
narrator's comments on the anarchists in the preceding paragraph
do not strike us as particularly deep—'depth' would seem to require

a more nuanced attitude than that we associate with the authorial narrator's rather harsh irony here. As one effect of the self-characterization, then, is to reduce the authorial authority on which many of the novel's effects depend, it can be seen as reinforcing the personal element in the authorial narrator's discourse. Such a view could be extended by suggesting that this peculiar instance of authorial self-appraisal is another, and perhaps more sophisticated, attempt on Conrad's part to indicate a certain distance from his narrator: in this particular sentence, the authorial narrator's irony seems to extend even to himself.

Here as in Chapter 2, the narrative succeeding this passage seemingly effortlessly reverts to the form of authorial narrative typical of the whole novel. There is a sense, therefore, in which the kind of interpretative comment I have just made is dependent not only on rereading, but also on a relatively high degree of textual insulation from the surrounding context. I do not say this to qualify my last critical points, but rather to establish a contrast against which the manipulative and formative skills of the authorial narrator can be more accurately measured. This is another way of saying that the novel's constant foregrounding of the authorial narrator's main characteristics and functions serves to make the problems of narrative consistency and method less conspicuous.

The next notable narrative variation is also related to Verloc:

Then after slipping his braces off his shoulders he pulled up violently the venetian blind, and leaned his forehead against the cold window-pane—a fragile film of glass stretched between him and the enormity of cold, black, wet, muddy, inhospitable accumulation of bricks, slates, and stones, things in themselves unlovely and unfriendly to man. (56)

The narrative and thematic nucleus of this passage is the metaphor 'a fragile film of glass', which invites two comments. First, this metaphor is very suggestive thematically. It embodies an exceptional concentration of textual meaning: although related to Verloc, it acutely pinpoints the vulnerability and loneliness of several of the most important characters in the novel. If we go on to suggest that, although most unambiguously applicable to the Verloc family, this kind of textual meaning has a wider relevance too, then we have also implied that the metaphor serves both to increase the significance of the Verlocs' domestic drama in itself and to relate it more closely to other, supplementary thematic aspects.

Secondly, the metaphor is actually more complex than indicated so far. The 'film of glass' includes two metaphorizing sememes, both of which are partly defined by 'fragile' as adjectival specification. As metaphorized sememe, the 'window-pane' is prefixed by 'cold', an adjective which is effectively repeated later in the sentence. The verb 'stretch' extends the semantic range of both the metaphorizing and metaphorized sememes, making the metaphor more dynamic and thus connecting it more directly with the novel's progressive action. Several commentators on the novel have drawn our attention to what Jeremy Hawthorn calls its 'treatment of persons as things and things as living beings'.[4] Such a notion may also be related to this complex metaphor, and especially to the way in which it blends into, or fails to separate man from, the enormous 'accumulation of bricks, slates, and stones, things in themselves unlovely and unfriendly to man'.

To single out certain aspects of Conrad's narrative method for relatively detailed analysis inevitably results in more superficial critical treatment of other aspects that can also be important. I mention this general problem as a way of indicating that several chapters of *The Secret Agent* might well have been considered in greater detail than I can do here. In Chapter 4, for instance, the combination of ellipsis and delayed decoding serves to circumvent and temporarily to suppress an authorial description of the accident in which Stevie is killed. Information on the killing is instead provided by Ossipon, as he casually remarks to the Professor that 'There's a man blown up in Greenwich Park this morning' (70). As this ellipsis too refers to one of the central events in *The Secret Agent*, it is reminiscent of Conrad's decision not to describe in detail the actual revolution in *Nostromo*. Very broadly, these shifts or deviations of narrative focus can be seen as both reflecting and constituting Conrad's tendency, in his fiction, to give the social and personal effects of events priority over the events themselves. In *The Secret Agent* this tendency is confirmed in Chapter 5, where more detailed news of the explosion is presented analeptically, as factual information inserted into the authorial description of the impression the victim's remains make on Chief Inspector Heat:

---

[4] Hawthorn, *Conrad: Language and Fictional Self-Consciousness*, 74. See also Avrom Fleishman's wide-ranging and persuasive thematic discussion in *Conrad's Politics*, 187–214. Fleishman's more recent essay 'The Landscape of Hysteria in *The Secret Agent*' includes observations on narrative method, see Murfin (ed.), *Conrad Revisited*, 89–105.

The Chief Inspector, stooping guardedly over the table, fought down the unpleasant sensation in his throat. The shattering violence of destruction which had made of that body a heap of nameless fragments affected his feelings with a sense of ruthless cruelty, though his reason told him the effect must have been as swift as a flash of lightning. The man, whoever he was, had died instantaneously; and yet it seemed impossible to believe that a human body could have reached that state of disintegration without passing through the pangs of inconceivable agony. No physiologist, and still less of a metaphysician, Chief Inspector Heat rose by the force of sympathy, which is a form of fear, above the vulgar conception of time. Instantaneous! (87–8)

This authorial description invites us to understand the man's death as a metaphor of pure terror. As a result of the device of delayed decoding, the man is not as yet identified as Stevie. This increases the thematic potential of the passage, whose narrative movement can be summarized thus: although removed from the scene of death and presented by the local constable, the sight of this 'heap of nameless fragments' strongly moves the Inspector; the impression instantly provokes reflections; these reflections lead into those of the narrator, who also seems stricken by this violent death. It is as though the authorial narrator is unprotected by his habitual ironic stance here; this exceptional absence of irony may be partly explained by the seriousness of the passage and by the later identification of the body as Stevie's. Although the concluding exclamation 'Instantaneous!' reminds us, through this variant of narrated monologue, of the personal element in the description, the authorial perspective is apparent throughout. It is particularly striking in the reflection starting with 'and yet it seemed impossible', which resembles the authorial description of the death of Nostromo. The presentation of this death as a metaphor of pure terror, then, is not only a reflection of the authorial narrator's contempt for anarchist activity. It has also a wider thematic dimension, furthered by generalizing reflections and reinforced by the absence of irony. There is even, I would suggest, a curious sense in which it is related to Conrad's sustained attempt to explore, through his fiction, 'The inexplicable mysteries of conscious existence' (88).

Cedric Watts has argued that the plot of *The Secret Agent* can be divided into an overt plot and a covert plot:

The overt plot of the novel shows how the forces of law and order in London prevail over the forces of anarchy, subversion and disruption. The covert plot, which is sustained by a series of ironic symmetries, resembles by inversion a mirror-image of elements of the main plot; and it suggests that if law and order prevail, the ostensibly right thing is often done for the wrong reason, and that there are troubling resemblances between the world of the authorities and the world of subversion. The relationship in the narrative between overt and covert is variable and shifting; they blend, part and blend again.[5]

Although I do not directly apply Watts's understanding of two forms of plot to my analyses, his suggestive notion is related to several of my main points about Conrad's narrative method, and not only in this chapter on *The Secret Agent*. Watts notes that, if Chapter 2 inaugurates the overt plot, Chapter 6 can be seen as inaugurating the covert plot. A main character closely associated with the covert plot is the Assistant Commissioner. As Watts puts it, the covert plot, 'by showing an Assistant Commissioner motivated to guard the tranquillity of an affluent society-hostess, suggests that the views of Verloc and his wife Winnie, if jaundiced, are not entirely false'.[6] This 'hostess' refers to the Assistant Commissioner's dubious motive for doing what may ostensibly be the right thing: she is a close friend of his wife and also of Michaelis, whom the Commissioner therefore seeks to protect. Thus the official and the private areas are intertwined; and there is both dramatic and authorial irony in the Commissioner's words about Verloc to Sir Ethelred in Chapter 10: 'From a certain point of view we are here in the presence of a domestic drama' (222). The dramatic irony resides in the invitation to compare what the Commissioner (as character) says about Verloc with what actually happens to the latter; and it is reinforced by his ignorance of how accurate the statement is as a formulation of part of the novel's thematics. But dramatic and authorial irony appear to blend when we think of the Commissioner's odd mixture of private and official motives: the suggestiveness of his remarks—so accurate that the qualification 'From a certain point of view' becomes comic—does not make him immune to a pervasive authorial irony by no means reserved for the anarchists only.

The constituent elements of the novel's narrative method are variously related to the interplay of the overt and covert plots. In the opening of Chapter 6, elements of the covert plot are pointed at

---

[5] Watts, *The Deceptive Text*, 111.
[6] Ibid. 114.

indirectly in an extended analepsis. Although presented by the authorial narrator, the analepsis is both motivated by and closely linked to the Assistant Commissioner's reminiscing thoughts, centred on his more private interests and Michaelis in particular. That the narrator is clearly sceptical of the Commissioner's tendency to mix the official and the private domains is evident enough in such a comment as this: 'The Assistant Commissioner made a reflection extremely unbecoming his official position without being really creditable to his humanity' (112). Again, this form of authorial scepticism is essentially presented through a combination of authorial distance and irony, both of which depend on an unquestionable superiority of authorial knowledge and insight. While quoted monologue indicates the narrator's omniscience, his insight most notably manifests itself in several authorial generalizations.

In the last part of the chapter the authorial narrator's knowledge is given a more explicitly rational slant. Rejecting what is 'inexplicable', he seems to reassert that his primary concerns are to observe, dramatize, and explain his characters and the actions they are engaged in. The rational basis for the narrator's knowledge is noticeable in his generalizations too; and as I am here thinking of a common-sense form of rationality it might serve as partial explanation of his tendency to make rather categorical and simplifying statements. There is a distinction to be drawn between this kind of knowledge, which in a sense is evaluative in spite of the narrator's authority and omniscience, and the more direct and indisputable knowledge observable in the quoted monologues. But here other difficulties can arise, as when the authorial insistence on omniscience becomes awkwardly explicit. An example of this is the narrator's peculiar, and not very persuasive, way of insisting that Chief Inspector Heat uses the particular phrase ' "fired out" (this was the precise image)' (125).

In Chapter 7, which describes the Assistant Commissioner's meeting with Sir Ethelred, there are numerous examples of a lighter, more humorous form of irony. The introduction of 'the great personage', for instance, is essentially comic rather than ironic; and the comic element is confirmed by minor variations of Sir Ethelred's phrases 'No need to go into details... Be lucid, please' (139). It is further strengthened by the Assistant Commissioner's eager response to his wish: 'I am trying to be as lucid as I can in presenting this obscure matter to you without details' (142). The humour partly derives from the repetition of 'lucid' and 'no details' at key points in the dialogue between the two. Although this cannot be described as a sophisticated narrative variation, it is effective enough; and as readers of this sombre novel we welcome a somewhat lighter interlude.

To make this point is not to imply that the chapter is peripheral to the main thematic thrust of the novel. Sir Ethelred and the Assistant Commissioner discuss some of its most central issues, such as the explosion and the roles of Verloc and Chief Inspector Heat. The linkage that is gradually established between the more comic aspects of Chapter 7 and the book's broader ironic pattern extends the range of the authorial narrative method of the novel. For instance, as the Assistant Commissioner, in the quotation above, accurately characterizes the orientation he has just given his superior, the comic effect of this concluding statement does not eliminate its underlying ironic reflection. It is as though the authorial narrator momentarily adopts the attitudinal perspective of the Assistant Commissioner. As the authorial narrator himself observes earlier in the chapter, the relevant 'affair' of the Greenwich explosion consists precisely of a number of more or less obscure details; and to exclude these details is tantamount to ignoring the human drama of suffering and loneliness which the action of the novel presents. Sir Ethelred in effect shuts himself off from this drama, and not only by virtue of his profession (and class), but also by attaching greater importance to principle than to the details on which the principles are based and in which they can result. Detail and fact are closely related; and both are closer to the book's drama of human suffering than is abstract principle.

To consider the Assistant Commissioner as relatively knowledgeable is not to imply that he has suddenly become invulnerable to authorial irony—with the partial exceptions of the Professor and Stevie, no character in the novel is. What needs to be affirmed is rather that the irony, which may appear rather inflexible, is sometimes modified. One of the ways in which this is achieved is by making the Assistant Commissioner a conscious ironist himself; see, for instance, his responses to Toodles, Sir Ethelred's 'unpaid' secretary who has been expressing his fears for the life of the great man, concluding that the country cannot spare him. ' "Not to mention yourself. He leans on your arm," suggested the Assistant

Commissioner, soberly' (145). Especially if linked to the novel's pervasive authorial irony, the calculated irony of this riposte definitely places the Assistant Commissioner at a higher level of insight than that granted to Toodles.

A related way of increasing the Assistant Commissioner's importance as a character is to connect the authorial comments on him with the imagery as it is gradually extended and integrated into the novel's narrative method. As the Assistant Commissioner leaves his office, 'His descent into the street was like the descent into a slimy aquarium from which the water had been run off' (147). A couple of pages further on, as the Assistant Commissioner embarks on his unofficial mission to Verloc, this image is transformed into an equally striking metaphor: 'He advanced at once into an immensity of greasy slime and damp plaster interspersed with lamps, and enveloped, oppressed, penetrated, choked, and suffocated by the blackness of a wet London night, which is composed of soot and drops of water' (150). The unpleasant suggestiveness of the metaphor is enhanced not only by the novel's insistence on the close relation between animate and inanimate, but also by its resemblance to the metaphor of 'a fragile film of glass' associated with Verloc, whom the Assistant Commissioner now is about to seek out.

As we proceed to Chapter 8, it is noteworthy that the detailed description of the cab-drive of Stevie, Winnie, and her mother to the almshouse (where the latter has gained admission) is broadly analeptic. Since the trip takes place just before the explosion, we are more responsive to what Stevie says and how he acts. This kind of alertness, essentially provoked by means of the analeptic description, is richly rewarded: as Stevie's words, actions, and feelings acquire deeper meaning when associated with his imminent violent death, so the authorial commentary on Stevie similarly becomes more interesting if related to the action of the novel as a whole. Consider, for instance, this passage:

The cabman grunted, then added in his mysterious whisper: 'This ain't an easy world.'

Stevie's face had been twitching for some time and at last his feelings burst out in their usual concise form. 'Bad! Bad!'

His gaze remained fixed on the ribs of the horse, self-conscious and sombre, as though he were afraid to look about him at the badness of the world. And his slenderness, his rosy lips and pale, clear complexion, gave him the aspect of a delicate boy... (167)

The suggestiveness of this passage works at different levels. To start with, the narrator's use of the adjective 'delicate' (neatly correlated, one may notice on rereading, with the verb 'snap' which concludes the description of Stevie drawing circles in Chapter 3) stresses Stevie's vulnerability and sensitivity as well as prefiguring the explosion. Secondly, the exclamation itself, rephrasing the cabman's description of the world, takes the form of a remarkably condensed thematic statement which, though most directly applicable to Stevie, clearly exceeds his role in the novel. Such an understanding is supported some pages further on, as the authorial chracterization of Stevie blends into narrated monologue: 'And Stevie knew what it was to be beaten. He knew it from experience. It was a bad world. Bad! Bad!' (171).

Finally, the authorial commentary which frames the exclamation reveals some of the authorial narrator's peculiar sympathy for Stevie. Noticeable throughout the novel, this sympathy is clearly expressed in an authorial comment such as this: 'Stevie was no master of phrases, and perhaps for that very reason his thoughts lacked clearness and precision. But he felt with greater completeness and some profundity' (171). This form of authorial sympathy modifies our impression of the authorial narrator. He emerges as more caring and understanding when describing Stevie, whose thoughts and feelings he seems more intent on presenting and exploring than on exposing to his habitual irony. Yet it is characteristic of *The Secret Agent* that this deviation from the narrator's ironic attitude alerts us to a further irony which seems to accompany the narrator's disillusioned insights: since Stevie perishes, his morality—which, the narrator comments, 'was very complete' (172)—seems to contribute to his vulnerability rather than to his ability to survive.

Towards the end of the chapter, the narrative focus shifts from Stevie to Winnie and Verloc. The transition is made via Stevie's impression of Verloc, rendered as a combination of referential narrative statement and narrated monologue. The dramatic irony of the latter is effective enough: 'Mr. Verloc was obviously yet mysteriously *good*' (176). The authorial comments on the Verloc couple extend the basis needed for the dramatized presentation of their confrontation in Chapter 11. Winnie, for instance, 'felt profoundly that things do not stand much looking into' (177); this intuition of hers is repeated three times. More interestingly, the way in which the authorial narrator's voice modulates between the perspectives of Winnie and Verloc anticipates the more elaborate perspectival variations in Chapter 11.

As this is the central, climactic chapter in the novel, I propose to analyse its narrative method in some detail. Again, this choice of interpretative focus does not mean that I regard Chapters 9 and 10 as unsuccessful or redundant. Chapter 9 takes place just before and after the explosion; and, as several of the book's commentators have noted, it is instrumental in bringing the public and domestic aspects of the action closer to each other. As Chapter 9 culminates with Winnie's belated understanding of what has actually happened to her brother, it prepares the ground for the encounter between her and Verloc in Chapter 11. The insertion of Chapter 10 before this confrontation not only retards the novel's climax and increases suspense; more indirectly, this chapter also justifies the domestic emphasis of the following one by bringing the public aspect of the case to some sort of conclusion. Performing key roles in the final dialogues with both Sir Ethelred and Vladimir, the Assistant Commissioner is surely the predominant character of the chapter; and Vladimir is 'almost awed' (226) by his cleverness. For all his professional competence, however, the Assistant Commissioner can still make the mistake of sending Verloc home to be murdered.

The painstakingly slow and gradually intensified narrative movement towards the climactic confrontation between Winnie and Verloc in Chapter 11 is a major achievement of Conrad's authorial method in *The Secret Agent*. Its essential constitutive elements are so well integrated and accumulated that a systematized presentation of them must inevitably be complicated. Still, much of the narrative success of the chapter would seem to derive from an exceptionally productive combination of authorial omniscience and perspectival modulations. The omniscience is already noticeable as the chapter opens. The quoted monologue applied to Verloc's thought (' "She knows all about it now," he thought to himself') both establishes the necessary connection with the ending of Chapter 10 and introduces a long, authorial statement on Verloc's thoughts and regrets:

Mr. Verloc had never expected to have to face [Winnie's grief] on account of death, whose catastrophic character cannot be argued away by sophisticated reasoning or persuasive eloquence. Mr. Verloc never meant Stevie to perish with such abrupt violence. He did not mean him to perish at all. Stevie dead was a much greater nuisance than ever he had been when alive... Stevie had stumbled within five minutes of being left to himself. And Mr. Verloc was shaken morally to pieces. He had foreseen everything but that. (229–30)

There is no reason to question the veracity of this omniscient observation, which, it might be noted, further increases the authority of the Assistant Commissioner by supporting his evaluation of Verloc in the last conversation with Sir Ethelred (219–20). Paradoxically, the narrator's omniscience modifies authorial irony here. Although his ironic attitude is still noticeable, it is less striking; and the main reason is suggested by the detailed presentation of Verloc's mental state (and particularly his sincere remorse). It is as though the authorial narrator's irony is modified by the seriousness and suffering of the human drama he is about to describe. As the importance of authorial irony is reduced, the dramatic ironies, often proleptically coloured, become more frequent.

Employing the shifts of perspective as a criterion, the narrative movement towards the climax of the chapter can be divided into three. Although the authorial voice remains largely constant and predominant throughout the chapter, it is sometimes personally coloured, especially in the narrated monologues and in the imagery. On balance, however, these variations are minor, and distinctly less significant than the perspectival shifts. At the first stage of the narrative process towards the climax of the confrontation (i.e. the murder of Verloc), the modification of authorial irony functions as a narrative variation designed to bring the perspectives of the narrator and Verloc temporarily nearer each other. The variation is made more sophisticated as it is integrated into a productive combination of omniscient narrative statements, narrated monologue, and the few words the dying Verloc manages to utter to Winnie.

When Verloc reflects that Stevie 'had turned up with a vengeance!' (230), this narrated monologue increases his sincerity by confirming his feelings as described by the authorial narrator just before. For the reader, then, there is little reason to doubt the sincerity of the remorse expressed in Verloc's first words to Winnie: 'I didn't mean any harm to come to the boy' (231). For Winnie, however, the remark must sound both hypocritical and provocative, as the second stage (which modulates towards her perspective) confirms. What needs to be stressed here is the importance of the temporary perspectival alliance between the narrator and Verloc for the vivid impression of total breakdown of communication. To put this another way: as the statements and reflections of the authorial narrator comply with, and go quite far to explain, the few words uttered by Verloc to his wife, Winnie's complete lack of normal response ironically prefigures her later, violent response in the form of a killing. The two short sentences she actually speaks both support this reading. 'I don't want to look at you as long as I live,' she says (233), and then, several pages later, comes the question: 'What are you talking about?' (240).

The first section or stage, assigned by the authorial narrator to Verloc's bewildered thoughts, can be seen as lasting approximately until this question of Winnie's. The section as a whole confirms the importance of the narrative characteristics already indicated. Authorial irony may reappear, but is often, though not always, modified. For instance, the authorial irony of such a statement as 'Mr. Verloc was a humane man' (233) is qualified as we read that 'the eventuality he had not foreseen had appalled him as a humane man and a fond husband' (235). In comparison with such modifications, some of the narrator's remarks on Verloc may seem simplifying and awkward. This criticism could also be made of a combination of quoted and narrated monologue such as this:

He thought: She will have to look after the shop while they keep me locked up. And thinking also how cruelly she would miss Stevie at first, he felt greatly concerned about her health and spirits. How would she stand her solitude—absolutely alone in that house? (236)

Yet the combined effect of dramatic irony and prolepsis is considerable. Indeed, the murder is prefigured so many times that one may wonder how the element of surprise can be retained at all. Once again, I would suggest that the reasons are essentially to be sought in the perspectival changes, related as they are to the authorial descriptions of Winnie at the next stage of the chapter.

The shift of authorial perspective from Verloc to Winnie is gradually and carefully made. It occurs in the paragraphs surrounding Winnie's apparently absent-minded question, starting with the mention of 'the inappropriate character of his wife's stare' (239–40) and ending with his well-meant advice to her: 'You go to bed now. What you want is a good cry' (241). In the following paragraph, the narrative perspective has departed from Verloc and is approaching that of Winnie. As it is then attuned to her thoughts and feelings for quite some time, the omniscient authorial statements here balance those relating to Verloc in the first section of the chapter. However, the narrative form of this second stage is somewhat different from the preceding one. It starts with some general, and not very persuasive, authorial observations on women. But then the quality of the reflections improves as they focus more specifically on Winnie, providing a partial explanation of her state of shock after Stevie's death. The narrator comments that her temperament

forced her to roll a series of thoughts in her motionless head. These thoughts were rather imagined than expressed. Mrs. Verloc was a woman of singularly few words, either for public or private use. With the rage and dismay of a betrayed woman, she reviewed the tenor of her life in visions concerned mostly with Stevie's difficult existence from its earliest days. (241)

On later readings of the novel, this authorial comment is one of several which evoke a strong sense of inevitability in the process towards the killing of Verloc. More important in our critical context is the word 'visions', which introduces an analeptic interlude where Winnie's memories of her childhood are presented as fragmented images given linguistic shape by the narrator. His mention of her last 'vision', which clearly illustrates how strongly the images have impinged on her senses, also establishes a link between her memories and the present situation. She is thinking of Verloc and Stevie leaving the shop together:

And this last vision had such plastic relief, such nearness of form, such a fidelity of suggestive detail, that it wrung from Mrs. Verloc an anguished and faint murmur, reproducing the supreme illusion of her life, an appalled murmur that died out on her blanched lips. 'Might have been father and son.' (244)

If 'anguished murmur' makes us think of Stevie, this is but one out of several narrative comments which establish a physical and mental resemblance between Winnie and her brother that is most striking at the moment when she kills Verloc. More broadly, both the content of the 'visions' and their analeptic form effectively illustrate the breakdown of communication between the two. Ironically, Winnie's remark encourages Verloc to try once again to make contact and explain his actions, but to no avail. Winnie's confused thoughts follow instead their own pattern; and the only conclusion she can reach is presented directly, as a quoted monologue: 'He took the boy away from his home to murder him. He took the boy away from me to murder him!' (246).

Characterizing this thought as 'a fixed idea' (249), the narrator connects it with Winnie's transformation into a woman released from her family ties: 'She had her freedom. Her contract with existence, as represented by that man standing over there, was at an end. She was a free woman. Had this view become in some way perceptible to Mr. Verloc he would have been extremely shocked' (251). This authorial comment illustrates the thematic density of the narrative in this chapter. If the reference to Verloc confirms that their communication problem has become insoluble, the narrator's authoritative description of Winnie as 'a free woman' increases suspense by making her subsequent actions less predictable.

To make this point is to suggest a partial reason why the various prolepses of the chapter's climax (the killing of Verloc) do not damagingly reduce narrative suspense. Not just Verloc's, but also *the reader's* impression of Winnie has been well established earlier in the novel, particularly through the convincing authorial description of her dedication to Stevie. If the prolepses are related both to the important element of suspense and to the earlier characterizations of Winnie, then Conrad's ability to manipulate, through his authorial narrator, our response as readers seems remarkable in this chapter. Having said this, 'response' as used here must be qualified as referring to the development of the novel's action rather than to the more inclusive and complex thematics based on the dramatized events. Several of the prolepses of the killing cannot be appreciated prior to a second reading of the novel. This applies, for example, to the references to Verloc's use of 'the sharp carving knife' (253). The prolepses can embed both irony and grim humour, as when Verloc expresses 'his firm belief that there were yet a good few years of quiet life before them both... The words used by Mr. Verloc were: "Lie low for a bit" ' (250). This of course is what he is to do, though literally and not metaphorically, first on his couch and then forever in his grave. If dramatic and authorial irony blend here, there are also instances where authorial irony is more unambiguously reasserted, as in narrated monologue such as, 'If only that lad had not stupidly destroyed himself!' (253).

The transition from the chapter's second stage (attuned to Winnie's perspective) to the third (the description of the murder) is blurred. Gradually the authorial perspective begins to shift more frequently from Winnie to Verloc and back to Winnie; and in between these perspectival variations the detached authorial irony again becomes more noticeable. In the description of the actual killing, the authorial commentary is combined with careful observation of relevant details which—grouped around the recurrent phrase 'leisurely enough'—enable us to visualise the scene with almost unpleasant accuracy.[7]

However, to note that the authorial description of the actual killing is in part constituted by relevant and suggestive details is not to imply that irony is absent from it. For instance, dramatic irony enters into the last words Verloc speaks to his wife; and it is noticeable not only in the actual words, but also in Winnie's interpretation of them: ' "Come here," he said in a peculiar tone, which might have been the tone of brutality, but was intimately known to Mrs. Verloc as the note of wooing' (262). Again, we notice a perspectival affinity between the authorial narrator and Winnie. An interesting variation from the moment of the killing onwards is that while the narrative perspective remains attached to that of Winnie (in the sense of offering a detailed, omniscient account of her reaction to what she has done), a distancing movement begins which results in increased attitudinal distance between Winnie and the authorial narrator (and, since we are manipulated into trusting the latter's evaluations, between Winnie and the reader as well).

Although he regards Chapter 11 as 'a successful dramatic scene', Guerard finds that it is 'too fully and too carefully explicated'.[8] The analysis presented here, however, would rather second F. R. Leavis's appreciation of the chapter's 'economy of form and pattern that gives every detail its significance'.[9] It must be added, though, that Guerard modifies his criticism; and his accompanying point about the success of the following twelfth chapter is reasonably

---

[7] And yet, as Terry Eagleton observes, the killing 'is presented with extreme obliquity, squinted at sideways rather than frontally encountered'. See Eagleton, 'Form, Ideology and *The Secret Agent*', in *Against the Grain: Essays 1975–1985* (London: Verso, 1986), 25.

[8] CN 230.

[9] Leavis, *The Great Tradition*, 236–7. Leavis's discussion is included in Ian Watt (ed.), *The Secret Agent: A Casebook* (London: Macmillan, 1973), 118–32. Watt's useful casebook contains both a critical survey and a number of the most important essays on the novel, including his own 'The Political and Social Background of *The Secret Agent*,' 229–51. See also CMP 131–59.

convincing. Guerard considers the 'macabre comedy' of Chapter 12 'so successful, and Ossipon's growing horror and disgust so vivid, that it effectively destroys much of our sympathy for Winnie'.[10] This comment might suggestively be related to the narrator's increased attitudinal distance from Winnie at this late stage of the narrative. Although this distancing process starts towards the end of Chapter 11, it is extended and confirmed in Chapter 12. An essential constituent aspect of the distancing movement is the combination of authorial omniscience and more pointed attitudinal distance. Consider, for instance, the authorial commentary which follows some of Winnie's bewildered words to Ossipon, on whom she is pinning her last hope:

'Haven't you guessed what I was driven to do!' cried the woman. Distracted by the vividness of her dreadful apprehensions, her head ringing with forceful words, that kept the horror of her position before her mind, she had imagined her incoherence to be clearness itself. She had no conscience of how little she had audibly said in the disjointed phrases completed only in her thought. (282)

That Ossipon has in fact *not* guessed gives the narrator ample opportunity to unmask his feigned intrepidity as the connection between Winnie's changed personality and Verloc's death dawns upon him. The ironic effect of such a combination as 'robust anarchist' and 'terrified' is obvious enough; and the narrator sardonically observes that 'Comrade Ossipon might have been said to be terrified scientifically in addition to all other kinds of fear' (290). To return to the authorial comment on Winnie in the quoted passage, we note that one of the ways in which the narrator increases his distance from Winnie is by substituting 'woman' for his common and more familiar 'Mrs. Verloc'. The distancing movement suggested by this change is then confirmed as the narrator goes on authoritatively to characterize Winnie's words as incoherent rather than clear. In the last sentence of the quotation too, it is evident that authorial distance from Winnie is not just associated with attitude in a restricted evaluative sense, but also with markedly different, indeed contrastive, levels of insight. If related specifically to the narrative method of the novel, this sentence could be seen as suggesting a partial authorial explanation of the need for narrated

[10] CN 230.

and quoted monologue in order to supplement the characters' speech. However, the authorial emphasis of the passage is on 'incoherence' rather than 'clearness'. To put it another way, the narrator does not insist on the coherence and lucidity of his own words. Relating my understanding of this passage to the text as a whole, it would seem to support my notion of the novel as tending towards incoherence or fragmentation not only on the level of language, but also on the related levels of narrative and thematics.

In the last chapter the narrator's distance from all the characters is again marked, and is integrated into the novel's broader narrative movement towards conclusion. There is a widening of narrative perspective towards the end; the distancing process observable late in Chapter 11 and in Chapter 12 blends into a more generalized authorial comment on both the domestic and public aspects of the story. Conrad's method of widening the narrative perspective here is quite sophisticated. One noteworthy aspect of it is the narrated monologue attached to the Professor's gloomy thoughts on bombs and destruction: 'The sound of exploding bombs was lost in their immensity of passive grains without an echo. For instance, this Verloc affair. Who thought of it now?' (306). The strong implication of these thoughts is that the incidents dramatized in the novel are already on their way to be forgotten. That the Professor rather than Ossipon asks this question strengthens the implication, not only because his authority as a character surpasses that of the anarchists (though not invulnerable to authorial irony, he is clearly exonerated from the harsher ironies levelled at such a character as Yundt), but also because the subsequent account of Ossipon and the newspaper report of Winnie's suicide go a long way to confirm his assumption. The Professor's question then, could be seen as contributing both to the novel's scepticism in a broad sense and to its more specific scepticism of newspapers and journalists.

Yet this particular kind of scepticism does not seriously interfere with the function of the newspaper report as a narrative variation in its own right, extending narrative perspective by adding another one to those of Ossipon and the narrator. It must be added, though, that the latter predictably takes an ironic view not only of the highly-wrought style in the newspaper report, but also of Ossipon, 'becoming scientifically afraid of insanity lying in wait for him amongst these lines' (307). For Ossipon, the last lines of the newspaper paragraph keep recurring like an insistent refrain. As the lines are repeated many times, we are invited as readers to share Ossipon's impression of being continually, even painfully, exposed to Winnie's death as an *'act of madness or despair'* (307, 310–11). We may well be critical of the rather mechanical way in which the newspaper sentence is repeated over and over again. Still, it could be countered that the narrator's scepticism of journalists' understanding of his own narrative (and the incidents and issues dramatized in it) does not drain the sentence of its odd mixture of cliché and thematic suggestiveness. As the last reference to *'madness or despair'* serves as a transition to the concluding narrative focus on the Professor, so this suggestiveness is extended through the contrast between his hidden 'force' and the world's ignorance of him. Clearly, the concluding image of the Professor, passing on 'unsuspected and deadly, like a pest in the street full of men' (311), can be variously interpreted. If we relate it to the thematic elements in the newspaper report, then it can be seen not only as a last fictional statement on the fundamental loneliness of human beings, but also as alluding to the two characters who provide the strongest links between human loneliness and the Professor's force, Stevie and Winnie, paradoxically both the agents and the victims of destruction.

II

Although Conrad's authorial narrative in *The Secret Agent* is not as wide-ranging and multi-faceted as that of *Nostromo*, we have seen that it includes a number of variations. These are essentially modulations of narrative distance, irony, and perspective. I have emphasized the functions of the authorial narrator not only because he possesses an overview of the action and a knowledge of the characters which seems almost total, but also because his detachment is crucially important in establishing and determining the complex irony of the novel. However, in spite of the prevalent concern with description and information the narrator is by no means neutral. One indication of his partial or more subjective stand is the frequent combination of information and evaluation. The evaluation is predominantly indirect, and the main constituent aspect of this indirectness is authorial irony. However, although both characters and events are often evaluated indirectly through irony, it needs to be stressed that authorial attitude to the characters varies, ranging from the scorn and contempt of the narrator's descriptions of some of the anarchists to the sympathy and pity characteristic of his portrayal of Stevie.

It would seem, therefore, that although the narrator's narration, perspective, and evaluation in *The Secret Agent* can broadly be characterized as ironic, such a description needs to be qualified in order not to over-simplify. Although Chatman rightly notes that 'ironic narration permeates the novel',[11] his accompanying point that irony is 'the narrator's regular vocal stance' would, on the basis of this textual commentary, seem somewhat too categorical. One possible way of bringing together the observations made on the novel's narrative variation, including the variation of irony, might be to discuss the authorial narrator's relation to Conrad on the one hand and to some of the most important characters on the other. The inescapable difficulties associated with this kind of approach spring in part from the complexity of the novel. I shall comment briefly on the narrator's relation to the Assistant Commissioner, the Professor, Verloc, and Winnie. The case of Stevie is intriguing and will be singled out for particular comment.

1. If, however, we start by asking what the narrator's relation to Conrad is, then the possible answer to such a question—here as in the case of *Nostromo*—would have to be very tentative. As in the former novel, the predominantly ironic stance of the narrator may be shared by Conrad, but not necessarily, and not always. Furthermore, and once again in a manner reminiscent of *Nostromo*, the opinions and attitudes of the narrator are made more unstable through personal colouring, as in the narrated monologues where the attitudinal perspective of the narrator may blend with that of a character. The effect is quite complex: while this kind of personal colouring would seem to increase the narrator's distance from Conrad, the accompanying perspectival approximation of the narrator and a character can temporarily increase the latter's authority, at least in the sense of offering a partial protection from authorial irony.

Building on the textual commentary, the most important observation to make here is perhaps to stress how indirect and complicated the relationship between Conrad and his narrator is, for there

---

[11] Chatman, *Story and Discourse*, 230.

is a significant correlation between the degree of indirectness in this relationship and the varying relation between the narrator and the characters. Moreover, we have noted some textual instances where Conrad seems to be distancing himself more explicitly from his authorial narrative device, as in the paragraph in Chapter 8 where the narrative suddenly seems to turn personal, then reverting to the more impersonal variant already established.

In the discussions of *The Nigger of the 'Narcissus'*, *The Shadow-Line*, and *Lord Jim*, we have seen that some passages can be described as lyric. These passages are characterized by a kind of prose intensified through the use of poetic devices such as simile, metaphor, personification, and repetition. Additionally, these lyric passages describe an experience more closely related to memory and feeling than to knowledge and intellect. As a corollary, the attitudinal distance between Conrad and his narrator can temporarily be reduced; and as the markers of epic distance become less noticeable, an impression of intensified, descriptive memory can be established. This brief recapitulation provides the necessary basis for my main point here: there is a significant connection between the absence of such lyric passages from *Nostromo* and *The Secret Agent* (and, as we shall see, *Under Western Eyes*) and the pervasive and complex irony of these novels. Although the relationship between Conrad and the authorial narrator in *The Secret Agent* (or *Nostromo*) may sometimes seem close, it is much more complex than in the lyric passages; and a main reason for this increased complexity is suggested by the two novels' multi-faceted irony, which in itself has a distancing effect. This is not to insist that it is necessarily wrong to speak, for instance, of 'Conrad's irony' in *The Secret Agent*, but then it would be essential not only to stress how paradoxical and complex the author's attitude to his fictional world is, but also to note how close the connections are between the complexity of Conrad's attitude (including 'irony') and the intrinsic variations of irony as an integral aspect of the narrative method of the novel.

2. The narrator's relation to the Assistant Commissioner is different from that to the other officials, since the commissioner has a more profound insight into the inherent contradictions of the crime he is investigating. We have noted some of the ways in which this relative insight is given to him, including the narrative tactic of making him a conscious ironist (in the talk with Toodles, for

instance), which in itself elevates him somewhat towards the level of the narrator's authorial irony.

At the same time, the relative insight or intelligence granted to the Assistant Commissioner ironically enhances the dubiousness of his motives for action, at both the official and the private levels. As we have noted, these motives are mixed, with the suggestion that the private ones are dominant. From Chapter 6 onwards, the structural and thematic importance of the Assistant Commissioner increases; he emerges as the most important of the officials belonging to the public realm of the novel. However, although the narrator stresses how actively the Assistant Commissioner is searching for Verloc, he also suggests a certain affinity between the two. This applies not only to the dubious mixture of motives for action associated with both characters, but also to an interesting similarity in the imagery related to them. We have briefly considered the most remarkable examples of this kind of resemblance, the metaphor of 'a fragile film of glass' associated with Verloc in Chapter 3 and that of 'greasy slime and damp plaster' associated with the Assistant Commissioner in Chapter 7. Although the thematic and symbolic suggestiveness of these metaphors exceeds that of both these two characters, the metaphors increase their thematic significance and interlink them in a resourceful way.

3. The narrator's relation to the Professor is curiously indeterminate, suspended between a certain respect for the consistency of his views (especially as opposed to the anarchists' lack of such consistency) and a very marked attitudinal distance from him, as in the last paragraph of the novel. Clearly, at one level the Professor's criticism of the anarchists is convincing enough: he represents at least a danger or 'force' while they, as Vladimir senses in his broken Latin quotation, can seem a mere voice.

Although the narrator appears to agree with the Professor's criticism up to a point, it must be stressed that his relation to the anarchists is much more nuanced than that of the Professor. While the narrator's contempt for Yundt is quite unqualified, his more favourable disposition towards Michaelis is suggested, for instance, by the combined authorial emphasis on his isolation from others and his capacity for human emotion. Ossipon would seem to occupy an intermediate position between Yundt and Michaelis. Paradoxically, one of the textual instances where the reader may find himself or herself partly in accord with Ossipon's views, or rather with his reaction, is his conversation with the Professor in Chapter 4: although we may admire the Professor's integrity, we are still, like Ossipon, somewhat shocked at his terrifying logic of destruction. One out of several perceptive observations Suresh Raval makes on the Professor (and *The Secret Agent*) is that 'there is a strong distinction to be drawn between the moral nihilism of the Professor and the skeptical stance of the narrator'.[12] One reason why it is important to stress this distinction is that there has been a tendency (partly, no doubt, because of the overt way in which the Professor is contrasted with the anarchists) to imply a closer alliance between him and the narrator than the text's authorial narrative actually warrants.

Considering Raval's distinction between the Professor's 'moral nihilism' and the narrator 'sceptical stance', the relative simplicity of the former position needs to be emphasized. Now elements of simplicity or simplification will of course always accompany religious or ideological fanaticism. However, one essential constituent aspect of the Professor's moral nihilism is the hope he attaches to destruction: he thinks it may provide a basis for a more just society. To nurture such a hope in itself increases the Professor's distance from the narrator, wholly incompatible as it is with the latter's sceptical stance. Having said this, however, I have reached the point where Raval's discussion provokes a minor dissent. For Raval, the narrator, in contrast to the Professor, 'knows the world cannot be destroyed. As he sees it, society will continue on its presumably endless, uncertain journey, and evil, exploitation, injustice, and suffering will continue to prevail.'[13] What makes this kind of statement problematic is that it introduces an element of stable certainty into the narrator's sceptical stance which it does not necessarily accommodate. I certainly agree with Raval's observation that 'the narrator has no formula for social change',[14] but to say this is not quite the same as maintaining that the narrator 'knows the world cannot be destroyed'.

There are at least two problems involved here. First, even though we have noted the range of the authorial narrator's knowledge, it seems disputable, from this analysis of the novel's narrative

---

[12] Raval, *The Art of Failure*, 119.
[13] Ibid.
[14] Ibid. 121.

method, to say that we can know, as readers, what the narrator knows about the future of the world. The narrator is characteristically reticent in these matters; and there is a link between this form of reticence and his scepticism. Secondly, although *The Secret Agent*, unlike *Nostromo*, cannot be described as a fictional presentation of the process of history, it does not follow that its dramatization of certain aspects of history at one particular stage is ahistorical. It might be suggested, for instance, that Hillis Miller's notion of apocalyptic elements in 'Heart of Darkness' could be extended to refer, albeit in a somewhat different sense, to *The Secret Agent* as well.[15] These brief reflections do not interfere with Raval's persuasive description of the narrator's 'sceptical stance'. Here, as in the discussion of the authorial narrator in *Nostromo*, I would suggest that a main reason why the adjective 'sceptical' can more appropriately be applied to the narrator than, say, 'pessimistic' is connected with a complex combination of, on the one hand, the characteristic indeterminacy of his attitudinal position and, on the other hand, various textual signals or traces of a pervasive existential and epistemological uncertainty. This kind of uncertainty accentuates his need for distance from the characters, particularly those whose problems may somehow reflect his own.

4. The narrator's relation to Verloc is also more complex than it at first seems. His distance from Verloc is apparent right from the start; and this form of distance is connected with attitude and evaluation as well as knowledge and insight. However, having established a firm impression of Verloc as mediocre and unattractive at an early stage of the narrative, the narrator can then manipulate the reader into modifying his or her views of Verloc as his various activies are described—spy for a foreign government, police informer, salesman of pornography, husband. We have seen how this is done in the conversation Verloc has with Vladimir in Chapter 2; and the association of Verloc and the metaphor of 'a fragile film of glass' in Chapter 3, for instance, can similarly be seen as part of the narrator's gradual diversification of his relation to him. Along with this process, however, there are other narrative variations which retard or even counter it. An example would be the authorial contempt for Verloc towards the end of Chapter 3.

One implication of this process of attitudinal diversification is

---

[15] Cf. ch. 2 n. 12.

that it becomes more difficult for the reader consistently to dissociate himself or herself from Verloc's mediocrity. Though we may, to begin with, be strongly critical of him, some of his thoughts and reactions later on in the narrative may seem unpleasantly familiar. An illustrative example is Verloc's reaction to the killing of Stevie: for all his irony, the narrator does not indicate that Verloc does not regret the accident. It even prompts Verloc into some new reflections, though it must be added that these selfishly revolve around himself. Yet this absence of authorial irony leads to another, since Winnie's inability to perceive her husband's regret serves to initiate the process towards two more killings, of both Verloc and herself.

5. Until Chapter 11, the narrator's relation to Winnie is stable and relatively uninteresting. Her ignorance of Verloc's diverse activities may appear less than convincing, though it is partly explained by the references to her passionate devotion to Stevie. These references are important in establishing a partial basis for the action of Chapter 11. Some of them are clearly proleptic, such as the narrator's observation, 'She could not bear to see the boy hurt. It maddened her' (38). In Chapter 11, however, the apparent stability of the narrator's relation to Winnie is upset. One consequence of this change is in itself noteworthy: Winnie is transformed from a minor to a major character at what is, by any standards, a very late stage in the novel.

The increased complexity of the narrator's relation to Winnie in Chapter 11 is generated by two supplementary narrative movements: one which temporarily reduces the narrator's distance from Winnie, and another which, subsequent to the killing of Verloc, again increases distance. It should be pointed out, though, that the increased complexity and interest of Winnie as a character are not *only* due to technical variations: they are also related to the interplay of the central event on the diegetic level (her stabbing of her husband) and the presentation of this event. One observation pertaining to the narrator's increased distance from Winnie towards the end of Chapter 11 and in Chapter 12 is that it is not as clearly associated with authorial irony as is often the case elsewhere in the novel. It is as if the narrator, though forced into distancing himself from Winnie because of her violent act, still cannot bring himself to make her a victim of his habitual irony. As a consequence of this suspension of authorial irony towards Winnie, the main target of the narrator's irony in Chapter 12 is Ossipon, and this in spite of the increased narrative distance from Winnie that we have noted. To make this last point is to suggest that there is an element of authorial sympathy or pity observable in the narrator's relation to Winnie; this element is much more noticeable and significant in his relation to Stevie.

6. As Thomas Mann has noted in an essay on *The Secret Agent* that continues to repay attention, 'Stevie is far and away the finest figure in the book, and conceived with the liveliest and most affecting sympathy'.[16] The narrator's relation to Stevie is intriguing, but difficult to comment on in a systematic manner. One of the problems raised by the case of Stevie is that his interpretative potential as an integral part of the novel's narrative method and thematics greatly exceeds his function as a character in a more conventional sense. Stevie's capacity for independent action, for instance, is very limited; yet paradoxically his statements, or fragments of statements, testify to an ethical integrity surpassing that of any other character in the novel.

If we go on to ask how the form of moral simplicity represented by Stevie can be compatible with, or even endorsed by, an authorial narrator as sceptical as that of *The Secret Agent*, then a partial response could be to stress how closely our understanding of Stevie is linked to our knowledge of what happens to him. It is the combination of his dedication and caring nature on the one hand, and his destruction on the other that confirms, rather than compromises, the sceptical stance of the narrator. However, although Stevie functions essentially as a contrastive character unable to survive in the world of the novel, this does not mean that the sceptical narrator does not value the moral attitude Stevie embodies and suggests. In this relation there is, as we have seen in the discussion of Chapter 8, a form of authorial sympathy which both modifies and to some extent explains the narrator's scepticism.[17]

[16] Thomas Mann, 'Joseph Conrad's *The Secret Agent*', in Watt (ed.), *Casebook*, 110. The essay first appeared as the preface to a German translation of the novel (*Der Geheimagent*, 1926). Mann goes on to argue that 'here Russian influence is plain: without Dostoevsky's Idiot Stevie is unthinkable'. Dostoevsky's influence on Conrad is hard to ascertain, but as it is likely to be more important than Conrad claimed that it was, Mann's suggestion is not uninteresting. It might be added, though, that Stevie's affinity with Benjy in Faulkner's *The Sound and the Fury* (1929) is perhaps stronger than his resemblance to Dostoevsky's character.

[17] Aaron Fogel finds that Conrad draws on various traditions of sympathy in *The Secret Agent*. See Fogel, *Coercion to Speak: Conrad's Poetics of Dialogue* (Cambridge, Mass.: Harvard University Press, 1985), 146–79.

Apart from the striking passage on Stevie and the cabman in Chapter 8, the powerful metaphor of his drawing of circles in Chapter 3 constitutes the most significant authorial description of him (and possibly the best description in the novel as a whole).

Mr. Verloc, getting off the sofa with ponderous reluctance, opened the door leading into the kitchen to get more air, and thus disclosed the innocent Stevie, seated very good and quiet at a deal table, drawing circles, circles, circles; innumerable circles, concentric, eccentric; a coruscating whirl of circles that by their tangled multitude of repeated curves, uniformity of form, and confusion of intersecting lines suggested a rendering of cosmic chaos, the symbolism of a mad art attempting the inconceivable. (45)

At the centre of the passage there is 'a coruscating whirl of circles'. This nucleus of the metaphor is in a way a description both of Stevie's drawing activity and the activity of the characters in the novel. The main constituent element of the metaphor—'circles'—is repeated three times before the nucleus; and it has also a double specification attached to it (the circles are 'innumerable' and they are both 'concentric' and 'eccentric'). The 'coruscating whirl of circles' not only constitutes the metaphorical nucleus, but also incorporates an interpretative element; this more subjective element (the narrator's impression of Stevie's circles as a 'coruscating whirl') is then confirmed and extended in the concluding part of the passage. Here the interpretative element becomes clearer as the narrator specifies the metaphor both in relation to Stevie and in relation to the complex thematics explored throughout the novel.

Reflecting on photography in *Camera Lucida*, Barthes introduces a distinction between *studium* and *punctum*.[18] The distinction is both subtle and complex and cannot be systematically presented here, but while the *studium* refers to the more general (though culturally coded) elements of a photograph, the *punctum* can be a particular detail, which, one you have noticed it, keeps arresting your attention again and again. The *punctum* is thus more subjective; yet its impact can improve the understanding of the whole picture. Now photography is of course, like painting, a spatial art, and hence even more different from narrative fiction than, say, poetry. Yet in spite of this basic generic difference some of Conrad's

---

[18] Roland Barthes, *Camera Lucida: Reflections on Photography*, trans. Richard Howard (London: Jonathan Cape, 1982), 26–7 and *passim*.

most suggestive metaphors, both in the lyric passages we have considered and elsewhere, are distinguished by a peculiarly spatial quality. It is not coincidental that we feel we can *see* Stevie's circles: the effect is established through a sophisticated combination of repetition (especially of 'circles'), perspective (we are, sharing the narrator's perspective, looking as it were over Verloc's shoulder), and explication (particularly that following the metaphorical nucleus).

If we attempt to translate the metaphor into ordinary syntactic discourse, much of this spatial quality is lost. I have already mentioned that, as I read and reread the passage, I tend to relate this central metaphor to the novel's central event, the destruction of Stevie which takes place in a textual gap or lacuna. This particular association constitutes for me the basis for a kind of *punctum*. It does not make me visualize other characters or occurrences in the novel but makes me rather think of another spatial structure which, in its own way, visualizes the association of Stevie's circles and destruction for me: Kandinsky's first abstract watercolour which he completed in 1910,[19] only three years after the publication of *The Secret Agent*. Especially if related to Conrad's novel (and I repeat that this is a subjective experience of *punctum*), there seems to be an exploding dynamism in this watercolour—a violent disintegration starting from no apparent centre. Some of the dashes of colour (red, blue, yellow) resemble meteors which, moving at high speed but with no set direction, suggest 'a rendering of cosmic chaos'.

Subjective as an experience of *punctum* is, it can sometimes enrich or improve our understanding of a work of art, including a novel. If Stevie's circles make me think of Kandinsky, this may be because some of the central aspects of his watercolour accentuate certain basic textual and thematic structures in the novel. Three seem particularly important: the impression of absence of centre or ground, the sense of instability, danger, and imminent destruction, and finally the sense of a different kind of stability which in the watercolour is related to the stability of spatial form, but which in *The Secret Agent* is related to the text's formal and thematic contradictions and to the disillusioned insights associated with the narrator's sceptical stance.

[19] For a reproduction of the watercolour see, for instance, *Kindlers Malerei Lexikon*, III (Zürich: Kindler Verlag, 1966), 524.

There is a sense, then, in which Miller's second form of repetition is more directly applicable to *The Secret Agent* than *Nostromo*. If in *Lord Jim* the tension between two forms of repetition is linked to the relationship between Marlow and Jim (and Marlow's attempt to understand Jim), and if in *Nostromo* the suggestiveness of this distinction may be less apparent because of the enormous thematic range and collective focus of the novel, what we have in *The Secret Agent* is in a way a fictional presentation of a set of existential and ideological contradictions and unresolved problems variously related to the second form of repetition.

As the presentation or textual revelation of these contradictions are intimately related to the novel's narrative method, the contradictions which the authorial narrator presents simultaneously suggest a partial reason for his need for distancing irony and a sceptical stance. *The Secret Agent* is one of the most illustrative examples in the Conrad canon of a fictional text in which the narrative method both generates, complicates, and sets at odds dissimilar thematic and ideological elements. As Terry Eagleton puts it in a terse, perceptive account of the novel: 'The complexity of the text is the product of certain contradictions between its component elements—contradictions which are in turn produced by the mutually conflictual relations of those elements to mutually conflictual aspects of the Conradian ideology *as that ideology is produced by the novel*.'[20]

One of the most fundamental contradictions is attached to Stevie. For if the narrator's very considerable (though varying) distance from the other characters of the novel is indicative of his scepticism about both the characters and the contradictions which their attitudes, actions, and interests reveal, the violent destruction of the only character who embodies the narrator's positive alternative to this predominant group would seem to suggest a concluding ironic comment on the narrator's own irony. Yet this irony is modified by Stevie's dual function: if his function as a character on the diegetic level may in part conform to the first form of repetition, his 'coruscating whirl of circles' can well stand as an emblem of the second form. Furthermore, if the narrator's relatively close relation to Stevie makes him curiously vulnerable to the irony he himself has established elsewhere, this is not necessarily a narrative weakness in

---

[20] Eagleton, 'Form, Ideology and *The Secret Agent*', 31.

a novel in which Conrad's narrative method may sometimes provide the impression of a calculated, almost cynical detachment. Because of the narrator's peculiar and moving relation to Stevie, however, the irony of *The Secret Agent* is also, though in a manner quite different from *Nostromo*, made more nuanced and resigned, thus confirming the narrator's sceptical disillusionment.

12

Under Western Eyes:
Modulation of Simplistic Personal
Narrative through Authorial Irony

The complexity of *Under Western Eyes* (1911) matches that of any other novel Conrad wrote. It belongs among the most important political novels of our century; it is a searching psychological study; it is also a sustained reflection on, and dramatization of, very basic problems of writing and language—and more specifically narrative method. The novel was immensely difficult for Conrad to write;[1] it is a demanding book to read, too, for its many, and diverse, constitutive elements are neither easily understood nor always obviously interrelated.

There is an implicit interpretative problem here on which I shall comment briefly before commencing the textual commentary and interpretation presented in this chapter. As in the case of, for instance, *Nostromo*, the sheer complexity of *Under Western Eyes* unavoidably makes the reader limit his or her attention to only a selection of its constitutive elements, for example the narrative function of the language teacher. This need not be a consciously selective attention, but perhaps rather a very understandable consequence of the fact that the novel contains many more such elements than can possibly be registered, let alone remembered, on a first (or even a second or third) reading. This particular difficulty should be kept in mind both in one's own understanding and analysis of the novel and when considering other interpretations of it. For the critic the difficulty is further enhanced in the sense that a more systematic or superimposed selection is added to the 'natural' one of the reader. Although such a critical emphasis is nearly always necessary to support a point or pursue a given argument, it inevitably entails certain drawbacks with regard to the response to, and hence also the critical understanding of, the impact and inherent variety of the text.[2]

The structure of this chapter is similar to that of previous ones in

---

[1] See Najder, *Chronicle*, 354–9, esp. 355.
[2] Cf. ch. 1 n. 29.

that the textual commentary proceeds consecutively, while the subsequent generalizations are based on observations that are part of this commentary. The study's critical concern with narrative method inevitably entails a relatively superficial treatment of other, albeit related, important issues, such as the novel's significant political dimension. The complexity of the book even necessitates some limitations of critical attention within the textual range of narrative method: hence my primary focus is on the diverse narrative functions of the text's predominant personal narrator, the English teacher of languages. In the concluding part of the chapter his functions are then related to a distinction between four types of text in *Under Western Eyes*, and to a short discussion of the thematic characteristics of the 'A-text' which I see as the novel's authoritative one.

Starting *Under Western Eyes* the reader first encounters the 'Author's Note'. Some of the novel's commentators still pay scant attention to the fact that Conrad wrote this note many years after the novel appeared, in connection with the publication of the Collected Edition of his works in 1920. This considerable temporal lapse need not in itself make the note uninteresting, but it inevitably reduces its relevance as authoritative authorial comment on, and explanation of, the novel. If added to my general reservations about making direct or unqualified reference to Conrad's non-fictional comments and views in order to explain his fictional texts, this fact makes me sceptical about too direct an application of the note's assertions to the fictional structure which the text itself constitutes. Thus there is reason for dissent when Terry Eagleton, in his chapter on the novel in *Exiles and Émigrés*, establishes a close relationship between Conrad's views as expressed in the 'Author's Note' and the 'official account' of the novel.[3] Such an 'official account'—to the extent that the term is viable at all—would rather have to be sought through laborious abstraction from the novel's thematics as engendered and shaped by its complex narrative strategies.

This is not to say that there are no interesting notions in the 'Author's Note'. In particular the 1917 Russian Revolution has increased the interest of Conrad's characterization of *Under Western Eyes* as 'a sort of historical novel dealing with the past' (p. vii). Yet Conrad's description remains dubious. For surely all novels have to deal with the past in the sense that there is a certain, though

---

[3] Terry Eagleton, *Exiles and Émigrés: Studies in Modern Literature* (London: Chatto & Windus, 1970), 23.

variable, distance between what is written and the writer; and further on in the note Conrad qualifies his characterization by suggesting that the novel may be more psychological than historical.[4] Although one could say that these two elements are variously present in any novel, Conrad here touches on a basic aspect or problem of this particular text. Building on his characterization, and using a simplifying formulation, we could describe *Under Western Eyes* as a psychological study of a group of characters (focusing on Razumov) placed in a setting which has proved exceptionally important historically. What such a description omits is the novel's persistent emphasis on the problems of narration and writing in the dramatized presentation of the psychological study.

The narrative function of the language teacher is central to this thematic aspect of *Under Western Eyes*. In his 'Author's Note' Conrad defends his narrator as 'useful to the reader both in the way of comment and by the part he plays in the development of the story' (p. ix). This extra-textual authorial comment accentuates Conrad's deliberate choice of the language teacher as a medium of narration: he represents a removed and detached, but still subjective, view which is brought into close contact with major characters and events, and which provides a unique mixture of information (presented by the narrator as a historical account) and evaluation and reflection. What is interesting about this comment (apart from its demonstration of the weight Conrad attached to the language teacher as a narrative device) is essentially the emphasis on the narrator as 'indispensable' (p. ix). It would seem that here, at least, the text supports its author's claim, for, regardless of how one responds to and evaluates the language teacher's presence and function in *Under Western Eyes* there can be no doubt that the novel would have been totally different without him. Discussions about the language teacher's 'relevance' to *Under Western Eyes* may therefore appear somewhat futile and even irrelevant. Instead it might be more useful to discuss his narrative and thematic functions in the gradual development of the text, and this is attempted below.

---

[4] The general problem of narrative and attitudinal distance in Conrad is particularly acute in *Under Western Eyes* because of the author's problematic relationship to Russia. See, in addition to n. 1, Edward Crankshaw, 'Conrad and Russia', in Sherry (ed.), *Conrad: A Commemoration*, 91–104. According to Crankshaw, in *Under Western Eyes* Conrad 'sought to exorcise his obsessional sense of evil by examining its origins in the coolest and most neutral light: through the eyes of the English language teacher' (103). Cf. Andrzej Busza, 'Rhetoric and Ideology in Conrad's *Under Western Eyes*', in Sherry (ed.), *Conrad: A Commemoration*, 105–18.

I

Part First of *Under Western Eyes* opens with the reflections of the language teacher, who throughout the novel functions as the personal narrator through whom the fictional text is transmitted to the reader. Anticipating the predominant position of Razumov as a character by drawing attention first to his name and then to his diary, the beginning also hints that the language teacher is to perform a crucial function not only as a narrator in the technical sense (as teller of a story), but also as a reflective observer. His function, it is suggested at once, is not merely narrative but thematic as well. As the overall narrative confirms the validity of this prefiguration we tend, on later readings of the novel, to register it as a prolepsis about the narrator's centrality at both the narrative and thematic levels.

It is noteworthy that the narrator's opening disclaimer about possessing 'high gifts of imagination and expression' (3) is different from his reservations in the following paragraphs concerning his limited understanding of things Russian. If the first statement functions rather mechanically as part of the narrative convention to which the language teacher conforms, the latter modification follows instead from reflection on the narrator's, and Conrad's, own medium—language. Recurring in more or less explicit form throughout the novel, such reflections on language and communication establish one of its major thematic focuses. These first reflections are hesitant and sceptical: 'To a teacher of languages there comes a time when the world is but a place of many words and man appears a mere talking animal not much more wonderful than a parrot' (3). Combined with the preceding observation in the same paragraph, 'Words, as is well known, are the great foes of reality', this narrative statement introduces, as several of the novel's commentators have noted,[5] serious reservations about the legitimacy and reliability of words right from the start.

As the reader is directly addressed in the following paragraph, the

---

[5] See, for instance, Jeremy Hawthorn, *Conrad: Language and Fictional Self-Consciousness*, 109. Hawthorn's chapter on *Under Western Eyes* is one of the best discussions of the novel. See also *CN* 231–53; *CMP* 160–85; *CWD* 184–209; and Raval, *The Art of Failure*, 126–47. Two interesting articles are Paul Kirschner, 'Revolution, Feminism, and Conrad's Western "I"', *The Conradian*, 10 (1985), 4–25; and Josiane Paccaud, 'The Name-of-the-Father in Conrad's *Under Western Eyes*', *Conradiana*, 18 (1986), 204–18.

narrator goes on to relate his narrative to 'documentary evidence', claiming that his account is 'based on a document' (3). The character of the document is 'something in the nature of a journal, a diary'; and we are given an introductory description of Razumov, the supposed author of the diary. Already here, in the introduction to Part First, there is a notable gap between the narrator's reservations—'Yet I confess that I have no comprehension of the Russian character' (4)—and the following, surprisingly unqualified, observations on Razumov and his background.

If the introduction (3–7) to Part First indicates how strongly dependent the narrator is on his source material (Razumov's diary), the opening of Chapter 1 exemplifies his characteristic, and often confusing, tendency to blur information which presumably stems from the diary with his own reflections and ideas. Razumov is now placed in a wider setting, within 'the moral corruption of an oppressed society' (7). Compared to the preceding introduction, the narrator's presence is so much toned down in this chapter that the narrative may seem authorial in spite of its personal foundation, and in spite of the narrator's various reservations. More broadly, I would argue that the relative success of Part First is to be sought in one of the most productive narrative variations in *Under Western Eyes*: that a narrative which defines and introduces itself as personal takes on authorial appearance in several sections of the text. It is as though, in a manner somewhat reminiscent of *Nostromo*, part of the function of the personal narrator is to provide a basis for an authorial narrative which not only influences the various personal ones, but also characterizes them and moves beyond them. In contrast to *Nostromo* there is here no identified authorial narrative at the extradiegetic level. But, as I shall argue below, the novel considered as a whole can be seen as an 'A-text' which incorporates the document ('B-text') prepared by the narrator, and which bears an interesting resemblance to the authoritative authorial narrative of *Nostromo*.

The reason for the 'authorial effect' of the personal narrative in the early chapters of Part First is not only suggested by the language teacher's spatial and psychological detachment from the events he relates; it is also due to the manner in which he presents, and edits, the information he allegedly has from Razumov's diary. In spite of his claims to the contrary, part of this narrative performance is not altogether different from that of an authorial narrator in the tradition of Hardy or Dickens.[6] The decisive events of the early chapters are effectively presented, in dramatized form (including extensive use of dialogue) and with a remarkable fullness of knowledge. The omniscience becomes the more striking in the light of the narrator's introductory reservations, but once this observation is made I should add that the question of narrative consistency is here less important than that of narrative effect: severe restrictions of the narrator's knowledge (the kind of restricted knowledge the introduction makes us expect) would have been wholly incompatible with the predominant narrative and thematic thrust of Part First. In the discussion of *The Nigger of the 'Narcissus'*, we have seen that the technical problems associated with the narrative variation of the novella are sometimes made conspicuous. A similar observation could be made on the problems of narrative reliability and consistency resulting from the strategy adopted in *Under Western Eyes*; there is an interesting similarity here between the early novella and the relatively late novel.

It is consistent with the paradoxical juxtaposition of personal reservations and authorial effect that the first two chapters of Part First take the reader directly into the novel's dramatic action. An early culmination is reached when Haldin unexpectedly confesses to Razumov that 'It was I who removed de P—this morning' (16)—a confession that makes Razumov feel 'the safety of his lonely existence to be permanently endangered' (21). Razumov's reaction to Haldin's confession at once pinpoints and anticipates a central thematic concern of the novel. It does so by contributing to what Jeremy Hawthorn, in his introduction to the World's Classics edition of *Under Western Eyes*, calls its 'view of the interpenetration of the social and the personal'.[7] For if there is, as the text invites us to infer, a worryingly close connection between Haldin's confession to Razumov and the latter's betrayal of him, then there is also, as Tony Tanner points out in a useful essay on the

---

[6] For an essay on the affinity of Conrad and Dickens, see Robert L. Casiero, 'Joseph Conrad, Dickensian Novelist of the Nineteenth Century: A Dissent from Ian Watt', *Nineteenth-Century Fiction*, 36 (1981), 337–47. For a discussion of some aspects of Hardy's narrative method, see my 'Hardy's Authorial Narrative Method in *Tess of the D'Urbervilles*', in Jeremy Hawthorn (ed.), *The Nineteenth-Century British Novel* (London: Edward Arnold, 1986), 156–70.

[7] Jeremy Hawthorn, intro. to the World's Classics edn. of *Under Western Eyes* (Oxford: OUP, 1983), p. ix.

novel, a persistent textual invitation to connect the question: why does Razumov betray Haldin? with another one: why is he driven to confess the deed?[8] The connection between the two questions is paradoxical but strong, and the novel's 'A-text' is made more coherent through their interdependence.

When the personal narrator's presence is reaffirmed early in Chapter 2, this typically happens through further observations on his deplorably limited understanding of the events he relates. Interestingly, the narrator now attempts to establish a sort of attitudinal alliance between himself as Western narrator and 'the Western reader' (25). It is a rather 'negative' alliance in that it seems to consist mainly of a shared—or rather, what the narrator supposes to be shared—contempt for Russia and scepticism about the story which the narrative unfolds. Especially if compared with the certitude of other statements of the narrator's, the reservations seem contrived and unconvicing, and the more so as they are constantly reiterated. However, although this form of repetition is a rather mechanical narrative variation, it paradoxically strengthens the curious impression the novel gives both of spatial and attitudinal distance and of a strangely undefined menace. The inconsistency of the narrator is noteworthy: appearing to forget his own reservations, he assumes more knowledge of Razumov in the middle of the chapter than at the beginning of it.

The opening of Chapter 3 incorporates an expressive modulation of the personal narrator's function. The mechanically repetitive notes on 'the difficulty of the task' (66) of telling the story are relatively unimportant, but then the reservations are used as a basis for introduction of the key word 'cynicism', which keeps recurring (as noun or adjective) throughout the novel, and which gradually comes to function as a leit-motif with far-reaching thematic reverberations. The narrator is here clearly reflective and evaluative, not merely a neutral recorder. This tendency is strengthened by his precise characterization of Razumov's 'five lines' (66) as 'his conservative convictions, diluted in a vague liberalism natural to the ardour of his age'(67). As the chapter, which culminates in the conversation Razumov has with Councillor Mikulin, gets under

---

[8] Tony Tanner, 'Nightmare and Complacency: Razumov and the Western Eye', *Critical Quarterly*, 4 (1962), 197–214; here quoted from C. B. Cox (ed.), *Conrad: A Casebook*, 173.

way, the narrator's presence is again reduced. Instead the narrative, in spite of the fact that it is still technically personal, reverts to the fluently descriptive and authoritatively omniscient form so characteristic of Part First. The predominance of this particular form is one reason why the narrator's sudden comment on page 86 seems pointed and artificial. Still, this comment ('I may remark here that the diary proper... ') is consistent enough with the narrative stance the narrator has adopted and the reservations he has already made about his lack of imagination and his limited knowledge of Russia. Furthermore, the intrusion has the effect not only of reaffirming the spatial and attitudinal distance between the narrator and the characters he describes, but also of confirming the differences between these characters and the reader. At one level, an intrusive narrative comment such as this one is an illusion-breaking device that augments the metafictional character of *Under Western Eyes* and warns the reader against identification with its fictional characters.

The narrative function of the excellent ending of Part First is essentially twofold. First, at the structural level, Mikulin's question establishes a link between St Petersburg and Geneva, the setting of the remaining action of the novel. Only later are we informed that Razumov's actual function in Geneva (the ostensible one being to introduce himself and act as a revolutionary emissary) is to spy on the exiled Russian revolutionaries gathered there. His mission is not in fact detailed until on page 308, in the crucially important extended analepsis concentrating on the part of his dialogue with Councillor Mikulin which the ending of Part First leaves out, and this increases the narrative economy of the novel by bringing its four main parts into closer relation to one another.

Secondly, Councillor Mikulin's calculated and softly-pronounced 'Where to?' (99) constitutes the first instance of a phrase which is repeated and explained on page 308, and also pinpoints Razumov's impossible post-betrayal situation: regardless of all the rational arguments he can possibly advance in support of his decision to betray Haldin, he is seen to be waging a vain battle against the constant and increasing pressure of conscience. That this particular form of pressure is greatly enhanced by his experiences in Geneva (and especially his infatuation with Miss Haldin) is one indication that the implications of Councillor Mikulin's question cannot be properly appreciated until on a second reading.

If the ending of Part First reads like effective authorial narrative, the opening chapter of Part Second sounds like a different novel. The main reason for this very substantial tonal shift is the reaffirmation of the personal narrator's presence. Attention is drawn to the Englishman as he directs his gaze towards Russia and tries to understand that enigmatic country; and there is renewed stress on the narrative activity as a reporting rather than an inventive one. However, an inserted remark somewhat later in the chapter constitutes a generalization which seems to run counter to the earlier qualifications: 'That propensity of lifting every problem from the plane of the understandable by means of some sort of mystic expression, is very Russian' (104). And this is not all, as the narrator goes on to advance his own theories which he then relates to the 'artlessness' (100) of his story. The theories' factual basis is blurred, and they are not exempt from Western prejudices.

The implication of such inconsistencies seems to be that the reader is meant to question the validity of the language teacher's narrative *qua* direct or literal transmission of Razumov's diary. In Part Second, the teacher's narrative function is further complicated by his presence at the diegetic level of the text and his contact with some of its main characters, especially Miss Haldin. At the same time, and this is sometimes overlooked by critics of the novel, it is precisely the narrator's contact and growing friendship with Miss Haldin that initiate his interest and give a credible motivation for his narrative undertaking. Thus at the end of the chapter—when the apparently insurmountable difficulties of understanding arising from differences in nationality and background are stressed once again—the effect is somewhat different because of the relationship the narrator has established with the Haldins. There is an obvious sense in which his reliability and narrative potential gain from the contact.

The narrator's growing concern for Miss Haldin and her mother is effectively revealed through his disappointment and annoyance when he finds Peter Ivanovitch in their home. Having read the feminist's book (the summary account of some of its contents forms a lighter, more unpretentiously entertaining episode in *Under Western Eyes*), the narrator has a rather negative opinion of him already, but here he appears to regard Peter Ivanovitch as some sort of rival. We do not quite believe his assertion that 'I trust that an unbecoming jealousy of my privileged position had nothing to do with [his presence]' (126). The incident and the comments it provokes are instrumental in indicating the narrator's increasing personal involvement in the subject-matter of his narrative.

An interesting variant on relatively simple, conscious irony is observable both in the narrator's first description of Peter Ivanovitch and in the latter's advice to Miss Haldin: 'be a fanatic' (129) and 'You must descend into the arena, Natalia' (131). So she does eventually, but the proleptic element embedded in this advice cannot be noticed prior to a second reading, when the irony becomes authorial and is instead directed towards the narrator himself. Broadly, Peter Ivanovitch adds a good deal of colour to *Under Western Eyes*. More specifically, his importance for the narrative includes the unexpected way in which he refers to 'That young man newly arrived from St. Petersburg' (127). This mention of Razumov not only increases suspense; it also enhances textual coherence by establishing the most direct connection with Part First.

When Miss Haldin shows the narrator the letter she has received from her brother Victor, renewed emphasis is laid upon the fact that the language teacher's comprehension of Razumov's diary is far from perfect. This important letter is not only a supplementary written source of the teacher's narrative; its references to Razumov also increase Miss Haldin's interest in the latter. As Miss Haldin tells the narrator about Razumov's arrival, his response, 'Compromised politically, I suppose' (135), suggest a latent jealously on his part, but it becomes much more suggestive if related to Razumov's act of betrayal and his actual mission in Geneva. That we *can* register and ponder these crucial facts is of course due to the knowledge we have gained from Part First, but our source of this information, the narrator, is now curiously ignorant of the part of the story he has already presented. However, in spite of this problem of chronological inconsistency, the gains are considerable, not least in establishing an effective dramatic irony: through her ignorance of what has actually happened Miss Haldin evokes both sympathy and pity.[9]

It is in the same conversation with Miss Haldin that the narrator advances his strange theory of 'a real revolution' (134). The theory may not be very important in itself, but it constitutes one of the rare instances where the language teacher expresses his personal opinion

---

[9] The gains are discussed by Daleski, see *C W D* 188.

on a matter not related to his problems as a narrator. Thus his views here enhance his importance as a character, and could be related to Razumov's manifesto 'Evolution not Revolution'[10] (66) in Part First. They provoke Miss Haldin to assert that 'I would take liberty from any hand as a hungry man would snatch at a piece of bread' (135), a statement that is given additional thematic weight through its function as epigraph to the novel. This epigraph is puzzling as well as intriguing. As Avrom Fleishman has pointed out,[11] it is not only highly unusual in being a quotation from the text it introduces, but it actually misquotes this text by omitting the preposition 'at'. Fleishman draws on the epigraph by way of distinguishing between different textual levels in Under Western Eyes; and we shall return to this helpful distinction after the textual commentary.

When early in Chapter 4 the narrator comments explicitly on his own problematic position as narrator-character, it is essentially to confirm his earlier reservations: 'but I had no illusions as to my power. I was but a Westerner... I was too curious, and too honest, perhaps, to run away' (141). However, when Miss Haldin too describes him as 'as curious as a child', his riposte, unconvincingly, is 'No. I am only an anxious old man' (143). The narrator seems very confused here, both as to his status in this fascinating but unfamiliar new environment and as to his primary personal characteristics. When Miss Haldin starts telling him about her visit to the Château Borel, he insistently claims to be interested in 'all the details' (143). As a *remembered* account, Miss Haldin's incorporated story is of course impossible: its 'details' include extended dialogue in inverted commas. This would seem another example of productive narrative inconsistency in Under Western Eyes. For as Miss Haldin informs the narrator about her talk to the *dame de compagnie*, we note that her story has significant, though indirect, bearing on that of Razumov. For instance, her exclamation 'Do you understand how frightful that is—nothing to look forward to!' (150) is clearly related to Razumov's gloomy thought, given as

---

10 Hawthorn notes that in Conrad's manuscript of the novel 'it looks as if he had started to write "Revelation" and then changed his mind—if so, an interesting association of the religious and the political in his thoughts'. See the World's Classics edn., 385.

11 Fleishman, 'Speech and Writing in *Under Western Eyes*', ch. 9 of his *Fiction and the Ways of Knowing: Essays on British Novels* (Austin & London: University of Texas Press, 1978), 123–35. Cf. the section on *Under Western Eyes* in my 'Repetition and Narrative Method', in Hawthorn (ed.), *Narrative*, 124–7.

narrated monologue, on page 69: 'Looking forward was happiness—that's all—nothing more.'

Considering the narrator's general, if somewhat assumed, reticence and great admiration for Miss Haldin, his spontaneous interruption of her narrative is a surprising move. Indicating his increasing personal involvement, the interruption illustrates to what extent the language teacher not only narrates, but also performs an editing activity: 'The above relation is founded on her narrative, which I have not so much dramatized as might be supposed' (161). In the light of these comments the contrast which the narrator goes on to draw in the following paragraph between his activity and that of a novelist becomes even more suspect, if not directly misleading. Still, for all its artificiality, the contrast provides Conrad with an opportunity to reaffirm that part of the narrator's reporting activity is based on information from reliable sources.

It is consistent enough that the narrator, unaware as he is of Razumov's background at this stage of the action, should be bewildered by his behaviour in Geneva. In the following chapter this discrepancy (i.e. between limited and full insight or knowledge) is commented on explicitly in a description the narrator gives of the tormented Razumov:

He looked as though he had not slept very well of late. I could almost feel on me the weight of his unrefreshed, motionless stare, the stare of a man who lies unwinking in the dark, angrily passive in the toils of disastrous thoughts. Now, when I know how true it was, I can honestly affirm that this *was* the effect produced on me. It was painful in a curiously indefinite way—for, of course, the definition comes to me now while I sit writing in the fullness of my knowledge. But this is what the effect was at that time of absolute ignorance. (183)

In the context of Part Second, the importance of this form of narrative break is strengthened by the fact that it is very rare. Stressing the language teacher's omniscience at the time of writing, and reminding the reader of the crucial temporal gap between this writing situation and that of the events described, the break confirms and extends the centrality of the personal narrator in the novel. At the same time, at this stage (approximately mid-way through the novel) we are more aware of the discrepancy between the narrator's own statements on his text and the textual complexity of *Under Western Eyes* as a whole. The way in which the discrepancy is engendered and developed is a main characteristic of the novel.

In Chapter 5 of Part Second there is an important perspectival shift from the language teacher to Razumov. The latter is mystified by the narrator's seemingly unmotivated interest and involvement. Although this perception is not wholly invalid, Razumov's situation is now so precarious and increasingly desperate that almost anybody seems to represent a potential danger to him. As the chapter dramatizes essential aspects of Razumov's problem through the dialogue between him and the narrator, we note that much of the narrative effect depends on the reader's knowledge of Razumov's identity. The following remark, interpreted by the narrator as an unexpected gesture of confidence, illustrates this particularly clearly: 'The fact is, I have received a sort of mission from them' (195). At the time of the conversation the narrator is not very enlightened by this comment, but the reader will at least put it into relation with the occurrences dramatized in Part First. It is noteworthy, however, that neither party is here in a position wholly to understand the remark, for in order to do so we need to have read the extended analepsis at the beginning of Part Four. This sentence alone, then, offers an unambiguous illustration of the need to reread the novel for a full appreciation of its varied narrative and thematic effects. Reminding the reader of Part First, 'mission' also prefigures the dramatized specification of its conditions in Part Four.

Early in Part Third the language teacher's narrative problems are toned down and there is instead a chronological continuation of the action, with stable focus on Razumov. As the narrative moves considerably faster here, a connection is established between this increased speed and the importance attached to suspense at the diegetic level. However, although the narrative of Part Third exhibits relatively few variations, this does not in itself make this part uninteresting in a discussion of narrative method: it is relevant that earlier narrative characteristics are confirmed, including some which reveal that the language teacher's attitude and assertions as a narrator are not wholly consistent. He tends to reassert points already made, but the relation of these points to the narrative he actually presents becomes increasingly problematic.

An example of this growing problem, which in its own way

becomes a narrative and thematic characteristic of the novel, occurs just after Miss Haldin's proleptic statement on Razumov's attitude to her: 'I think that he is observing, studying me, to discover whether I am worthy of his trust . . . '(202). The prolepsis embedded in this remark will almost inevitably strike anyone rereading the novel: it is Miss Haldin who is to receive Razumov's first confession in Part Four. Miss Haldin's comment provokes the teacher of languages to reflect that

The dead brother, the dying mother, the foreign friend, had fallen into a distant background. But, at the same time, Peter Ivanovitch was absolutely nowhere now. And this thought consoled me. Yet I saw the gigantic shadow of Russian life deepening around her like the darkness of an advancing night. It would devour her presently. I inquired after Mrs. Haldin—that other victim of the deadly shade. (202)

There is both a general and a more narrowly contextual side to the problem raised by these reflections. At the level of the broad narrative progression of the text, the description of Russia seems rhetorically pompous, and the constellation of metaphors not very suggestive. It also sounds repetitive, reaffirming the opposition between the narrator's reservations about his ability to understand Russia on the one hand, and his generalizations about the country on the other. Considered as a reflection following the narrator's conversation with Miss Haldin, the passage indicates such a sceptical, if not to say hostile, attitude to Russia that the narrator's earlier modesty and reservations come to seem rather contrived. Thus a conspicuous contrast develops between his sceptical attitude to the country and his sincere interest in it, an interest to which his narrative amply testifies.

The last paragraph of Chapter 1 of Part Third takes the form of an incorporated, reflective passage where the language teacher again defends the 'sincerity' of Razumov's written record:

The very words I use in my narrative are written where their sincerity cannot be suspected. The record, which could not have been meant for any one's eyes but his own, was not, I think, the outcome of that strange impulse of indiscretion common to men who lead secret lives... Mr. Razumov looked at it, I suppose, as a man looks at himself in a mirror, with wonder, perhaps with anguish, with anger or despair. (214)

If the previous quotation we considered exemplifies the narrator's tendency to indulge in generalizing descriptions about a subject he

knows very little about, this one reaffirms his insistence on
Razumov's diary or 'memorandum' (214) as the primary source of
his narrative. At such a relatively late stage this claim, too, seems
repetitive; and neither are the reflections on Razumov's possible
reasons for writing the diary very persuasive. Moreover, the textual
position of the self-reflective comment further complicates the
narrative assertions it embodies: it is preceded by the important
conversation between Razumov and Peter Ivanovitch in which the
former identifies himself with Russia ('I am *it!*' (209)), and which
includes lavish use of quoted monologue. It is of course most
unlikely that all these quotations should be included in Razumov's
'memorandum'. The whole of *Under Western Eyes* concerns the
problem of narrative reliability and unreliability, but this problem
becomes particularly pressing in a passage such as this one. As
observable here it can be related to Wayne C. Booth's comments on
'The Unreliable Narrator' in connection with his discussion of
Henry James's thought-provoking *Notebooks*.[12] Pondering the best
way of telling his short story 'The Next Time', James wonders
whether his narrator ought to be able to recognize the ironies of the
story in order to convey them to the reader: 'Can I take such a person
and make him—or her—narrate my little drama *naïvement*?'[13]
James doubts if he can without 'wasting my material and missing
my effect', and as far as 'The Next Time' is concerned this is
probably correct. I am certainly not suggesting a direct comparison
of two texts as different as 'The Next Time' and *Under Western
Eyes*, but the reference to James, for whose literary craftmanship
Conrad had great respect, may make us see more clearly not only
how different the function of the language teacher is from that of
James's ideal narrator, but also how paradoxically complicated the
narrative and thematic effects of *Under Western Eyes* are. As we
shall see, this applies in particular to the effects and implications of
the novel's 'A-text'.

In the following chapter the assertion about narrative authentic-
ity is reaffirmed. Now the language teacher would have the reader
believe that even the account of Razumov's thought is authentic: 'He
thought to himself (it stands confessed in his handwriting), "I won't
move from here till [Peter Ivanovitch] either speaks or turns away.

---

[12] Booth, *The Rhetoric of Fiction*, 340–5.
[13] Quoted in *The Rhetoric of Fiction*, 343.

This is a duel" ' (229). Here, then, the language teacher's narrative presents Razumov's diary as a literal transcription of his thoughts at the relevant point in time. The unlikelihood of such a transcription need hardly be detailed. Generally speaking, however, the narrative presentation of Razumov's talks to the revolutionaries and his attempts to gain their confidence contains few narrative insertions. It even becomes somewhat monotonous, since the authorial-type narrative is distinctly less effectively dramatic here than in Part First. A further connection between Part Third and Part First is established as Sophia Antonovna, the 'woman revolutionist' (257), asks Razumov about 'the other—this wonderful Haldin appearing only to be regretted—you don't know what he intended?' (259). The reader is reminded of the question which General T—ordered to be put to Haldin just before his execution, and which Councillor Milkulin reads out to Razumov at the end of Part First:

'Question—Has the man well known to you, in whose rooms you remained for several hours on Monday and on whose information you have been arrested—has he had any previous knowledge of your intention to commit a political murder? . . . Prisoner refuses to reply.' (93)

Particularly if combined with Sophia Antonovna's appreciative view of the late Haldin, this passage both highlights and prefigures Razumov's lasting moral predicament. Had Haldin affirmed the question, Razumov would of course have been heavily compromised, and his safety much more seriously endangered. Preserving his 'stubborn silence' (93), Haldin rejects this opportunity to avenge himself upon the person who betrayed him. The contrast in personal loyalty is striking, and functions as a basis for the authorial irony noticeable in Sophia Antonovna's remark on page 260: 'And what is death? At any rate, it is not a shameful thing like some kinds of life.' This is a relatively simple variant of authorial irony in *Under Western Eyes*, aimed at Razumov rather than the language teacher: 'Razumov felt something stir in his breast, a sort of feeble and unpleasant tremor' (260). At the time of writing, the teacher of languages is probably aware of this form of implicit criticism, which we could describe as a blend of authorial and personal irony.

Razumov's reaction to the information about Ziemianitch's suicide constitutes the next stage in his changing process. The effect the information has on Razumov is paradoxical, and yet sufficiently well prepared to be credible: since his position is now more secure due to Ziemianitch's death, 'he felt the need of perfect safety, with its freedom from direct lying' (278, cf. 279–80 and 284). It is thematically significant that this indication of Razumov's irresistibly growing remorse comes precisely at the point when he is suddenly less endangered than previously. The novel's concern with the moral issue of human responsibility is strengthened by the protagonist's mental reaction to the form of external alleviation which the unexpected death of Ziemianitch implies.

Up to the meeting with Julius Laspara, the language teacher is unusually reticent. Refraining from inserting his usual comments and reservations, he gives instead an apparently omniscient portrayal of Razumov's agonizing situation. However, as Razumov is introduced to Laspara, the anarchist 'of indefinite nationality' (285) who strongly encourages him to write, Razumov's riposte (rendered as quoted monologue) implies an important reference to the narrator's main source: 'I shall write—never fear. Certainly. That's why I am here. And for the future I shall have something to write about' (289). Razumov's intention to write anticipates not only the concluding part of his diary but, more specifically, his written confession to Miss Haldin. Its ambiguity is also an indication that writing—in various of its multidimensional aspects—is a fundamental problem which in this novel is given its own thematic import, but not without retaining a very close relation to the text's narrative method. In a curious way the narrator copies Razumov's lonely writing activity; the major differences are those of age, nationality, and involvement. However, the similarities between the novel's narrator and its protagonist should not be overlooked. As Berthoud observes, Razumov's political creed (cf. page 66) could also stand as a paradigm of the narrator's convictions as they are extractable from his narrative presentation.[14] The missing narrative qualifications in the section we have just considered could be interpreted as an indirect suggestion of sympathy for Razumov, and possibly also as a partial recognition on the narrator's part that in a different society he might, at least in theory, have found himself in a position comparable to that of Razumov. The consequences of complacent liberalism vary greatly.

Part Four opens with an extended homodiegetic analepsis.[15]

---

[14] *CMP* 170.
[15] Cf. ch. 2 n. 10.

There are several reasons why Genette's accurate term is preferable to the more common 'flashback' here. After the narrator's introduction there is a chronological break and a movement backward in story time, but the analepsis is clearly internal since it is focused on the lacuna or textual gap between the ending of Part First and the beginning of Part Second: Razumov's mental state after the execution of Haldin, his contact with Councillor Mikulin, and the motives for his appearance in Geneva. Moreover, the fact that the analepsis is homodiegetic makes the action of *Under Western Eyes* more coherent and confirms the novel's emphasis on Razumov as main character.

It is an indication not only of the narrator's self-consciousness, but also of the way in which it is restricted, that he himself mentions the word 'retrospect' at the beginning of Part Four. If 'retrospect' can be seen as a more imprecise synonym of 'homodiegetic internal analepsis', the narrative restriction (which includes an extraordinary lack of self-criticism) is suggested by the reader's increased scepticism, at this rather late stage of the narrative, about the narrator's vocabulary and insight. It must be stressed here that to comment on a certain similarity between the narrator and Razumov is not to suggest that the former has now achieved a much better understanding of the subject matter of his narrative. Although there are flashes of insight, his commentary all too easily reverts to the form of reservations which have begun to strike us as highly repetitive, if not positively boring. Our general scepticism is confirmed by the authorial irony in the note in the first paragraph on the connections between 'this narrative where the aspects of honour and shame are remote from the ideas of the Western world' and 'what every reader has most likely already discovered himself' (293). For certainly our discoveries of moral and other differences between Western and Eastern Europe are intimately related to our growing doubts about the narrator's ability to understand the characteristics of the latter.

The analepsis occurs just at the point in the text where it is likely to make the maximum effect. The preceding Part Third has dramatized Razumov's growing moral dilemma, particularly as provoked through the contact, and apparently growing infatuation, with Miss Haldin. His mission as spy has placed him in a situation that is rapidly becoming unbearable. Now the analepsis, interposed between the account of Razumov's anguished state of mind just

before confessing his betrayal of Haldin and the narrative presentation of the tripartite confession itself, fills in the lacuna already
mentioned between his act of giving up Haldin and the start of his
Geneva activities. Although the far-reaching thematic implications
of the analepsis cannot be explored here, it must be noted that it
augments, rather than reduces, the moral seriousness of the betrayal
by describing the subsequent spying engagement as an almost
unavoidable consequence of it.

The last observation applies not least to the description of
Razumov's state of mind in the days preceding the conversation
with Councillor Mikulin. This dialogue constitutes the structural
and thematic centre of the analepsis. Once again, the language
teacher is surprisingly well informed:

... the consciousness of [Razumov's] position presented itself to him as
something so ugly, dangerous, and absurd, the difficulty of ever freeing
himself from the toils of that complication so insoluble, that the idea of
going back and, as he termed it to himself, *confessing* to Councillor
Mikulin flashed through his mind.

Go back! What for? Confess! To what? 'I have been speaking to him with
the greatest openness,' he said to himself with perfect truth. (297)

The last part of the quotation illustrates how productively narrative
and quoted monologue are combined in this novel. The two devices
are closely related here, and depend on the narrator's pointed
omniscience. If the quoted monologue is the less successful in this
case, this is essentially due to the phrase 'perfect truth': at this stage
of the narrative we have reservations about the narrator's ability to
ascertain the 'truth' of Razumov's thoughts and actions.

The thematic impact of Razumov's conversation with Councillor
Mikulin is increased by the form of narrative reticence that can be
observed in the analepsis; the language teacher's self-imposed comments on his own narrative are less conspicuous and disturbing
here. Razumov's 'moral loneliness' (307, cf. 301–3) is repeatedly
referred to, also as a motivating factor contributing to his accepting
the 'mission' Councillor Mikulin wants him to undertake. The most
direct link with Part First is established on page 308, where repetition of the key question 'Where to?' (cf. 99) is succeeded by this very
dense passage:

It was to be a dangerous mission to Geneva for obtaining, at a critical
moment, absolutely reliable information from a very inaccessible quarter of

the inner revolutionary circle. There were indications that a very serious plot was being matured . . . The repose indispensable to a great country was at stake . . . A great scheme of orderly reforms would be endangered . . . The highest personages in the land were patriotically uneasy, and so on. In short, Councillor Mikulin knew what to say.

The persuasiveness of Councillor Mikulin's eloquent and, in its way, very consistent reasoning is enhanced through the use of ellipsis. This device has not just a stylistic but also a narrative function in *Under Western Eyes*; and it is related, as Hawthorn has shown,[16] to the novel's sophisticated presentation of bodily communication. An interesting effect of ellipsis as employed in this passage is the implied suggestion that Razumov's use of rational arguments in order to justify the betrayal of Haldin (cf. 37–8) makes him more vulnerable to the sort of arguments put to him by Councillor Mikulin; this is indeed the main reason why the latter's reasoning must seem consistent and persuasive to Razumov. The observation can be extended to suggest that Razumov's 'official' action in Geneva, the action, that is, which he carries out for Councillor Mikulin and the Russian authorities, is not only an unavoidable consequence of the betrayal itself, but also of its supposedly rational motivation. Once this point is made, however, an immediate qualification must be added. If Razumov was unable to foresee the mission to Geneva at the time of giving up Haldin, he was still less able to discern the ultimate consequence of a counteracting process, which is initiated by the moral culpability of betraying a person who confides in you. As the novel dramatizes this process, it shows it to be as irreversible as the first. Miss Haldin serves as its most important catalyst; and it is not brought to satisfactory conclusion until Razumov's third and final confesion is completed.

In the opening of Chapters 2 and 3 of Part Four the textual position of the narrator is again more prominent, but the narrative focus remains on Razumov. In Chapter 2 the narrator notes that 'The Westerner in me was discomposed' (317); in the following chapter he places renewed stress on his feeling of 'European remoteness', and characterizes his perspective as that of 'a helpless spectator' (336). Rather monotonously repetitive, such comments confirm the established position of the narrator as the naïve

---

[16] Jeremy Hawthorn, 'Bodily Communication in *Under Western Eyes*', *Anglo-American Studies*, 3 (1983), 5–20.

transmitter of occurrences and processes that are more complex than he realizes. But Chapter 2 incorporates a reflective passage which to some extent contradicts this description:

It is strange to think that, I won't say liberty, but the mere liberalism of outlook which for us is a matter of words, of ambitions, of votes... may be for other beings very much like ourselves and living under the same sky, a heavy trial of fortitude, a matter of tears and anguish and blood. Mrs. Haldin had felt the pangs of her own generation. (318)

It would seem evident that these reflections are distinctly shrewder than the narrator's previous ones have led us to expect, not only by qualifying his earlier, more uncritical and categorical defence of Western values, but also by being better attuned to the moral implications and values which the text gradually constitutes. Broadly, the narrator's repetitious reservations and simplifying generalizations have by now made us uncertain about his ability to acquire new insight into the subject matter of his story; and the above quotations from page 336 confirm a doubt of this kind. Still, it is significant that the present, more untypical reflection follows not only the narrator's prolonged contact with Mrs and Miss Haldin, but also a correspondingly sustained exposure to the integrity of their moral and political convictions. The English teacher of languages has come to respect and admire both of them, and this deference, which must have been quite unexpected for him, seems to have effected a partial revision of his initial prejudices.

It would also seem that there is an important connection between this observation and that made above concerning a certain sympathy for Razumov on the part of the narrator. It should be stressed, however, that, important as they are, these indications of increased affinity between the narrator and the novel's main characters do not invalidate the main points about narrative distance, limited understanding, and simplifying narrative transmission. One of the chracteristics of the narrator is his tendency to revert all too easily to his customary reservations and simplifications (compare, for instance, page 374). But on the basis of the uneasy combination we have noted between the language teacher's narrative distance from his subject matter and his narrative affinity with it, two more specific points can be made. First, the quality of the narrator's comments and reflections is uneven, in the sense that the customary emphasis on distance and detachment may suddenly give way to a

surprising understanding of the characters' problems and an unexpected similarity of perspective. Secondly, this form of variation
makes the narrator more interesting, and not only as narrator but
also as character. As his views become less predictable, the tedious
effect of mechanical repetition is reduced. Moreover, the narrator's
scattered insights come to function as a device which constitutes a
narrative link between the 'B-text' the narrator presents and the
novel's total 'A-text', thereby increasing the novel's textual coherence. This point will be extended below.

Critical evaluation of the dialogue between Razumov and Miss
Haldin in Chapter 3 will to a large extent depend on which aspects
of their conversation one chooses to emphasize. Razumov's struggle
to formulate the confession of his betrayal of Miss Haldin's brother
is rendered most convincingly: the dialogue is vivid, dramatic, and
has an inherently logical progression. These qualities may also be
observed in a narrative comment such as this one: 'she was unable to
see the truth struggling on his lips. What she was conscious of was
the obscure form of his suffering' (354). If, on the other hand, one
chooses to focus on the use of narrative convention here, then one
rapidly concludes that it is forced indeed, almost to the point of
becoming comic. It is of course most unlikely that the narrator
should actually overhear their conversation in the first place. Still
more problematic are his awkward attempts to explain his presence:

[Razumov and Miss Haldin] seemed brought out from the confused
immensity of the Eastern borders to be exposed cruelly to the observation
of my Western eyes. And I observed them. There was nothing else to do.
My existence seemed so utterly forgotten by these two that I dared not now
make a movement. (346)

The explanation is not only awkward but disappointing as well:
merely repeating a view the narrator has already voiced several
times, it seems inconsistent with the understanding he appears to
show in the description of Miss Haldin on page 354. There is an
interesting incoherence here between the narrator's conventional
reaction and attitude at the beginning and end of the confession and
the insights embedded in the explanatory comments to the dialogue
itself. When Razumov's 'atrocious confession' (355) makes the
infuriated narrator address him directly at the level of action, the
narrator's reproach is hopelessly irrelevant; it also includes authorial
irony concerning himself rather than Razumov:

'This is monstrous. What are you staying for? Don't let her catch sight of you again. Go away! . . .' He did not budge. 'Don't you understand that your presence is intolerable—even to me? If there's any sense of shame in you . . .'

Slowly his sullen eyes moved in my direction. 'How did this old man come here?' he muttered, astounded. (355)

The authorial irony is noticeable above all in the narrator's appeal to Razumov's 'sense of shame'; and it becomes particularly evident for the reader who recalls Razumov's reaction to Sophia Antonovna's characterization of some kinds of life as 'shameful' (260). As it would of course have been much more 'shameful' of Razumov *not* to confess, the narrator's lack of understanding is extreme here.

If Razumov's first, oral and gestural, confession to Miss Haldin constitutes the dramatic climax of the novel, it is consistent with its focus on the problems of writing and communication that in the following chapter a written confession extends and explains the oral one. Underlining Razumov's loneliness, this second confession to Miss Haldin is characterized by his relentlessly honest attempt to state both the initial, misguided motives for the betrayal of her brother and his subsequent remorse. The narrator's introduction to this written confession, which Razumov sends to Miss Haldin, again draws attention to his editing activity: he presents only the sections of the letter he considers most relevant, and 'which have been already made use of in the building up of this narrative' (357). A related indication of the way in which the narrator edits Razumov's writings is the blurred transition between the beginning of the letter and the diary proper. Narrative omniscience is marked in both cases; the letter is essentially characterized by a greater personal intensity and by the absence of narrative commentary.

The basis for the narrator's pervasive omniscience becomes especially problematic and obscure as Razumov's letter abruptly ends. The source of the narrator's information after Razumov has stopped writing on page 362 is unclear; and the following description of the protagonist is, with its incorporated quoted monologues, probably the novel's clearest break with the narrative convention employed. It should be stressed, however, that the main reason why we react more strongly to the stretching of the convention here than elsewhere is to be sought in the abrupt transition from the (supposedly accurate) rendering of the letter to the following authorial-type, personal narrative. The language teacher's omniscience is not more remarkable here than at various other stages of the text, but the abruptness of the transition makes the inherent technical problem more conspicuous.

As regards the narrative presentation of Razumov's third, public confession before the revolutionaries he has been spying upon, there is at least a semblance of narrative source observable in the narrator's claim to have based his account on Laspara's 'version of that night's happenings' (364). At the same time this version is characterized by the narrator as 'very summary', and the presentation of the dramatic confession seems freely constructed. This is not to suggest that it is unsuccessful; there is, overall, no direct correlation between narrative plausibility (with regard to narrative convention) and narrative quality in *Under Western Eyes*. On the contrary, the writing of this section (363–71) has an absorbing, dramatic progression that is brought to an arresting conclusion with Nikita's brutal deafening of Razumov.

Conrad's insertion of Razumov's explanatory comments before the third confession not only strengthens this progression and increases narrative suspense, but also gives Razumov the opportunity to give some idea of his 'obscure solitude' (366) at the time he was contacted by Haldin. This short account recapitulates in compressed, but not distorted, form some of the thematic highlights of Part First, thus further improving the thematic connections between the novel's first and concluding parts. There is no reason to question the sincerity of Razumov's claim to have had 'certain honest ideals in view' (366) when giving up Haldin. Nobody knows better than Razumov himself what a fatal mistake this act was; what needs emphasis is rather the impressive, carefully-calculated way in which his public confession before the revolutionaries is performed. That Razumov is described as 'the puppet of his past' (362) at the time of his confession tells more about the narrator's limited understanding of his moral growth than about Razumov himself.

In the novel's concluding chapter the narrator's presence is again much more pointed, and some of his habitual reservations are voiced yet again. Talking to Miss Haldin just before her return to Russia, the narrator feels more extraneous: 'To my Western eyes she seemed to be getting farther and farther from me, quite beyond my reach now, but undiminished in the increasing distance' (374). There are elements of circular structure observable as the narrator and Miss Haldin depart; their contact, according to the narrative convention employed, has provided the basis for the fictional text. As Miss Haldin passes on to the narrator the diary Razumov sent to her, a structural linkage is established to Razumov's first confession and the opening of the novel. The weight attached to the diary as 'documentary evidence' (3) is confirmed here at the end.

Following yet another reference by the narrator to his limited 'Western' (377) understanding, a narrative reach of two years is introduced: 'My information was completed nearly two years later' (377). This epilogue takes the form of a summary account by Sophia Antonovna, whom the narrator 'quite accidentally' meets, and who provides information on Miss Haldin's and Razumov's present whereabouts. The relation of the epilogue to the preceding main narrative is strengthened by the relatively neutral, reporting function of Sophia's information: in Russia she has actually met Razumov, who, crippled and ill, has become a sort of revolutionary sage. Her final characterization of Razumov is accurate and appreciative. 'There's character in such a discovery' (380), she says, thinking of the remorse and moral pressure which necessitated his confession. The narrator's comment after Sophia's story reasserts his function as witness rather than as commentator and interpreter, but at this concluding stage it essentially serves to confirm a repetitious reservation we have become thoroughly used to.

II

If the narrative function of the language teacher in *Under Western Eyes* enhances rather than impairs the narrative variation and complexity of the novel, this is surely because the function is more diverse than he seems to think. It is, however, a diversity of a complicated and paradoxical kind. To provide a basis for a short consideration of this form of narrative variation I use Avrom Fleishman's helpful distinction between four types of text in *Under Western Eyes*.[17] The A-text, according to Fleishman, is the fiction written by Conrad, including the title, the author's name, the dedication, the unusual epigraph, and (in his view but not mine) the 'Author's Note'. The B-text is the document prepared by the narrator

---

[17] See n. 11 above.

and regarded by him as authentic. Third, there is a C-text, which Fleishman relates to the narrative convention of *Under Western Eyes* which requires that the language teacher's report be based on written documents as well as his direct observation of the action. The most important of these documents are the newspaper report of Haldin's arrest, Peter Ivanovitch's autobiography, sources relating to Mr de P—, Razumov's written confession to Miss Haldin, and finally Razumov's notebook. In addition to these three texts Fleishman sees the contours of a D-text, consisting of Haldin's letters to his sister and his spoken words to Razumov.

The vagueness noticeable in the narrator's description of the journal is typical of his attitude to his source material. The scheme demands that he claim to stay close to his source, but the vagueness makes it easier for Conrad to blur the distinctions between Razumov's voice and that of the language teacher. One of the narrative characteristics of *Under Western Eyes* is that although the C-text contains a variety of voices, they are all modulated through the ever-present voice of the language teacher. There is a sophisticated interplay of voice and perspective in this novel: the narrative perspective of the language teacher as personal narrator influences the tone, and partly also the content, of the voices he claims to report, and yet the perspective is not wholly unaffected by these voices. This constant modulating activity on the part of the narrator is one reason why we do not react more strongly as the various gaps among the constitutive parts of the C-text are overcome. Or perhaps we should say they are filled in because the narrator not only repeats and edits the C-text, but also imagines and silently fills in what took palce in between the textual fragments available to him. In spite of his claims to the contrary, his activity often approaches that of a writer of fiction; and it is precisely this apparently unproblematic combination of insistence on a factual narrative and presentation of a much more creative or invented one which most forcefully characterizes the B-text as representative of Hillis Miller's first form of repetition. From this observation I shall go on to suggest that the most interesting narrative variation in *Under Western Eyes* takes the form of a tension between the B-text and the A-text: this tension is dramatized as a process during which the attitudes and views of the narrator are not so much openly contradicted as gradually undermined by the narrative movement itself. This second discourse, which is embedded in that of the narrator, finally emerges as the novel's authoritative one; and the form of repetition detectable in it is, predominantly, the second.

One possible way of indicating how the two coexisting discourses, the overt one of the B-text and the covert one of the A-text, are opposed is to look more systematically at the narrator's principal reservations and then to indicate how these narrative characteristics are not only subjected to irony or openly contradicted, but paradoxically confirmed. The reservations provide in one sense an example of repetition at the surface level of recurrent phraseology. By insisting that his story is non-imaginative, but then going on to present one which, as we have noted, may be indistinguishable from omniscient, authorial narrative, the narrator unknowingly activates the novel's second discourse, the A-text which not only includes but also transcends the B-text, and through which the central questions of understanding, distance, loneliness, fragmentation, and moral responsibility are thematized. It is primarily the narrator's own resistance to these textual pressures (in other words his inability to learn from his own narrative) that associates him with the first form of repetition. I am not saying that he is not at all changed by the incidents and characters the action confronts him with—witness the observations on the understanding he may sometimes show. But his role as the representative of commonsense rationality (a role, as Berthoud and other critics have noted, duplicated to a remarkable extent by Razumov) implies an identity and ground which is incompatible with the A-text's fundamental fragmentation and deep scepticism about writing as a means of improving the human condition.

There are three reservations which the narrator is anxious to make at the outset of his narrative. The first is his disclaimer of any 'gifts of imagination and expression' (3). If this particular reservation had occurred only once the narrative effect would have been limited. Even modest repetition would not be disturbing, considering the demands of convention we have noted. But the way in which the reservation is repeated over and over again provokes the reader to compare its implied assertion with the narrative as it actually unfolds. Finding that the assertion is actually belied by the narrative the language teacher himself presents, we begin to regard his reservations as a peculiar mixture of assumed modesty and severely limited understanding of his own narrative activity.

The second reservation concerns the limited value the narrator attaches to language: 'Words, as is well known, are the great foes of reality' (3). Combined with the thematic implications of the A-text this statement becomes ambivalent, but it is an ambivalence or obliqueness which concerns only the *possibilities* of language and writing as a means of existential orientation and basis; the acuteness of the problem as such is emphasized rather than modified. This emphasis is noticeable in the final reservation, 'Yet I confess that I have no comprehension of the Russian character' (4), which is later repeated as a comment on the D-text. Confronted with one of Haldin's letters to his sister, the narrator 'glanced down at the flimsy blackened pages whose very handwriting seemed cabalistic, incomprehensible to the experience of Western Europe' (133). The difficulties of understanding are presented as insurmountable, but at this stage of the narrative the reservation is already contradicted both by implication and by the narrator himself, for example in his generalizations on pages 104–9. And yet the end effect of the novel is to reaffirm the immense difficulties connected with the understanding of the motives and action of others.

In one of the most stimulating essays written on this novel, Penn R. Szittya follows Berthoud in emphasizing the paradoxical similarities between the language teacher and Razumov. Szittya makes more of this point than Berthoud does: 'As the major theme of the novel is duplicity', he writes, 'the characteristic feature of its construction is doubleness or duplication.'[18] For Szittya, there is a close relation between the 'double narration' of the narrator and Razumov and the metafictional character of the text as a whole. He sees *Under Western Eyes* as 'metafiction—fiction about fiction, and especially about itself. Its concerns are with the sufficiency of fictions as bases for life; with the possibility of interpretation; and ultimately with the insecurity of the novelist's work'.[19]

As my interpretation of the novel concedes only a partial agreement with this interesting, bipartite point Szittya makes, a brief exposition of my dissent may help us towards a conclusion of this chapter. First, Szittya's emphasis on the close relation between the narrator and Razumov implies a corresponding stress on the relation which we, following Fleishman, have noted between the novel's

[18] Penn R. Szittya, 'Metafiction: The Double Narration in *Under Western Eyes*', *ELH* 48 (1981), 818.
[19] Ibid.

B- and C-texts. There is no need to deny the thematic importance of the motif of duplicity at this level—that the relation is a surprising and paradoxical one corroborates, rather than reduces, its significance. However, my discussion of the novel's narrative method has shown that there are very important differences of character between the narrator and Razumov, and that these essential differences are—in spite of the interspersed indications of a surprising similarity—basically confirmed rather than resolved. It seems forced to suggest, as Szittya does, that 'Razumov is a double of the first person narrator'. Neither does it appear persuasive to argue, as he goes on to do later in the essay, that the superficial similarities between the two 'seem to be signposts for a deeper psychological affinity'.[20] On the basis of the above analysis we could, however, rephrase Szittya's observation by suggesting that although the narrative of *Under Western Eyes* indicates that the similarities between the narrator and Razumov exceed the level of superficial resemblance, it remains doubtful whether the text provides evidence indicating that these similarities—such as the two characters' common loneliness and their shared concern with writing—signal a psychological affinity at a deeper level. On the contrary, the textual suggestions of similarity are counteracted by the narrator's reversion to qualifications and simplifying comments. Furthermore, an essential point to make about the character of Razumov is the importance of his moral growth; the text contains few indications of a corresponding growth on the part of the language teacher.

Secondly, Szittya's stress on the thematic connections between B-text and A-text becomes even more problematic if related to his view of the novel as an instance of metafiction. This aspect of *Under Western Eyes* is not to be overlooked, but I would argue that it is rather through the complicated, paradoxical relation between the A- and B-texts that the reader is most strongly reminded of the metafictional character of the narrative and the fragmentary nature of the world this fiction sets out to portray. Relating both these two adjectives ('metafictional' and 'fragmentary') to the A-text of the novel, I shall conclude this chapter by attaching some comments to each of them.

The observations on Conrad's narrative method in this study suggest an understanding of his fiction as complex, multi-faceted,

---

[20] Ibid. 819.

and partly unresolved thematically. As we have seen, however, there are considerable differences within the Conrad canon here; and *Under Western Eyes* is perhaps the Conrad text which does most to justify this generalization. Essentially, it is the contrast between the narrator's B-text and the all-embracing, surrounding A-text which serves first to establish, and then to retain, the fragmentation of the world—and world experience—the novel describes. In this sense the narrator's severely limited understanding of the subject matter of his narrative is very much part of the A-text's complicated thematics. As Tony Tanner observes, the narrator tries to impress on the reader 'the remoteness, the alienness, the regrettable primitiveness of his material'.[21] We have noted the narrator's repeated mention of his remoteness from Russia and his corresponding inability really to understand the subject matter he is writing about (at this level, his reasoning is consistent enough). Although these reservations and the emphasis on spatial and attitudinal distance are to some extent counteracted by the narrator's generalizations and display of knowledge, their in-built contradictions serve to augment fictional fragmentation. This is a two-way process: reducing the reader's ability to form a coherent picture of the novel's Russian characters, the narrator's inconsistencies and simplifying explanations also make us doubt the integrity of his own psyche and perhaps even the coherence of his Western culture. And yet, as we also have seen, large sections of *Under Western Eyes* are characterized by a surprisingly suggestive psychological realism. One problem thus raised is to what extent rational objections apply to the language teacher as a narrator: this novel demonstrates that even in reflective, modernist fiction there is no direct relation between narrative consistency and thematic effect. The essential point to make here is that in *Under Western Eyes* the main thematic effects are paradoxical: running counter to and superseding the narrator's predictions, they reveal an absorbing drama of confidence, betrayal, remorse, and confession. The relation of these motifs to the problem of fragmentation is one indication of the complexity of the thematics of *Under Western Eyes*.

One reason why this particular relation is insufficiently heeded by Szittya may be that it complicates his view of the novel as 'metafictional'. It is certainly true that it incorporates metafictional elements,

---

[21] Tanner, 'Nightmare and Complacency', 165.

of which the problem of writing may be the most intriguing. Neither is it necessary to object to the connections Szittya draws between *Under Western Eyes* as metafiction and the insecurity of Conrad as a novelist, though the point might appear too biographical to be of major critical interest. My dissent is provoked by Szittya's view of the novel as essentially metafictional, and exclusively or at least predominantly concerned with the fundamental insecurity of writing. Several of the novel's commentators have observed that it presents writing as a mediated, and artificial, form of human communication. But as my interpretation has shown, the novel's metafictional concern with writing does not prevent it from presenting, through this very medium, a dramatic, moving, and inherently persuasive life story. Concluding, then, I would emphasize the complicated relation between the sustained concern that *Under Western Eyes* shows with the problems of writing and communication and with the psychological issues which we have noted, and which stand as a paradigm of Razumov's development towards the confessions with which the novel culminates. Though problematic, writing has its advantages too: Razumov is forced by his loneliness and moral anguish to write, but he also manages to use writing as a means of freeing himself from his guilt. Our interest in the narrator, however, is inextricable from his function as writer of a text much more complex than he can possibly realize.

13

Conclusion

My critical focus on the devices, functions, variations, and thematic effects or implications of Conrad's narrative method logically entails some uncertainty as to whether a short, generalized conclusion can do justice to the range and complexity of the method I have investigated. Yet this interpretative problem indirectly illuminates an essential aspect of Conrad's narrative method: one rather obvious, but important concluding point to stress must be its technical sophistication, intrinsic variation, and thematic productivity. Arguably, this study presents substantial critical evidence to demonstrate that the narrative method and resulting thematics of a number of Conrad's fictional texts justifies and confirms his position as one of the most important and original writers of early modernist fiction. Moreover, there are interesting ways in which Conrad's fiction prefigures not only that of high modernism (Joyce, Woolf, and especially Faulkner), but also, as Edward Said implies in his 1984 essay on Conrad,[1] later post-modernist fiction.

Unavoidably, my critical focus on narrative method as manifested through textual structure delimits the extent to which I have been able to explore the thematic effects of Conrad's narrative method. Still, many effects have been noted; and they demonstrate, on the whole, a very close relationship between narrative method and thematics. This study could be described as 'philological' in the sense that it attempts to do justice to Conrad's fiction as it is presented on the pages of his published work. Such a critical approach is related to structuralism and the variants of close reading associated with New Criticism. But while structuralism often tends to emphasize static (though also, it must be added, basic and textually significant) narrative and thematic contrasts and parallels, I have attempted to pay attention to the kinesis and intricate modulations of Conrad's narratives as well.

Although, then, this study is not only related but also indebted to textual close reading as practised by New Criticism, it is less

[1] Said, 'Conrad: The Presentation of Narrative', 101 and *passim*.

concerned than is New Criticism (and here I am thinking more of the large portion of Conrad criticism that proceeds, mostly implicitly and semi-consciously, from New Critical assumptions than of the school itself) with such terms as structural coherence and artistic or thematic unity. One suggestion of this study is that there is no simple correlation between fictional achievement and narrative and thematic unification in Conrad. Many of the problems Conrad explores are intrinsically difficult, in part even insoluble. This applies, for instance, to the contradiction which for Jacques Berthoud makes Conrad's work tragic, that 'between private vision and public action'.[2] These thematic qualities of Conrad's fiction are accentuated by the insistent way in which they are related to the characteristics and problems of written and oral communication. As such concerns—including problems of coherence, communication, and repetition—are highlighted by contemporary post-structuralism, literary criticism as practised in this study is also related to this interesting and complex critical trend.

In the epilogue to the most persuasive and wide-ranging developmental study of Conrad that we have, Ian Watt argues that although 'Conrad's career as a writer had started very late... his maturity of experience had rapidly found its expressive complement in a new and highly original kind of narrative technique'.[3] Although in one sense this concluding statement is true enough, my sustained critical focus on the narrative method of a dozen Conrad texts of varying lengths has led to the conclusion that the relationship between narrative technique and thematics in Conrad is more complicated and reciprocal than Watt suggests. Moreover, there does not, on the basis of this study, seem to be any direct or obvious correlation between narrative success and date of composition in Conrad's fiction. Although, on the whole, the artistic quality of the fiction subsequent to *Under Western Eyes* deteriorates, texts such as *Victory*, 'The Tale', and (particularly) *The Shadow-Line* are notable exceptions. More importantly, Conrad's narrative method matured very rapidly. As Cedric Watts has demonstrated, even the method of *Almayer's Folly* is more sophisticated and thematically productive than has generally been recognized.[4] Particularly if

---

[2] *C M P* 191.
[3] *C N C* 357.
[4] Watts, *The Deceptive Text*, 47–53.

related to the developmental approach of much Conrad criticism, such considerations go quite far to justify a systematic, rather than developmental, approach to his narrative method. It must be added, however, that although this book can be described as systematic in that it presents relatively detailed analyses of the narrative method of three short stories, three novellas, and four novels, the discussions of the narratives within each of these three main groups proceed chronologically. Thus the systematic and the developmental approaches are interlinked, with the former as the more important.

As I now proceed to bring together some of the most essential concluding points about the narrative method of the dozen Conrad texts analysed in the chapters above, it must be emphasized once again that such a summarized account unavoidably entails both simplifications and omissions. Following an outline of the problem to be investigated and the introduction of my main critical concepts in Chapter 1, Chapter 2 has attempted to supplement this theoretical basis for the study by contrasting the narrative method of two additional Conrad texts, 'Heart of Darkness' and *Chance*. We have seen, then, that a main reason why the narrative method of the former work is greatly superior to that of *Chance* is suggested by the way in which Marlow's story, filtered through an unidentified, 'simpler' personal frame narrative, is based on—even necessitated by—his trying Congo experience. There is a remarkably productive interplay of narrative method and thematics in 'Heart of Darkness': as the dramatic story of Marlow's journey unfolds, it lends intrinsic justification to the characteristics of his act of narration. In contrast, the garrulous Marlow of *Chance* shows no corresponding existential involvement in his narrative, which gradually deteriorates after a promising beginning. The relation between narrative method and thematics is more arbitrary and problematic in *Chance* than in 'Heart of Darkness', partly because the three narrative frames of *Chance* seem an over-sophisticated device in relation to the simplicity of the 'heroic vision' associated with Anthony, but also because Marlow's frequent generalizations appear more artificially superimposed here than in 'Heart of Darkness'. One conclusion suggested by the comparison of these two works is that narrative quality in Conrad seems to improve if the experience underlying the narrative has seriously affected not just the narrator's philosophy of life, but also his attitude to the problems of narration and mediation. However, this observation applies more unambiguously to Conrad's personal than to his authorial narrative. The use of the 'oblique narrative' convention in 'Heart of Darkness' functions exceptionally well as a means of extending Marlow's involvement to include the reader, at least in the sense of guiding and manipulating his or her response to and understanding of the tale.

In Chapter 3 we have seen that 'An Outpost of Progress' is an impressive early short story in which Conrad ably employs omniscient authorial narrative to dramatize thematic concerns which he was to explore at greater length, and in greater depth, later on in his writing career. As far as narrative method is concerned, 'An Outpost of Progress' anticipates *Nostromo* rather than 'Heart of Darkness'. The function of irony is clearly much more diverse in the later novel than in the short story, and so are the variations of authorial distance from the various characters. Still, taking into account the early date of composition and textual concentration of 'An Outpost of Progress', these two devices function well here too.

If the authorial narrative of 'An Outpost of Progress' is panoramic, terse, and omniscient, the narrative of 'The Secret Sharer' is intensely personal. Related to that of *Under Western Eyes*, the thematics of 'The Secret Sharer' remains vaguely suggested rather than, as in the novel, seriously explored. This problem (for it is more of a problem here than in 'An Outpost of Progress') can be partly explained by connecting the personal narrative of 'The Secret Sharer' with the narrative principle of suspense, which, combined with the strong impression of similarities and contrasts between the captain-narrator and Leggatt, belong among the most important constituent aspects of its narrative method. Because the similarities and contrasts are very noticeable, and because of the combination of the suspense principle and the relative shortness of the tale, the moral issues it dramatizes are blurred rather than given the kind of serious fictional treatment which other Conrad texts indicate that they deserve.

The thematics of 'The Tale', too, is problematically ambiguous and unresolved. This is a late short story in which the relation between the surrounding authorial narrative and the commander-narrator's personal account is conspicuously unclear: the transitions between the two main narrative levels can be abrupt; and the authorial narrator's comments on his personal narrator-protagonist (as well as on the latter's narratee) contain disturbing elements of cliché. Yet the personal narrative of the commander is rendered effectively and economically, and it gives a vivid dramatization of the problem that confronts him. Aspects of this problem are understood by the commander (and implicitly by the authorial narrator) as essentially epistemological, but his growing awareness of the moral complications of his decision concerning the neutral ship indicates that the thematics of the short story is also existential and ethical.

Proceeding from consideration of the short fiction to Conrad's novellas, I have first analysed the narrative method of *The Nigger of the 'Narcissus'*—a crucially important text not only in its own right, but also as far as the evolution of Conrad's narrative method is concerned. This novella has a compelling narrative rhetoric and thematic suggestiveness which goes far to override its flaws and inconsistencies, where the technical problems pertaining to the variations of perspective and voice are made conspicuous. The focus of the narrative of *The Nigger of the 'Narcissus'* is on the crew of the *Narcissus* rather than, as in 'The Secret Sharer' or 'The Tale', on single characters. The description of the crew and its tasks in the well-defined setting of a ship serves to constitute a thematics less complex than in a novella such as 'Heart of Darkness', but it remains an essential aspect of the thematics of Conrad's fiction as a whole. In the attempt to establish, dramatize, and develop more 'positive' constituent aspects of Conradian thematics (such as solidarity and the work of the crew aboard the ship) the combination of authorial and personal narrative in *The Nigger of the 'Narcissus'* achieves considerable success.

While the combination of authorial and personal narrative in *The Nigger of the 'Narcissus'* could be seen as a more sophisticated, and technically also more problematic, variant on the authorial narrative in 'An Outpost of Progress', the authorial narrative of 'Typhoon' is relatively simple. However, we have seen in Chapter 7 that the novella evinces significant modulations of perspective, and that the combination of these perspectival variations with varying attitudinal distance contributes substantially to the dramatization of the development of MacWhirr's character as he is confronted by the challenge, and test, of the typhoon. Paradoxically, narrative and thematic simplicity promotes thematic persuasiveness in 'Typhoon': as the elemental drama of the *Nan-Shan* struggling with the typhoon accentuates human qualities such as courage and perseverance, so it is precisely this lonely, testing ordeal of MacWhirr's that constitutes the basis for his fundamental change in the course of the narrative.

The narrative success of *The Shadow-Line* is intimately connected with the narrative and thematic dominance of the personal narrator of this late novella. This exceptional centrality, and the way in which it is integrated into the narrative method of the text, serve to make the relation between narrative and thematics particularly close and reciprocal here; it also makes the novella more coherent and unified thematically than is often the case in Conrad. The narrative potential associated with temporal distance, which is closely linked to the protagonist's process of learning, is effectively exploited. One reason for the suggestiveness of *The Shadow-Line* is to be sought in its high degree of narrative and thematic unification, which is closely related to personal narration as a sustained act of intensified memory. Focused on his instructive experience, this act of memory persuasively dramatizes the personal narrator's initiation into a society which gives him both the independence and the responsibility of a captain.

Thus the three novellas interpreted in this study testify to a considerable narrative variation within this sub-genre of Conrad's fiction. The length of the novellas—approximately 100 to 150 pages each—allows Conrad to explore, at least to some extent, the thematic issues raised in these narratives while at the same time some of the potentially damaging effects of repetitious, lengthy narrative (such as in *Chance*) are counteracted by the relative shortness.

Moving on from discussion of Conrad's short stories and novellas to analysis of four of his major novels, we have seen that in these longer texts narrative and thematic complexity increases radically. Much of *Lord Jim* revolves around the relationship of Jim and Marlow. Problematic and distressing, it contributes to the pervasive scepticism of the novel; yet at the same time it develops into a deep and intrinsically convincing friendship. Though ostensibly personal, the function of Marlow's narrative in *Lord Jim* is often interestingly authorial, and shows Conrad's narrative method at its most sophisticated and powerful. It reveals an intricate interplay of perspective, voice, and various forms of narrative distance. Moreover, considering its sophistication and textual extension, it remains surprisingly intense. Although this intensity is partly due to the seriousness of Jim's moral problem, it is even more strongly related to the tension observable in Marlow's attitude to Jim: the tension between a fundamental, existential doubt and an unplanned, growing friendship. The two constituent elements of the tension are reciprocal in that although the friendship is important and rewarding for both Jim and Marlow, it is precisely Marlow's frustrating inability to comprehend and help Jim that most decisively contributes to his growing doubt and, as a corollary, his slanting movement towards an existential and epistemological position conforming to the second form of repetition. This tension, and Marlow's change of character associated with it, are intimately connected with Marlow's crucial narrative function in *Lord Jim*. As Marlow comes to doubt Jim's belief in the sovereign power, the thematic association of this doubt with the threat of loss of ground, direction, and coherence not only enhances the complexity of Jim as a character, but also makes the relationship between main narrator and main character more interesting and unpredictable. It needs to be stressed to what extent this thematic association is dependent not only on the characteristics and modulations of Marlow's activity as narrator, but also on the way in which his narrative is related to his pensive narratees and reinforced by the surrounding authorial narrative. While Marlow's story in 'Heart of Darkness' is relayed to the reader through a less subtle, though gradually wiser, personal frame narrator, the mere fact that the authorial frame narrator in *Lord Jim* refrains from imposing evaluative judgements on Marlow is an indication of the latter's narrative and thematic authority as a personal narrator with an original and productive authorial function.

The panoramic and all-inclusive authorial narrative of *Nostromo* is of a very different, though equally impressive, kind from the narrative method of *Lord Jim*. *Nostromo* demonstrates how flexible Conradian authorial narrative can be: its various constituent elements are interlinked and developed in a highly sophisticated manner. Two key devices are narrative omniscience and narrative mobility, both of which contribute essentially to the novel's characteristic flexibility and range. In part three of Chapter 10 I have suggested that the best indication of this range is provided by the narrative device of irony as it functions as an integral part of the narrative method of the novel: irony serves both as a means of diversifying characterization and as an authorial attitude necessitated by its thematic concerns and disillusioned insights. With regard to the first function of irony, the authorial narrator employs different and supplementary forms of ironic modulation both by way of characterization and in order to introduce and develop essential aspects of textual content. These aspects are diverse: they include moral issues such as personal integrity and depravity as well as socio-economic questions such as economic exploitation and the relationship between power and influence. The authorial narrator's attitude is most directly related to the variations of narrative perspective and distance. It is as though the narrator needs a very substantial, and often ironic, distance from the novel's action and characters in order to retain a lasting narrative focus on the sombre subject matter of his tale. Even if distance decreases and irony temporarily disappears, as in the description of Decoud on the Great Isabel, both devices recur before long and are further modulated. There is an important relation between this form of ironic attitude and the pervasive scepticism of the novel. Furthermore, the need for distance associated with this variant of irony reinforces the more technical motivation for the authorial narrative of *Nostromo*: as the novel's narrative flexibility and thematic range are dependent upon authorial omniscience and panoramic overview, so the distance related to such omniscience is paradoxically motivated by the narrator's serious, even threatening, involvement in his narrative.

Although Chapter 10 has demonstrated that there are important ways in which the flexible, all-embracing authorial narrative of *Nostromo* is connected with, and serves to engender, the thematics of the novel, still its narrative seems to entail certain limitations as to which (or what kind of) thematic generalizations can plausibly be made about the work. Generating literary meaning, narrative method also imposes limitations on the range of this meaning, especially if it becomes overtly thematic or ideological in a sense which removes it from the literary basis of the surface narrative. This observation also applies to some of the thematic generalizations that have been made about *The Secret Agent*, a novel reminiscent of *Nostromo* both thematically and with regard to narrative method. These two major novels represent the peak of Conrad's fictional achievement with authorial narrative. In *The Secret Agent* as in *Nostromo*, the authorial narrative is flexible and wide-ranging; and in the later novel too Conrad employs irony as an integral part of his narrative method. Moreover, in both works the interrelationship of narrative method and thematics is partly indicated by the way in which authorial irony both helps to constitute and reflects a pervasive, and thematically significant, scepticism. In contrast to the exceptional thematic range and characteristically collective focus of *Nostromo*, however, the authorial narrative of *The Secret Agent* is centred on important issues related to the opposition between the public and private spheres, or more specifically on aspects of both that are at once typical and extreme. As the authorial narrative develops, dissimilar thematic and ideological elements are set at odds, through both dialogue and authorial description, and they are only partly or unsatisfactorily resolved. There are complex connections in *The Secret Agent* not only between unresolved contradictions of this kind and the fates of the main characters (especially those of the novel's private sphere), but also between a strong sense of fragmentation and chaos and the sceptical and disillusioned stance of the authorial narrator. Nowhere is this impression of unresolved contradictions and bewildering fragmentation stronger than in the authorial narrator's portrayal of Stevie. As Stevie is destroyed as a result of the ideological forces and personal weaknesses the novel depicts, the tragic fate of this simple and good character, whom the narrator treats with sympathy and little or no irony, reinforces and enhances the sceptical disillusionment of both the authorial narrative and the thematics it informs.

If both *Nostromo* and *The Secret Agent* are characterized by a productive flexibility of authorial narrative, the narrative complexity of *Under Western Eyes* is essentially paradoxical: it revolves round and develops from a covert contrast between the personal narrator's pronounced views and the thematic implications of the narrative as a whole. Emphasizing the interpretative necessity of distinguishing between the novel's 'A-' and 'B-texts', I have argued in Chapter 12 that the narrative originality of *Under Western Eyes* resides essentially in the manner in which the language teacher's personal narrative is undermined and modulated by means of authorial irony. Writing and human communication are more crucial issues in *Under Western Eyes* than in most of Conrad's other works. The novel dramatizes a thematic concern with the possibilities and problems of narrative method as a form of linguistic mediation and human communication. In this sense the novel is one of Conrad's most acutely personal works, and also one of his most distinctly modernist texts. The problems of writing and communication in *Under Western Eyes* are closely related to the narrative presentation of a fragmented fictional universe. This fragmentation is primarily established through the contrast between the 'B-text' of the language teacher as personal narrator and the novel's surrounding 'A-text'. Paradoxically, the narrator's severely limited understanding of the subject matter he presents is an integral part of the complicated thematics of the 'A-text'. Reducing the reader's ability to form a coherent picture of the Russian characters in the novel, the narrator's peculiar combination of reservations, inconsistencies, and simplifying generalizations also makes us doubt his own intellectual integrity and perhaps even the coherence and superiority of his own Western culture. Yet *Under Western Eyes* demonstrates that even in reflective, modernist fiction there is no direct relation between narrative consistency and thematic effect. Large sections of the novel are distinguished by a strikingly effective psychological realism which seems to defy, or run counter to, the problematic position and function of the language teacher. That this psychological realism can be presented and persuasively explored through a personal narrative which is repeatedly subjected to the authorial irony of the 'A-text' is a measure of the achievement of the narrative method of *Under Western Eyes*.

The analyses of the fictional texts, then, have demonstrated that Conrad's narrative method is wide-ranging, diverse, and thematically highly stimulating. As the form of narrative diversification and sophistication observable in Conrad demands careful close reading, general statements about his narrative method do but scant justice to its remarkable variation. The narrative devices and functions in Conrad's fiction are not always thematically productive, but in an impressive number of cases they are, and often in paradoxical and surprising ways. It must be remembered that narrative failure is more easily illustrated than narrative success; this is an additional reason why the comments on Conrad's less successful narratives have been limited to a few works. The narrative sophistication of his fiction is revealed to be even more striking if his texts are reread: we then often see thematic implications of narrative devices or functions which at first seem redundant, obscure, even baffling. Conrad's narrative method cannot, in a majority of cases, be fully appreciated unless the relevant text is reread. This characteristic of his narrative is already observable in *Almayer's Folly*, and it is most apparent in such texts as 'Heart of Darkness' and the four major novels.

If this study of Conrad's narrative method differs from earlier ones in being more consistently focused on the narrative devices and functions that are significantly related to, and serve to establish and shape, the thematic concerns of the texts, it also breaks new ground by attempting to employ a critical terminology that is suited to, and suggested by, the fictional texts subjected to analysis. Thus this study of the narrative method of one exceptionally original and influential modernist writer can also be seen as an attempt to contribute to the more general and theoretical study of narrative. Generalizations about narrative need not necessarily always be based on a broad selection of texts and authors, but may also proceed from more detailed analyses of the works of one writer. Thus Conrad's uses of personal and authorial narrative, though mainly and most directly illuminating with regard to his own fiction, may also indicate essential narrative and thematic characteristics of other modernist fiction. I hope, then, to have shown that there are certain critical advantages associated with studying general issues of narrative in the context of one writer's work. This applies, for instance, to the dialectical relationship between narrative method and thematics, which is more easily lost sight of in the context of a more comprehensive study. Moreover, this book would seem to demonstrate that several of the generalizations one can make about fictional narrative presuppose critical reference to relatively detailed textual commentaries. Although the borderlines between critical commentary and interpretation are frequently blurred in Conrad criticism, this need for textual reference offers additional support to my emphasis on textual commentary and close reading of the texts analysed.

While it is true that Conrad's work may usefully be grouped into authorial and personal narratives, we have seen that several of his most important texts contain elements of both. There is a remarkable narrative flexibility within both these two main variants of Conrad's narrative; the best example can probably be found in the extraordinary range and flexibility of the authorial narrative of *Nostromo*. Even though Conrad's personal narrative in *The Shadow-Line* and *Under Western Eyes* has great thematic richness, it is intimately related to, and in part dependent upon, the introduction and use of Marlow as narrator. Marlow's function as narrator is complex; it varies considerably from work to work, and although his role is generally of crucial importance, we cannot assume that his character is identical at each appearance.

Index